Critical Care Nursing

CONTRIBUTING AUTHORS

ALLEN C. ALFREY, M.D.
Associate Professor
University of Colorado
School of Medicine

JOHN H. ALTSHULER, M.D.
Assistant Clinical Professor of Medicine
(Hematology and Pathology)
University of Colorado
School of Medicine

MARGARET ANN BERRY, R.N., M.A., M.S.
Research Assistant
Department of Physiology
University of Colorado
School of Medicine

BOYD BIGELOW, M.D.
Assistant Clinical Professor of Medicine
University of Colorado
School of Medicine
Medical Director, Pulmonary Department
St. Anthony's Hospital, Denver, Colorado

ANNE T. BOBAL, R.N., B.S.
Clinical Specialist, Hemodialysis Unit
Veterans Administration Hospital
Denver, Colorado

H. L. BRAMMELL, M.D.
Assistant Professor of Cardiology
University of Colorado
School of Medicine

JOSEPH O. BROUGHTON, M.D.
Clinical Instructor in Medicine
University of Colorado
School of Medicine
Medical Director,
  Inhalation Therapy Department
Mercy Hospital, Denver, Colorado

KAREN D. BUSCH, R.N., M.S.
Associate Director, Nursing Service
Colorado Psychiatric Hospital
Denver, Colorado

DONALD E. BUTKUS, M.D.
Instructor in Medicine
University of Colorado
School of Medicine

LANE D. CRADDOCK, M.D.
Assistant Clinical Professor of Medicine
University of Colorado
School of Medicine
Director, Cardiopulmonary Department
General Rose Memorial Hospital
Denver, Colorado

ALVA R. DEGNER, R.N.
Head Nurse, C.C.U. and Medical I.C.U.
General Rose Memorial Hospital
Denver, Colorado

ROBERT W. HENDEE, JR., M.D.
Clinical Instructor, Neurological Surgery
University of Colorado
School of Medicine

SHIRLEY J. HOFFMAN, R.N., B.S.
Clinical Specialist in Cardiology
Presbyterian Medical Center
Denver, Colorado

JANET KERKMAN, R.N., A.R.I.T.
Clinical Specialist
St. Anthony's Hospital
Denver, Colorado

M. LYNN McCRACKEN, R.N., M.S.
Crisis Nurse Consultant
Colorado-Wyoming Regional Medical
  Programs
Denver, Colorado

NAOMI DOMER MEDEARIS, M.A., M.B.A.
Associate Professor
Coordinator, Organization and Staff
  Development Programs
University of Colorado School of Nursing
Continuing Education Services

JOAN MERSCH, R.N., M.S.
Clinical Specialist
Stanford Medical Center
Palo Alto, California

STUART SCHNECK, M.D.
Professor of Neurology
University of Colorado
School of Medicine

JANET S. SMITH, R.N., M.S.
Division Director of Health Occupations
  Department
Community College of Denver
Denver, Colorado

VIRGINIA WARD
Executive Director
Colorado Nurses' Association

PHILLIP S. WOLF, M.D.
Assistant Clinical Professor of Medicine
University of Colorado
Director, Coronary Care Unit
General Rose Memorial Hospital
Denver, Colorado

CAROLYN M. HUDAK, R.N., M.S.
Assistant Professor
Coordinator, Adult Health Practitioner Program
University of Colorado School of Nursing
Continuing Education Services
Formerly Instructor, Intensive Care
Nursing Program

BARBARA M. GALLO, R.N., M.S.
Assistant Professor
Instructor, Adult Health Practitioner Program
University of Colorado School of Nursing
Continuing Education Services
Formerly Coordinator, Intensive Care
Nursing Program

THELMA LOHR, R.N., M.S.
Associate Professor
Coordinator, Mental Health Programs
University of Colorado School of Nursing
Continuing Education Services
Formerly Coordinator, Intensive Care
Nursing Program

Critical Care Nursing

J. B. LIPPINCOTT COMPANY
PHILADELPHIA • *TORONTO*

Library of Congress Cataloging in Publication Data
Main entry under title:

Critical care nursing.

1. Cardiovascular disease nursing. 2. Intensive
care units. I. Hudak, Carolyn M., ed. II. Gallo,
Barbara M., ed. III. Lohr, Thelma L., ed.
[DNLM: 1. Intensive care units—Nursing tests.
2. Nursing care. WY156 H883c 1973]
RC674.C75   610.73'6   73-6780
ISBN 0-397-54130-9

ISBN 0-397-54130-9
Library of Congress Catalog Card Number 73-6780
Printed in the United States of America

3 5 7 9 8 6 4

Distributed in Great Britain
Blackwell Scientific Publications, Oxford, London, and Edinburgh

CONTENTS

UNIT III
A Specific Crisis Situation

UNIT IV
Professional Practice in the Critical Care Unit

FOREWORD

In 1965 the Interorganizational Committee of the Colorado League for Nursing and the Colorado Heart Association requested the Continuing Education Services of the University of Colorado School of Nursing to plan and conduct a one-week workshop for nurses who were working in coronary care units in the State of Colorado. The first one-week course became a two-week course when the nurse participants felt they needed more training in reading ECG monitoring strips, drug therapy, complications, and the nursing care of the coronary patient and his family. After the successful completion of these two one-week sessions for the same nurse participants, the suggestion was made by the Nursing Consultant of the Heart Control Branch of Health, Education, and Welfare in Washington, D.C., that Continuing Education Services of the University of Colorado School of Nursing submit a grant proposal to the Nursing Division of Health, Education, and Welfare for funds to conduct further intensive courses in "Training Today's Nurse for Coronary Patient Care." The grant was submitted and subsequently awarded. Seventy-seven nurses from eleven states came for training in cardiac massage, mouth-to-mouth resuscitation, defibrillation, reading of monitoring strips, and the nursing care of the coronary patient and his family.

It was through this experience and the course evaluations made by participants and staff that the four-week intensive course, "Training Today's Nurse for Coronary Patient Care," was designed. The course was offered over a 2½-year period to 253 nurses from 27 states. It was during this time that many nurses from other critical care areas requested assistance in continuing their education.

The continuing-education educators concerned with this specialty in nursing believed there was a core content which every nurse working in a critical care area needed to know. The course was redesigned for nurses in all critical care areas. Theory sessions included, in depth, the interrelatedness of the four major body systems. Clinical experiences were selected for each of the participants as their educational needs and job assignments dictated. A project proposal was submitted to the Colorado-Wyoming Regional Medical Program. Funding from this source was available for three years. Two hundred and three nurses from twenty-seven states participated in experiences designed for their own learning and in experiences intended for course evaluation.

In current practice, continuing education is aimed largely at updating and increasing knowledge and skills of the practitioners in the nursing profession. However, the new technologies and the development of critical care units have brought about responsibilities which at one time were considered outside the scope of nursing. Today's nurses are the key persons in the critical care areas and they must become experts in the care of people. It is imperative that nurses think of their patients and their families as human beings with needs to be met. Critical care unit nurses must focus on and sharpen their abilities to work with people rather than on the disease-and-treatment orientation of the past. It remains essential that critical care unit nurses be alert to the patient's level of illness and to minute changes through constant observation, supervision, and evaluation of his status and progress and utilize all the knowledge and skill at their disposal. But it is also essential that these nurses be alert to the total individual and his environment—his needs, strengths, and his level of wellness.

Basically these nurses are bedside nurses with optimum teaching-learning opportunities. Nurses working in intensive care units and crisis areas must be willing to function as interdependent members of the health team and to exercise their expert nursing judgments in caring for and about patients and their families.

Nurses' knowledge, observations, judgments, and ideas are of vital importance in a critical care area. Through these they can create a climate that is conducive for all health workers to contribute to meeting the needs of the patient and his family.

This is but an example of the challenge that is nursing today and the dramatic advances in the biomedical world. These innovations demand that nurses continue their education so that they may keep up with present advances and be prepared for the future which cannot be predicted.

The main purpose of this book is to assist nurses in continuing their own education in the aspect of critical care nursing. Readers will be particularly interested in the holistic approach based on the interrelatedness of the four major body systems and the philosophy of nursing developed by the writers.

Elda S. Popiel, R.N., M.S.
Professor and Assistant Dean
Continuing Education Services
University of Colorado School of Nursing

PREFACE

The idea and materials for this book have evolved from four years experience with intensive care nursing content for the practicing nurse. Through the Continuing Education Department of the University of Colorado School of Nursing, we have conducted a five-week, ongoing course, "Intensive Care Nursing—A Core Program" for registered nurses. Our approach has been a holistic one based on the interrelatedness of the four major body systems—respiratory, cardiovascular, renal, and nervous—with man's hierarchy of needs as a framework. Continuous use of evaluation tools has helped to identify the strong points of the content and that which needed revision. This has led to the design and content appearing in this book.

The intent in the preparation of this work was to focus on the rational bases underlying medical and nursing intervention. We support the premise that in the illness state, when the patient can no longer effectively control his own environment and requires assistance from an outside source, the nurse is the appropriate health team member to assume the role of patient negotiator. This role will be especially challenging in the critical care setting where the patient's internal and external environment is in a constant state of change. In order to accept this challenge, the nurse's practice must be geared to predicting and anticipating possible events in a patient's clinical course based on understanding of the patient's underlying pathology. To this end we have moved from a review of normal system functioning to a more detailed coverage of pathophysiological, psychological, and social aspects of various illness states. The major emphasis is on the change from normal body functioning as a basis for therapeutic intervention. Laboratory data and its significance for the nurse as well as pharmacologic information are integrated throughout the text.

Some material in the book, such as the chapter on arrhythmias, is presented in work manual form to allow the reader to "digest" it at an individual pace and to provide an exercise for periodic review.

This book should be a major resource for the practicing nurse dealing with any patient in crisis, whether inside or outside the critical care unit. It will also be helpful to students who need a resource for increasing their understanding of a specific patient-care aspect, as well as to educators and those persons involved in inservice and continuing education programs related to crisis nursing.

We wish to express our appreciation for the assistance and involvement of the contributing authors and to those colleagues and past course participants who were a vital part of the Intensive Care Program and whose contributions are reflected throughout this work. We wish to acknowledge the expert assistance of Janet Kerkman, R.N., and Fern DeLouche, R.P.T., in preparing the material on the respiratory system. We are particularly grateful to our secretary, Mrs. Maxine Evertz, for her perseverance in typing the manuscript and keeping us "consistent," and to Miss Cindy DeCounter for her secretarial aid. To David Miller, Managing Editor, Nursing Department, J. B. Lippincott Company, a special thanks for his unique ability to provide encouragement and support.

Carolyn M. Hudak
Barbara M. Gallo
Thelma L. Lohr

INTRODUCTION

The sun shone down on the gleaming white edifice called *The Hospital.* The telerecorder rang sharply in the receiving heliport and the teletype began its nervous chatter. The receiving room nurse walked over to read the message: "Caucasian, male; fifty-five years of age; shortness of breath; crushing chest pain; collapsed over desk; history of two previous similar attacks." She punched out the message on the electronic call board, indicating the estimated time of arrival.

When the sound of the helicopter blades increased to a deafening level, the nurse moved out to the landing pad. As the copter touched down, the doors in the fuselage opened and the life-support capsule was lowered into the waiting cradle car on the track. As soon as the nurse removed the sky hooks from the ends of the capsule, the helicopter lifted off with a pulsing roar. The nurse activated the electronic conveyor track and the capsule moved into the receiving room.

Once inside, the nurse quickly opened the capsule and took from the pocket the field-punched computer cards. As she passed the call board, she activated the call switches from The Learned Ones who would be concerned with #125-A-70-90056, the newly arrived case. While she awaited their arrival, she fed the cards into a computer and the information was instantaneously displayed on the video screen in all four corners of the receiving room and at the diagnosis console. Suddenly the doors marked "Biological, Psychological, and Sociological" burst open and The Learned Ones and their assistants quickly entered the room. Glancing furtively at the video printouts, each addressed his attention to the problems of #125-A-70-90056 which were in the area of his specialty. One by one they took their respective problem area and with it in its minicapsule, left by way of the doors "Biological, Psychological, and Sociological." When all had left and only the capsule and clothing of #125-A-70-90056 remained at the diagnostic console, the nurse signaled for the sanitation specialist to prepare the room for the next arrival.

In white coveralls and armed with a collection of aerosols filled with various sanitizers, the specialist began to clean the life-support capsule, assisted by the receiving room attendant. The two chatted cheerfully as they did their work. After they had folded the clothing left inside the capsule they noticed a kind of ethereal cloud inside the capsule. Selecting a stronger sanitizer, the specialist sprayed the cloud more thoroughly. Much to his dismay the cloud did not disappear. A second glance showed that the clothing was no longer neatly folded.

The specialist summoned the nurse from the receiving room office. She too tried without success to disperse the cloud and fold the clothes. Then she notified the offices of the director of nurses and the supervisors of biological, psychological, and sociological nursing problems. They arrived from the various areas, but they too were unsuccessful. The Learned Ones were recalled, but again all efforts met with failure. As the crowd of professionals stood pondering over the puzzling conditions inside the capsule, a small voice was heard:

"But what about me? I am MORE than the sum total of my parts!"

UNIT I
Holistic Approach to Critical Care Nursing

1

Critical Care Nursing: What Makes It Special?

CAROLYN M. HUDAK, R.N., M.S.
BARBARA M. GALLO, R.N., M.S.
THELMA L. LOHR, R.N., M.S.

It is our contention that the essence of the concept of critical care nursing lies not in special environments or amid special equipment but rather in the decision-making process of the nurse and her willingness to act upon her decisions.

Critical care nurses have been pioneers in what professional circles are now calling the "expanded role." From the days of the 24-hour recovery room which substituted for the absence of an intensive care unit, nurses in these areas have had to look beyond just "taking vital signs." Before the term "critical care nursing" evolved, the critical care nurse was the one who could see beyond the patient's blood pressure, pulse, and respiration. She felt a pulse and noted its quality; she made a mental note of the skin temperature and its state of hydration; she compared the pulse rate with the temperature and blood pressure and asked "why" if her anticipated correlation was not there. In short, she functioned according to her intellect. She anticipated events based on what she knew about normal physiology and her patient's condition, and if findings other than those she anticipated materialized, she asked herself "why" and proceeded to gather additional clinical data to answer that question. If she did not answer the question, her response was based on intuition, "That patient just doesn't look good to me!" We believe that predictability based on intuition actually involved a response to clinical cues which nurses had not attempted to identify concretely. For example, the patient doesn't "look good" because:

his respirations are more shallow;
his color is duskier than previously;
his eyes have an anxious stare;
he is more restless now;
he is perspiring.

The critical care nurse of today seeks the *rational base* for all her interpretations and actions.

What are the processes a nurse goes through to arrive at a decision which guides her intervention? A postoperative patient presents with a blood pressure of 88/60, pulse 100, respirations 28, and diaphoresis. How does the nurse arrive at a decision to medicate the patient for pain as opposed to alerting the physician that the patient may be hemorrhaging? What findings are there to support either premise? Does he complain of pain? Does he "splint" the area when he moves? Is his dressing wet? Is urine output diminished? Is there any evidence of bleeding into the incisional area? What is the pulse quality? Does the CVP lend any clues? Depending on her findings, the nurse may decide to medicate the patient for pain.

In turn, critical care nursing also involves evaluating the outcome of a given intervention and proceeding appropriately. For example, after medicating the post-op patient described above the nurse will *anticipate* a given outcome. If the vital sign parameters noted above are due to pain, the nurse will anticipate a return to that patient's previous "normal" values if pain relief is achieved. If this anticipated outcome is not realized, she then asks "why?" and proceeds to gather additional data to answer that question. We believe that the essence of critical care nursing is to be found in that decision-making process, which is based on a sound understanding of physiological and psychological entities.

The expression of the decision is the art of nursing intervention which will produce a given clinical picture. This art of intervention requires the ability to deal with critical situations with a rapidity and precision not usually necessary in other health care settings. It requires adeptness at integrating information and establishing priorities, for when illness strikes one body system, other systems become involved in the effort of coping with the disequilibrium. The person admitted to an acute care unit usually receives excellent care for the affected body system, but problems in other systems are not recognized early, if at all. Critical illnesses will always endanger and involve the respiratory, cardiovascular, renal, and central nervous systems as well as the self-esteem of each person.

We believe the nurse needs to actively engage her mental image of the person and his body processes to gather all the data possible for the decision making process. Therefore, the following framework is proposed as a basis for the study of persons with critical illnesses and *critical care nursing*.

Man seeks to preserve his life by directing all of his energies toward the most basic unmet needs. For example, a person with inadequate cardiac output will have all his compensatory mechanisms working to maintain the circulation of oxygen, thus meeting the most basic requirement for life. In this

HIERARCHY OF MAN'S NEEDS FOR CRITICAL CARE NURSING

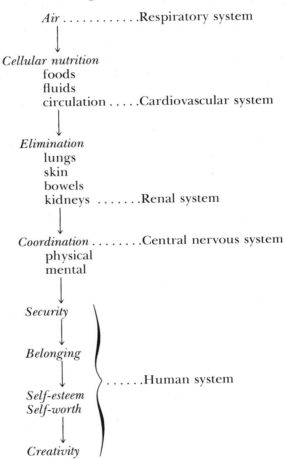

Self-Preservation
The Nurse as the Negotiator

Air . . . . .Respiratory system

↓

Cellular nutrition
    foods
    fluids
    circulation . . . . .Cardiovascular system

↓

Elimination
    lungs
    skin
    bowels
    kidneys . . . . . . .Renal system

↓

Coordination . . . . .Central nervous system
    physical
    mental

↓

Security

↓

Belonging

↓   } . . . . . .Human system

Self-esteem
Self-worth

↓

Creativity

situation, energy is directed away from subsystems such as the gastrointestinal, skin, and kidney functions, creating a degree of physiological amputation. Anxiety and the need for a sense of security is always present, but it is not the most basic need at this time. Later, when needs for air, cellular nutrition, and elimination are met, man directs his efforts toward seeking security, a sense of belonging, and self-esteem. Although each of us has physiological and psychological mechanisms which compensate for disequilibrium, there are situations in which we cannot adapt without outside intervention. It is in these situations that the critical care nurse becomes the patient's advocate and fosters adaptation.

Man's attempts to cope with his environment include avoidance, in which he flees from the situation; counteraction, in which body defenses try to destroy the stressor, often at the expense of other systems; and adaptation, in which man seeks to establish a compatible response to the stress and still retain a steady state. Although all mechanisms foster self-preservation, nursing intervention is aimed at adaptation. By fostering responses that encourage useful functioning both physiologically and emotionally, we enhance adaptation and aid the patient in conserving his energy. On the other hand, when our intervention or lack of it does not foster adaptation, the patient's energy is wasted and a state of entropy exists, that is, the patient will have a diminished capacity to deal with a changing situation. Thus, entropy is increased when a patient's energy is devoted to maladaptive functioning which perpetuates the disequilibrium, and entropy is minimized when the patient expends energy which fosters his adaptation to the disequilibrium. An example of maladaptation versus adaptation is seen in the patient with restrictive lung disease who develops a lung infection resulting in $\uparrow CO_2$ and $\downarrow O_2$. This patient cannot compensate because of his restrictive lung disease, thus his established pattern of breathing is maladaptive, perpetuating the problem of gas exchange. On the other hand, adaptive nursing intervention involves helping the patient to breathe more deeply and to foster the drainage of secretion either by having him do breathing exercises or by use of mechanical aids. Although the energy is still expended, it is expended usefully. This concept of minimizing entropy is consistent with the ultimate goal of health care—to restore the person to a steady state with minimal stress to the rest of the body.

Because of the degree of patient contact, critical care nurses have more influence than other health care personnel in either fostering adaptation or encouraging entropy. That influence may be a burden as well as a challenge. It does not however, negate the responsibility of other health care personnel to act on behalf of patient adaptation.

Fostering adaptive functioning means that the nurse negotiates for the patient. She becomes his advocate. Because the critically ill patient often cannot effectively cope with both the physiological problem *and* the rest of his environment, it becomes necessary for the nurse to do for the patient what he is unable to do for himself so that his energy is conserved. As negotiator the nurse must refrain from adding burdens which increase the patient's need to interact when it will not foster adaptation. For example, patient energy spent in fearful suspense about the equipment nearby is not as helpful as energy spent in asking and then listening to a reply about it. Or, energy spent in persistently requesting a loved one to be present may not be as helpful as energy spent interacting with that person.

Fostering safety for the critically ill patient involves decreasing his vulnerability both physiologically and emotionally. The feeling of security is lost or at least significantly decreased whenever there is a decrease in one's control of body functions. Loss of control may vary from fatigue and weakness to paralysis. It may result from pathology, from the environment (such as restraint by I.V. tubing or machinery), or from both, or from fatigue and sleeplessness resulting from physical discomfort, or physiological fatigue, i.e. dyspnea and sensory overload. Regardless of the decrease or loss of control, the nurse intervenes in order to increase the patient's feeling of safety. She may accomplish this by technical skill, tools, medication, interaction, by providing assisted breathing with a respirator, by encouraging breathing exercises, or by staying with the patient during a time of anxiety or loneliness. Recognizing a patient's safety needs is an important element in the holistic approach to patient care. In addition, it is this very consideration of the "whole" patient which allows us to establish priorities as patient negotiators.

Negotiating for the patient is not without its hazards. This kind of caring and giving requires our energies in place of those which the patient is temporarily lacking. Therefore, to maintain our own emotional reserves, we also need to support each other as colleagues in the critical care unit and to enhance each other's feelings of belonging and self-esteem. Other hazards involve speaking on behalf of the patient often as a minority voice and in the face of administrative, physician, or peer pressure. It means experiencing the joy of patients who recover or the sadness and anger for those who do not.

It is apparent to us that this philosophy of nursing need not and should not be confined to acute care areas. It is every patient's right to expect this type of intelligent care; it is the nurse's responsibility and challenge to provide it.

Furthermore, we believe that many of the responsibilities now defined in expanded role terms will in the not too distant future be the standard levels of practice for professional nurses. The "doing" part can and is being delegated to other members of the health team; it is the "thinking" part which nursing must continue to develop and retain.

Already we are seeing a reversal of the trend to centralize patients receiving critical care nursing. The rationale for this reversal lies in the desire to maintain consistency in providing care. This purpose is lost if the patient is moved from one area to another with different staff along the course of his hospitalization. The critical care nurse may eventually find herself delivering care both in the hospital and in the community. With her background of technical and intellectual skills she will be most qualified to meet the challenge of patient needs.

2

Emotional Response to Illness

KAREN D. BUSCH, R.N., M.S.
BARBARA M. GALLO, R.N., M.S.

When man's dynamic stability is threatened or impinged upon and his usual coping mechanisms begin to fail him, he enters a state of illness. Much of this book is focused on supporting and implementing man's response to the threat of illness through physiological maintenance and adjustments. It is the purpose of this chapter to consider the intimate relationship between man's emotional response to illness and its effect upon his adaptation to his temporary and/or permanent limitations. Concepts of anxiety, grief, and adaptation to illness will be presented for the purpose of developing related nursing interventions based on principles of sound theory.

Illness, or the threat of it, acts as a stressor which leads to an ambient state of tension. The existence of tension produces a response toward adaptation, and this tension state is known as *entropy*. For example, if a man is dehydrated he drinks when he becomes aware of his thirst. The tension state of thirst activates his response of drinking. If he drinks salt water, neither the stressor nor the tension state of thirst will be relieved and his state of entropy will increase. If he drinks fresh water his dehydration will be relieved and therefore his thirst, and he will place himself in a state of negative entropy, thus freeing his energies to cope with other stressors of life (Fig. 2–1).

Just as thirst is the motivating tension state to relieve dehydration, the phenomenon of anxiety is the tension state which activates man's response to the threat of illness. When energy is channeled and directed toward *reducing the stressor* it minimizes entropy. But energy is often directed toward merely relieving the tension state and may only perpetuate entropy, as with the thirsty, dehydrated man who drinks salt water.

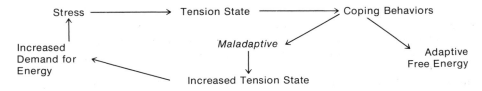

Fig. 2-1. Negative Entropy.

ANXIETY

Any stressor which threatens man's sense of wholeness, containment, security, and control will bring anxiety into play. Illness is such a stressor. The physiological responses of rapid pulse rate, increased blood pressure, increased respirations, dilated pupils, dry mouth, and peripheral vasoconstriction may go undetected in the seemingly cool, calm, self-controlled patient. These autonomic responses of anxiety are always a reliable index when behavioral responses do not conform to the professional's expectations. Behavioral responses indicative of anxiety are often familial and culturally learned. They vary from quiet composure in the face of disaster to panic in the presence of a honeybee.

Nevertheless, such extremes of control or panic utilize valuable energy; and when this energy is not directed toward eliminating the stressor it serves only to perpetuate the state of entropy. Thus the goal of nursing care is always to promote physiological and emotional equilibrium, thereby minimizing entropy and freeing the patient's energy resources for healing and recuperation.

Whenever possible the threatening stressor is reduced or eliminated. When this is done the problem is quickly resolved and the patient is returned to equilibrium. Usually, however, the stressor is not so easily eliminated; instead many other stressors are introduced in the service of remedying the original state of entropy. For most people hospitalization is that kind of secondary stressor. Their presence in the critical care unit is to them the tangible proof that their fears are justified, that their life may be in jeopardy, and that they are wholly at the mercy of strangers who, they feel, must regard them as inferior for not understanding what is happening or how those awesome gadgets work their reputed cures.

When it is impossible to remove the provocative stimuli, it is the nurse's function to make an assessment of the coping mechanism that the patient might utilize in his current precarious state. Those coping behaviors may be directed toward eliminating either the stressor of illness or the stressor of the anxiety state itself. Thus the nurse must evaluate each behavior in the light of whether or not it functions to restore a steady state. She can support or encourage those behaviors which are consistent with movement toward a steady state; or she may need to modify or find substitutes for those behaviors which are disruptive to or threaten a steady state. And at times it is necessary to teach or introduce new coping mechanisms to enhance movement to the overall goal of homeostatic equilibrium.

For example, in an acute period a patient may be more capable of experiencing concern and worry over the variety of equipment which surrounds him rather than of focusing on the threat to his life. This activity may allow him some necessary denial of the reality of his crisis, but the worry itself may drain him of his needed energy. Information and explanation of the machinery may serve to reduce his secondary anxiety, while expert nursing care may serve to reassure him nonverbally of his security without stripping him of his defense of denial.

Commonly anxiety is experienced when there is a threat of helplessness or lack of control. Thus nursing measures which reinforce every possible control the patient may have help to increase his sense of autonomy and reduce the overpowering sense of loss of control. Providing order and predictability allows the patient to anticipate and prepare for what is to follow. Perhaps it creates only a mirage of control, but anticipatory guidance keeps the patient from being caught off guard and allows him to muster those coping mechanisms which he can bring to bear.

Allowing small choices when the patient is willing and ready decreases the patient's feeling that he is totally at the mercy of others. Is he ready for a pain medication? Would he prefer to lie on his right or left side? In which arm would he like his I.V.? How high does he want the head of his bed? Does he want to cough now or in twenty minutes following pain medication? All serve to let the patient participate in ways which allow him to exert a minimal amount of control and predictability. It may also help him accept the lack of control around procedures for which he has little choice. Minute decisions like these allow him to exercise some controls in a way designed to help reduce the anxiety-provoking sense of helplessness.

A second overriding cause of anxiety is a sense of isolation. Rarely is one more lonely than in the midst of a socializing crowd of strangers. In such a situation individuals either attempt to include themselves, remove themselves, or distance themselves with feigned interest in a magazine, scenery or anything else that offers them relief from the sense of not belonging. The sick person surrounded by active and busy persons is in a similar situation but with fewer available resources to reduce his sense of isolation. Serious illness and the fear of dying separate the patient from his family. The reassuring cliche "You'll be all right" serves to enhance the sense of distance the patient is experiencing. It shuts off his expression of fears and his questions of what is to come next. The efficiency and activity engulfing him reinforce his sense of separateness as he lies isolated in his bed.

A third category of anxiety-provoking stimuli includes those that threaten the individual's security. Needless to say, entrance into the critical care unit serves as dramatic confirmation to the family and patient that their security on all levels is being severely threatened. Most individuals associate the critical care unit with a life-and-death crisis. By now many individuals associate the deaths of relatives and friends with the critical care unit.

But to the nurse the unit may represent a closer and safer vigilance of life. Her attention is directed more to the preservation of life than to the fears and preparations of dying that may be occupying the minds of the patient and his family. Upon the patient's admission to the unit insecurity is undoubtedly about life itself. Later, questions of length of hospitalization, return to work, well-being of the family, permanent limitations and the like arise to keep a state of insecurity ever present.

RESPONSE TO LOSS

The threat of illness precipitates the coping behaviors associated with loss. For some patients it is an adaptation to dying; for others it is the loss of health or loss of a limb, a blow to one's self-concept, or the necessity to change one's life style. Any of these require a change in one's self-image—a loss of the familiar image and its replacement with an altered self-image. Nevertheless the dynamics of grief present themselves in one form or another. Engel has conveniently categorized the response to loss in four phases:[1] shock and disbelief, developing awareness, restitution, and resolution. Each phase has characteristic and predictable behaviors which dynamically take the patient step-by-step through the healing process. Through the recognition and assessment of the various behaviors and an understanding of their underlying dynamics the nurse can plan her intervention to support the healing process.

Shock and Disbelief

In this stage the patient demonstrates the behaviors characteristic of denial. He fails to comprehend and experience the emotional impact and rational meaning of his diagnosis. Because the diagnosis has no emotional meaning the patient often fails to cooperate with precautionary measures. For example, he may attempt to get out of bed against the doctor's orders, may deviate from his diet, may fail to inform the nurse of minor pain, and may assert that he is there for a *rest!* Denial may go so far as to allow the patient to project his difficulties onto what he perceives as ill-functioning equipment, mistaken lab reports, and—more likely—on the sheer incompetence of physicians and nurses.

When such blatant denial occurs it is apparent that the problem is so anxiety-provoking to the patient that it cannot be handled by the more sophisticated defense mechanism of rational problem solving. Thus the stressor is obliterated. This phase of denial may also serve as the period when the patient's resources, temporarily blocked by the shock, can now be regrouped for the battle ahead. The principle of intervention consists not in stripping away the defense of denial but in supporting the patient and acknowledging his situation through nursing care.

The nurse accepts and recognizes his illness by watching the monitor or changing his dressings. She communicates her acceptance of the patient through her tone of voice, her facial expression, and her use of touch. She can reflect back to the patient his statements of denial in a way that allows him to hear them—and eventually to examine their incongruity and apply reality—as by saying, "In some ways you believe that having a heart attack will be helpful to you?" She can also acknowledge the patient's difficulty in accepting his restrictions by such comments as, "It seems hard for you to stay in bed." By verbalizing what the patient is expressing in action she gently confronts his behavior but does not cause anxiety and anger by reprimanding and judging him. Thus in this phase the nurse supports denial by allowing for it, but she does not perpetuate it. Rather she uses herself to acknowledge, accept, and reflect the patient's new circumstance. It is interesting to note that although denying illness can prevent adaptation at a new level, denial also has its advantages. High deniers with myocardial infarctions have a higher survival rate than moderate or low deniers.[2] They also often return to work sooner and reach higher levels of rehabilitation. This points out the effectiveness of denial as a coping mechanism as well as the hazards of stripping it away before the patient is ready.

Development of Awareness

In this stage of grief, the patient's behavior is characteristically associated with anger and guilt. He may present himself as overtly angry. His anger is most likely to be directed at the staff for oversights, tardiness, and minor insensitivities. Demanding and whining in this state often serve to alienate the nurse. The patient who does not demand or whine has probably retreated into the withdrawal of depression. He will demonstrate verbal and motor retardation, will have difficulty sleeping, and may prefer to be left alone.

At this time the ugliness of reality has made its impact. Displacement of the anger on others helps to slow down the impact. The expression of anger itself helps give the patient a sense of power in a seemingly helpless state. The depression is characteristic of other depressions, such as anger turned inward. The demanding and whining is an attempt to regain the control the patient senses he has lost.

During this phase the nurse is likely to hear irrational expressions of guilt. The patient seeks to answer "Why me?" He will attempt to isolate his human imperfections and attribute the cause of his malady to them. He and his family may participate in looking for a person or object to blame.

Guilt feelings around one's own illness are difficult to understand unless one examines the basic dynamic of guilt. Guilt arises when there is a decrease in the feeling of self-worth or when the self-concept has been violated. In this light, the nurse can understand that what is behind an expression of guilt is a negatively altered self-concept. Blame thus becomes nothing more than projection of the unbearable feeling of guilt.

Nursing intervention in this phase must be directed toward supporting the patient's basic sense of self-worth and allowing and encouraging the expression of direct anger. Nursing measures which support a patient's sense of self-worth are numerous: calling the patient by name, introducing him to strangers (particularly when they are to examine him), talking *to* rather than *about* him, and most of all providing and respecting the patient's need for privacy and modesty. The nurse needs to guard against verbal and nonverbal expressions of pity. She will do better to empathize with the patient's specific feelings of anger, sadness, and guilt rather than his condition.

The nurse can create outlets for anger by listening and by refraining from defending either herself, the doctor, or the hospital. A nondefensive, accepting attitude will decrease the patient's sense of guilt, and the expression of anger will avert some of the depression. Later when the patient is apologetic for his irrational outburst the nurse can interpret the necessity of this kind of verbalization as a step toward rehabilitation.

Restitution

Engel called this phase the "work of mourning." In this stage the griever puts aside his anger and resistance and begins to cope constructively with his loss. He tries new behaviors consistent with his limitations. His emotional level is one of sadness, and much of his time may be spent crying. As he adapts himself to his new image he spends considerable time going over and over significant memories relevant to his loss. Behaviors in this stage should include the verbalization of fears regarding his future. Often these go undetected because they are unbearable for the family to hear. After severe trauma which includes scarring or removal of a body part or loss of sensation, the patient may question his sexual adequacy and the future response of his mate to his changed body. He probably also questions his new role in his family and job and has a variety of concerns that are specific to his own life style.

Thus in the mourning process such manifestations as reminiscing, crying, questioning, expressing fears, and trying on new behaviors serve to help the patient modify his old self-concept and begin working with and experiencing his revised concept.

Nursing intervention in this stage should again be supportive to allow this adaptation to occur. Listening to the patient for lengthy periods of time will be necessary. If the patient is able to verbalize his fears and questions about the future, he will be better able to define his anxiety and to problem-solve. Furthermore it will help him put his fears into a more rational perspective as he hears himself talk about them. He may require privacy, acceptance, and encouragement to cry so that he can find respite from his sadness.

During this stage the nurse might have the patient consider meeting someone who has successfully adapted to similar trauma. This measure would provide the patient with a role model as he begins to take on a new identity, which often occurs after the crisis period.

Additionally, the patient with appropriate support from his nurse will begin to identify and acknowledge changes that are arising out of his adaptation to illness. Relationships can and do change. Because friends respond to an invalid differently, the patient will not feel or believe that he is being treated like his old self. During this time the family has also been going through a similar process. They too have experienced shock, disbelief, anger, and sadness. When they are ready to problem-solve, their energies will be directed toward wondering how the changes in the patient will affect their mutual relationship and their life style. They too will experience the pain of turmoil and uncertainty. Nurses must serve the family also. By providing ventilation and acceptance of their feelings of repulsion and fear, the nurse can help the family to be more useful and accepting to the patient. Through intensive listening the nurse provides an accepting sounding board and then redirects the members of the family back to each other so that they can receive mutual support.

Resolution

Resolution is the stage of identity change. At first the patient can be observed to be overidentifying himself as an invalid. He may discriminate against himself and make derogatory remarks about his body. Another method is to detach the traumatized part such as a stoma, prosthesis, scar, or paralyzed limb by naming it and referring to it in a simultaneously alienated and affectionate way. The patient is alert to the ways in which health care workers respond to his body and to his comments about himself, and may be testing out their acceptance before he ventures into the outside world. Chiding him or telling him that many others share his problem will be less helpful than acknowledging his feelings and indicating acceptance by continuing to care for and talk with him.

As the patient adapts with the passage of time, the sting of the endured hurt leaves and the patient moves toward identifying himself as an individual who has certain limitations due to his illness, rather than as a "cripple" or "invalid." He no longer uses his defect as the basis of his identity. As the resolution is reached, the patient is able to depend on others when necessary, and he should not need to push himself beyond his endurance or to overcompensate for his inadequacy. Often the individual will look back upon the crisis as a growing period. He will have hopefully achieved a sense of pride at accomplishing the difficult adaptation. He is able to reflect back realistically upon his successes and disappointments without discomfort. At this time he may find it useful and gratifying to help others in the stage of restitution during their identity crisis by sharing himself as a role model.

Unfortunately the hospital nurse rarely is in a position to observe the successful outcome. It is useful for her to know the process in order that she may work with an attitude of hope and communicate this hope, especially when her patient is most self-disparaging.

The goal of nursing care in this stage is to help the patient attach a sense of self-esteem to his rectified identity. Nursing intervention revolves around helping the patient find the degree of dependency that he needs and can accept. She must accept and recognize with the patient his vacillation between independency and dependency, and must encourage a positive emotional response to his new state of modified dependency. Certainly she can support and reinforce his growing sense of pride and his accomplished rehabilitation. For those nurses who have had the experience of working through the process with one individual, the problem will be to stand back and allow the patient to move away from them.

Adaptation to Illness

Another method of assisting and evaluating a patient's response to his illness is Martin and Prange's *Adaptation to Illness*.[3] By comparing man's emotional adaptation to his physical state of illness or well-being it is easy to identify problem areas.

Martin and Prange theorize that there is an emotional lag in which man becomes physically ill before he adapts emotionally; it follows that in the process of recuperation man becomes well before he adapts emotionally. Thus in the shaded area of Fig. 2-2 the patient is likely to be denying his illness. Again, he is likely to be uncooperative in his treatments and resist restrictions placed upon him. As he adjusts to his sick role things should go fairly smoothly. This is a receptive time for the patient to learn about his illness. Because progress heightens anxiety, teaching is usually more effective during this period of acceptance than during the times in which the patient is moving either into or out of the sick role. As the patient improves physically, the nurse and others begin to raise their expectations for his activity and independence. However, since his emotional adaptation has not caught up with his physical state the patient will move forward only with trepidation. He will demonstrate greater concern over his physical state and increase his demands for help. Preparation for his return to health, acknowledgment of his concerns over increased activity, and the reassurance of watchful eyes will help alleviate his anxiety as he progresses.

One principle that greatly affects understanding of the patient's response is the fact that during stress the patient will regress as an attempt to conserve his energies. Thus during times of acute exacerbation or the raising of expectations, or during any significant change, the initial response will be

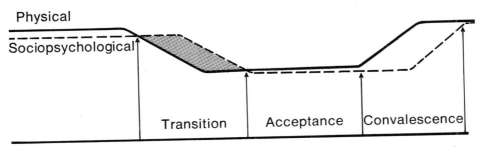

Fig. 2-2. The solid line represents a normal level of physical well-being, the broken line a corresponding degree of sociopsychological integration.

to regress to an earlier emotional position of safety. Weaning from a respir-ator, removal of monitor leads, or increased activity and reduction in medica-tion often trigger anxiety and regression. This regression may even include a retreat into increased dependency, depression, and anger. At that time comfort may be found in regressing into a state the patient has already discovered he can live through and/or master. The regression is usually temporary and brief and serves to pinpoint the cause of anxiety. At this time health personnel may become disappointed, anxious, or angry with the patient's backsliding and may wish to retreat from him. It is more helpful, however, to acknowledge that regression is inevitable and to support the patient with intervention appropriate in earlier stages.

Transfer from the Critical Care Unit

Regression is often elicited when the patient is told that he is ready to be transferred to a room in the general hospital. The stage of illness greatly influences the patient's response to transfer. If the patient is transferred while he is denying his illness, the move will be done with ease since it further fortifies his feeling that he isn't very sick. On the other hand, if the patient is transferred when he is improving physically more than he acknowledges emotionally, then anxiety will be heightened. The patient is saying, "I'm sick, and being transferred means you think I'm getting better when I'm not." In trying to cope with the anxiety generated by the move, he will regress and become more dependent. Transferring a patient when he first acknowl-edges the severity of his illness may create discomfort for his nurses, since the patient is likely to be frightened, angry, uncooperative, and demanding.

Preparing the Transfer

Regardless of the timing, in preparing for transfer both nurses and patients need to accept the fact that their relationship with each other will be ending. This may be done by reminiscing over an initial meeting or a special moment and by talking about the move.

If the patient is feeling dependent, then more time may be needed to talk about how it will be to leave. Often, because of discomfort at saying goodbye, nurses withdraw under the guise that it is easier for the patient to ignore the termination process. This unexplained withdrawal may be interpreted by the patient as a lack of interest or anger over earlier unresolved outbursts when he had been experiencing a change in body image and lowered esteem because of his illness.

The news of transfer often comes without warning or preparation. Even though the patient may be pleased with his progress, he is at the same time concerned about losing the reassurance of special equipment, close sur-veillance, and the presence of familiar faces. It has long been advocated that continuity of care be provided by thoughtful preparation. Introduction to the new nurses who will take over care of the patient, as well as follow-up visits by the critical care nurses, will increase familiarity, enhance security, and let the patient know that he is important. Removing equipment before the time of transfer will lessen the strain of having to give up his room, equipment, and nurse all at the same time.

Urine catecholamine studies on patients transferred to a general unit from a coronary care unit indicated that increased stress with transfer, occurred in five out of seven patients.[4] All five of these patients had a cardiovascular complication such as arrhythmia. In a follow-up study however, seven patients were prepared for transfer from the beginning of their stay. They had follow-up visits by the nurse and care by the same physician. No cardiovascular complications occurred and only two had a rise in urine catechols at the time of transfer. Even with preparation for transfer, regression and anxiety may occur; however, by acknowledging his concerns and receiving support from the nurse, the patient will again mobilize his energy.

Because these processes have proven predictable, they give the nurse a basis for her care and provide rationale for appropriate intervention. In spite of the predictability of these responses in human behavior, they still have an impact upon the individual and are unique to him. By the time they are modified by his personality and by sociocultural and economic variables they have become a significant part of his life, and are indeed made unique as they are made a historical and living part of his identity.

REFERENCES

1. George L. Engel, "Grief and Grieving," *American Journal of Nursing,* Vol. 64, No. 9 (September 1964), pp. 93–98.
2. Thomas Hackett, N. H. Cassem, and Howard Wishnie, "The Coronary Care Unit—An Appraisal of Its Psychological Hazards," *New England Journal of Medicine,* Vol. 279, No. 25 (December 19, 1968), pp. 1365–1370.
3. Harry W. Martin and Arthur J. Prange, "Adaptation to Illness," *Nursing Outlook,* Vol. 10 (March 1962), pp. 168–171.
4. Robert F. Klein et al., "Transfer From A Coronary Care Unit—Some Adverse Responses," *Archives of Internal Medicine,* Vol. 122 (August 1968), pp. 104–108.

Adverse Effects of Critical Care Units

JANET S. SMITH, R.N., M.S.

The necessity of employing highly technical and precise measures to preserve life in a crisis situation commonly found in critical care units can create an environment totally alien and threatening to the patient. The complicated equipment necessary for maintenance of life requires unquestionable expertise on the part of personnel involved in the care of the patients. However, if life-preserving measures are to have any meaning to the patient, the nurse must be aware of factors other than the physical need and the mechanical workings of the necessary respirators, monitors, and the increasing array of machines which medical technology is producing.

The psychological care necessary for the patient in the critical care unit demands more than assistance in dealing with a critical illness. In addition to the effects of fear of their illness, the sounds and activities of the units are continually bombarding the patients twenty-four hours a day. Normal defense mechanisms which allow us to cope with threatening situations are diminished in all patients and absent in the "unconscious" patient. The ability to run from a frightening or painful stimulus is gone, as is the ability to analyze a situation objectively and plan how to control it.

To appreciate how devastating confinement to a critical care unit can be, the nurse needs only to think of her own feelings about reversing roles with a patient. When asked if they would volunteer to spend twenty-four hours in the patient role in the crisis care unit, nurses respond readily with a definite "No!" In view of their awareness of the environmental threats of such units nurses must function as the negotiator for the patient. To be an effective negotiator the nurse must acquire knowledge about the effects of sensory input on the human organism.

SENSORY INPUT

The broad concept of sensory input deals with stimulation of all of the five senses: visual, auditory, olfactory, tactile, and gustatory. Stimuli to all of the senses may be perceived in a qualitative manner as pleasant or unpleasant, acceptable or unacceptable, desirable or undesirable, soothing or painful. Individual perception of stimuli may vary drastically. Some individuals may consider the sounds and smells of a metropolitan business section to be pleasant, acceptable, desirable — or painful. Everyday activities including the choice of food or drink are based on the individual's perception of what is liked or disliked. Thus people tend to choose whenever possible, the environment or stimuli from the environment that is most acceptable to them, but patients in the critical care unit have no control over the choice of their environment or many of its stimuli.

In addition to the quality of a stimulus the nurse must consider the quantity also. Too much of a desirable stimulus can become as unacceptable as a little of an undesirable stimulus. An example of excessive quantity of a good thing is gorging oneself with a favorite food to the point of revulsion. In the critical care unit, excessive and constant noise, bright light and hyperactivity can be as distorting and bothersome as gloom, silence, and indolence.

In dealing with the control of environmental stimuli in a critical care unit, the nurse must then be aware of both the quality and the quantity of sensory input. If sensory stimuli are diminished too drastically the patient is exposed to sensory deprivation, which can cause severe disorganization of normal psychological defenses.[1] When sensory stimuli occur in excessive quantity the phenomenon of sensory overload will create an equally undesirable response to the environment.

SENSORY DEPRIVATION

Sensory deprivation is a general term used to identify a variety of symptoms which occur following a reduction in the quantity of sensory input and/or the degree of structure or quality of sensory input.[2] Other terms used to denote sensory deprivation or some form of it include *isolation, confinement, informational underload, perceptual deprivation,* and *sensory restriction.* A variety of symptoms or changes in behavior has been noted in normal adults following exposure to sensory deprivation for varying lengths of time. These include loss of sense of time; presence of delusions, illusions, and hallucinations; restlessness, and any of the types of behavior or symptoms present in psychoses.

Sensory deprivation need not be present for a period of days or weeks for psychopathological reactions to occur. In one study conducted on a normal young male subject, an eight-hour period of sensory deprivation elicited an acute psychotic reaction followed by continuation of delusions for several days, and severe depression and anxiety for a period of several weeks.[3] The degree of sensory deprivation possible in a laboratory setting is greater than that likely in a critical care unit, but it must be remembered that the subject was aware of the time involved in the experiment and also possessed clinically normal defense mechanisms, whereas hospital patients do not have these advantages. It is not presently known how the stress of illness will affect human subjects exposed to sensory deprivation, but there is no reason to assume that such stress will make patients any less susceptible to adverse reactions to such deprivation. On the contrary, it would appear more logical to assume that patients faced with coping with illness would have increased susceptibility to more severe responses to sensory deprivation. The main types of patients most susceptible to the adverse effects of sensory deprivation would appear to be the defenseless or unconscious patient, the very young patient, the very old patient, and the postoperative patient.

Although it has been known for more than twenty years that sensory deprivation can lead to psychotic behavior, the nursing profession has done very little to apply this knowledge to its planning for patients in critical care units. Hospital personnel have long demonstrated at least a passing concern over the control of excessive noise causing sensory overload by the use of the familiar "Quiet, Please" signs in hospitals and other health care facilities, but a survey of the literature and an examination of many critical care units fail to demonstrate a similar concern for creating an environment intended to diminish the effects of sensory deprivation.

If unstructured sound or noise was all that was necessary to prevent the phenomena caused by sensory deprivation, most crisis care units would never need to be concerned with the concept at all. It is not, however, *quantity* alone that must be considered; even more important is the inclusion of planning the *quality* of stimuli in the external environment. A British investigator supports such a conclusion by stating that "Reality testing can only occur when there is a continual input of meaningful information from the outside world. When this is markedly reduced, as under experimental conditions of sensory deprivation, reality testing is impaired and internal mental events are taken to be events in the external world."[4]

REALITY TESTING

For reality testing to occur there must be familiar environmental stimuli. However, the sounds of the critical care unit cannot be said to be meaningful to more than a few medical and nursing personnel who spend long periods of their working life in such an environment. Therefore the nurse in the critical care unit should be certain that the environment offers the patient adequate stimuli to provide for reality testing. As human beings we take our physical environment for granted, but if we suddenly awoke in a world without grass or sunlight or the sounds of traffic or human speech we would not have the necessary stimuli to keep our minds in contact with reality. We would try to interpret the unknown stimuli on the basis of what we have always been familiar with. In reality, however, our interpretations may be wrong. This is especially true of patients who suffer temporary loss of any of the senses, particularly vision or hearing, since we normally utilize a combination of senses to interpret our environment.

This lack of reality testing may offer at least partial explanation for the high incidence of psychosis in patients commonly assigned to critical care units for long-term care due to an "unconscious state." The fact that no physical reason has ever been identified to explain posttraumatic psychosis offers additional support to such an assumption. Nursing is limited in its consideration of the unconscious patient who is often found in critical care units because authorities in the field have perpetuated the concept that such patients are insensitive to their environment and have perceptual disturbances that affect their responses to the environment. In view of the necessity of reality testing and the lack of meaningful information to allow such testing in the critical care unit, it is reasonable to explain some of the reactions of patients, including even the unconscious patient, as being caused by the lack of meaningful input which can be referred to as sensory deprivation. There is more empirical data to support this assumption than there is evidence for believing that posttraumatic psychosis is due to physical phenomena.

One example of such a situation caused by sensory deprivation in the critical care unit occurred during an experiment conducted by the writer with an unresponsive patient assumed to be unconscious by both the medical and nursing team members. She was a twenty-year-old college student with severe basal skull trauma and multiple injuries who was unresponsive throughout the eight-day period she spent in a critical care unit. When she began responding verbally, her first words to her mother were: "Am I free now? I was in the hands of the Soviet Union!" An immediate interpretation of such a statement could reasonably be that she was totally out of contact with reality due to the injury and had dreamed such an episode. It is just as reasonable to assume that she could have perceived that the actions in the unit and treatments she received due to her condition were related to torture and she was the victim for some unknown reason. She had no noticeable motor control of her facial muscles, so she was "blind." She had a tracheostomy that required frequent suctioning. She was almost immobile because of fractures and spasticity necessitating plaster casts or cloth restraints on all extremities. It is reasonable to assume that such a situation could cause her to believe she was being tortured, since she had no means of interpreting her experience realistically from meaningful cues in the environment.

Many other situations and case histories can be reported to stress the importance of planning for and providing meaningful sensory stimulation for the patient cared for in all hospital units but especially the ones in critical care units. Nurses can play a significant role in alleviating the unnecessary stress caused by sensory deprivation by recognizing the need for the structuring of sensory input. The use of auditory stimuli such as the explanation of any treatment or procedure to be performed on a patient is a basic requirement and must not be overlooked as insignificant; but explanation alone is not adequate to prevent adverse effects of sensory deprivation. This type of communication can be considered a minimal requirement in a broader area of communication which can be called security information.

SECURITY INFORMATION

Security information helps prevent unnecessary anxiety and disorientation regarding date, time, and place. It also includes explanation of treatment and procedures. This is particularly important for patients with deviations in levels of consciousness due to trauma, drugs, or toxicity. Orientation to date and time could be encouraged not only by including the information in conversation but by providing large-faced clocks that are readily visible to the patient, and similar placement of large calendars displaying the day, month, and year in large figures. The simplicity of such information sometimes causes it to be overlooked, but it can affect the patient's comfort by providing information we take for granted. In addition, it is essential to provide this information because the patient's state of orientation is often based on his answers to those questions.

A nursing history included in the initial phase of planning can help make nursing intervention an effective part of the total care. Such a history requires that individualized questions be asked of both patient and family members. A brief outline of a normal 24-hour period of activity and sleep habits gives a good starting point in compiling a useful nursing history. A concerned and well-informed nurse can determine the times when the individual's physiological functions are at both maximal and minimal levels. For example, urine output is minimal during the night when sleep normally occurs. Treatment and procedures not predicated by moment-to-moment conditions and necessary activities such as bathing can then be performed when maximum energy is available—or avoided if possible when lower energy levels are present. Physiological functions reach their lowest levels in the middle of the night, whereas in the early morning hours functions are beginning to move up to a maximum level. Therefore normal fluctuations in vital signs should be expected and patients should not be subjected to activity or stressful procedures in the early morning hours. Such predictability of peaks and troughs of physiological functions is possible due to increasing knowledge of periodicity, a topic which is briefly discussed later in this chapter.

Additional information which may be included in the nursing history could be anything from likes to dislikes to the favorite type of music or TV programs. It would be desirable to provide exposure to familiar stimuli such as playing a favorite record from home or finding the right radio station to listen to if the patient is not able to do it, or requesting a taped message sent from a loved one who cannot visit. Such action will offer meaningful sensory stimulation to the patient in an otherwise unfamiliar environment. A simple rule to use in collecting a nursing history is to determine what is significant or familiar to the patient and expose him to it if possible.

The family and friends should be involved in planning and providing such sensory input, especially for unconscious patients. One of the most miserable feelings must be that of uselessness on the part of a family member or friend at the bedside of an unresponsive loved one. During a survey conducted in critical care units preceding a research project on unconscious patients, this writer was repeatedly impressed by the scene of a mother, father, husband, wife, or other close relative standing at the bedside and staring with a variety of emotions at the unconscious patient. A simple direction, or granting of permission in some cases, to touch the patient's hand and talk to him brought a look of relief and gratitude to their faces. With further assistance on what to say to the patient, the visitor became very effective in preventing sensory deprivation by discussing people or subjects familiar and of interest to the patient.

The value of simple conversation about everyday activities is underestimated in the care of the unconscious patient in critical care units. This is pointed out vividly in the following incident recorded in "A Study of Sensory Response in the Unconscious Patient":*

Critical Incident

Interest in nursing implications inherent in care of the unconscious patient beyond the physical dimensions was initiated while caring for a patient in her late fifties, comatose as a result of metastatic carcinoma of the brain. The investigator carried on a one-sided conversation about many things, including a daily introduction of self, explanations of care to be given, and discussion of the day and the weather. There was no perceptible response from the patient. Her condition appeared to be slowly deteriorating. Contact with the patient was lost after four days due to an assignment change.

About two months later while boarding a train the investigator was approached by a woman on crutches who called the investigator's name and asked if she were a nurse. Following an affirmative response and recognition of the previous nurse-patient interaction the investigator and the patient conversed for several hours. The discussion revealed much about the initial relationship between them. The patient expressed how she had felt during the days she lay in the hospital bed totally defenseless and at the mercy of those on the nursing team and that the investigator had been the only person who had identified herself and talked to the patient.

Of particular interest to the patient was information as to the nurse's time of leaving and when she would return. When the investigator had informed her she would be leaving for another assignment she said she had felt like crying because she anticipated receiving no further information about the outside world. The patient recalled much more about the interaction than the investigator.

---

*Janice Shirley Smith, "A Study of Sensory Response in the Unconscious Patient," thesis submitted to the faculty of the Graduate School of the University of Colorado in partial fulfillment of the requirements for the degree of Master of Science, School of Nursing, 1970.

Such experiences indicate that even in today's modern nursing world the little things, such as consideration of the patient as an individual deserving common courtesies, are still important to patients. It cannot be taken for granted that such behavior should be automatic on the grounds that nurses are trained to be comfortable around the hectic environment of a critical care unit, and rapidly forget the sense of awe or fear that was present the first time they saw the unit. It might be helpful for the nurses in the critical care unit to stop for a moment each day and project themselves mentally into the patient's role to determine what information or activity might be desirable. Such an act might be effective in salvaging whatever human dignity is left for the patient after being subjected to the regressive procedures of being bathed, fed, and forced to meet toileting needs in bed shielded from other patients only by a cotton curtain with wide openings at top and bottom.

SENSORY OVERLOAD

The area of sensory overload has not received as much attention as sensory deprivation, but some of its effects on man are known. One of the best documented adverse effects is that of decreased hearing following long-term exposure to high noise levels such as those found in factories or machine shops. It is also recognized that tension and anxiety increase when an individual is exposed to noise for continuous periods of time without quiet periods of rest. Edgar Allan Poe capitalized on such knowledge in horror stories dealing with the effect of continuous rhythmical sounds such as the dripping of water or the whirring of machinery, as in "The Pit and the Pendulum." In more recent periods we have heard of the use of continuous noise as a means of torturing prisoners of war. We too must capitalize on this information. When patients become increasingly anxious or restless, environmental causes such as noise as well as physiological reasons such as hypercarbia must be considered in trying to determine the cause of such behavior.

Many years ago Florence Nightingale expressed her awareness of the effects of noise on patients: "Unnecessary noise is the most cruel absence of care which can be inflicted on either sick or well".[5]

Clues about the significance of both the quantity and quality of noise are offered by a study conducted in a recovery room. It was found that high levels of noise increased the need for pain medication. It is interesting to note, however, that the most pronounced reaction on the part of the recovery-room patient was that of resentment of the sound of occasional laughter from the recovery-room personnel.[6]

The presence of continuous noise in crisis care units must be minimized at least for some time in every 24-hour period. The cardiac monitors with their beeping should not be kept in areas where patients must hear them continuously. The physical planning for units must include provision for facilities where patients on continuous respirators are not in the same open area as other patients. However, ways have not yet been devised for protecting patients who are on the respirator from the machine's incessant cycling noise. Nor is it presently known how or if the sound of the machine has any adverse psychological effect on the patient. In view of the recent and ongoing advancement in technical methods necessary for retention of life, problems such as this will continue. When technology becomes more advanced and heroic life-saving measures succeed in significant numbers of patients needing such treatment we will then be able to focus attention on their less apparent psychological needs.

The effect of continuous sound on the intricate physiological functions of the human organism is not fully known, but assumptions can be made that a variety of adverse responses can be expected. Even without such empirical data to support the need to control unnecessary noise we can look at our own life style to see how we react to continuous or loud noise. It is normal to attempt to plug our ears in the presence of a loud noise such as a firecracker, and it is just as normal to choose to sleep in a quiet room with the sounds of the outside world shut out by well-constructed walls or special soundproofing. It is perhaps not feasible to control noise in the environment of critical care units to the same extent the patient is accustomed to, but it is both feasible and essential that nurses exert a conscious effort to avoid unnecessary noise in such an environment.

Another facet of controlling unnecessary noise involves preventing exhaustion. There is adequate knowledge available in the areas of sleep research to prove that sleep is essential for both physical and mental well-being. Therefore nurses need to plan for and provide an environment which will not only allow but also encourage sleep for patients in critical care units. This sounds deceptively simple until one realizes what is necessary in meeting such a need. A darkened room makes it impossible to have the security of visual observation of the critically ill patient, but few people can sleep in a lighted room even if the lighting level is low or soft. Normal practice is to sedate many patients in such a unit, but the nurse must realize that drug-induced or interrupted sleep is not adequate for any significant period of time. The human organism must have normal uninterrupted periods of sleep that are long enough to allow all stages of sleep to occur. This normally means a period of a minimum of three to four hours, but even that is probably not adequate for most people for a period of more than a day or two.

PERIODICITY

Another area of knowledge necessary for the nurse in the critical care unit deals with the broad concept of periodicity. Other terms include: *circadian rhythm, biological clock, internal clock,* and *physiological clock.* It has been recognized for a number of years that all living matter not only has an identifiable life cycle but also possesses short-term cycles which are rhythmical in nature; disruption of that rhythm can cause deviations from the normal or cessation of life. The human organism possesses a 24-hour cycle that is resistant to change, and long-term disruption can be fatal. Each of the biochemical and biophysical processes of the human body possesses a rhythm with peaks of function or activity which occur in consistent patterns within the normal 24-hour day we are accustomed to. Knowledge of when physiological functions are at their lowest level would allow for more intelligent assessment of the significance of vital-sign fluctuation, and even the quantity of urine output since the kidneys possess their own unique rhythm as demanded by our sleep and activity patterns. Drug dosage, sleep periods, and stressful procedures such as surgery may also someday be based on knowledge of individual circadian rhythms, thus avoiding further stress in the most vulnerable part of the cycle and capitalizing on the strongest parts of the cycle.

The environment of a critical care unit possesses the unique ability to deprive a patient of meaningful sensory input while exposing him to a continual bombardment of unfamiliar stimuli causing potential sensory overload. A period of casual observation of sounds and activity in such a unit will identify a wide variety of sounds not present in the normal environment outside the hospital setting. The only readily identifiable familiar sound is that of the ringing of the telephone, and even that can create frustration. For example, think about your internal response to a ringing telephone. After years of conditioning, a ringing telephone elicits an automatic movement to answer it and a feeling of frustration when it is left unanswered. This can create additional stress for an immobile patient in a strange environment.

The unfamiliarity of the environment is a potential double threat to patients already faced with coping with a severe crisis that demands more energy than may be available. The challenge is in recognizing the potential for using the presently rampant environment of the crisis care unit as a controlled and therapeutic tool in the total care of the patient in the unit.

Effective planning can reverse the current traumatic situation present in most critical care units. Total control of the sounds and activities is not possible in the physical setting present in most units used in hospitals today, but the nurse can exert her influence in the knowledgeable planning of future units. It is not possible to give concrete directions that will fit all situations, but it is important to know that sensory input can be hazardous if it is excessive, meaningless, or too continuous. This knowledge, combined with the awareness that the patient is not as familiar or respectful of the life-saving but noisy technical advances called machines, will make the nurse in the critical care unit a knowledgeable and effective practitioner and negotiator for the patient.

A great number of nursing measures are presently possible, and identification of them will result in a significant advance in the area of individualization of care. Nursing has used the phrase "individualization of care" for a long time, but now needs to apply it to the critical care units more extensively than ever before. The area of individualization of physical care has been more tangible, and was therefore the initial area of care focused on. However, the psychological care of the patient should now receive more emphasis. Some of our actions have been traditional rather than logical with empirical data supporting them. Knowledge available today indicates that actions must be justified in light of weighing the potential adverse effects against the validity and necessity of an action that may cause undesirable effects. In other words, it is necessary to determine whether or not the omission of the act is more threatening than its commission, as in arousing a patient to take a BP at the expense of disrupting the REM (rapid eye movement) stage of sleep. The robot action of following a routine without theoretical knowledge involved in decision making is no longer a function of the nurse. Instead it is necessary to make decisions based on sound rationale, with knowledge of the consequences, and evaluation of the effects.

REFERENCES

1. G. C. Curtis et al., "A Psychopathological Reaction Precipitated by Sensory Deprivation," *American Journal of Psychiatry*, Vol. 125 (August 1968), pp. 255–260.
2. H. B. Adams et al., "Sensory Deprivation and Personality Change," *Journal of Nervous and Mental Disease*, Vol. 143 (September 1966), p. 256.
3. G. C. Curtis, et al., "A Psychopathological Reaction Precipitated by Sensory Deprivation," *American Journal of Psychiatry*, Vol. 125 (August 1968), pp. 255–260.
4. J. P. Leff, "Perceptual Phenomena and Personality in Sensory Deprivation," *British Journal of Psychiatry*, Vol. 114 (December 1968), pp. 1499–1508.
5. T. W. Hurst, "Is Noise Important in Hospitals?," *International Journal of Nursing Studies*, Vol. 3 (September 1966), pp. 125–131.
6. Barbara Minckley, "A Study of Noise and Its Relationship to Patient Discomfort in the Recovery Room," *Nursing Research*, Vol. 17, No. 3 (May–June 1968), pp. 247–250.

BIBLIOGRAPHY

Adams, H. B., et al., "Sensory Deprivation and Personality Change," *Journal of Nervous and Mental Disease*, Vol. 143 (September 1966), pp. 256–265.

Blake, Florence G., "Immobilized Youth," *American Journal of Nursing*, Vol. 69, No. 11 (November 1969), pp. 2364–2369.

Catlin, Francis, "Noise and Emotional Stress," *Journal of Chronic Diseases*, Vol. 18 (June 1965), pp. 509–518.

Comer, Nathan L., Leo Madow, and James J. Dixon, "Observations of Sensory Deprivation in a Life-Threatening Situation," *American Journal of Psychiatry*, Vol. 125 (August 1967), pp. 164–169.

Curtis, G. C., et al., "A Psychopathological Reaction Precipiated by Sensory Deprivation," *American Journal of Psychiatry*, Vol. 125 (August 1968), pp. 255–260.

Gerdes, Lenore, "The Confused or Delirious Patient," *American Journal of Nursing*, Vol. 68 (June 1968) pp. 1228–1233.

Golub, Sharon, R.N., "Noise, the Underrated Health Hazard," *R.N.*, (May 1969), pp. 40–45.

Hurst, T. W., "Is Noise Important in Hospitals?," *International Journal of Nursing Studies*, Vol. 3 (September 1966), pp. 125–131.

Leff, J. P., "Perceptual Phenomena and Personality in Sensory Deprivation," *British Journal of Psychiatry*, Vol. 114 (December 1968), pp. 1499–1508.

Minckley, Barbara, "A Study of Noise and Its Relationship to Patient Discomfort in the Recovery Room," *Nursing Research,* Vol. 17, No. 3 (May–June 1968), pp. 247–250.

Sister Regina Elizabeth, "Sensory Stimulation Techniques," *American Journal of Nursing,* Vol. 66 (February 1966), pp. 281–286.

Smith, Janice Shirley, "A Study of Sensory Response in the Unconscious Patient," a thesis submitted to the faculty of the Graduate School of the University of Colorado in partial fulfillment of the requirements for the degree of Master of Science, School of Nursing, 1970.

Ziskind, Eugene, and Theodore Augsburg, "Hallucinations in Sensory Deprivation (Method or Madness)," *Diseases of the Nervous System,* Vol. 28 (November 1967), pp. 721–726.

Zubek, J. P., "Effects of Prolonged Sensory and Perceptual Deprivation," *British Medical Bulletin,* Vol. 20, No. 1 (1964), pp. 38–42.

4

Anatomy, Physiology, and Pathophysiology of the Cardiovascular System

MARGARET ANN BERRY, R.N., M.A., M.S.
H. L. BRAMMELL, M.D.

ANATOMY AND PHYSIOLOGY OF THE HEART

During the seventy years in the life of the average individual, his heart pumps five quarts of blood per minute, 75 gallons per hour, 70 barrels a day, and 18 million barrels in a lifetime.[1] The work accomplished by this organ is completely out of proportion to its size, but this fact is not so surprising when one considers the economy of size in the overall architecture of the entire body. The surprising thing is that for most people the heart presents no illness problem, and it functions normally throughout their life span. For the individual who does develop a cardiac problem, the result is much different. When a pathological condition manifests itself in this very vital organ, the effects are extremely dramatic and the outcome often drastic. It is for this reason that you the reader are presently addressing yourself to the problems that arise from functional deviations of the heart. To assess, manage, and evaluate nursing problems with which you must deal, it is necessary to have a solid foundation in understanding normal structure, function, and pathogenesis of cardiac action. Nursing appropriately addresses itself to supporting the medical regime developed for the individual patient. However, its primary concern should lie in the conservation of the patient's resources by accurately predicting when and where critical problems may present themselves which will deter the success of the medical and nursing plan and the improvement of the individual's health status. The information contained in this chapter will therefore be concerned with the normal structure and function of the heart and with the pathogenic variables which lead to the development of coronary heart disease, as well as those which progressively produce more dysfunction in the circulatory system.

Man is a biopsychosocial being constantly faced with the necessity of interacting with his environment and all other organisms and forces within it. Although it is necessary to approach the study of structure and function in a dissective manner, every effort will be made to recall the reader to the consideration of the *gestalt* of cardiac function as it operates to maintain the individual's steady state in harmony with his environment.

As multicellular organisms evolved, two crucial problems arose: (1) providing each cellular unit with those substances needed to carry on its differentiated function, and (2) removing waste products from the immediate vicinity. In response to these fundamental demands, a circulatory system evolved along with a pumping unit—the heart. As the complexity of the organism increased, this system became further elaborated, culminating in the four-chambered heart of the mammal or class *Mammalia* of which man is but one species.

Although man enjoys a terrestrial existence, his individual cells are dependent upon their abilities to exchange materials across membranes which are constantly bathed in aqueous solutions. Fundamentally, then, man is still an aquatic animal at the cellular level, and his functions are controlled and mediated by the efficiency with which materials are moved to and from cells. For this reason the heart is completely dependent upon its own effectiveness as the circulatory pump to provide for its differentiated function—that of constantly moving aqueous solutions into and out of the vicinity of individual cells through a highly developed tubular system.

Microstructure of Cardiac Muscle

In the human organism there are three kinds of contractile tissue found in various locations in the body: *striated muscle,* sometimes referred to as skeletal or voluntary muscle; *smooth* or *involuntary muscle;* and *cardiac muscle.* The cells of striated muscle have lost their distinctive cell walls and therefore are syncytial in nature. There are cross-striations which appear when the tissue is studied under the microscope. These "stripes" are due to the different optical densities of the chemical contractile elements actin and myosin. These two substances are found in all contractile tissues of the body, and the characteristic linear arrangements coupled with the cellular arrangement allow one to histologically differentiate between the three types of muscle cells.

Figure 4-1 diagrammatically shows the three types of contractile tissue. Figure 4-1A is striated muscle as just described. As shown in Figure 4-1C, smooth muscle is made up of individual spindle-shaped cells which are densely packed into layers. When these cells are stretched the total muscle layer is thinned out. When the contractile elements shorten, the total effect is one of thickening the muscle layer. It is easily seen that this type of contractile tissue is characteristically found surrounding the lumen of tubular structures such as gut and vessel walls. When the muscle contracts, the diameter of the lumen is decreased and the contents are propelled along the tube in a linear fashion.

Cardiac muscle combines properties of both the other two types of contractile tissue. It is striated like skeletal muscle, but is not a structural syncytium. The fibers are composed of separate cellular units joined end to end by intercalated discs as seen in Figure 4-1B. The cells bifurcate and branch connecting with adjacent fibers forming a three-dimensional complex network. The elongated nuclei, like smooth muscle, are found situated deep in the interior of the cells and not adjacent to the sarcolemma.

Although it was stated that cardiac muscle is not a structural syncytium, it functions as one. It is believed that this is due to the presence of the intercalated discs which because of their low electrical resistance permit the rapid spread of excitation from cell to cell and thus allow essentially simultaneous contraction.

Yet another difference, perhaps the most important difference between cardiac muscle and skeletal muscle cells, is that of automaticity, whereby cardiac muscle cells are capable of initiating rhythmic action potentials and thus waves of contraction without any outside humoral and/or nervous intervention.

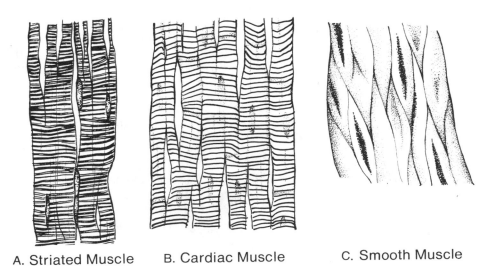

A. Striated Muscle   B. Cardiac Muscle   C. Smooth Muscle

Fig. 4-1. Histological features of the three types of contractile tissue.

The syncytial organization of cardiac muscle is such that there are two "lattice works"—the atrial syncytium and the ventricular syncytium. Though physically discontinuous, these two syncytia are functionally connected by the specialized conduction system. These specialized cardiac muscle fibers provide for communication of the contractile stimulus from one to the other. The Purkinje system is composed of the A-V node and the A-V bundle, which further subdivides into the right and left ventricular branches. These two branches then spread across the entire myocardium of each ventricle. The fibers then fuse with the syncytial muscle fibers so that their membranes are continuous and any impulse traveling along the membrane of a Purkinje fiber is transmitted directly to the ventricular myofibril.

Figure 4-2 is a schematic representation of the distribution of the Purkinje system and the location of the S-A node where the contractile impulse is initiated.

In summary, the microstructure of human cardiac muscle provides the knowledge necessary to understand the structural components which contribute to normal cardiac function. This microstructure orders the overall characteristics of cardiac function which result in a very efficient propulsive unit in the circulatory system.

General Characteristics of the Developing Heart

The human heart begins its function at an extremely early age in the individual. The rhythmic contraction of cardiac muscle is initiated long before there is much form to the organ itself, to say nothing of the undifferentiated state of the body form of the whole embryo. In fact, the early heart is little more than a tube when the first wave of contraction is initiated. This innate heart beat is referred to as a "myogenic" beat—that is, it is initiated in the muscle itself and needs no nervous stimulation for its initiation or main-

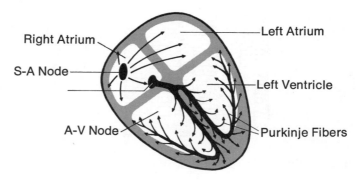

Fig. 4-2. Distribution of the Purkinje system and the location of the sinoatrial node in the human heart.

.tenance. Once the rhythmic contractions have started they will continue without interruption until the death of the individual. Nervous stimulation may alter the rhythm and/or the rate, but the contractile characteristic of cardiac muscle resides in the biochemical properties of the chemical substances found in the tissue itself.

The structural developmental sequence of the heart is very interesting and of great importance to a discussion of those pathological conditions which arise from congenital cardiac defects. A discussion of structural development of the heart can be found in any good textbook which deals with the description of human development. For purposes of this discussion, however, it is sufficient to briefly touch on the development of the individual contractile units. The musculature of the atria develops and functions independently of the musculature of ventricles. Timewise, this development is simultaneous. Therefore, when the myogenic beat is initiated in the atrial musculature, it occurs soon after in the ventricular lattice. The atria contract at a faster rate than do the ventricles because the muscular walls of the atria are both thinner and smaller, permitting the spread of excitation to reach all parts much more quickly. The initiation of the contraction is an electrochemical stimulus and is dependent upon changes in the membrane potential for the spread of excitation to all parts of both the atrial and ventricular musculatures.

The difference in the "natural" rates of contraction between the atrial and ventricular lattices is of prime importance when dealing with the effect of abnormalities in the conduction system. These differences in myogenic contractile rates are the main reason that the disruption of the normal conduction patterns in each lattice work is incompatible with life and why restoration of normal coordinated rhythmicity is absolutely essential. If the normal rhythmicity is not restored, the result is that approximately two atrial contractions occur for each ventricular contraction. The ultimate problem is one of incomplete emptying of the chambers and valvular regurgitation. When dealing with patients whose normal cardiac conduction mechanisms are disrupted, the nurse must be cognizant of the impending dangers and exigencies of the situation.

Conducive and Contractile Characteristics of Cardiac Muscle

All membranes of the cells in the human body are charged—that is, they are polarized and therefore have electrical potentials. This means simply that there is a separation of charges at the membrane. In humans all cell membranes regardless of type are positively charged, there being more positively charged particles at the outer surface of the cell membrane than at the inner surface.

Figure 4-3A illustrates this "resting state." This does not mean that there is an absence of negatively charged particles at the outer surface, nor that there is an absence of positively charged particles at the inner surface. It merely

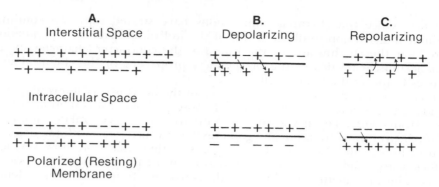

Fig. 4-3. The nature of cellular membranes in the human body.

means that there is a net difference in the number and kind of charged particles at the outer surface as compared to the inner surface.

Cardiac muscle membranes are polarized and the electrical potential can be measured, as is the situation in any of the cells in the human body. The potential results from the difference of intra- and extracellular concentrations of electrolytes. The electrolyte mainly responsible for the charge at the membrane is potassium with some contribution from sodium and chloride. When compounds or salts of the elements are dissolved in aqueous solutions, they dissociate into their charged particles called *ions*. It is through the selective control of the concentrations of these ions that the electrical membrane potential is maintained.

Since the cell membrane is permeable to certain ions whose concentration gradient favors diffusion into the cell, energy must be expended to remove them from the cytoplasm and out through the cell membrane by means of a chemical carrier and the expenditure of energy. The process is called "active transport." For each molecule of ion pumped from the cell, one molecule of adenosine triphosphate (ATP) is required to provide the energy necessary to affect the chemical bond between the ion and the chemical carrier. The process of maintaining membrane potentials in living cells is an *endergonic* (energy-consuming) phenomenon.

When a stimulus is applied to the polarized cell membrane, the membrane which ordinarily is only slightly permeable to sodium permits sodium ions to diffuse rapidly into the cell. The result is a reversal of net charges; the outer surface is now more negative than positive and the membrane is said to be "depolarized" (Fig. 4-3B). As soon as the impulse moves along the membrane, the separation of charges is restored by way of the sodium pump and potassium diffusion restoring the original state or "repolarizing" the membrane (Fig. 4-3C). This method for transmitting impulses of physical, chemical, or electrical origin is not peculiar to cardiac muscle membranes, but indeed is common to all excitable membranes in the human body.

The Purkinje system is composed of very specialized cardiac muscle fibers which have the ability to depolarize and recover at a much more rapid rate than ordinary cardiac myofibril membranes. Also, the membrane of the cells of the S-A node is extremely sensitive to minute changes in electrochemical conditions in the posterior wall of the right atrium where it is situated. As a result, it initiates the impulse of depolarization leading to contraction of the atrial musculature. The impulse is passed to the A-V node by adjacent atrial cells.

The A-V node lies on the posteriomedial surface near the right atrioventricular valve (tricuspid). The membranes of the node fibers have a slower depolarization rate and thus there is a slight delay before the impulse reaches the midline bundle and spreads to the right and left ventricular branches. This delay allows the atria to completely empty their contents into the two ventricular chambers before there is any contraction of the myocardium of those chambers.

The discussion on membrane dynamics and the characteristics of the conduction of impulses in cardiac muscle readily indicates the importance of the electrolytes sodium, potassium, chloride, and calcium. Of these four, sodium plays the most obvious role in membrane action potentials. The role of potassium ions is in establishing membrane potentials. Calcium is chemically involved in the combination and release of the contractile substances of actin and myosin and membrane thresholds. The importance of understanding the separate and collective functions of these electrolytes is prerequisite to an understanding of normal cardiac function.

Control of Rate and Rhythm of Cardiac Function

It was emphasized in the section on cardiac embryogenesis that cardiac muscle has a myogenic beat. The S-A node of the heart, without any outside influence, will discharge an impulse to the atrial muscular lattice 70–80 times per minute, while the A-V node, if not fired by the S-A node, will stimulate the ventricular lattice to contract 40–60 times per minute. Because the S-A node not only discharges at a faster rate than does the A-V node or the bundle fibers, but also recovers at a much more rapid rate, it controls the rhythmic discharge and resultant contractile rate of the heart. For these reasons it is called the "pacemaker." In order for the heart to function efficiently as a pump, both atria must contract simultaneously. This presents no real problem, inasmuch as the spread of excitation from the S-A node to the membranes reaches the A-V node in only 0.08 second. There is a delay at the A-V node which is sufficient to permit complete emptying of the atrial contents into the ventricular chambers.

The rate at which the S-A node can initiate cardiac contractions does not allow the heart to change either its rate or its rhythm to meet the physiological demands of the body. The nervous innervation via the autonomic nervous system performs this function. The distribution of the parasympathetic and sympathetic nerve fibers is shown in Fig. 4-4.

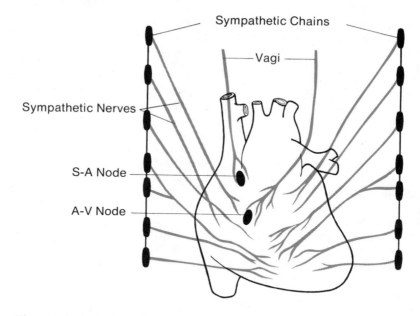

Fig. 4-4. Distribution of autonomic nervous fibers to the human heart.

The effect of sympathetic stimulation of the heart is one of increasing the rate of contraction; that of parasympathetic stimulation is a decrease in the contractile rate. Both responses are mediated by chemical mediators which are secreted by the nerve endings themselves. In the case of vagal (parasympathetic) fibers, the chemical substance is acetylcholine, and for the sympathetic fibers the substance is the familiar norepinephrine. The effects of both substances are the result of changing the rate of depolarization in S-A cells.

It is during the spread of excitation to the ventricular walls that the value of the Purkinje system is most easily demonstrated. Both ventricles must contract simultaneously and after the completion of atrial contraction. Since the Purkinje fibers conduct impulses 3–7 times as rapidly as cardiac muscle fibers, they contribute to the rhythmicity of cardiac function and increase the efficiency of the heart as a pump by some 25 percent.

The very quality of cardiac muscle that provides for its maximum efficiency can become the etiology of some very serious problems in rhythmicity. The five most common causes of abnormal rhythm of the heart rate are:

1. Abnormal rhythmicity in the pacemaker itself.
2. Shift of the pacemaker activity to some other site.
3. Blocks in transmission of the impulse through the heart.
4. Abnormal pathways of transmission are developed.
5. Spontaneous generation of abnormal impulses while the pacemaker is still firing.

These pathological problems will be dealt with in detail throughout other areas of this book. A listing of the possibilities is sufficient at this time to point out the extreme importance for the nurse addressing herself and her activities to the care of patients with life-threatening heart disease to adequately understand the mechanism for the establishment of normal rate and rhythm and its control.

The reader will recall that the divisions of the autonomic nervous system operate in direct opposition to one another and thus provide a system of checks and balances upon each other. For example, if in response to heavy exercise the sympathetic nerve fibers serving a large leg muscle receive impulses as a result of increased local levels of carbon dioxide in the muscle itself, they then transmit the impulse to the cardiac centers in the hypothalamus of the brain. From the hypothalamus the impulse is in turn transmitted to the fibers directly connected to the cardiac muscle membranes. This action results in decreasing the time required to depolarize the membrane and causes contraction of the myofibrils. The total effect is one of increased rate of contraction of the heart, and ultimately increased circulation to the large leg muscle itself. This effect would continue indefinitely were it not for the stimulation of vagal fibers in the myocardium which would secrete acetylcholine, increasing the time necessary for repolarizing the membrane of the cardiac muscle. This increase would result in a slowing of the contractile rate and allow for a return to normal rate and rhythm.

As a result of the electrochemical nature of the excitatory impulse characterizing the depolarization of the cardiac membrane, it is possible to pick up and record these action potentials from the surface of the body. As stated earlier, the membrane potentials are the result of separation of charged particles situated at the surface. As the impulse spreads and passes to all parts of the cardiac musculature, electrical currents spread into the tissues surrounding the heart. This is not a surprising fact when one recalls that the chemical composition of extracellular fluids is not different in any of the tissues of the body. A small number of these currents reach the surface of the body, and if electrodes are placed at opposite sides of the heart the potentials generated can be recorded. The reader readily recognizes this recording as an electrocardiogram. Electrocardiogram tracings are covered in detail in another chapter, and therefore it will be sufficient to emphasize that the deflection of the recording needle is the direct result of the depolarization and repolarization of the membranes of the atrial and ventricular musculatures.

Figure 4-5 is a schematic presentation of a normal tracing. These tracings provide a means of constant monitoring of what is happening internally to the conduction system of the heart. It is this feature of extending one's five senses to allow for internal assessment via an external means that makes the knowledge of how cardiogram tracings are possibly relevant to nursing.

The Cardiac Cycle

In the foregoing sections the more subtle and less obvious features of cardiac function have been discussed. There are more obvious functional charac-

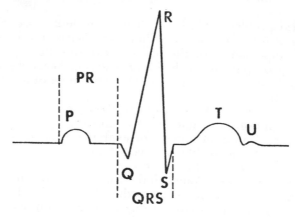

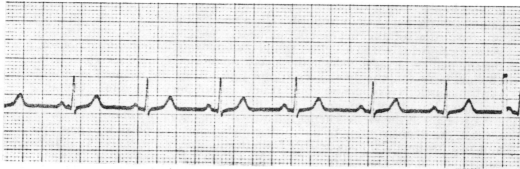

Fig. 4-5. Normal electrocardiogram tracing.

teristics with which you are familiar but until now they have been ignored. Pulse, blood pressure, and heart sounds are very important indicators of cardiac function and will now be discussed in light of the characteristics which have just been presented.

When atrial contraction is completed and the ventricular contraction is initiated, three events occur simultaneously. The atrioventricular valves shut to prevent the regurgitation of blood back into the relaxed atria. The leaves or "cusps" of the bicuspid and tricuspid valves close and the blood rushes against them resulting in the production of the first heart sound, "lub." At the same time, there is a surge of fluid pressure against the walls of the major arteries as a result of increased volume of blood pumped from the ventricles. This surge is felt in the peripheral circulation and is known as the *pulse*. The contractile phase or period is known as *systole,* and thus the blood pressure of this period of ventricular systole is called the *systolic pressure.* Immediately following the period of ventricular systole comes the relaxation or "refractory" period which is called *diastole.* One result of ventricular relaxation is the closing of the semilunar valves in both the systemic and pulmonary aortae to prevent backflow of blood. The closing of these valves results in the second heart sound, "dub." The fluid pressure of the blood against the arterial walls drops to its lowest level during diastole and is known as the *diastolic pressure.* Following the period of complete recovery of both lattice works, "absolute refraction," this chain of events is reinitiated with a new contractile impulse being initiated at the S-A node.

The cyclical chain of events is schematically summarized in Fig. 4-6.

This scheme points out how there are several simultaneously occurring events which can be assessed at any given time. It is of the utmost importance for the nurse to be fully aware of a number of routes available to her in gathering data on the state of the patient's cardiac function at any given moment. The gathering of data from multiple sources provides her with a "set" to analyze and a base upon which she can plan her *modus operandi.*

Coronary Circulation

Blood supply to the myocardium is derived from the two main coronary arteries which originate from the aorta, immediately above the aortic valve. The left coronary artery supplies the major portion of the left ventricle, while the right coronary artery supplies the major portion of the right ventricle.

Shortly after its origin, the left coronary vessel branches into the anterior descending artery which traverses the groove between the two ventricles on

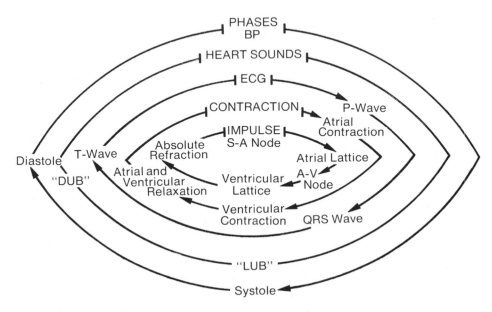

Fig. 4-6. The cardiac cycle.

the anterior surface of the heart and the circumflex artery which passes to the left and posteriorly in the groove between the left atrium and the left ventricle. The circumflex branch may terminate before reaching the posterior side of the heart, or it may continue into the posterior groove between the left and right ventricles. The coronary circulation is referred to as *dominant left* if this branch of the left coronary artery supplies the posterior aspect of the heart, including the septum.

Eighty percent of human hearts are *dominant right*. When this situation prevails, the right coronary artery passes posteriorly and is responsible for the blood supply to the posterior side of the heart and the posterior portion of the interventricular septum.

Pathogenesis of Coronary Heart Disease

It is estimated that 95 percent of all cases of myocardial damage are due to intrinsic disease of the coronary vessels as a result of arteriosclerotic changes in the vessel walls. Arteriosclerotic changes in coronary vessels do not absolutely parallel systemic sclerotic changes and thus may be more severe than the observed peripheral alterations would indicate. The most common characteristic of the diseased vessel is the presence of patchy atheromatosis scattered in the lining of the vessels and projecting into the lumen. Because of this propensity for atherosclerotic vessel changes, it is imperative that a brief discussion of the etiology of these vascular changes be included, as well as the correlation of vascular dysfunction and its effect upon functional anatomy of the myocardium.

As vessels respond to the local physiological demands for nutrients, oxygen, and the removal of waste products, the diameter of the lumen changes in response to the sympathetic innervation of the muscularis. In effect, over long periods of time the endothelial lining develops minute breaks in the integrity of the lining and atheromatous plaques begin to form. These plaques contain lipid deposits and large amounts of cholesterol. Later, fibroblasts invade the plaques, resulting in the development of inelastic deposits which not only restrict the physiological response to demands but progressively can restrict the lumen of the artery. The etiology of atherosclerotic changes in the arteries of man is almost certainly a derangement of lipid metabolism. It can be increased lipid mobility, dietary lipid overload, and/or an error in the metabolic breakdown of lipids. It has also been demonstrated that the vessel wall has the ability to secrete cholesterol in response to the breaks in the lining of the vessels. This fact would account for the extensive atherosclerotic changes sometimes seen in individuals whose serum levels are well within normal limits.

Although sclerotic changes are usually associated with the normal aging process, there is an increasing incidence in the middle-aged affluent male in our American population. There is a sex differential which must also be taken into account, inasmuch as there are twice as many men who die of atherosclerotic changes than do premenopausal females. This differential levels off after age 50. It would appear that estrogens protect the female from developing atherosclerotic vessel changes. There is also evidence that atheromatous plaque formation in the major vessels tends to run in families.

Certain physiological states predispose to the development of atheromatous plaques. Severe diabetes and hypothyroidism, conditions which are accompanied by hypercholesterolemia, are two examples. Another physiological etiological factor is any situation that results in diabetogenic conditions by immobilizing fat stores and increasing blood glucose by glycogen turnover and gluconeogenesis. All three of these conditions are mediated through the glucocorticoids from the adrenal cortex as a part of the general adaptive syndrome in response to stress.

Any situation which causes hyperemia, tissue damage, or hypothalamic sympathetic stimulation also causes a functional stimulation to the heart. Consequently the coronary circulation responds to permit junctional hyperemia in the myocardium. If the vessels are inelastic or are partially occluded due to atherosclerotic changes in the vessel walls, the result is myocardial ischemia in certain areas instead of hyperemia. If the coronary arteries become completely occluded by the development of a thrombus and/or plaques, then the result is ultimately necrosis of myocardial fibers. Such necrotic changes are irreversible and the damaged fibers are replaced by inelastic scar tissue. If the occlusion is sufficiently large, or is in a main artery, death results from one or a combination of the five following situations:

1. Decreased cardiac output.
2. Hemostasis in the pulmonary circulation and resultant edema.
3. Hemostasis in the systemic circulation and resultant edema.
4. Fibrillation of the heart.
5. Occasionally, rupture of the cardiac wall itself.

In conclusion, any situation that tends to elicit a sympathetic or adrenal stress response tends to contribute to the establishment of the prerequisite conditions for the development of atherosclerotic changes in the coronary circulation. If the general physical condition of the individual is one that can handle the stress and strain of daily living, the amount of atheromatous plaque development is commensurate with the age, sex, and genetic characteristics of the individual. It is when the person's physical condition is so deteriorated or when he lives under such an increased amount of tension-producing stress that the changes become excessive and the conditions for the development of coronary vascular disease are met. The nurse who cares for such an individual must be able to assess the current status of the environment as well as the patient's biopsychosocial state if she is to maintain the resources available for recovery and prevent further deterioration of the situation. An understanding of the multiple causal factors which lead and/or contribute to the patient's acute condition is prerequisite to planning a means of preventing further strain on an already damaged vital organ.

PATHOPHYSIOLOGY OF HEART FAILURE

The heart is a complex musculoelectric structure that has the single function of pumping blood. In order to do its job well, a good heart pump requires good muscle, a good valving system, and an efficient pumping rhythm. An abnormality of sufficient severity of any component of the pump can affect its pumping efficiency and might cause the pump to fail.

Reserve Mechanisms of the Heart

When the heart is stressed, it has several reserve mechanisms that it can call upon to maintain good pumping function—to provide a cardiac output sufficient to meet the demands of the body. First, the individual cardiac muscle cells may hypertrophy. The process of hypertrophy requires considerable time and is not an acute adjustment to stress. However, if the stress is applied long enough, such as with systemic or pulmonary hypertension or significant stenosis of the aortic or pulmonic valve, the muscle of the chamber pumping against the resistance may hypertrophy to such a degree that it effectively outgrows its blood supply and becomes ischemic. When this happens, hypertrophy ceases to be a useful compensatory mechanism and the heart's pumping ability decreases.

A second normal reserve mechanism of the heart is dilatation. Whereas in hypertrophy the individual muscle cell becomes larger, in dilatation the muscle cell stretches. The relationship between the cardiac output, (the amount of blood the heart pumps in each unit of time), and the length of the heart muscle cell at the end of diastole is expressed in the well-known Starling relationship which states that as the end-diastolic fiber length increases, so does the cardiac output. Like hypertrophy, however, its usefulness is self-limiting. There is a point beyond which the stretching of the muscle fiber does not lead to an increase in cardiac output and the heart's effectiveness as a pump decreases. This is partly explained by the Laplace theorem which states that the tension in the wall of a chamber such as the left ventricle is directly related to the pressure in that chamber and its radius. Put another way, as the radius of the chamber increases (dilatation), so does the tension in the wall as long as the pressure in the chamber does not fall. Since wall tension is directly related to the demand of the myocardium for oxygen, it is not difficult to see that eventually the radius will dilate to such a distance that the demand of the heart for oxygen cannot be met. In this instance, dilatation has proceeded to the point where it is no longer providing an increase in cardiac output and the pump has begun to fail.

A third response of the heart to stress is an increase in heart rate. This adjustment is rapid and has been experienced by everyone during periods of exercise or anxiety. Increasing the heart rate is an excellent way to quickly increase the cardiac output and meet the demands of the body for blood. In most normal people, the heart rate can increase to the range of 180/minute with an associated progressive increase in cardiac output. The critical heart rate is greater in young people and falls with advancing age. Like hypertrophy and dilatation, however, there is a limit to which an increase in heart rate is a useful reserve mechanism. As heart rate increases, the period of diastolic ventricular filling decreases, and at heart rates much above 180/minute the time available for ventricular filling is so small that filling is inadequate and cardiac output starts to fall. In persons with coronary artery disease and significant obstruction to one or more coronary arteries, a substantial increase in heart rate can be a potentially dangerous event. Coronary artery blood flow to the left ventricle takes place primarily in diastole. With increasing heart rates, decreasing diastolic filling time, increased demands of the heart for oxygen (because of the rapid rate), and coronary blood flow may become critical and angina pectoris, congestive failure, or occasionally myocardial infarction may be produced. An increase in heart rate then is a readily available response to stress and is generally useful, but like all good things it can occasionally be carried too far.

A fourth reserve mechanism of the heart is to increase its *stroke volume* — the amount of blood that it ejects into the circulation with each systole. It can do this by either increasing the percentage of the end diastolic volume ejected with each beat (increase the ejection fraction), or by increasing the venous return to the heart. This is commonly accomplished by the reflex increase of sympathetic nervous system activity which increases venous tone. Venous pressure is then raised and thus venous return to the heart is increased. Venous return is also increased with elevated body temperature which shortens the time required for blood to make a complete circulation through the body; by recumbency, in which case the volume of blood that is held in the legs as a result of gravity is largely returned to the central circulation and presented to the heart; or by taking a deep breath which increases intrathoracic negativity, thereby "sucking" more blood into the chest. Also, any increase in intravascular volume will increase venous return. By either an increase in ejection fraction or venous return, stroke volume and cardiac output will increase.

Heart Failure

When the normal cardiac reserves are overcome, the heart fails to do its job as a pump and heart failure is present. Heart failure was defined many years ago by Lewis very simply and appropriately as "a condition in which the heart fails to discharge its contents adequately." This definition is as good today as it was in the 1920s. As stated earlier, dysfunction of any of the components of the pump may result in failure.

Causes of Failure

Abnormalities of the *muscle* causing ventricular failure would include myocardial infarction, ventricular aneurysm, extensive myocardial fibrosis, endocardial fibrosis, or excessive hypertrophy due to pulmonary hypertension, aortic stenosis, or systemic hypertension. *Valve* malfunction can lead to pump failure by causing either obstruction to outflow of the pumping chamber such as valvular aortic stenosis or pulmonary stenosis (pressure load), or the valve may be regurgitant such as with mitral insufficiency and aortic insufficiency, both of which present an increased volume of blood to the left ventricle (volume load). Valve abnormalities that impose either a pressure or a volume load on one or more chambers usually are slowly progressive conditions which cause the heart to utilize its long-term defense mechanisms of hypertrophy and dilatation. Both these mechanisms may be overcome and lead to pump failure.

Less commonly, an acute volume load is imposed on the heart causing a rapid onset of pump failure. Bacterial endocarditis of the aortic or mitral valves or rupture of a portion of the mitral valve apparatus is the usual cause. In these cases, one tries to support the heart during the period of acute insult so that the long-term compensatory mechanisms can be utilized. However, if not successful, replacement of the diseased valve is indicated.

Disorders of cardiac *rhythm* can produce or contribute to failure in several ways. Bradycardia allows for increased diastolic filling and myocardial fiber stretch with an associated increase in stroke volume (Starling relationship). Cardiac output is therefore preserved. This is well tolerated in healthy persons and bradycardia is, in fact, an effect of high levels of physical conditioning. However, in the diseased heart contractility is decreased, the useful limits of the Starling relationship are exceeded, and cardiac output may be insufficient. On the other hand, with tachycardia, diastolic filling time is decreased, myocardial oxygen demand is increased and the diseased myocardium may tolerate the burden poorly and fail. Furthermore, frequent premature contractions may decrease the cardiac output, a circumstance that may be poorly tolerated in a marginal situation.

Responses to Failure

When the heart's normal reserves are overwhelmed and failure is noted, certain physiologic responses to the decrease in cardiac output are important. All of these responses to a decrease in cardiac output represent the body's attempt to maintain a normal perfusion of vital organs. The primary acute adjustment to heart failure is an increase in sympathetic nervous system influence on the arteries, veins, and heart. This results in an increase in heart rate, an increase in venous return to the heart, and increased force of contraction; in addition, through constriction of the peripheral arteries, it helps to maintain a normal blood pressure. As a result of the autonomic nervous changes and other factors the blood flow to the essential organs, specifically the brain and heart, is maintained at the expense of less essential organs such as the skin, gut, and kidneys. With severe congestive heart failure there is sufficient decrease in blood flow to the skeletal muscles to cause an acidosis that must be considered when the patient is being treated.

When the kidneys sense a decreased volume of blood presented to them for filtration, they respond by retaining sodium and water and thereby try to do their part in increasing the central blood volume and venous return. With an increase in blood volume and venous tone there is an increase in venous return to the heart, an increase in end-diastolic fiber length (dilatation) and within limits, an increase in stroke volume and cardiac output. However, with a failing heart, an increased circulatory volume may be too great a burden for the ventricle and failure may be worsened. In some patients with prolonged failure, individual heart cells will hypertrophy, increasing pumping efficiency, and the clinical findings of heart failure may improve.

Recognition of Failure

It is useful to think of the clinical features of heart failure as coming from failure of either the left ventricle, the right ventricle, or both. When the left ventricle fails, its inability to discharge its contents adequately results in dilatation, increased end-diastolic volume, and increased pressure at the end of diastole. This results in inability of the left atrium to adequately empty its contents into the left ventricle and pressure in the left atrium rises. This in turn is reflected back into the pulmonary veins which bring blood from the lungs to the left atrium. The increased pressure in the pulmonary vessels results in pulmonary vascular congestion which is the cause of the most specific symptoms of left ventricular failure.

The symptoms of pulmonary vascular congestion are dyspnea, orthopnea, paroxysmal nocturnal dyspnea, acute pulmonary edema, and cough. *Dyspnea* is characterized by rapid shallow breathing. Occasionally a patient may complain of insomnia, restlessness, or weakness which is caused by the dyspnea. *Orthopnea,* the inability to lie flat because of dyspnea, is another common complaint of left ventricular failure related to pulmonary vascular congestion. It is important to note if the orthopnea is truly related to heart disease or whether elevating the head to sleep is merely the patient's custom. For example, if the patient states that he sleeps on three pillows, one might hasten to believe that the man is suffering from orthopnea. If, however, when asked why he sleeps on three pillows he replies that he does this because he likes to sleep at this elevation, and has done so since before he had symptomatic heart disease, the condition does not qualify as orthopnea. *Paroxysmal nocturnal dyspnea* is a well-known complaint characterized by the patient's awakening from a sound sleep in the middle of the night because of intense shortness of breath. Nocturnal dyspnea is thought to be caused by a shift of fluid from the tissues to the intravascular compartment as a result of recumbency. During the day the pressure in the veins is high, especially in the dependent portions of the body due to gravity, increased fluid volume, and increased sympathetic tone. With this increase in hydrostatic pressure, some fluid escapes into the tissue space. With recumbency, the pressure in the dependent capillaries is decreased and fluid is resorbed into the circulation. This increased volume places an additional burden on an already congested pulmonary vascular bed, and dyspnea is the resultant symptom.

Acute *pulmonary edema* is the most florid clinical picture associated with pulmonary vascular congestion. It is characterized by intense dyspnea, cough, orthopnea, profound anxiety, cyanosis, sweating, noisy respirations, and very often chest pain and a pink frothy sputum from the mouth. It constitutes a genuine medical emergency and must be managed vigorously and promptly.

One symptom of pulmonary vascular congestion that is often overlooked but may be a dominant symptom is an irritating *cough*. This symptom is related to congestion of bronchial mucosa and an associated increase in mucus production. It may be productive or dry and hacking in character.

In addition to the symptoms which result from pulmonary vascular congestion, left ventricular failure is also associated with nonspecific symptoms which are related to the decreased cardiac output. The patient may complain of weakness, fatigability, lethargy, difficulty in concentrating, or diminished exercise tolerance. These symptoms may be present in chronic low output states.

Physical signs associated with left ventricular failure that are easily recognized at the bedside include third and fourth heart sounds and rales in the lungs. The *fourth heart sound* or atrial gallop is associated with atrial contraction and is best heard with the bell of the stethoscope very lightly applied at the cardiac apex. It is heard just before the first heart sound and is not always a definitive sign of congestive failure. A fourth heart sound is extremely common in patients with acute myocardial infarction, and likely does not have prognostic significance, but may represent incipient failure. On the other hand, a *third heart sound* or ventricular gallop is an early sign of left ventricular failure. Most physicans would agree that treatment for congestive failure is indicated upon the appearance of this physical sign. The third heart sound is heard in early diastole after the second heart sound and is associated with the period of rapid passive ventricular filling.

The fine moist rales most commonly heard at the base of the lung posteriorly are common recognized as evidence of left ventricular failure, as indeed they may be. It is, however, important to note that the patient may have good evidence for left ventricular heart failure on the basis of a history of symptoms suggesting pulmonary vascular congestion or the finding of a third heart sound at the apex and have quite clear lung fields. It is not appropriate to wait for the appearance of rales in the lungs before instituting therapy for left ventricular failure.

Other signs of left ventricular failure which may be noted in addition to a third heart sound and rales in the lungs include bronchial wheezing, pulsus alternans (an alternating greater and lesser volume of the arterial pulse), and the square-wave response noted on Valsalva maneuver. Radiographic examination of the chest may often be helpful in making a diagnosis of heart failure. Careful evaluation of the chest X-ray may demonstrate changes in the blood vessels of the lungs which result from an increase in pulmonary venous pressure. X-ray findings may be present in the absence of rales, and careful examination of the chest film may be quite rewarding.

Failure of the right ventricle alone is often the result of such conditions as severe pulmonary hypertension (primary or secondary), stenosis of the pulmonary valve, or a massive pulmonary embolus. The right ventricle tolerates a volume load well in adults, and pure right ventricular failure is usually due to resistance to outflow. More commonly however, right ventricular failure is the result of failure of the left ventricle. In this situation symptoms and signs of both left and right ventricular failure are present, and the symptoms of left ventricular failure may improve as the right ventricle fails.

In contrast to left ventricular failure, in which specific symptoms can usually be related to a single underlying mechanism — pulmonary vascular congestion — the symptoms of right heart failure are not so specific and many are related to a low cardiac output. Fatigability, weakness, lethargy or difficulty in concentrating may be prominent. Heaviness of the limbs, especially the legs, an increase in abdominal girth, or inability to wear previously comfortable shoes reflect the ascites and edema associated with right ventricular failure.

When the right ventricle decompensates there is resistance to filling of the ventricle, dilatation of the chamber, and an increase in pressure in the right atrium. This increasing pressure is in turn reflected upstream in the vena cava and can be recognized by an increase in the venous pressure. This is best evaluated by looking at the veins in the neck and noting the height of the column of blood. With the patient lying in bed and the head of the bed elevated between 30 and 60 degrees, the column of blood in the external jugular vein will be, in normal individuals, only a few millimeters above the upper border of the clavicle if it is seen at all. When recording an observation of venous pressure, the height of the column of blood above the sternal angle and the elevation of the head of the bed should be recorded. This will then provide a useful basis for comparison of future observations.

Edema is often considered a good sign of heart failure, and indeed it is often present when the right ventricle has failed. However, it is the least reliable sign of right ventricular dysfunction. Many people, particularly the elderly, spend much of their time sitting in a chair with the legs dependent; as a result of this body position the decreased turgor of subcutaneous tissue associated with old age, and perhaps primary venous disease, such as varicosities and ankle edema, may be produced which is not a reflection of right ventricular failure. When edema does appear related to failure of the right ventricle it is dependent in its location. If the patient is up and about it will be noted primarily in the ankles and will ascend the legs as failure worsens. When the patient is put to bed the dependent portion of the body becomes the sacral area and edema should be looked for there. With congestion of the liver this organ may enlarge and become tender, ascites may be present, and jaundice may be noted.

The Valsalva maneuver has a long and interesting history and may have use in the diagnosis of heart failure. It has also been implicated as causing an occasional fatality either through the production of a cardiac arrhythmia or through the dislodging of venous thrombi producing massive pulmonary embolization. A standard Valsalva maneuver is produced by blowing into a mercury manometer to a pressure of 40 mm Hg and sustaining this effort for 10 seconds. Naturally a patient does not do this on his own during the day but may closely simulate this effort during a prolonged effort of straining at stool. Intermittent positive-pressure breathing may produce short periods of a similar type of strain as may a cough or sneeze. In the normal response to the Valsalva maneuver there are four phases. Phase I occurs with the onset of strain at which time there is an increase in intrathoracic pressure which leads to a rise in the arterial blood pressure. During Phase II, as a result of the increased intrathoracic pressure and limitation to venous return to the heart, there is a decrease in right atrial filling, a decrease in left ventricular stroke volume, and a fall in the arterial blood pressure and pulse pressure (the difference between the systolic and diastolic pressure). This fall in pressure stimulates the receptors in the carotid sinus, aortic arch, and common carotid artery which are sensitive to pressure and which in turn cause an increase in sympathetic activity, resulting in an increase in heart rate and peripheral vasoconstriction. At the bedside Phase II is characterized by an increase in heart rate and a fall in blood pressure.

With Phase III or release of the strain there is an increased venous return to the right heart and an increase in blood volume in the pulmonary vascular bed. This is ultimately transmitted to the left side of the heart with an associated increase in the left ventricular stroke volume as the left ventricle once again fills. Because it takes a few seconds for the pulmonary vascular bed to fill with blood before it reaches the left heart, there may be a continuous fall in cardiac output and blood pressure immediately upon the release of the strain.

Phase IV is called the overshoot and is characterized by bradycardia and a rise in blood pressure over the resting observed values. This occurs because the increased left ventricular stroke volume is ejected into a constricted peripheral vascular bed. This constricted bed causes an increase in peripheral resistance and the pressure therefore rises, whereupon the pressure-sensitive receptors sense the higher pressure, and parasympathetic activity through the vagus nerve is stimulated, causing a reflex slowing of the heart. The overshoot period then is characterized by blood pressure that is greater than the initial resting values and a bradycardia.

In the patient with heart failure the response to the Valsalva maneuver is quite different. As the strain begins there is a rise in intrathoracic pressure. This rise in pressure is transmitted and is noted as an increase in the peripheral arterial pressure. However, as the strain continues there is no decrease in pressure and there is no increase in the heart rate. Upon release of the maneuver the blood pressure returns to the baseline values and there is no overshoot. This kind of response in which there is just a rise in arterial pressure without any heart-rate changes and no overshoot response has been called the *square-wave response.*

General Management of Failure

The physiologic responses to heart failure form a rational basis for treatment. The goals of the management of congestive heart failure are to reduce the workload of the heart, to increase cardiac output and myocardial contractility, and to decrease retention of sodium and water. Since the heart cannot be put to complete rest in the same fashion that a broken bone can be immobilized in a cast, the best that one can do is to put the entire patient to rest, thereby decreasing the overall demand on the heart pump. Bedrest is therefore an important part of the treatment of congestive heart failure. In addition to decreasing the overall work demands made on the heart through inactivity, bedrest assists in lowering the workload by decreasing the intravascular volume through diuresis.

Studies of prolonged bedrest have demonstrated that within 48 to 72 hours of inactivity there is a decrease of plasma volume of 300 ml. or more. While this is not a great volume in terms of the overall intravascular fluid compartment, it does assist in decreasing the volume load that is presented to the failing heart. It therefore assists in decreasing dilatation of the heart chambers and reestablishing a compensated state. This effect results from stimulation of atrial stretch receptors which sense the increased volume of blood returning to the right side of the heart that would be sequestered in the lower extremities if the patient were upright. These receptors then "turn off" the production of antidiuretic hormone and a diuresis follows.

If the patient remains in bed for a prolonged period of time the total number of red cells in the circulation decreases, so that if a patient is at bedrest for a month his total intravascular fluid compartment may be diminished by as much as a liter. Furthermore, with prolonged bedrest there is loss of subcutaneous tissue turgor, muscles atrophy, and an inadequately understood state of deconditioning of the peripheral blood vessel follows. The net effect of these changes is to render the patient less able to tolerate a change in position from recumbency to sitting or standing so that he is likely to exhibit symptoms of postural hypotension. These symptoms include tachycardia, lightheadedness, dimness of vision, nausea, sweating, pallor, and finally syncope. With syncope there is usually a profound bradycardia. This is the syndrome of orthostatic intolerance. The symptoms of orthostatic intolerance can be prevented by providing external support for the veins of the lower extremities, although the basic physiologic changes are not altered. This provides a good reason for using elastic stockings as a patient is permitted up from a period of bedrest. By the use of good firm support stockings symptoms of orthostatic intolerance can largely be prevented. Of course the elastic stockings have further benefit while the patient is in bed by preventing venous stasis and decreasing the threat of thrombosis and pulmonary emboli.

Digitalis is the primary therapy for increasing myocardial contractility and cardiac output. This drug is one of the most useful drugs in cardiology and also potentially one of the most dangerous. In the failing heart digitalis slows the ventricular rate and increases the force of contraction, making the function of the heart more efficient. As cardiac output increases, a greater volume of fluid is presented to the kidneys for filtration and excretion, and intravascular volume decreases. In an extremely grave situation such as cardiogenic shock in which the function of the pump is profoundly and often fatally compromised, sympathomimetic amines are often used. The most common drugs used at this time are isoproterenol and norepinephrine. A relatively new drug, glucagon, has been used with some success in this situation. However, it must be given intravenously and frequently in order to achieve any lasting effect. It has the unfortunate side effect of nausea and vomiting in a significant percentage of instances. When the heart has failed so badly that shock is present and the sympathomimetic amines are required to maintain blood pressure, there is usually an associated metabolic acidosis that is often quite severe. Treatment of this acidosis is required if the patient is to survive.

In the early stages of pump failure, retention of sodium and water is easily handled by bedrest, salt restriction, and digitalis. With moderate and severe degrees of failure, oral or parenteral diuretics are of great benefit in reestablishing a normal intravascular volume. There are several extremely potent diuretics that are currently available. When used intravenously they can produce a profound diuresis in a short period of time. This decreases the intravascular fluid volume, decreases the venous return to the heart, decreases end-diastolic fiber length (decreases dilatation), thereby decreasing myocardial oxygen demand and assisting the heart to once again become compensated. The same effects are achieved by oral diuretics, although more slowly. Most situations in which a diuretic is indicated can be well managed with an oral preparation. All diuretics, regardless of the route of administration, may cause significant changes in the serum electrolytes, especially potassium and chloride. Therefore regular determination of serum electrolytes is an important part of following the patient. This is particularly true when the patient is also receiving digitalis, because low potassium produced by diuretics predisposes to digitalis toxicity—a life-threatening but avoidable complication. Because of this possibility potassium supplements are customarily ordered when diuretics are given.

In addition to digitalis, diuretics, and bedrest, fluid intake and the amount of salt in the diet may be restricted. The limitation of fluids may be quite severe so that the patient's insensible loss via his respiratory tract and skin will be greater than his fluid intake. This is an important adjunct when the patient's kidneys are not functioning well and when diuretics work poorly, if at all.

Failure with Acute Myocardial Infarction

The acute myocardial infarction patient is the primary concern of the coronary care unit and may develop heart failure on the basis of muscle dysfunction, electrical system dysfunction, or rarely on purely mechanical grounds. Heart failure may present as primarily left- or right-sided failure. Left-sided failure is certainly the more common and in its most severe form presents as acute pulmonary edema, cardiogenic shock, or rupture of a papillary muscle. Acute pulmonary edema is usually associated with a large myocardial infarction and increases in frequency with advancing age at the time of infarction. The clinical picture was described earlier. Acute pulmonary edema is a dramatic medical emergency that requires intensive treatment usually involving morphine, digitalis, diuretics, oxygen, and phlebotomy.

Pulmonary edema results from pressure in the pulmonary vascular bed exceeding the opposing forces which tend to keep blood in the vascular channels. This pressure runs in the neighborhood of 30 mm Hg. When this pressure is exceeded there is a transudation of fluid into the alveoli which in turn diminishes the area available for the normal transport of oxygen into and carbon dioxide out of the pulmonary capillary bed. The patient may therefore become quite cyanotic during an episode of pulmonary edema. Morphine is the single most useful drug in the treatment of pulmonary edema. It achieves its primary usefulness through a peripheral vasodilating effect, forming a peripheral pool of blood. This blood is removed from the central circulation, decreasing venous return. In addition, morphine allays the great anxiety associated with the severe dyspnea and quiets the patient, thereby decreasing the respiratory pump mechanism; it decreases arterial blood pressure and resistance, lessening the work of the heart. Digitalis is always indicated in situations of acute left ventricular failure. Digitalis increases contractility and slows the heart rate, thereby increasing pumping efficiency.

Phlebotomy is often useful in the patient with acute pulmonary edema, since it removes a volume of blood from the central circulation, decreases venous return and filling pressure, and provides rather prompt reversal of some basic hemodynamic problems. Phlebotomy may be bloodless (rotating tourniquets), or whole blood may be directly removed from the circulation. While often helpful in managing acute pulmonary edema, phlebotomy may be dangerous in the patient who does not have an increased intravascular volume. This situation most commonly occurs in patients with acute myocardial infarction in which there is primary muscle disease and rapid onset of pulmonary edema before the kidneys can compensate for a diminished cardiac output by sodium and water retention. The patients with a normal blood volume usually have a normal-sized heart on chest X-ray. Removing a unit of blood from the circulation either by use of tourniquets or by vena section may cause a significant drop in blood pressure in these patients. On the other hand, the person with more chronic congestive heart failure with an increased intravascular volume and dilatation of the heart is often an excellent candidate for rotating tourniquets or vena section.

In addition to drugs and phlebotomy the patient should be placed in a position of comfort, usually lying at about 45 degrees to the horizontal. If there is an associated ectopic tachycardia with the acute pulmonary edema direct current cardioversion may well be indicated.

Cardiogenic shock may be seen in up to 10 percent of patients with acute myocardial infarction and is recognized clinically by a systolic blood pressure less than 80 mm Hg (often it cannot be measured); a feeble pulse that is often rapid; pale, cool, and sweaty skin that is frequently cyanotic; restlessness, confusion, and apathy. Coma is not usual. Urine output is decreased and may be absent. These manifestations of shock are a reflection of the inadequacy of the heart as a pump, and usually reflect a profound degree of pump failure characterized by inadequate cardiac output, high peripheral resistance (arteriolar constriction), and low arterial pressure.

Not all clinical circumstances of cardiogenic shock are associated with an inadequate cardiac output, however. Depending on modifying circumstances, such as fever, the cardiac output may occasionally be normal or even increased. Unfortunately, cardiogenic shock is not a completely understood situation at this time. Accordingly, the treatment of cardiogenic shock is generally unsatisfactory and at the very least requires administration of alkali to correct the metabolic acidosis, oxygen, and agents to elevate the blood pressure. Depending upon the venous or pulmonary artery pressure the administration of small amounts of fluid may be indicated. Digitalis, norepinephrine, or isoproterenol may be selected. Mechanical devices such as intra-aortic balloon counterpulsation, direct ventricular assistors applied to the left ventricle, or left heart bypass are occasionally used but are best considered experimental at the present time. The general outlook for patients with cardiogenic shock is poor.

An uncommon cause of acute left ventricular failure in acute myocardial infarction is rupture of a papillary muscle. There are two papillary muscles in the left ventricle which are thumblike projections of muscle to which the restraining "guidewires" of the mitral valve, the chordae tendineae, are attached. The papillary muscle may be involved in the infarction process and very occasionally may rupture. When it does there is a sudden loss of restraint of one of the leaflets of the mitral valve, and free mitral regurgitation occurs with each contraction of the left ventricle. This sudden profound pressure and volume load on the left atrium is reflected back through the pulmonary veins and the acute onset of symptoms of pulmonary vascular congestion is noted. This is usually manifested as severe dyspnea and frank pulmonary edema. At the bedside a loud murmur lasting throughout systole is present. Very often nothing can be done to save the patient, although occasionally emergency mitral valve replacement can be successfully accomplished.

Sudden failure of the right ventricle can be seen occasionally in a patient with an acute myocardial infarction as a result of rupture of the intraventricular septum. Like rupture of the papillary muscle, septal rupture is distinctly uncommon but when it does appear is noted usually in the first week of the illness. Septal rupture is clinically characterized by chest pain, dyspnea, shock, and a rapid onset of evidence of right ventricular failure. There is a loud murmur that lasts throughout systole at the lower left sternal border and is often accompanied by a thrill which can be felt by placing the hand over the precordium at the left sternal border. This differs from the papillary muscle rupture murmur which is not generally accompanied by a palpable thrill.

As with all myocardial ruptures, the prognosis of septal rupture is extremely poor. However, it is possible to occasionally repair these ventricular septal defects by emergency surgery using cardiopulmonary bypass.

Electrical failure of the heart in the crisis care unit is the most important complication of acute myocardial infarction. Arrhythmias are seen in over 75 percent of all coronary care patients and their accurate recognition allows appropriate preventive therapy and aggressive treatment of those rhythms which are life-threatening. Some arrhythmias are harbingers of a potentially fatal arrhythmia which may be avoided if correct treatment is undertaken early. Life-threatening arrhythmias are seen with infarctions of all sizes and are not confined to the patient who has a large area of damage. Many patients who die from an arrhythmia are noted at postmortem study to have a relatively small area of infarction. It has been correctly said that these patients have hearts that are "too good to die." The greatest advances that have been made by the coronary care unit have resulted from continuous monitoring, recognition, and proper management of arrhythmias.

Mechanical failure of the heart seen in acute myocardial infarction is another relatively rare event and is due to rupture of the free wall of the left ventricle and the spilling of blood into the pericardial cavity. This results in acute compression of the heart or tamponade and the inability of both chambers to fill adequately. There is then very sudden pumping failure with associated shock and death. Rupture of the free wall may be preceded by or associated with a return of chest pain as the blood dissects through the necrotic myocardial wall. Most ruptures occur during the first two weeks following the acute infarction episode at a time when the damaged myocardium is softest. As with rupture of the papillary muscle and interventricular septum, rupture of the free wall of the left ventricle carries with it an extremely poor prognosis.

REFERENCE

1. Carl J. Wiggers, *The Heart*, Scientific American, Reprint #62, 1957.

5

Management Modalities

ALVA R. DEGNER, R.N.
LANE D. CRADDOCK, M.D.
STUART A. SCHNECK, M.D.
PHILLIP S. WOLF, M.D.
CAROLYN M. HUDAK, R.N., M.S.

MONITORING TECHNIQUES

Monitoring the patient with cardiac disturbances is now an accepted and routine practice.

Modern electronics is constantly improving monitoring equipment and modifying the electrode for monitoring. At this point in time, disposable floating electrodes are by far the most suitable. They provide the most comfort for the patient and the least amount of artifact if applied according to the manufacturer's instructions. Needle electrodes are uncomfortable and provide a source of infection because of the break in skin integrity. Metal disc electrodes are cumbersome and restricting to the patient. Considerable artifact occurs because of the inability to seal the disc adequately to the skin.

Operating instructions provided by manufacturers of electronic monitoring equipment should be followed to insure proper functioning.

The most desirable electrode placement is that which provides easy identification of P waves and an adequate QRS signal to accurately operate the rate meter and alarm system. Figures 5-1 through 5-4 suggest methods for lead placement. To obtain an adequate recording, the nurse should feel free to experiment with lead placement and not be bound by a "routine."

Special Nursing Precautions for the Monitored Patient

1. No ungrounded electrical equipment should be used in conjunction with a monitor due to the danger of stray current "shocking" the patient or inducing ventricular fibrillation.

2. The alarm system should always be in operation. If frequent false alarms occur, check the system between the patient and the monitor. Also check for a source of extraneous electrical signals.
3. The limits of the high- and low-rate alarms should be set at an appropriate level for each patient.
4. Most disposable electrodes have a low incidence of skin irritation and can be left on the patient for several days. However, leads should be repositioned when irritation is noted. An anesthetic type ointment can be applied to the irritated area.
5. If the insertion of a pacemaker is anticipated, avoid placing the electrodes at a possible insertion site.

Telemetry

Twenty-five to thirty percent of deaths due to a myocardial infarction occur after the patient has left the coronary care unit. It is impossible to keep these patients in an acute care unit for their entire convalescence. Telemetry provides a means of monitoring the ECG in situations where the use of conventional equipment is impractical or impossible. It allows the patient to be ambulatory and eliminates the problem of cumbersome patient cables by employing a small pocket-size radio transmitter. The patient's ECG is transmitted to a receiver in a specialized area and recorded on an ECG oscilloscope.

Electrode placement and techniques of monitoring are similar to those of conventional monitoring except that the ground electrode is eliminated. Because the patient is often ambulatory, stabilization of the electrode is vital to good monitoring.

ARTIFICIAL CARDIAC PACING

Electrical stimulation of the heart was tried experimentally as early as 1819. In 1930 Hyman noted he could inject the right atrium with a diversity of substances and restore a heartbeat. He devised an "ingenious apparatus" that he labeled an artificial pacemaker, which delivered a rhythmic charge to the heart. In 1952 Zoll demonstrated that patients with Stokes-Adams syndrome could be sustained by the administration of current directly to the chest wall. Lillehei in 1957 affixed electrodes directly to the ventricles during open-heart surgery. In the period of 1958 to 1961 implantable pacemakers for treatment of complete heart block came into use in a rather extensive fashion. Over subsequent years, various improvements and refinements have been made for both short-term temporary pacing and long-term permanent pacing.

Indications for Artificial Pacing

Indications for short-term cardiac pacing include:
1. Emergency pacing for prolonged Stokes-Adams attack.
2. Myocardial infarction associated with second- or third-degree A-V

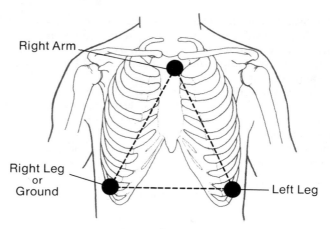

Fig. 5-1. 3-Lead system when lead selection is not part of monitor.

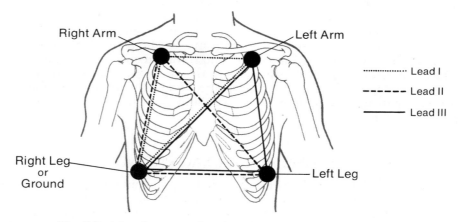

Fig. 5-2. 4-Lead system when lead selection is part of monitor.

block, bilateral bundle branch block, or severe bradycardias not responsive to drug therapy.

3. In preparation for long-term pacing to improve the patient's clinical state, guard against serious arrhythmias and allow for evaluation of the benefits of long-term pacing.

4. Coverage against the risk of cardiac arrest during the implantation of the permanent pacemaker.

5. Coverage for anesthesia and surgery in patients with a history of cardiac arrest or complete heart block.

6. Control of rate during periods of implanted pacemaker failure.

7. Treatment of complete heart block developed during cardiac surgery.

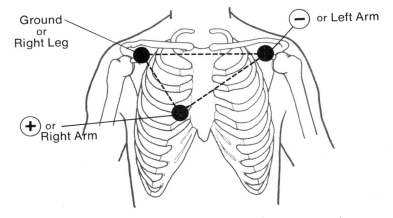

Ground or Right Leg

⊖ or Left Arm

⊕ or Right Arm

Fig. 5-3. Marriott's MCL[1].

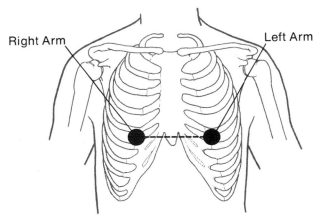

Right Arm

Left Arm

Fig. 5-4. For telemetry no ground electrode is necessary.

8. Overdriving the heart in order to control tachyarrhythmias or to suppress ectopic ventricular activity.

Indications for long-term pacing include:
1. Inadequate cardiac output as shown by cerebral symptoms, congestive heart failure, or renal insufficiency.
2. Recurrent Stokes-Adams attacks.

Methods of Pacing

The electrical stimulus can be delivered to the heart in three basic ways:
1. External—by means of an electrode placed on the chest wall.

2. Transthoracic—by inserting a needle electrode through the chest wall into the myocardium.
3. Direct—by passing a small electrode through the venous system into the right ventricle or by attaching electrodes to the epicardial surface of the heart via a thorocotomy.

The technique for establishing the various pacing systems is described in order to give the nurse greater understanding of the procedure so that she is better prepared to assist with it and to explain it to the patient.

EXTERNAL CARDIAC PACING

After Zoll's work external cardiac pacing became the accepted approach for treating ventricular asystole. However, this method has now been largely abandoned because of its unpredictable effectiveness, being utilized only as a desperation technique in emergency situations. This approach to pacing causes severe pain, skin burns, and skeletal muscle contractions resulting from the high voltage and current required. Therefore it is unsuitable for the preventive treatment of warning arrhythmias or as long-term prophylaxis against recurrent cardiac standstill. Its single advantage is the ease and rapidity with which it can be initiated. The technique of external pacing is as follows:

1. A small metal electrode is attached to the chest wall in the left precordial area and is anchored with adhesive tape. The ground electrode is placed on the right side of the chest in a similar manner.
2. The electrodes are then attached to the power supply which may be part of the monitoring system or a separate battery pack.
3. With external pacing the energy level of the power supply is set at the maximum level.
4. Rate should be set at 70–80 impulses per minute.
5. If the heart is not stimulated within one minute, cardiopulmonary resuscitation should be initiated immediately.

TRANSTHORACIC OR PERCUTANEOUS PACING

Wires inserted percutaneously into the wall of the right ventricle via a needle introduced through the chest wall can produce ventricular stimulation. The advantage of this method is the rapidity and ease with which pacing can be initiated and the availability of the necessary equipment. It is not suitable for long-term pacing or as a prophylaxis against warning arrhythmias. There is a small risk of coronary artery puncture and hemopericardium associated with this method. The technique of transthoracic pacing is as follows:

1. A #20 spinal needle with a stylet is introduced through the anterior chest wall at the fifth or sixth left intercostal space near the sternum. The needle is advanced at a 30 degree angle toward the right second intercostal space about 5 mm into the myocardium.
2. The stylet is removed and a stainless steel noninsulated surgical wire is advanced through the needle about 1 cm. beyond the tip.
3. The needle is removed and the electrode is connected to the negative pole of the external power source.

4. In order to create a circuit, a ground electrode is accomplished by placing a wire suture in the chest wall and connecting it to the positive pole of the power source.
5. The energy level of the power supply is set at 10–15 milliamperes and a pacing rate of 70–80 impulses per minute is appropriate.

DIRECT EPICARDIAL PACING

Effective pacing can be accomplished by implanting the electrode system directly on the myocardium. This is done under general anesthesia via a left anterolateral thorocotomy.

This method is being abandoned in favor of endocardial electrodes because it involves a thorocotomy, while the transvenous method can be done under local anesthesia. The life span for both pacemakers is approximately the same. Since the procedure involves direct visualization of the heart, there is greater operative risk, a longer hospitalization, and more postoperative complications.

Some physicians prefer this approach in children and young adults because of yet unknown hazards of the long-term presence of an endocardial electrode and the chance of electrode displacement due to growth. This method is also utilized as a temporary adjunct after open-heart surgery. In these cases the electrodes are sutured to the heart and brought out through the chest wall. The wires can be pulled out when they are no longer needed. The technique of epicardial pacing is as follows:

1. A thorocotomy is performed under general anesthesia.
2. The electrode tips are sutured to the apex of the right or left ventricle.
3. The wires are connected to the power pack which is implanted in a subcutaneous pouch in the axillary region or the abdominal wall.

DIRECT ENDOCARDIAL OR TRANSVENOUS PACING

Transvenous electrodes presently are the most utilized and satisfactory method of pacing. This method can be employed as a temporary or permanent measure.

The catheter electrode is introduced into a superficial vein (brachial, external jugular, femoral, or subclavian), threaded through the vena cava and right atrium and is lodged against the endocardial surface of the right ventricle. The electrical stimulus is provided by an external generator source or an implanted power supply. The technique of temporary transvenous pacing is as follows:

1. The vein is selected and the skin area is cleansed with an antiseptic solution.

   Brachial vein—usually requires a cutdown. Patient's arm must be immobilized as the electrode can easily become dislodged. Phlebitis is a rather common complication.

   Femoral vein—involves a percutaneous puncture. The patient's mobility is markedly reduced.

   External jugular vein—a cutdown is required. It is desirable to reserve this site since it is most often used for the permanent transvenous electrode. This site does permit patient mobility and the use of both arms.

Subclavian vein—a cutdown is not required and insertion is therefore more expedient. It allows for patient mobility and the use of both arms. It also results in greater catheter stability and a lesser incidence of infection and phlebitis. Complications encountered with use of this site include pneumothorax, hemothorax, subcutaneous emphysema, brachial plexus injury, septicemia, local hematoma, and air embolism.

2. The puncture site is infiltrated with a local anesthetic.
3. The needle is inserted into the vein and the catheter is threaded into position in the right ventricular apex.
4. The catheter is ideally positioned under fluoroscopy but this is not always feasible. An alternate method of positioning the catheter may be accomplished by attaching the electrode to the V lead of the electrocardiogram machine with an alligator clamp. When the tip of the catheter is in the right atrium, the amplitude of the P wave and the QRS will be about the same. When the tip has crossed the tricuspid valve the QRS amplitude will increase markedly. The ECG will reveal a current of injury pattern when the tip touches the endocardium.
5. The catheter should be sutured to the skin to avoid dislodgment. An antibiotic ointment and sterile dressing is then applied to the puncture site.
6. If a bipolar catheter is used, the two wires extending from the electrode can be connected to the positive and negative pole without differentiation. If a unipolar catheter is used, the wire from the catheter is connected to the negative terminal and the ground suture is connected to the positive pole.
7. The ma (milliamperage) is turned to the lowest setting which provides a 1:1 response plus a small margin of safety. Usually 1.5–2.5 ma is adequate.
8. The pacing rate is predetermined by the physician, depending on the indication for the pacemaker.

Special nursing responsibilities:
1. The patient must be prepared by explaining the purpose of the pacemaker and the procedure.
2. If the catheter electrode is positioned by ECG, attach the limb leads to all extremities and use the V lead as the attachment for the electrode. It is vital that all equipment be grounded to prevent electrocution by current leakage passing through the catheter.
3. Establish a patent intravenous site.
4. Have a 100-mg. bolus of lidocaine available in case ventricular irritability occurs.

5. Have an Isuprel infusion readily available to maintain the patient until the pacemaker is ready.
6. Defibrillator should be on standby.
7. Assist in the observation of the ECG recording.
8. Encase the pacemaker battery pack in a rubber glove so that current leakage from other equipment will not be delivered to the heart. When touching the terminals always wear rubber gloves.

Technique for permanent implantation of transvenous pacemaker:
1. Local anesthesia is used at the cutdown site and the incision for the battery pack.
2. The electrode is passed through either the jugular vein or the subclavian vein.
3. Fluoroscopy is utilized to position the catheter in the right ventricular apex.
4. The power pack is embedded in the axillary area and the electrodes are connected subcutaneously either over or under the clavicle.

Types of Pacemaker Generators

Pacemakers are basically of two types. The fixed rate or asynchronous system and the demand or synchronous system.

FIXED RATE—ASYNCHRONOUS—PARASYSTOLIC

The electrical mechanism of this pacemaker discharges at a fixed rate which is independent of the electrical activity of the heart. It is not changed by any physiological parameter which might require an increased rate with subsequent increased cardiac output. The constant threat of the patient's own rhythm competing with the pacemaker makes this a very undesirable type of generator. The fixed-rate pacemaker should be used only when it is unlikely that the patient will return to normal sinus rhythm. This generator is less prone to failure because of the simplicity of its design. (See Fig. 5-5.)

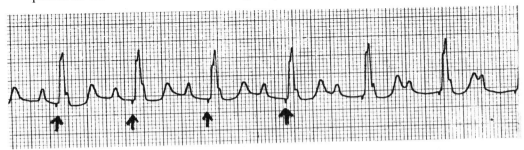

Fig. 5-5. Fixed-rate pacemaker artifact.

DEMAND — SYNCHRONOUS — NONPARASYSTOLIC

The "Ventricular Inhibited Demand Device" is stimulated only when the patient's ventricular rate falls below the preset rate of the generator. The pacemaker senses the signal of the QRS coming back through the electrodes and suppresses the output of the generator. It is important to obtain a stable electrode position to provide an ECG signal of sufficient amplitude to be sensed. The pacemaker can be falsely inhibited by a P or T wave. However, improved sensing filters have reduced this hazard. Ventricular fibrillation due to competition is almost nonexistent. Figures 5-6 and 5-7 illustrate a demand pacemaker firing when the patient's ventricular rate falls below a preset rate.

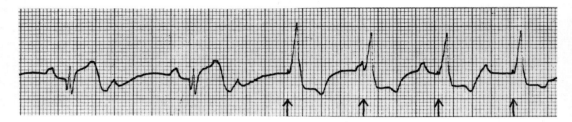

Fig. 5-6. Demand pacemaker.

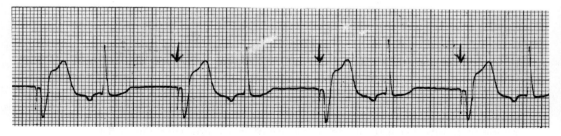

Fig. 5-7. Demand pacemaker with every other impulse artificially stimulated.

A "Ventricular Standby or Synchronous" device senses the QRS (either normal or ectopic) and superimposes the pacing impulse into the absolute refractory period. If a spontaneous beat fails to occur, the pacemaker will discharge at a preset escape interval.

The "atrial-synchronous" mechanism is activated by the atrial P wave and allows for normal depolarization through the conduction system. The rate varies according to physiological demands. The problem with this method is that it also responds to pathological impulses and could result in rapid ventricular responses with atrial fibrillation or flutter.

Types of Catheter Electrodes

There are two basic electrodes. In order for electrical stimulation to occur, current must flow between two poles to create an electrical circuit. With the unipolar electrode the negative pole is within the heart and the positive pole is accomplished by a wire suture placed in the skin on the chest wall. The bipolar electrode has both poles at the tip of the catheter about 1 cm. apart. It is felt that a bipolar electrode will continue to pace even if contact is lost with the endocardium. However, the unipolar catheter will stop pacing if this contact is lost. The unipolar catheter also causes pain at the site of the indifferent electrode.

Pacing Rate

The most advantageous rate for pacing will depend on the specific indications and the clinical condition of the patient. The rate should be set to the point where cardiac output is maximal (50–105/minute). However, the optimal rate for achieving maximal cardiac output may not coincide with the best rate for suppressing ectopic activity. The oxygen demand of the myocardium is increased and results in angina if the rate is too fast. Also at rapid pacing rates inadequate ventricular filling takes place and the cardiac output is decreased. In complete heart block, the atrial rate is an index to the ventricular pacing rate necessary for adequate cardiac function. In other words, if the atrial rate is 70/minute, the pacemaker rate should be set at 70/minute.

Energy of Pacing

When the heart is stimulated by an electrical impulse it either contracts completely or not at all. The lowest level of energy at which the heart will contract is called the *threshold level*. If the pacing stimulus is less than the threshold level the heart will not contract. However, if the stimulus is greater than the threshold level it will not improve contractility.

When the catheter is positioned and connected to the power supply, the energy-level dial is gradually increased until a QRS is noted with each stimulus. This level is called the *threshold*. The threshold is measured in milliamperes (ma) and is usually less than 2 ma. The pacing threshold can vary, and a safety factor of an additional 1-2 ma is added to the determined threshold level.

The pacing threshold is affected by tissue excitability, electrode position, impulse duration, waveform and wave amplitude. The threshold is increased the first few days after insertion of the pacemaker due to local tissue reaction. Drugs affect the threshold in various ways. Sympathomimetic amines, adrenalsteroids, and glucocorticoids decrease the threshold. Beta-adrenergic and mineralcorticoids increase the threshold. Atropine, quinidine, Pronestyl, and lidocaine do not affect the threshold.

The relationship of extracellular to intracellular potassium concentration is important in determining the pacing threshold. When the serum potassium is elevated the threshold is decreased, and when the extracellular potassium is decreased the muscles become refractory to electrical stimulation.

Complications of Pacing

Complications related to insertion or presence of the electrode within the body:

1. There is a surgical risk if the epicardial technique is used. It often involves direct exposure of the heart in an elderly, debilitated patient. In the 7.5 percent mortality, intraoperative infarction has been observed. With endocardial technique there is less than a 1 percent mortality and less morbidity.
2. Infection or phlebitis at the venous entry site.
3. Pulmonary air embolism if the patient is improperly positioned at the time of the cutdown in the neck. The patient should be flat so that a positive venous pressure exists to prevent an influx of air into the venous system.
4. Ventricular irritability due to the electrode catheter.
5. Myocardial perforation with the use of stiff electrodes. This is more common when the catheter is positioned in the apex of the heart.
6. Pericardial tamponade, although this rarely develops with small electrodes unless the patient is anticoagulated.
7. Entanglement of the electrode around the chordal structures of the tricuspid valve.
8. Large thrombi occurring at the electrode tip or in the right atrium may lead to pulmonary emboli or obstructed blood flow.
9. Segments of a fractured electrode may migrate within the vascular system.
10. Electrical stimulation of noncardiac sites such as the phrenic nerve, diaphragm, and intercostal or retrosternal muscles.
11. Endocarditis due to adherence of the catheter to the tricuspid valve.

Complications related to subcutaneous implantation of the generator:

1. Infection or hematoma.
2. Battery extrusion.
3. Muscular contractions in the region of the implantation.

Complications related to improper pacer function:

1. Malfunction of the pacemaker is due to component failure, improper interfacing between the host and the pacer system, and physiologic changes within the heart.
2. Failure of the power supply presents itself clinically either by complete cessation of pacing or by intermittent pacing.
3. Complete cessation of pacing may occur abruptly or be preceded by a prolonged period of disordered functioning (Fig. 5-8).

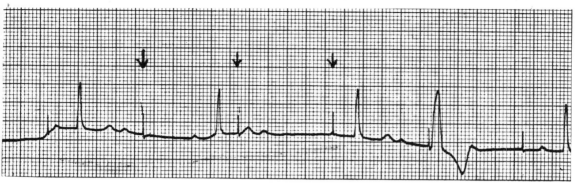

Fig. 5-8. Nonfunctioning pacemaker —
no ventricular response to pacemaker stimulus.

Clinical manifestations of cessation are (1) sudden death, (2) Stokes-Adams attack, or (3) if a spontaneous heart rate is present, failure of the demand mode will not be detected unless it is specifically tested. This can be done by slowing the heart with carotid sinus massage or converting the pacemaker to a fixed rate mode.

Causes of intermittent pacing are (1) Displaced catheter or perforation of the ventricular myocardium. This usually occurs during the first few weeks after implantation. Pacing may vary with the body position or respirations. (2) Partially fractured electrode due to faulty insertion. (3) Changing myocardial threshold. Threshold is affected by meals, exercise, infection, electrolyte imbalance, change in body metabolism, and myocardial fibrosis. (4) Extraneous electrical signals, such as occur when the power supply is close to intense high-frequency electrical fields such as microwave ovens, FM radio transmitter or TV stations. (5) Poor electrical connections within the power system such as a fractured electrode or an improper pacemaker electrode junction. (6) Competitive rhythms are especially hazardous with myocardial ischemia, electrolyte imbalance, or hypoxic states. In these conditions ventricular fibrillation is almost certain to ensue.

If there is an alteration in the pacing rate with either an increase or decrease in the preset rate, battery depletion is most likely the cause.

Other malfunctions include the loss of the specialized functions of the demand type systems and aberrant stimulation of the diaphragm, intercostal, or abdominal muscles.

Assessment clues to pacemaker malfunction for the nurse:

1. The apical heart rate is slower than that preset for the pacer.
2. There is development of abdominal muscle or diaphragmatic twitching (hiccoughs).
3. Appearance of a widely split second heart sound. This is suggestive of migration of the electrode from the right to the left ventricle.

4. Absence of pacer spikes with a bradycardia. This may indicate failure or electrode breaks.
5. Alteration in pacing spike rate. This indicates battery depletion or component failure.
6. A transistorized AM radio with tuning indicator placed between stations will pick up radio-frequency signals discharged by the pacemaker. The clicks counted in one minute from a fixed-rate pacer will equal the pacing rate. If there is a correlation between the clicks and the pulse, it indicates that the pacemaker is capturing and the demand mode is working. If there is a presence of clicks and an absence of spikes on the ECG it suggests an electrode fracture.

Follow-Up Care for the Patient with an Implanted Pacemaker

One week after implantation a baseline pulse rate is determined. Until this time, body heat will alter the rate. In determining the pulse rate a baseline 12-lead ECG, X-ray of the battery supply and a chest X-ray showing electrode placement should be taken. The patient should be seen by the physician or in a pacemaker clinic every 4–6 months the first year, every 2–3 months the subsequent six months, and every 1–2 months thereafter. The rate should be measured at each visit and once failure of the pacemaker is documented, the battery pack should be replaced without delay. The battery pack should be replaced prophylactically before depletion, usually at 24 months for the demand mode and at 30 months for the fixed-rate system.

Patient Teaching

A planned and systematic approach to teaching the patient to live with his pacemaker is a vital part of his nursing care. A helpful tool in patient teaching is a progress report which is accessible to the physician and other members of the team, along with written guidelines for the nurse instructing the patient. The following outline gives general instructions for areas to include in patient teaching.

Reason for pacemaker:
1. Determine the patient's impression. Clarify the difference between heart block and a heart attack.
2. If a patient's impression is correct, reinforce his knowledge. If incorrect, make the reason clear.
3. Explain the reason for the temporary pacemaker if used and describe the difference between it and the permanent pacemaker.
4. Describe the general anatomy of the heart and where the normal pacemaker is.

Durability of pacemaker:
1. Discuss the sturdiness. Explain that the pacemaker is strong. Give exam-

ples: Patient can continue with sports, housework, and other forms of activity.
2. Battery lifetime. Approximately two years, but point out that time can vary.
3. Procedure for battery change — hospitalized about three days; an incision is made at the same site; the old battery is removed and replaced by a new one.
4. Necessity for periodic checkups with physician. ECG and X-ray help evaluate the pacemaker function. Physician can check on patient's gen--eral state of health.

Psychological aspects:
1. Reaction. Allow patient to verbalize.
2. Fears. Patients often have fears of hurting the pacemaker. Allay these. Stress that there are signs of pacemaker failure that patient can watch for.
3. Acceptance. Try to determine how the patient has accepted it and what his attitude is.

Signs of pacemaker failure:
1. Dizziness. Define. It is not the transient dizziness experienced when getting up quickly.
2. Shortness of breath. Stress that a notable increase may be meaningful.
3. Pulse range. Depends on type of pacemaker and the rate at which it is set.
4. Fluid retention and weight gain. Describe — such as "puffy ankles" or "rings too tight."
5. Have him describe his symptoms prior to the pacemaker insertion.

Specific instructions:
1. Instruct in pulse taking if possible. Take pulse once a day upon awakening. If pulse is slower than set rate of fixed or demand pacemaker he should notify his physician.
2. Instruct regarding any medications he will be taking at home.
3. Passive and active range of motion exercises started on the affected arm 48 hours after implantation. Discuss benefits of regular exercise. Encourage to walk regularly but to avoid excessive fatigue.
4. Provide with extra copies of pacemaker warranty card. Instruct him to carry one on his person at all times.
5. Electrical hazards. Avoid contact with questionably defective electrical equipment. Avoid working directly over ignition systems or going into an area where there are high-voltage radio transmitters. Stay 10 feet away from microwave ovens. May use electrical devices, but discontinue use if he becomes lightheaded or dizzy.
6. Always inform a physician or dentist not familiar with his medical history that he has a pacemaker.
7. It is understood that the patient's family should be involved in this learning process.

CARDIOPULMONARY RESUSCITATION

Definitions

Because of the dual nature of resuscitation—that is, availability (ventilation) and transport (circulation) of oxygen—the more appropriate term is *cardiopulmonary resuscitation*.

Cardiac Arrest. This means abrupt cessation of effective cardiac pumping activity resulting in cessation of circulation. There are two types only: cardiac standstill (asystole) and ventricular fibrillation (plus other forms of ineffective ventricular contraction, i.e., ventricular flutter and rarely ventricular tachycardia). The condition referred to as "profound cardiovascular collapse" will not be specifically included since its recognition and definition are nebulous and management less specific. One form, referred to as cardiogenic shock, is included in Chapter 4.

Resuscitation. Liberally interpreted, this means the restoration of vital signs by mechanical, physiological, and pharmacological means.

The application of cardiopulmonary resuscitation is made possible by the concept of clinical versus biologic death. Clinical death is defined as the absence of the vital signs, and biologic death refers to irreversible cellular changes. As determined both experimentally and clinically, the interval between the two approximates four minutes.

Who Should Be Resuscitated

It is easier to say who should *not* be resuscitated, and this includes individuals with known terminal illness and those who are known to have been in clinical death for longer than five minutes. Both represent situations not only where resuscitation would likely prove impossible but where survival would be meaningless. All others should be regarded as candidates for resuscitation. The key here is to remember that resuscitation can always be abandoned, but it cannot be instituted after undue delay.

Recognition

The recognition of cardiac arrest depends on the finding of signs of absence of circulation: (a) unconscious state (preceded of course by less profound states of mental obtundation), (b) pulselessness, (c) dilated pupils, and (d) minimal or absent respirations. Two things should be noted: The pupils require a certain amount of time to dilate; this has been estimated at approximately 45 seconds and may be longer than 1 minute. It is therefore at times a valuable sign for pinpointing the time of cardiac arrest. Secondly, inadequate respiratory excursions may be noted in the early seconds of cardiac arrest, and these should not cause delay in recognition of the other signs.

Pulselessness is best determined by palpation of either the carotids or femoral arteries (the former is almost always immediately available, the latter not); less adequate is palpation of brachial or radial pulses. It should not be done by attempting to obtain a blood pressure.

An ideal situation should obtain in coronary care units or well-equipped critical care units: continuous monitoring, electronic warning signals, automatic conditioned response of a skilled team without the delay of feeling pulses, auscultating over the precordium, and the like.

The Troops

An organized approach to resuscitation is essential; regardless of how it is organized or of whom it is made up, resuscitation should be approached by a team made up of trained personnel and should include nurses, physicians, electrocardiographic technicians, inhalation-therapy technicians, and individuals to transport special instruments such as defibrillators, pacemakers, and special tray sets. It should also include an administrative or secretarial member who can do the legwork, make all necessary phone calls, and perform other miscellaneous duties that are minor but necessary and a part of every prolonged resuscitation attempt. We will describe a specific method geared to an institution with trained resuscitative personnel and found successful. The team includes the nurse as the primary member. The first nurse present becomes the initial captain of the team, and institutes the resuscitation attempt as outlined below. A single call, preferably by the secretary, should summon the entire team on an immediate, spontaneous basis—ECG technicians, inhalation-therapy technicians, available physicians including house staff and senior staff members in the area, nurses from the appropriate intensive care unit who will immediately transport the defibrillator, monitor, and pacemaker instrument to the site of the emergency, and the nursing supervisor. The last but not least member of the team is the switchboard operator or operators, who must react immediately in alerting the entire team in preference to all other duties. A single digit on the telephone dial should be utilized to alert the switchboard; they will often know where to find key physician members of the team and can summon them individually, whereas they may otherwise not be alerted.

Although minor variations in different approaches may bring the same results, the important thing is to have a definite routine kept rigorously up-to-date (including one's own experience).

It is to be emphasized that the nursing personnel and other key nonphysician members must have sanction to act spontaneously.

Steps in Management

There are two situations here—that where the patient's electrocardiogram is being continuously monitored, as in the coronary care unit, and that in an area where the patient is not under continuous monitoring, such as an ordinary hospital room or ward.

For the continuously monitored patient the arrhythmia sets the alarm, and if it is ventricular fibrillation, the patient is immediately defibrillated without attempted resuscitation by other means, after which a physician is summoned for evaluation.

In the event of cardiac standstill (asystole) the nurse immediately proceeds as below:

1. A sharp blow to the precordium. This requires virtually no time and may institute a cardiac rhythm; if so, it may be all the resuscitation required.

2. Call for help. This should require one simple phrase such as "cor zero," or "red alert," together with the location, to a second individual who then places the emergency call to bring the team together.

3. Obtain adequate airway, immediately institute artificial ventilation (mouth-to-mouth).

4. External cardiac compression. The technique is simple and it is applied by standing at either side of the patient, placing the heel of one hand over the lower half of the sternum, the heel of the other hand over the first, and applying vigorous compression directly downward, depressing the sternum between 1½ and 2 inches, releasing abruptly, and maintaining this rhythm at the rate of 60–80 times/minute. To be effective it must be learned correctly and applied skillfully. A little attention to instructors, two hands, and a lack of timidity are all that is required.

   If a single individual must apply both ventilation and massage, it is best to give two or three quick inflations by mouth-to-mouth or other readily available means of inflating the lungs, followed by 12–15 external cardiac compressions. This routine may be maintained until additional members of the team arrive.

5. External countershock should be applied as soon as the instrument is available. This should be done without knowing the specific rhythm diagnosis if there is a delay in determining this. If cardiac standstill is present, the countershock will take only moments and will do no harm. If ventricular fibrillation is present, the earliest possible countershock delivered is the one most likely to be effective and should be done at a time when the rhythm may more likely be maintained.

6. A specific *diagnosis* now is required (the word *recognition* has been used up to now, not diagnosis). As mentioned earlier this will be either cardiac standstill or ventricular fibrillation (continued in Item 9).

7. This item will be devoted to a very important member of the team—the nurse who is first available after two members are applying ventilation and massage will man the emergency cart, be responsible for preparation of drugs to be used, the preparation of an intravenous infusion set (with several types of venapuncture equipment) and do whatever is necessary to see that an intravenous infusion is started, thus paving the way for drug therapy. The importance of this underlies the continuously available venous cannula maintained in patients in critical care units.

   At this point the need for an intravenous infusion is obvious and must be obtained by whatever route is feasible. The simplest of all is the insertion of a needle, cannula, or scalp needle into an arm vein. Failing this, the femoral vein is readily accessible and a very large cannula can easily be inserted into the largest blood vessel in the body (the inferior vena cava) by simple puncture. A cutdown on a branch of the basilic system just above the elbow crease on the medial aspect of either arm or on the external jugular vein will allow insertion of a large cannula into the superior vena cava or right atrium. For those familiar with the technique of subclavian vein puncture, a large cannula can be rapidly inserted directly into the right atrium to serve the multiple purposes of rapid infusion or withdrawal and monitoring of central venous pressure and oxygen saturation, and has the added advantage of being well tolerated for long periods of time. The intracardiac route should be reserved for situations in which urgency takes precedence over availability of the intravenous route. This should be a rare occurrence.

8. Pharmacologic agents to be made ready immediately and appropriate preparations are as follows: (a) Sodium bicarbonate in a 5 percent solution, preferably in an intravenous drip preparation. THIS WILL BE STARTED BY RAPID DRIP OR GIVEN IN 50 CC. ALIQUOTS EVERY 5 MINUTES AND IS THE INITIAL DRUG USED. Tromethamine (THAM) can also serve as a buffer, but has disadvantages and is used much less often than sodium bicarbonate). (b) Epinephrine (Adrenalin) in a 1:1,000 aqueous solution. (c) Isoproterenol should be available in an intravenous preparation; 2 mg. in 250 cc. of appropriate vehicle solution is an adequate routine preparation. (d) Calcium chloride 10 percent solution. (e) Lidocaine (Xylocaine) should be prepared in an intravenous solution of varying concentration but 1 mg./ml. is an adequate solution for initial use. This drug is used most frequently by intravenous push in 50-mg. doses. (f) A vasopressor, preferably a peripheral vasoconstrictor such a methoxamine (Vasoxyl) or phenylephrine (Neo-Synephrine, an alphamimetic) or norepinephrine (both alpha and beta stimulating) should be available in an intravenous infusion of appropriate concentration. The critical emergency drugs given by I.V. "push" are all available in ready-to-use forms (sodium bicarbonate, epinephrine, calcium chloride, lidocaine) and should be readily available. Other preparations such as procainamide (Pronestyl), quinidine, diuretics such as ethacrynic acid (Edecrin) and furosemide (Lasix), mannitol, dexamethasone (Decadron), and propranolol (Inderal) should be available though not routinely prepared for immediate use. The inotropic and chronotropic agent glucagon has gained use in some situations. Its inotropic effect is substantial though less than that of isoproterenol and it has the advantage of a lesser chronotropic effect and generally induces less hyperexcitability. Its use is more or less experimental here and should not be thought of as a routine drug or as a substitute for isoproterenol. The catecholamine dopamine is being used on a trial

basis (not yet generally available) and has the advantage of not reducing renal blood flow. Its place, if any, in resuscitation remains to be clarified.

9. If cardiac standstill, epinephrine should be given routinely, usually 1 mg. intravenously, artificial ventilation and circulation continued; if unsuccessful, epinephrine should be repeated and the isoproterenol drip started. At this point, calcium chloride, 0.5–1.0 Gm. is given intravenously. If no response, continued artificial ventilation and circulation, continued intravenous epinephrine injections, and insertion of a transvenous pacemaker is indicated (less often a percutaneous transthoracic pacemaker is used).

10. If ventricular fibrillation, epinephrine is given intravenously (it is important that the continuous artificial ventilation and circulation are maintained and that interruptions not exceed 5 seconds) and external countershock is given at the maximum setting of the instrument with immediate resumption of artificial circulation and ventilation. If unsuccessful, the cycle should be repeated. If ventricular fibrillation persists in spite of the above or if reversion to ventricular fibrillation occurs each time it is applied, intravenous lidocaine is given by push in 50–100-mg. aliquots. Procainamide, if preferred, may also be given by intravenous push, and either drug may be given by intravenous drip. Beta blocking drugs (Inderal) may be the only effective agents here and have their prime indication in cardiac arrest. Quinidine is preferred by some, but its tendency to lower peripheral blood pressure and reduce myocardial contractility (resulting in a diminished cardiac output should a rhythm be resumed) constitute important disadvantages. It should also be emphasized here that regardless of the initial mechanism (whether it be an irritable or depressive phenomenon) once cardiac arrest has gained foothold with some duration it must be assumed that the heart is depressed, making the routine use of depressive drugs unwarranted. Since uneven tissue perfusion, particularly myocardial perfusion, may be a factor in perpetuating the ventricular fibrillation or standstill, a vasopressor agent of the peripheral constrictor type may be of value at this point. Digitalis and potassium chloride are rarely indicated in resuscitative attempts, their use being based on knowledge of special preexisting situations. As indicated above, depressive cardiac mechanisms are often the cause of repetitive ventricular fibrillation and paradoxically, pacing the heart (pharmacologically with isoproterenol or electronically by transvenous pacing catheter) is the treatment of choice in some cases (after resumption of rhythm, of course).

11. If above fail: (a) Pericardial tap should be performed, preferably by the subxyphoid route; although an uncommon factor in cardiac arrest it may result in dramatic recovery. (b) Consider further underlying causes subject to treatment such as pneumothorax (insertion of chest tubes); pulmonary embolism (assisted circulation, surgery); ventricular

aneurysm, rupture of papillary muscle or interventricular septum (assisted circulation, surgery); subvalvular muscular aortic stenosis with extreme gradients (propranolol, reserpine, etc.). Failing these, the decision to terminate resuscitative attempts is eminent, based on CNS changes and/or the assumption of a nonviable myocardium.

Postresuscitative Care

If there is resumption of spontaneous cardiac activity, the situation should be thoroughly evaluated as to the clinical state, underlying causes, and complicating factors in order to determine proper management. A routine as follows has been found successful: Intravenous diuretic (e.g., furosemide 80–240 mg.), a steroid such as dexamethasone for its salutary effect on cerebral edema, and electrical and physiological monitoring in an intensive care unit. A portable chest X-ray and an arterial sample for determination of pH and blood gases are obtained as soon as possible following resumption of cardiac rhythm. Continuous oxygen therapy is maintained; an intravenous infusion is of course essential. Routine measurements other than continuous electrocardiographic monitoring include frequent blood pressures (ideally done by intra-arterial cannula), hourly urine volumes, frequent bedside estimates of tissue perfusion, and central venous pressure measurements through a cannula extending into the superior vena cava or right atrium connected through a stopcock to a simple water manometer.

If central nervous system damage is evident, hypothermia should be instituted immediately, additional mannitol or intravenous urea should be given, and dexamethasone for cerebral edema should be continued. Monitoring otherwise as outlined above.

If oliguria or anuria is present, massive doses of furosemide should be given immediately. If no response to these, management as in acute renal insufficiency should be instituted.

The specific approach in the postresuscitative period will depend not only on the patient's condition at the time, but on the underlying disease process, the previous condition of the patient, and the events in the immediate postresuscitative period. More patients are being studied by catheter techniques acutely to evaluate them for emergency surgical procedures such as saphenous bypass grafts. The state of this art is changing rapidly.

Complications of Resuscitation

Resuscitation has come a very long way; it has changed drastically with time and undoubtedly will continue to do so. It has proven its worth beyond doubt. There are of course complications, and these include (a) injuries to sternum, costal cartilages, ribs, esophagus, stomach, liver, pleura and lung. Any one of these can be serious. (b) Another—fortunately rare—complication is the production of a live patient with permanent central nervous system damage such as to render him totally dependent. (c) There are also medical-legal considerations. This originally leaned against the attempt because of the frequency of undignified failures. More recently, however, the pendulum is swinging to the other side. This aspect should probably be ignored for the most part, since we are dealing with an earnest and reasonable approach to the treatment of sudden death in reversible situations, but it does emphasize that it should always be applied by well-trained, responsible people. The aim should be to reverse the reversible and not to inflict suffering by applying it to the irreversible. The alternative in both, of course, is death. The differentiation lies in good judgment which, as someone has said, "is difficult to learn, impossible to teach."

Central Nervous System Support after Cardiac Arrest

In order to comprehend fully the possibilities for central nervous system support after cardiac arrest, some features of the metabolic activity of nervous tissue must be understood. The nervous system is dependent on two major substrates for its metabolic processes—oxygen and glucose. Inasmuch as neither of these is stored in any appreciable extent in nervous tissue, they must be continuously supplied in large amounts. A very large proportion of the total body oxygen consumption is utilized by the brain in adults, and in children the brain utilizes nearly half of the total oxygen consumed by the body.

When the circulation fails, oxygen and glucose are no longer supplied to the nervous system. Almost immediately carbon dioxide and certain acid substances such as lactic acid begin to accumulate, and this causes dilation of cerebral blood vessels. In addition, the anoxia causes an increase in the permeability of these vessels, and fluid moves rapidly through their walls into the tissues. The end result of these two processes is cerebral edema. This is a serious complication of anoxia, for the swollen brain may compress the blood vessels at its base and—even though the circulation is restored as by successful cardiac resuscitation—the blood may thus be unable to pass through these compressed vessels. Cerebral infarction may then result. This entire process may take place in a matter of minutes and thus speed in resuscitation is essential.

Certain physiological facts are pertinent to this discussion. When cardiac arrest occurs at normal body temperature, consciousness is impaired in 8 to 12 seconds. The waves in the electroencephalogram will slow and within 20 seconds, at which time the oxygen tension in the brain has fallen to 50 percent of normal, the EEG is completely silent. Unlike the cerebral cortical neurons from which the EEG is primarily derived, the electrical activity of neurons in the brain stem, spinal cord, and cerebellum may continue for 30–90 seconds. Cerebral cortical neurons are irreversibly damaged in approximately 4–5 minutes, though occasional individuals have been severely injured in one minute while others have tolerated six minutes of anoxia. Irreversible cellular damage in the spinal cord and medulla, which contains the cardiorespiratory centers, may not occur for as long as 20 minutes. The cerebellum and basal ganglia are intermediate in their resistance. The exact reasons for this differential susceptibility are not known.

In view of these extremely serious and rapidly occurring events, physicians have sought for means to avoid or minimize the damage from anoxia. Though the idea that hypothermia exerted a protective effect in such a situation has been known for a long time, it was not until about 1950 that clinical applications of this concept began to be made. The evidence that cooling the brain decreases cerebral metabolism and protects against injury may be summarized as follows.

In dogs there is a 7 percent decrease in the amount of oxygen utilized by the brain for each degree centrigrade that the body temperature is lowered. Extrapolated to the human situation, this means that if the temperature is lowered to 30°C, the usual working range for hypothermia, there is only need for 50 percent of the oxygen requirement at normal body temperature (37°C). In order to achieve this, shivering (which raises muscle need for oxygen) must be avoided, and this can be done with proper medication.

A second benefit of hypothermia is that cerebral volume is decreased by approximately 5 percent at 30°C. This may not seem like a significant change, but it can represent the difference between the presence or absence of cerebral infarction. Since the skull is an unyielding bony box, anything that can be done to decrease the expansion of the brain against it is of value. The use of dexamethasone or urea will also assist in decreasing cerebral edema by producing a diuresis and decreasing intersticial fluid.

There is a small amount of experimental data which supports the idea that hypothermia protects the brain against injury. Tying the middle cerebral artery in a dog at normal body temperature will produce a large area of infarction, whereas little or no infarction results from the same procedure at 25°C. A standard cerebral injury in a dog at normal body temperature will produce a sizable area of hemorrhage, edema and infarction while the extent of injury is far less at 25°C. If the middle cerebral artery in a dog is ligated or the standard injury is again made at normal body temperature and then the dog is cooled at 25°C in 90–180 minutes, there is again less cerebral injury and a higher survival rate. This latter example is more akin to the clinical situation in man wherein the anoxia occurs first and then hypothermia is used.

It has been shown in humans that temporary occlusion of a major cerebral vessel for 10–12 minutes is possible at 30°C without causing infarction. It has also been a clinical impression, though unsupported statistically, that hypothermia in severe cases of cardiac arrest with prolonged periods of hypoxia has been of benefit in decreasing morbidity and mortality.

One problem that is difficult to answer in a general way is when to use hypothermia. In most cases cardiac resuscitation will have been rapid enough so that the patient quickly regains a normal neurological state. We suggest that when resuscitation has been difficult and hypoxia prolonged, cooling the patient may be of benefit. The length of time hypothermia is maintained is dependent on the neurological signs that exist. If rigidity is lessening, fixed dilated pupils are returning to normal and coma is lightening, then a slow decrease in hypothermia may be utilized. The method of inducing hypothermia will vary in each hospital, but electric cooling mattresses have usually been satisfactory.

If the above discussion emphasized one point it is that speed and adequacy of resuscitation are vital to protect the brain. If more than 5–6 minutes have passed before an adequate circulation and respiratory exchange are established, then survival without severe neurological damage, even with hypothermia, is unlikely.

Drug Therapy in Cardiopulmonary Resuscitation

Drugs indicated for use in cardiopulmonary resuscitation are detailed here to expand the nurse's understanding of the rationale for their use as well as the desirable and undesirable features of each.

Oxygen, while strictly speaking not a drug, is an agent that has important pharmacologic applications. During cardiac arrest oxygen must be given through a face mask or endotracheal tube at a high flow rate. The advantages of oxygen, besides supplying oxygen to body tissues, are its effects on peripheral resistance and coronary blood flow. It has been demonstrated in normal persons that oxygen given by facial mask will increase the peripheral resistance and raise the blood pressure, and this effect will increase blood flow through the coronary arteries. Hence the heart derives a greater blood supply, and the blood that it does receive is more richly oxygenated.

The second drug always used in the patient who has just had a cardiac arrest is sodium bicarbonate. A less common agent used to counteract acidosis is tromethamine (TRIS, THAM). This buffer is not widely circulated in contrast to bicarbonate and probably has no advantage over bicarbonate. So for purposes of this discussion, sodium bicarbonate is the drug of choice.

Why is bicarbonate used in all patients? Immediately upon the heart arresting, the body's oxygen supply is abruptly curtailed. As a result, the tissues, particularly the liver which is the primary source of metabolism, must function without oxygen. This process is called *anaerobic glycolysis*. Glycolysis refers to the breakdown of glycogen (starch stored in the liver) to provide energy for the body. Anaerobic means "in the absence of oxygen." During anaerobic glycolysis changes occur in the chemical breakdown of glycogen and the reactions that follow and the end result is an accumulation of lactic acid. The lactic acid which is then released into the blood stream causes profound acidosis.

Acidosis can be defined as a state in which the blood becomes acid and the pH, instead of being 7.35–7.45, may drop to 7.2 or lower. Recall that as the pH drops, the blood is more acid; as the pH rises, the blood is more alkaline. The acidosis as it occurs, in turn, has very harmful effects. These include (1) impaired contractility of the heart; the heart is unable to generate much power as long as acidosis exists; (2) blood pressure falls, and any attempts to raise it by using vasopressor therapy are unsuccessful until the acidosis is corrected. Giving sodium bicarbonate will reverse both the decreased contracitility of the heart and the shock, and will make the patient much more responsive to other agents used in treatment.

In dogs with experimentally induced cardiac arrest, the pH drops from 7.4 to 7.1 in 20 minutes. This is with external cardiac massage and ventilation. So it is evident that even in the best circumstances, with good ventilation and good massage, the pH of the blood rapidly becomes acid and must be corrected.

How much should be given? No one is terribly certain about the amounts to give, although it is generally agreed that the patient who has just arrested probably needs 2 ampules of bicarbonate immediately. This will supply 88 to 100 miliequivalents of bicarbonate. The preparations of sodium bicarbonate that are commercially available contain 44.6 miliequivalents (mEq.) per ampule, vial, or syringe. This is usually a volume of 50 cc. After the initial 2 ampules, 44.6 mEq. every 5–10 minutes until the patient is fully revived is recommended. Some institutions provide an intravenous solution of 5 percent sodium bicarbonate which the nurse is authorized to start. This should follow the same dosage scale so that the patient gets approximately 50 miliequivalents every 5 minutes.

What is the danger of bicarbonate? For practical purposes, it is difficult to overalkalize the patient—that is, to give too much—unless the intravenous bottle empties too rapidly, in 20 minutes or so. The major disadvantage is that the sodium in the sodium bicarbonate can lead to pulmonary edema. Sodium in any situation where the patient is apt to retain fluid may provoke pulmonary edema and giving this hypertonic solution too rapidly intravenously can lead to such a consequence. Hence the need for not being overly vigorous.

The respiratory care team, if present, can assist in monitoring these patients and providing serial blood pH values. If these values are available every 30 minutes to 1 hour, the bicarbonate can be titrated to the patient's needs. Unit policies should permit the nurse to administer this drug, since the urgency for its use is great and the need for it is sudden. The faster the acidotic state is corrected, the greater the patient's chance for resuscitation.

The next drug which is used is epinephrine. Epinephrine is given in all instances of asystole—that is, when heart action stops entirely and there is no impulse generated by the heart electrically. This is also known as ventricular standstill. Epinephrine can be given by one of two routes: (1) directly into the heart itself—into the chamber of the left ventricle, or (2) into a vein if external massage is being performed. It is worthy of note that if the patient is getting effective external cardiac massage there is probably no advantage in giving drugs directly into the heart. Certainly there is some risk in needling the heart —the risks of tearing the muscle and of penetrating a coronary artery and causing fatal bleeding. Therefore this action should not be used indiscriminately. All drugs if given intracardially should be injected into the cavity of the ventricle and not into the wall of the muscle itself. Proper needle placement can be tested by drawing back on the syringe and observing a return of blood.

What about epinephrine for treating ventricular fibrillation? There is much controversy about this, primarily because epinephrine can induce ventricular fibrillation in the patient with an irritable heart. But there seems to be a place for its use in the patient who has fibrillated. This is seen typically in the operating room. For example, patients who have fibrillated at the time of heart surgery and are then defibrillated will often respond better if they are given epinephrine first. Epinephrine has the effect of so-called "coarsening" the fibrillatory waves. As is known, ventricular fibrillation on a cardiac monitor appears as a jagged, wavy line without any formed pattern. Epinephrine makes these waves broader and more uniform, and for some reason which is not clearly understood this tends to make the fibrillation more responsive to countershock.

Calcium chloride may be used and although it is not as effective as epinephrine, it is occasionally successful. It should be used in the patient who does not respond to other measures. Calcium chloride or calcium gluconate can be given intravenously and has the effect of strengthening the contraction of the heart (inotropic effect). In fact, one way of stopping the heart is to inject a large dose of calcium chloride intravenously and the heart will stop in the midst of a strong contraction—in systole. Hence the risk of giving calcium intravenously at a too rapid rate. Calcium is a helpful drug and ordinarily is reserved for the patient who does not respond to the measures mentioned before.

The pressoramines or sympathomimetics include drugs such as epinephrine, levarterenol (Levophed), isoproterenol (Isuprel), mephentermine (Wyamine), and metaraminol (Aramine). To discuss their action and their harmful effects, assume that the patient has just had a cardiac arrest. He has been successfully resuscitated with sodium bicarbonate, epinephrine, external cardiac massage, and countershock. He is now faced with the problem of shock which persists, no matter what is done for him. How do we manage such a patient? The role of oxygen was mentioned earlier. Analgesia would involve pain medication for severe chest pain, which in itself may lower the blood pressure through a vagal effect. Attention must be focused on blood pressure control. In the acute situation, the most important function is to raise the blood pressure with a drug that will constrict the vessels at the body's periphery.

Three drugs commonly used to elevate the blood pressure are norepinephrine, also known as levarterenol (Levophed), epinephrine (Adrenalin), and isoproterenol (Isuprel). Levophed decreases the pulse rate; all other drugs increase the pulse rate. Effects on the blood pressure differ also. Norepinephrine is a potent stimulus for the peripheral arteries to contract; this causes the blood pressure to rise. The great advantage in raising the blood pressure in the patient with cardiogenic shock (shock due primarily to cardiac causes such as infarction) is that this increases the perfusion or blood flow through the coronary arteries. Levophed does this best. Adrenalin will actually decrease the diastolic blood pressure and increase the systolic blood pressure, but not nearly to the extent that Levophed does. The same is true with isoproterenol (Isuprel). Isuprel has the effect of dilating the peripheral arteries —a very important action. It strengthens the contractility of the heart while at the same time dilating the peripheral vessels. This is an important distinction from Levophed, which constricts the peripheral vessels and increases peripheral resistance. Peripheral resistance is a reflection of how tightly the arteries at the periphery of the body are being constricted. Levophed is a potent constrictor, while the other drugs mentioned are dilators, the most powerful being Isuprel. It must be remembered that as heart rate and contractility increase, so does oxygen consumption. Therefore arrhythmias may occur on an anoxic basis.

Most pressoramines act on the heart and on the blood pressure but these actions may be opposites. Levophed has a direct effect on the heart increasing the contractal force and also raising the blood pressure. Epinephrine also acts in the same way. It is a more potent stimulus to the contraction of the heart and in large doses will raise the blood pressure. Aramine acts the same way as does Wyamine, except that Wyamine tends to dilate the vessels more at the periphery than the other drugs. Isuprel is a powerful cardiac stimulant, but at the same time decreases the peripheral resistance and lowers the blood pressure. Methoxamine (Vasoxyl), is the only drug in this group that has no action on the heart. Its action is focused entirely on the peripheral vascular bed, causing vasoconstriction and a marked rise in blood pressure. Quite a range of drugs is evident here, from Vasoxyl (which affects the heart not at all but affects the blood pressure to an important degree) to Isuprel (which affects the heart more strongly than any agent mentioned, while actually lowering the blood pressure). Intermediate in this group are drugs like Levophed which have some action on the heart and a powerful constrictor action peripherally. The effects of these drugs are summarized in Table 5-1.

The action of these drugs can be described as either direct or indirect. The drugs classified as direct, including Levophed, epinephrine, and Isuprel, act on the smooth vessels in the wall of the artery to cause constriction or dilation. The drugs labeled as indirect act by releasing norepinephrine which is stored at the site of nerve contact with smooth muscle in the artery. Drugs like Aramine and Wyamine do not act directly on the muscle wall but indirectly by releasing norepinephrine stored in the muscle wall. More descriptively, an impulse travels down to the nerve ending and dislodges molecules of norepinehprine, which then begin to work on the smooth muscle of the artery wall, making the muscle contract and thereby raising the blood pressure.

What is the drug of choice for the patient with cardiogenic shock? Frankly, the answer is not known. It is felt that two actions are important; to increase the cardiac output and to increase the strength of contraction. This role is fulfilled with drugs like Isuprel, epinephrine, and other agents which act on the myocardial muscle itself.

Glucagon, a hormone manufactured by the alpha cells of the pancreas, has recently come into use in situations of cardiogenic shock or severe congestive heart failure. Its main action is to increase the strength of myocardial contraction. It increases heart rate somewhat and may produce arrhythmias.

The big controversy remains: What to do about the peripheral arteries—should they be constricted to raise the blood pressure or should they be relaxed and dilated to lower the blood pressure? This controversy stems from the fact that patients in shock already have intense systemic vasoconstriction. What is the value of raising the peripheral resistance further when the vessels are already near maximal constriction? Furthermore, if the vessel is constricted peripherally and an agent is added which tightens down the constriction more, what does this do to the blood supply to the organs that are perfused by this artery? The answer is that very likely the blood supply will fall below that needed to sustain normal functioning of the organ and symptoms of failure (liver failure, renal failure) will ensue.

CARDIAC DRUGS

Although drug therapy has been included throughout the cardiovascular material, it is important to study the drug therapy for long-term maintenance of persons with myocardial pathology who have gotten along reasonably well without complications such as shock, pulmonary edema and/or congestive heart failure.

Atropine

Cardiac effects: Increase heart rate by blocking vagal effects on the S-A pacemaker; can lessen the degree of heart block if it is due to vagal influence.
Indications: Bradycardia, heart block, sinus arrest.
Contraindications: Patients with glaucoma or asthma.
Undesirable effects: Tachycardia, tachypnea, delirium, coma.

Digitalis

Cardiac effects: Has a vagal effect on the S-A and the A-V node inhibiting their activity. Beneficial effects are to slow the pulse, strengthen the force of cardiac contraction and raise the blood pressure slightly.
Indications: Heart failure—it is favorable to the failing heart which has a weakened beat and fast rate. Atrial or nodal tachycardias—inhibits ectopic areas of activity and slows conduction through the A-V node. May convert atrial or nodal arrhythmias to normal sinus rhythm. Digitalis is mediated by the vagus nerve. Since there are no vagus fibers below the A-V node, it is of no value in ventricular arrhythmias.
Contraindications: Rhythms suspected as being due to digitalis intoxication: ventricular tachycardia, 2nd-degree block, nodal rhythms of slow rate. The patient with impaired renal function is prone to digitalis toxicity since this drug is excreted by the kidneys. If the BUN is elevated, dosage should be decreased.

TABLE 5-1
DRUGS USED IN CARDIAC RESUSCITATION

AGENT	DOSAGE	HEMODYNAMIC/ CARDIAC EFFECTS	DISAD- VANTAGES	COMMENTS
Oxygen	L/min.	↑ Peripheral resistance ↑ Blood pressure ↑ Coronary blood flow		Can produce pulmonary changes if given at high concentrations under pressure for several days
Sodium bicarbonate	88 mEq. immediately 44.6 mEq. 5–10 min. until resuscitated	Correct acidosis	Can cause alkalosis, pulmonary edema	Serial blood pH values helpful in providing correct dosage. Policies should permit registered nurse to administer this drug at time of cardiac arrest
Epinephrine	1 cc. 1:1,000	Restore heart beat in asystole "Coarsen" waves in ventricular fibrillation ↑ Pulse and BP ↑ Cardiac output ↑ Heart contraction	Can induce ventricular fibrillation in irritable heart	Avoid intracardiac route if effective cardiac massage established to prevent myocardial tears
Calcium chloride Calcium gluconate	10 cc. 10 cc.	↑ Heart contraction	Causes cardiac arrest in systole if given too rapidly	Useful if patient does not respond to other measures Neutralizes potassium effects
Norepinephrine (Levophed)	4–8 cc. in 500 cc. of 5D/W	↑ Peripheral resistance ↑ Blood pressure ↑ Heart contraction	Causes tissue sloughing if infiltrates	Potent vasconstrictor
Isoproterenol HCL (Isuprel)	2 mg./500 cc.	↑ Heart contraction ↓ Peripheral resistance ↑ Cardiac output	↓ Blood pressure	Potent vasodilator Can cause tachycardia with rapid administration
Metaraminol (Aramine)	100–200 mg./500 cc. 5 D/W	↑ Peripheral resistance ↑ Cardiac output ↑ Blood pressure		
Mephentermine (Wyamine)	15–30 mg. I.M. or I.V.	↑ Cardiac output		Peripheral vasodilator
Methoxamine (Vasoxyl)		↑ Peripheral resistance ↑ Blood pressure		No direct action on heart

Undesirable effects: Often the first warning signals of digitalis intoxication which are appreciated are the arrhythmias. It may produce an arrhythmia which in its own right decreases cardiac output. The resulting arrhythmias are universal—PVC, VT, VF, AT, nodal rhythms, heart blocks. Seldom does it cause atrial fibrillation or flutter. Mortality of digitalis produced arrhythmias is estimated at 30 percent. PVC's due to digitalis toxicity are not controlled well by Xylocaine. Nausea, vomiting, abdominal cramps, diarrhea, colored vision, severe facial pain, or psychosis are a few of the whole host of problems digitalis can produce.

Diphenylhydantoin (Dilantin)

Cardiac effects: Mechanism unknown. Enhances A-V conduction. Effects are weaker than lidocaine and as transient. Antagonistic to digitalis and thus effective for digitalis intoxication and arrhythmias therefrom.

Indications: All arrhythmias but especially those due to digitalis intoxication. Should be given slowly I.V. (50 mg./minute) to avoid a drop in heart rate due to propylene glycol base.

Undesirable effects: Hyperplasia of gums, syndrome very similar to infectious mononucleosis, fever, thrombocytopenia.

Oxygen

Cardiac effects: Has a vagal action on the A-V node and slows pulse slightly (approximately 10 percent reduction in pulse rate). O_2 elevates blood pressure slightly. These effects are beneficial as they allow more time for diastole and improved pressure during diastole.

Indications: Usual routes of administration provide a concentration of 40 percent. Ordinarily it is continued for the first few days.

Contraindications: Some patients with chronic lung disease who have increased CO_2 retention which provides their drive for respiration. When given oxygen in abundance, their respiratory stimulus is removed and they become dusky, hypoventilate, or stop breathing altogether. For these patients oxygen must be given with assisted respiration and blood gas samples obtained.

Propranolol (Inderal)

Cardiac effects: Very powerful blocking agent of epinephrine and norepinephrine. Decreases heart rate, decreases heart contraction, constricts superficial peripheral circulation.

Indications: Only drug to slow down sinus tachycardia. Antiarrhythmia drug, especially for digitalis-intoxication arrhythmias.

Contraindications: It may accentuate heart failure and propranolol (Inderal) has such complete blocking action that digitalis and catecholamines have little or no effect until it wears off several hours later.

Lidocaine—Procainamide—Quinidine

Cardiac effects: Have direct effect on heart muscle by depressing myocardial activity (irritability of the heart), decreasing speed of conduction through the heart, and decreasing the strength of cardiac contraction. The above thus decrease cardiac output. They are also vasodilators. Beneficial effects include decreasing irritability of the heart and impulse formation from ectopic foci.

Indications: Lidocaine—ventricular arrhythmias; procainamide—ventricular arrhythmias; quinidine—atrial and ventricular arrythmias.

Contraindications: Persons with decreased cardiac output. Will produce shock, failure or both.

Undesirable effects: All may produce serious arrhythmias, heart blocks or cardiac standstill. Quinidine is the most toxic while lidocaine is the least toxic.

Lidocaine—causes less fall in blood pressure and decrease in myocardial contractibility. Can cause drowsiness, discomfort in breathing and sweating. In high doses, causes excitability of central nervous system resulting in grand mal seizures and respiratory arrest.

Procainamide—GI tract symptoms, anorexia, lupuslike syndrome.

Quinidine—can be fatal if given intravenously. Diarrhea, nausea, vomiting and the syndrome called cinchonism (tinnitus, vertigo, headache, and visual disturbance). These will disappear with withdrawal of the drug.

6

Assessment Skills for the Nurse

PHILLIP S. WOLF, M.D.
THELMA L. LOHR, R.N., M.S.
SHIRLEY J. HOFFMAN, R.N., B.S.
JOAN MERSCH, R.N., M.S.
CAROLYN M. HUDAK, R.N., M.S.

ARRHYTHMIA RECOGNITION—CARDIAC ARRHYTHMIAS AND CONDUCTION DISTURBANCES

Disorders of the heartbeat occur in 70 to 95 percent of patients with acute myocardial infarction. Their importance differs; some lack clinical significance while others are lethal.

The common arrhythmias seen in monitoring units, appear so faithfully in reproducible patterns that to facilitate your study and to prevent confusion by the numerous varieties of disorders, we have presented the arrhythmias singularly and the significant changes from the normal rhythm. Since they are out of context of a person's total clinical picture, the significance of and treatment of these arrhythmias might be altered.

The nurse's understanding of arrhythmias is helped by knowledge of the conduction system. Before beginning your study of this section, you might find it helpful to review the conduction system and the principles of electrocardiography.

The nurse must be able to recognize the basic waves, but more important, she must be able to interpret the rhythm strips by LOGIC. These skills are not mystical. They can be developed by all nurses who have a constant exposure to monitored patients.

Two very important features to look for when you begin your strip study are (1) the P waves, (2) the appearance of the QRS complex. Both of these provide excellent signposts for determining basic rhythms and are the basis for continued learning of the complicated arrhythmias. On occasion, it is impossible to specifically identify the rhythm from a single strip and it may be necessary to take a 12-lead ECG.

Recognizing that monitoring the electrical activity of a patient's heart is but one parameter for appropriate therapy, it is the nurse's responsibility to describe as accurately as possible not only the patient's monitor pattern but also her findings and judgments from observations of the body's main systems and their functions.

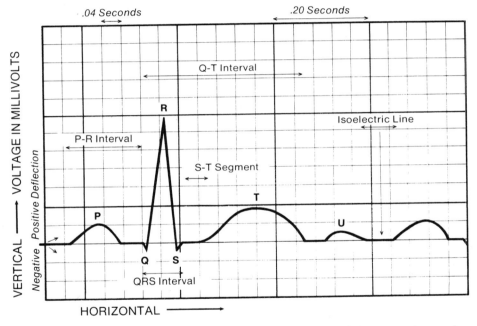

Fig. 6-1. Schematic representation of the electrical impulse as it traverses the conduction system, resulting in depolarization and repolarization of the myocardium.

Normal Sinus Rhythm

RATE	Normal limits, 60–100 beats/minute.
ISOELECTRIC LINE	The straight line seen when no electrical activity is occurring. The baseline of the tracing.
P WAVE	A deflection from the baseline produced by depolarization of the atria. The atrial repolarization is slow and of such low amplitude that the atrial T wave is not seen and/or is buried in the QRS complex.

P-R Interval | The time required for the impulse to travel through the atria into the first portion of the conduction system, the A-V node. Normal limits are 0.12–0.20 second, and is the interval from the beginning of the P wave to the start of the QRS complex.

QRS Complex | A deflection from the baseline produced by depolarization of the ventricles. Normal duration is 0.06–0.08 second.

S-T Segment | The isoelectrical interval between the *end* of the QRS complex and the *beginning* of the T wave.

Q-T Interval | The time required for the ventricles to depolarize and to repolarize. Usual duration is 0.32–0.40 second, and is the interval from the beginning of the QRS complex to the end of the T wave.

T wave | A deflection from the baseline produced by ventricular *r*epolarization and is of the same deflection as the QRS complex.

U wave | A small deflection following the T wave which is rarely seen. Its significance is uncertain, but it is typically seen with hypokalemia.

Rate Determination. The following is one of the various methods to determine rate:

Remembering that 1 large block of 5 small squares = .20 seconds, count 5 large blocks. This equals 1 inch of ECG paper = 1 second. Thirty large blocks = 6 inches = 6 seconds. Count the number of R waves in 6 inches. Multiply this number of R waves by 10–10 times 6 seconds = 1 minute. You now have an *approximate* pulse rate for the patient.

Caution. To gain an accurate count, one must count the apical pulse for a full minute.

Problem. Interpret the monitor strip below by supplying the required information.

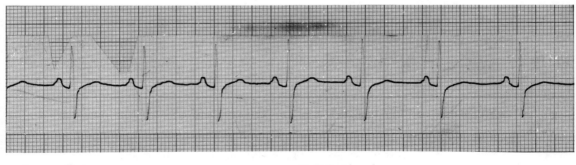

Rate _____   P–R Interval _____
P-Wave Rate _____   QRS Interval _____
R-Wave Rate _____   T-Wave Configuration _____

Sinus Tachycardia

DEFINITION: A rapid heart rate with impulses originating in the S-A node.

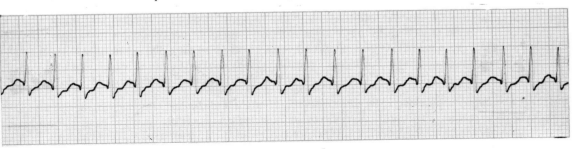

SIGNIFICANT ECG CHANGES

Rate: Range 100–180 beats/minute. Rhythm is regular, but may vary from minute to minute. The diastole duration is shortened.

INFORMATION ABOUT

Etiology: Sinus tachycardia may be a physiological response to any form of stress and is found in all age groups. It occurs in such diverse conditions as excitement, physical exertion, fever, anemia, hyperthyroidism, anoxia, and from drugs such as atropine, isoproterenol (Isuprel), and epinephrine. It may also occur with heart disease and is often present with congestive heart failure.

Dynamics: Sinus tachycardia results from sympathetic nervous system activity and the release of catecholamines (epinephrine and norepinephrine). These substances are released by the adrenal medulla and from nerve endings in the heart. Guyton records that sinus tachycardia results from two main causes:[1]

1. Stimulation of the heart by the sympathetic nervous system.
   (a) Causes the following reaction: increase in peripheral resistance, increase in arterial pressure, increase in venous return, increase in stimulation of the heart and increase cardiac output. It also causes vasodilation of the muscle and increases the blood flow there.
   (b) Elevation of body temperature: an above-normal temperature also increases the metabolism rate of the myocardium, exciting the muscle and increasing the rhythm rate.
   (c) Weakened heart muscle—decreases the blood flow into the arterial tree which stimulates the sympathetic nervous system, and in turn increases the rhythm rate to increase cardiac output.
2. Internal myocardium changes.
   Conditions of the heart such as inflammatory processes,

ischemia, etc., increase the irritability of the heart muscle and cause an increased excitability of the S-A node.

The person may experience a sense of "racing of the heart" and/or palpitations. The cause of sinus tachycardia determines its prognosis, not the continuation or duration of the arrhythmia which in and of itself ordinarily is harmless. In persons who already have depleted cardiac reserve, ischemia, and/or congestive heart failure, the persistence of a fast rate may worsen the underlying condition.

Treatment: Based on the underlying cause, treatment may include sedation and digitalis if heart failure is present.

Caution: Do not confuse *sinus* tachycardia with *paroxysmal* tachycardia, which will be discussed later.

Problem: To become adept in arrhythmia recognition, interpret the preceding strip by supplying the required information.

Rate _____   P-R Interval _____
P-Wave Rate _____   QRS Interval _____
R-Wave Rate _____   T-Wave Configuration _____

Sinus Bradycardia

DEFINITION: A slow heart rate with impulses originating in the S-A node.

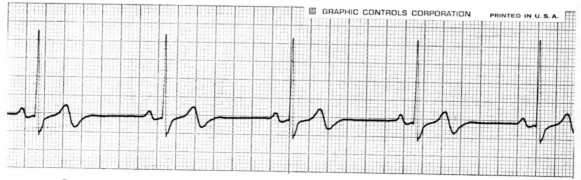

© GRAPHIC CONTROLS CORPORATION   PRINTED IN U.S.A.

SIGNIFICANT ECG CHANGES
Rate: Below 60 beats/minute. Rhythm is regular but may vary from minute to minute. The diastole duration is lengthened.

INFORMATION ABOUT
Etiology: Sinus bradycardia is common among all age groups and is present in both normal and diseased hearts. It is also seen in diverse conditions such as highly trained athletes, persons with severe pain, with myxedema, from the vagal effects of drugs (digitalis, reserpine) and as an occasional complication of myocardial infarction.

Dynamics: Sinus bradycardia results from excessive parasympathetic nervous system activity. Slow rates are tolerated well in persons with healthy hearts. With severe heart disease, however, the heart may not be able to compensate for a slow rate by increasing the volume of blood ejected per beat as does the healthy heart. This may cause fainting (insufficient blood flow to the brain), weakness (inadequate flow to the muscles), and/or angina, dangerous arrhythmia or congestive heart failure (diminished coronary artery flow).

Treatment: Usually none is indicated unless symptoms are present. If the pulse is very slow and symptoms are present, appropriate drugs are atropine to block vagal effect, Isuprel to accelerate the cardiac pacemaker and/or electric pacing.

Problem: To become adept in arrhythmia recognition, interpret the preceding strip by supplying the required information.

Rate _____   P-R Interval _____
P-Wave Rate _____   QRS Interval _____
R-Wave Rate _____   T-Wave Configuration _____

Sinus Arrhythmia

DEFINITION: All impulses originate in the S-A node, but the rate of discharge varies. Some occur prematurely while others are delayed, which causes the rate to alternately increase and decrease.

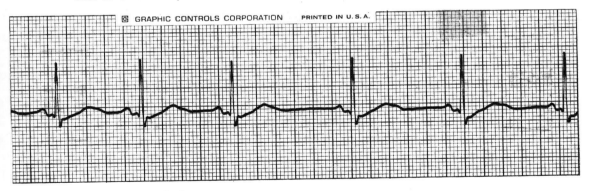

SIGNIFICANT ECG CHANGES
Rate: Usually varies with respiration. Heart rate usually increases with inspiration and slows with expiration.

INFORMATION ABOUT
Etiology This is a physiological variation, not a symptom of underlying heart disease. It is most common in children and young adults, but may be seen in older adults. It is not thought to indicate underlying heart disease.

Dynamics: Since the S-A node is controlled by the autonomic nervous system, it is believed that sinus arrhythmia, which is synchronized with respiration, is caused by one or a combination of circulatory reflexes. These reflexes cause the heart rate to slow with expiration and speed with inspiration. It does not disturb cardiac output or circulation, for the chambers fill and empty normally.

Treatment: None necessary.

Caution: To verify this phenomenon, it is necessary to take a strip long enough to include a full respiratory cycle.

Problem: To become adept in arrhythmia recognition, interpret the preceding strip by supplying the required information.

Rate _____   P-R Interval _____

P-Wave Rate _____   QRS Interval _____

R-Wave Rate _____   T-Wave Configuration _____

Premature Atrial Contraction (PAC)

DEFINITION: During the normal cardiac rhythm, a contraction occurs earlier than expected. The stimulus for this contraction arises from somewhere else in the atrium and NOT in the S-A node.

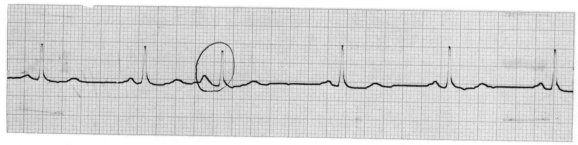

SIGNIFICANT ECG CHANGES

Rate: Normal range 60–100 beats/minute. The rhythm is regular except for the premature beats.

P Wave: Those originating in the S-A node are of normal deflection and duration, and occur at regular intervals. The P wave of the premature beat is usually slightly different in deflection, indicating the stimulus originates elsewhere in the atrium than the S-A node.

QRS Complex: Follows each P wave no matter what the form of the P wave. The QRS usually is of normal configuration, but it may appear distorted when the PAC is conducted aberrantly, or the QRS may not occur at all (PAC is blocked).

Pauses: The PAC is usually followed by a short pause which is less than "compensatory." (See Pauses under PVC's.)

INFORMATION ABOUT

Etiology: This is a common arrhythmia seen in all age groups. It may result from emotional stress, tobacco, caffeine, alcohol, or from underlying heart disease.

Dynamics: An impulse arises in the atrial musculature from an ectopic focus, causing atrial contraction. Usually the stimulus travels on through the A-V node and continues its normal course through the ventricles. If the PAC occurs too rapidly, some QRS complexes may be dropped because the A-V node is refractory from the previous stimulus and is unable to receive the current one. In most instances the atrial ectopic beat is followed by an incomplete compensatory pause which can be heard by ausculation, or the patient may have the sensation of a "pause" in rhythm or of a palpitation.

Treatment: Counting the apical pulse is important for premature beats are usually heard apically but not felt radially, resulting in a pulse deficit. Observation of the frequency of PAC's is needed, but treatment is not necessary in most cases. Mild sedation or the removal of the exciting cause are indicated if the PAC's are symptomatic. If the premature beats are the result of underlying heart disease, specific drugs may be ordered such as quinidine, digitalis, or Pronestyl.

Problem: To become adept in arrhythmia recognition, interpret the preceding strip by supplying the required information.

Rate _____   P-R Interval _____
P-Wave Rate _____   QRS Interval _____
R-Wave Rate _____   T-Wave Configuration _____

Atrial and Nodal Tachycardia

DEFINITION: These tachycardias are rapid, regular superventricular rhythms. The pacemaker of the heart shifts from S-A node to a rapidly firing atrial ectopic focus in paroxysmal atrial tachycardia (PAT) and to the A-V junction in paroxysmal nodal tachycardia.

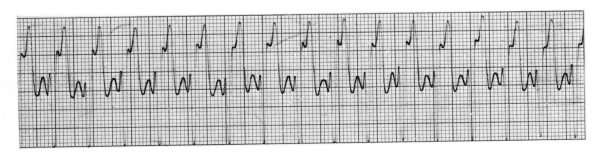

SIGNIFICANT ECG CHANGES

Rate: Range 140–220 beats/minute. The rhythm is regular and the paroxysms ordinarily last from a few minutes to a few hours.

P Waves: Usually upright with atrial tachycardia and inverted in Leads II, III, and AVF when the tachycardia is of nodal origin. If the rate is very rapid, the P waves may be buried in the QRS or superimposed on the T waves.

P-R Interval: If seen, it is usually shortened with nodal tachycardia and normal or shortened with atrial tachycardia.

QRS Complex: Usually of normal configuration, but may be distorted if aberrant conduction is present.

INFORMATION ABOUT

Etiology: These arrhythmias occur most often in adults with normal hearts. They may occur for the same reasons as PAC's. When disease is present, such abnormalities as rheumatic heart disease, coronary heart disease or digitalis intoxication may serve as the background for these arrhythmias.

Dynamics: Atrial tachycardia is typically preceded by a PAC. As with a PAC, the new pacemaker discharges impulses to which the atrium and/or conduction system responds, and it fires so rapidly that the S-A node temporarily loses its function as pacemaker. In nodal tachycardia, the A-V junction then discharges more rapidly than the S-A node. The impulses are continuous, regular, and follow on through the conduction system of the ventricles in normal sequence, but the atria are always stimulated in a retrograde fashion. During the paroxysms, the heart is contracting so rapidly that cardiac output may decrease. Extreme regularity (in a given person at a given time stays at a constant rate) is one of the hallmarks. Early symptoms are palpitations and lightheadedness. With underlying heart disease present, dyspnea, anginal chest pains, syncope and congestive heart failure may occur.

Treatment: Stimulation of the vagal reflex many times will stop the paroxysms and is worth a try. If the nurse is unfamiliar with these, she should NOT try them without proper instruction and supervision. This reflex may be elicited by massage with pressure on the carotid sinus (unilaterally), painful pressure on the eyeball at the onset of an attack, or the Valsalva maneuver. If these are unsuccessful, antiarrhythmic drugs are used—quinidine, digitalis, or procainamide (Pronestyl). If the attack persists, or if complications occur which demand more immediate action, countershock is indicated.

Problem: To become adept in arrhythmia recognition, interpret the preceding strip by supplying the required information.

Rate _____   P-R Interval _____

P-Wave Rate _____ QRS Interval _____

R-Wave Rate _____ T-Wave Configuration _____

Atrial Flutter

DEFINITION: Abnormally rapid but regular atrial contractions caused by impulses arising from an ectopic focus which becomes the pacemaker. The ventricular rate varies.

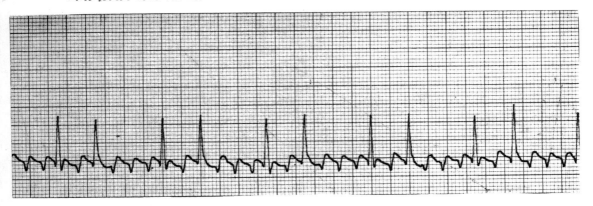

SIGNIFICANT ECG CHANGES

Rate: Atrial rate from 250–350 beats/minute. Ventricular rate depends upon the degree of A-V block.

P Wave: Regular and rapid in rate, they appear widened and have a characteristic sawtooth appearance. Since they occur at regular intervals, it is usual that one falls within the QRS-T complex.

QRS Complex: Normal configuration, except when aberrant conduction is present. They do not, however, follow every P wave, since the ventricles cannot respond this rapidly.

INFORMATION ABOUT

Etiology: The stimuli which cause PAC can also cause atrial flutter. This is not a common arrhythmia and most cases occur with cardiovascular disease. However, it can occur paroxysmally in persons with no known heart disease.

Dynamics: Again, the ectopic focus becomes the pacemaker and stimulates the atrium; the impulse is conducted through the A-V node to the ventricles in normal fashion. There are two theories currently considered as to the mechanism of atrial flutter. (1) A continuous impulse travels through the atrium, causing a "circus" movement at a very rapid but coordinated rate, and (2) a single ectopic focus discharges rapidly. Early in the arrhythmia the ventricles respond once to every two impulses from the atrium. Further A-V block develops or the arrhythmia persists and the ventricles respond irregularly to every 2–6 beats. If ventricular rate is within normal limits, the cardiac output will remain sufficient. If it is too rapid so that the chambers cannot fill, cardiovascular changes are immediate. These changes are described in atrial tachycardia. A rapid ventricular response cannot be tolerated for any length of time without serious consequences. This tachycardia is frequently accompanied by symptoms of chest pain, congestive heart failure, and cerebrovascular disturbance, because it most often occurs in persons with carviovascular disease.

Treatment: If the flutter has a sufficient degree of block so that the ventricular rate remains within normal limits, no treatment may be necessary. Since this usually is associated with heart disease, prompt treatment to control the rate and/or convert the rhythm to normal is indicated. Digitalis is usually the drug of choice for it may answer both purposes. It usually increases the degree of A-V block and thus controls the ventricular rate, or it may increase the irritability of the atrium, thus producing atrial fibrillation. Further treatment depends upon underlying conditions present. If complications occur suddenly and more immediate action than drug therapy is demanded, countershock is indicated. Further treatment depends upon the progression of the condition.

Problem: To become adept in arrhythmia recognition, interpret the preceding strip by supplying the required information.

Rate _____   P-R Interval _____
P-Wave Rate _____   QRS Interval _____
R-Wave Rate _____   T-Wave Configuration _____

Atrial Fibrillation

DEFINITION: An atrial arrhythmia occurring at an extremely rapid rate lacking coordinated activity. The atria produce stimuli rapidly, but the ventricles respond in a normal sequence to only impulses conducted by the A-V node, causing an irregular rate.

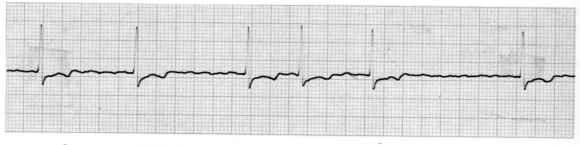

SIGNIFICANT ECG CHANGES

Rate: Atrial rate 400–600 beats/minute. Ventricular rate is irregular, 150–180 beats/minute.

P Wave:　　　Absent; irregular "fibrillary" (F waves) waves are usually seen.

QRS Complex:　Irregular rate, but the atrial impulses which do reach the A-V node are conducted in normal sequence.

INFORMATION ABOUT

Etiology:　　Atrial fibrillation may occur as a chronic condition or in paroxysms in the normal heart (see PAC). It occurs in the older adult especially those with coronary artery disease and mitral stenosis. Atrial fibrillation is often preceded by atrial premature contractions, tachycardia, and/or flutter.

Dynamics:　　The impulses originating either from many ectopic foci or from a circus movement, are so rapid that the atrium do not depolarize as a unit. The contractions are irregular in rate and force causing fibrillatory movement of the chambers. The A-V node is incapable of responding to the extremely rapid atrial rate. Those impulses that the A-V node does transmit cause the ventricles to respond with an irregular rhythm. The cardiac output falls because of (1) rapid rate (less time for the ventricles to fill), and (2) loss of effective atrial contractions. At the onset of paroxysms, the person frequently experiences palpitation, but if the arrhythmia is chronic with ventricular rate within normal limits, the person thereby may have no symptoms at all. Rapid ventricular rate leads to a decreased cardiac output with the consequences as outlined for other atrial arrhythmias and with mitral stenosis. Symptoms of another complication may arise from atrial fibrillation— peripheral arterial emboli. Due to the passive dilated state of the atria, thrombi can develop on the atrial wall and fragments dislodge, producing embolization. A pulse deficit is always present with atrial fibrillation. The radial pulse is slower than the apical pulse because some systolic contractions are feeble and not felt in the peripheral arteries.

Treatment:　　If the complications develop rapidly, countershock is indicated immediately. If cardiac output remains sufficient, then drug therapy is utilized. Digitalis is specific for its ability to increase A-V block, allowing more time for diastole and results in better filling of the ventricular chambers; thus, more blood volume per stroke. The rhythm may convert with digitalis to normal sinus rhythm. Quinidine is utilized for maintenance of normal sinus rhythm. It is also used for conversion and for maintenance of normal sinus rhythm.

Problem: To become adept in arrhythmia recognition, interpret the preceding strip by supplying the required information.

Rate _____　　　　　P-R Interval _____

P-Wave Rate _____　　QRS Interval _____

R-Wave Rate _____　　T-Wave Configuration _____

Atrial Standstill

DEFINITION: Complete cessation of the S-A node and atrial activity. The pacemaker shifts to a point below the atria, either in the A-V junction or an ectopic focus within the ventricular myocardium (idioventricular focus).

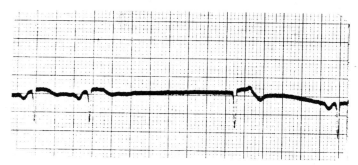

SIGNIFICANT ECG CHANGES

Rate: Ventricular rate is usually slowed.

P Waves: No P waves are seen. The baseline is isoelectric.

QRS-T Complex: Normal in sequence, deflection and duration if impulse originates in the A-V node. If originated in an idioventricular focus, it will appear widened and distorted, of positive or negative deflection.

INFORMATION ABOUT

Etiology: An arrhythmia so infrequently seen that it is rarely mentioned. It is usually the result of intoxication from quinidine, digitalis, or potassium. For a brief period, atrial standstill may also accompany a sudden injury to the myocardium, such as with an infarction.

Dynamics: The atria are motionless for there is no electrical activity. They remain dilated and nonfunctioning. The heart rhythm may cease altogether for 10–20 seconds, but usually some other area takes over as pacemaker. Most frequently, it is the A-V junction, but as stated an ectopic focus in the ventricular myocardium can assume the pacemaker function. The symptoms are those due to temporary standstill (fainting) or those due to underlying heart disease in the patient. Sudden death may occur if a lower pacemaker does not take over.

Treatment: Prompt reporting of this arrhythmia is vital to the patient's life. Digitalis and/or quinidine are stopped immediately. Hyperkalemia, if present, responds to appropriate therapy, such as intravenous sodium bicarbonate or glucose and insulin mixtures. An artificial pacemaker may be needed.

Problem: To become adept in arrhythmia recognition, interpret the preceding strip by supplying the required information.

Rate _____	P-R Interval _____
P-Wave Rate _____	QRS Interval _____
R-Wave Rate _____	T-Wave Configuration _____

A-V Junctional Premature Beats

DEFINITION: An impulse from an ectopic focus in the A-V node or A-V bundle occurs sooner than the normal impulse from the S-A node, initiating ventricular contraction.

SIGNIFICANT ECG CHANGES

P Wave: Inverted in Leads II, III, and AVF. The P waves may occur before, during, or after the QRS complexes.

P-R Interval: Usually shortened.

INFORMATION ABOUT

Etiology: Often the cause may be completely unknown, or due to those listed under PAC. In older adults it commonly accompanies coronary artery disease.

Dynamics: The A-V node or A-V bundle acts as pacemaker. The impulses pass through the conduction system of the ventricles in normal fashion, creating a normal QRS pattern. Stimulation of the atria by the A-V premature impulse occurs as the impulse travels backward through the atrial fibers in retrograde fashion. This causes an inverted P wave. Increase in A-V nodal irritability may lead to more serious A-V nodal arrhythmias, such as nodal tachycardia. Usually no symptoms accompany these premature beats.

Treatment: None if beats occur infrequently. If frequent, antiarrhythmia drugs may be given (digitalis, lidocaine, quinidine, procainamide). The same as for PAC's.

Problem: To become adept in arrhythmia recognition, interpret the preceding strip by supplying the required information.

Rate _____	P-R Interval _____
P-Wave Rate _____	QRS Interval _____
R-Wave Rate _____	T-Wave Configuration _____

Premature Ventricular Contractions (PVC)

DEFINITION: A ventricular contraction originating from an ectopic focus in the ventricular musculature which appears earlier than is expected.

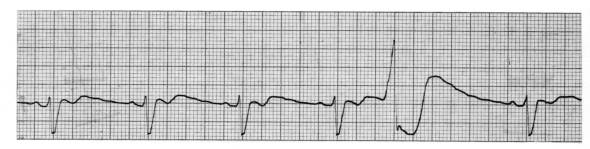

SIGNIFICANT ECG CHANGES

Rate: Within normal limits if the PVC's are infrequent.

P Waves: Not seen before the QRS of the premature beat.

QRS Complex: The QRS of the premature beat cannot be missed. It not only appears earlier than expected, but it is bizarre, widened, notched, and may be of greater amplitude.

S-T Segment: Not distinguishable with the PVC for the QRS and T wave merge with the PVC.

T Wave: After the PVC, it is widened and of greater amplitude, as is the QRS, and of opposite deflection to the QRS complex.

Pause: A compensatory pause follows the premature beat as the heart awaits the next stimulus from the S-A node. The pause is fully compensatory if the cycles of the normal and premature beats equal the time of two normal heart cycles.

INFORMATION ABOUT

Etiology: PVC's are the most common of all arrhythmias, and can occur in any age groups, with or without heart disease. They are very common in the person with myocardial disease (ischemia, myocardial infarction, cardiac surgery) or with myocardial irritability (electrolyte imbalance, overdose or intoxication from drugs). Other causes, as described in PAC, can also cause PVC's.

Dynamics: The impulse arises outside of the conduction network and within the ventricular muscle. This slows the spread of the impulse through the ventricles and produces a distorted QRS pattern. PVC's may occur after each normal beat (bigeminy) or after two normal beats (trigeminy). If they originate from different ectopic foci, the PVC's have a different configuration and are known as *multifocal.* Often there are no symptoms, but some persons may experience a "thump" or "skipping" sensation. PVC's may be the earliest sign of progressive heart disease, and/or myocardial irritability. When more frequent than 6–10/minute or close to the apex of the T wave, they may be precursors of more serious arrhythmias such as ventricular tachycardia, fibrillation, and/or standstill.

Treatment: Infrequent, isolated PVC's require no treatment. Multiple PVC's or PVC's encroaching upon the apex of the T wave are treated with antiarrhythmia agents. If serum potassium levels are low, potassium replacement may correct the arrhythmia, if due to drug toxicity (digitalis or emetine) withdrawal of the drug may correct the arrhythmia.

Problem: To become adept in arrhythmia recognition, interpret the preceding strip by supplying the required information.

Rate _____   P-R Interval _____
P-Wave Rate _____   QRS Interval _____
R-Wave Rate _____   T-Wave Configuration _____

Ventricular Tachycardia

DEFINITION: The ventricular ectopic focus emits impulses rapidly and regularly and the ventricular contractions are disassociated from the atrial contractions.

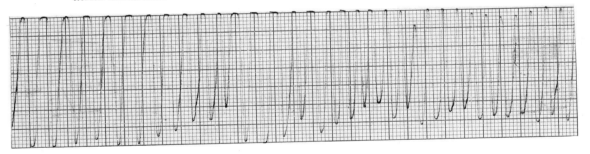

SIGNIFICANT ECG CHANGES
Rate; Ventricular rate range 140–220 beats/minute.
P Wave: Rarely seen due to superimposition on the rapid, prominent QRS-T complexes.
QRS Complex: Same characteristics of PVC's and they occur consecutively.
T Wave: Opposite in deflection to QRS complex.
INFORMATION ABOUT
Etiology: A rarity in adults with normal hearts, but common (20–30 percent) as a complication of myocardial infarction or digitalis intoxication.
Dynamics: The ventricles have one or more ectopic foci which emit stimuli regularly and rapidly. The ventricular contractions appear as a series of PVC's. The atria can continue to respond to the S-A node, but the two have no association. The rapid

rate leads to decreased cardiac output. Palpitations, chest pain, weakness and fainting are frequent symptoms. Hypotension or congestive heart failure may also follow due to decreased stroke volume.

Treatment: Lidocaine, procainamide (Pronestyl), quinidine, or Dilantin in adequate doses and potassium supplement given I.V. may terminate the ectopic foci. Electrical countershock is often very useful. If the arrhythmia is due to digitalis intoxication, the medication should be withdrawn and potassium given.

Problem: To become adept in arrhythmia recognition, interpret the preceding strip by supplying the required information.

Rate _____	P-R Interval _____
P-Wave Rate _____	QRS Interval _____
R-Wave Rate _____	T-Wave Configuration _____

Ventricular Fibrillation

DEFINITION: Rapid, irregular contractions of the ventricles which are uncoordinated and incapable of pumping blood.

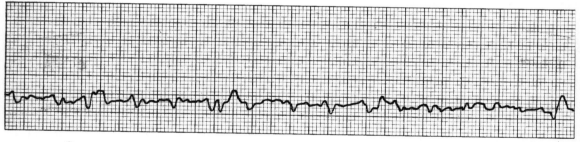

SIGNIFICANT ECG CHANGES

Rate: Indeterminate.

Complexes: None of the complexes of normal heart electrical activity are present. The baseline wavers with bizarre, distorted waveforms.

INFORMATION ABOUT

Etiology: Ventricular fibrillation is favored by several causes. Some of these include myocardial ischemia (as with infarction), PVC's occurring at the apex of the T wave, and drugs (digitalis or quinidine) in toxic doses.

Dynamics: The ventricles remain dilated and do not expel blood; thus circulation and perfusion cease and death ensues rapidly. Symptoms occur simultaneously with the arrhythmia. Loss of consciousness occurs within 8–10 seconds, and an anoxia seizure may occur. No pulse can be elicited, and the pupils are dilated. Clinical death is present and biological death follows in a few moments. It is the most common cause of immediate death, and is nearly always fatal if resuscitation is not immediately instituted. Rarely, ventricular fibrillation may terminate spontaneously within seconds.

Treatment: Prevention! This is much more realistic with patients who are monitored. Prevention may be attained with the anti-arrhythmic drugs for PVC's and ventricular tachycardia. Recognition of sudden death and the nurse's immediately initiating cardiac resuscitation measures (maintenance of ventilation and circulation) can adequately perfuse the patient until assistance arrives. Then defibrillation with d-c current to correct the arrhythmia, and I.V. sodium bicarbonate to correct the acidosis are instituted. (See cardiac resuscitation.)

Problem: To become adept in arrhythmia recognition, interpret the preceding strip by supplying the required information.

Rate _____   P-R Interval _____
P-Wave Rate _____   QRS Interval _____
R-Wave Rate _____   T-Wave Configuration _____

Sinoatrial Block

DEFINITION: The impulses, originating in the S-A node, occasionally fail to appear and one or more beats are totally dropped.

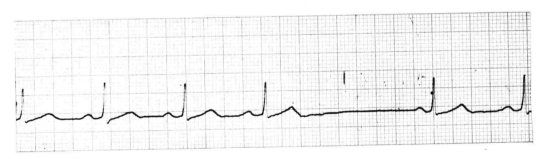

SIGNIFICANT ECG CHANGES

P-R Interval: No complex appears during the blocked impulse interval, indicating that an entire beat has been dropped. The time interval is exactly twice as long as the interval for each normal cardiac cycle.

INFORMATION ABOUT

Etiology: A rare arrhythmia which may be a spontaneous phenomenon, a result of excessive vagal stimulation, myocardial infarction affecting the S-A node, or digitalis intoxication.

Dynamics: The S-A node fails to emit an impulse. The pause is as long as a regular cardiac cycle, and the next P wave occurs at its designated time. There are usually no symptoms but with prolonged pauses, cardiac standstill may result in fainting.

Treatment: When due to drug intoxication, the offending agent is stopped. When due to vagal activity, atropine or Isuprel are sometimes useful. Transvenous pacing may be required for prolonged pauses because of the threat of cardiac standstill.

Problem: To become adept in arrhythmia recognition, interpret the preceding strip by supplying the required information.

Rate _____   P-R Interval _____

P-Wave Rate _____   QRS Interval _____

R-Wave Rate _____   T-Wave Configuration _____

First-Degree Block—Delayed A-V Conduction

DEFINITION: A delay in conduction through the A-V node.

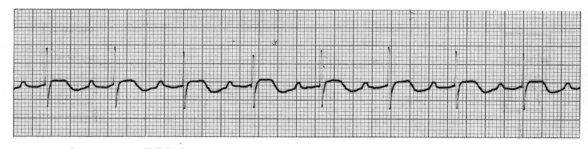

SIGNIFICANT ECG CHANGES

P-R Interval: Exceeds the upper limit of 0.20 second in duration.

INFORMATION ABOUT

Etiology: Occurs in all ages, and in both normal hearts and in heart diseases of all types. Drugs such as digitalis, quinidine, Pronestyl and lidocaine may prolong the P-R interval.

Dynamics: The impulse originates normally in the S-A node and travels through the atrium in normal sequence. The A-V node is at fault in that it delays the conduction for a longer time than usual. When the impulse does pass on through the A-V node, the ventricles contract normally. If delay is too long, an "escape" beat may originate from a lower pacemaker area. This is a "benign" conduction disturbance of no significance except as a possible precursor of second-or three-degree A-V blocks.

Treatment: Constant monitoring for progression to more serious blocks. No treatment needed.

Problem: To become adept in arrhythmia recognition, interpret the preceding strip by supplying the required information.

Rate _____   P-R Interval _____
P-Wave Rate _____   QRS Interval _____
R-Wave Rate _____   T-Wave Configuration _____

Second-Degree Block—Wenckebach Mobitz Type I

DEFINITION: With each beat, the delay of conduction through the A-V node is progressively increased. Eventually, a ventricular contraction does not follow.

SIGNIFICANT ECG CHANGES

P-R Interval: Progressively lengthens with each beat.

QRS Complex: Normal configuration, but progressively delayed after each P wave until one is dropped.

INFORMATION ABOUT

Etiology: Of the two types of second-degree block, the Wenckebach phenomenon is the more common. The causes are the same as for second-degree block, except that digitalis may cause *this* type of second-degree block.

Dynamics: The impulses originate normally in the S-A node and travel to the A-V node. A progressive delay at the A-V node occurs until the sinus impulse falls at the same time the A-V node is still in the refractory period from the previous impulse. Thus no QRS follows and a long pause appears. The next impulse finds the heart polarized and ready for stimulation and the phenomenon repeats itself. This arrhythmia alone does not significantly alter cardiac output.

Treatment: No treatment required.

Problem: To become adept in arrhythmia recognition, interpret the preceding strip by supplying the required information.

Rate _____   P-R Interval _____
P-Wave Rate _____   QRS Interval _____
R-Wave Rate _____   T-Wave Configuration _____

Second-Degree Block—Mobitz Type II

DEFINITION: Some atrial impulses are blocked from passage through the A-V node.

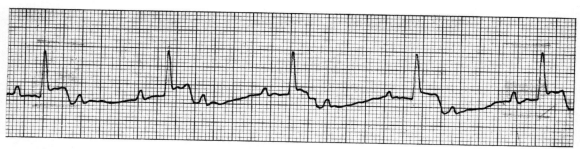

SIGNIFICANT ECG CHANGES

Rate: Ventricular rate is a fraction (1:2, 1:3, 1:4, etc.) of the atrial rate.

P-R Interval: May be lengthened.

INFORMATION ABOUT

Etiology: Same as for first-degree block except that digitalis is never a cause.

Dynamics: Atrial contractions result from regular S-A impulses. Only those impulses which penetrate the A-V node cause ventricular contractions. There are no symptoms unless ventricular rate is so slow that cardiac output is decreased and thus is inadequate for perfusion. This rhythm is potentially dangerous, as it may progress to third-degree block.

Treatment: Constant monitoring and observation of progression. Isoproterenol (Isuprel) or epinephrine; atropine; occasionally cardiac pacing.

Problem: To become adept in arrhythmia recognition, interpret the preceding strip by supplying the required information.

Rate _____   P-R Interval _____

P-Wave Rate _____   QRS Interval _____

R-Wave Rate _____   T-Wave Configuration _____

Third-Degree Block—Complete A-V Block

DEFINITION: The atria and ventricles contract independently of each other since the S-A impulse is not transmitted through the A-V node.

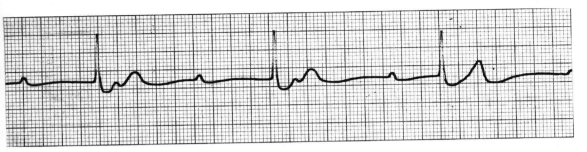

SIGNIFICANT ECG CHANGES

Rate: Atrial rate usually normal and regular. Ventricular rate regular but slower, usually 30–45 beats/minute.

P-R Interval: Variable sequences.

QRS-T Complex: Normal configuration if it originates in the A-V junction or bundles, and widened if from below this point.

INFORMATION ABOUT

Etiology: Occasionally congenital or may be secondary to myocarditis, myocardial infarction, cardiac surgery or digitalis intoxication.

Dynamics: The S-A node continues to pace in normal fashion, but the impulse is blocked at the A-V node. A pacemaker takes over either in the bundles or ventricular myocardium, initiating its own rhythm. If the ventricular rate is fast enough for adequate cardiac output, the person is asymptomatic with the arrhythmia. When the rate is slow and the cardiac contraction impaired (from underlying ventricular disease) output decreases. Heart failure may result, and runs of ventricular tachycardia, fibrillation or even standstill may cause syncope (Adams-Stokes episodes), hypoxic seizures, coma or death. Untreated cases with symptoms carry a poor prognosis and most such patients die within a year.

Treatment: Isoproterenol (Isuprel) is the drug of choice. Temporary or permanent pacing is often indicated. The nurse must be familiar with the beneficial effects and hazards of electrical pacing.

Problem: To become adept in arrhythmia recognition, interpret the preceding strip by supplying the required information.

Rate _____   P-R Interval _____

P-Wave Rate _____   QRS Interval _____

R-Wave Rate _____   T-Wave Configuration _____

Bundle Branch Block (BBB)

DEFINITION: A delay of conduction through the Bundle of His, right bundle and/or left bundle.

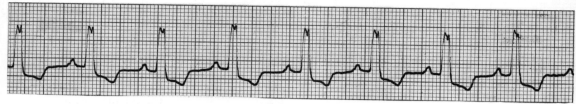

SIGNIFICANT ECG CHANGES

QRS Complex: Prolonged above 0.12 second. Typically, the QRS complex is notched and/or slurred, with a widening of the QRS complex. Right bundle branch block: the greatest deflection is negative in Lead I and positive in Lead III. Left bundle branch block: the greatest deflection is positive in Lead I and negative in Lead III.

T Wave: Widened, of greater magnitude, and in the opposite direction than the QRS complex.

INFORMATION ABOUT

Etiology: The most common causes of BBB are hypertension, myocardial ischemia, and myocardial infarction. It may also be the result of such drugs as digitalis, quinadine, Pronestyl or potassium, or of cardiac surgery. If due to drugs or surgery, the block may be transient and not permanent.

Dynamics: When conduction through the bundles is delayed, the impulse is conducted through the ventricular musculature. Transmission by this route is slower and right and left ventricular contractions do not occur simultaneously. This abnormal conduction causes the widened QRS. Incomplete bundle branch block is 0.1–0.12 second in duration. Complete block is greater than 0.12 second. Cardiac output is not decreased and thus the arrhythmia itself does not produce symptoms. The underlying heart disease determines treatment and prognosis.

Treatment: Nóne required.

Problem: To become adept in arrhythmia recognition, interpret the preceding strip by supplying the required information.

Rate _____   P-R Interval _____

P-Wave Rate _____   QRS Interval _____

R-Wave Rate _____   T-Wave Configuration _____

Note: Answers to the preceding arrhythmia problems are found in the following section.

REFERENCE

1. Arthur C. Guyton, *Textbook of Medical Physiology,* 4th ed., (Philadelphia: W. B. Saunders Co., 1971), p. 224.

ANSWERS TO ARRHYTHMIA PROBLEMS

Normal Sinus Rhythm (pages 85–86)

Rate 70

P-Wave Rate 70

R-Wave Rate 70

P-R Interval 0.16 sec

QRS Interval 0.04 sec

T-Wave Configuration same deflection as QRS

Sinus Tachycardia (pages 87–88)

Rate 200

P-Wave Rate 200

R-Wave Rate 200

P-R Interval 0.14 sec

QRS Interval 0.06 sec

T-Wave Configuration same deflection as QRS

Sinus Bradycardia (pages 88–89)

Rate 50

P-Wave Rate 50

R-Wave Rate 50

P-R Interval 0.18 sec

QRS Interval 0.06 sec

T-Wave Configuration same deflection as QRS

Sinus Arrhythmia (pages 89–90)

Rate 60

P-Wave Rate 60

R-Wave Rate 60

P-R Interval 0.18 sec

QRS Interval 0.06 sec

T-Wave Configuration same deflection as QRS

Premature Atrial Contraction (PAC) (pages 90–91)

Rate 60

P-Wave Rate 60

R-Wave Rate 60

P-R Interval 0.16 sec

QRS Interval 0.08 sec—normal configuration with
PAC

T-Wave Configuration same deflection as QRS

P wave of PAC is of different configuration. PAC occurs early. Pause is less than compensatory.

Atrial and Nodal Tachycardia (pages 91–92)

Rate   170   P-R Interval   undeterminable
P-Wave Rate   170   QRS Interval 0.08 sec
R-Wave Rate   170   T-Wave Configuration same deflection as QRS

P waves precede each QRS complex, upright on the T waves = atrial tachycardia.

Atrial Flutter (pages 93–94)

Rate   100   P-R Interval   0.16 sec
P-Wave Rate   330   QRS Interval 0.06 sec
R-Wave Rate   100   T-Wave Configuration same deflection as QRS

Rate is determined by the QRS rate of the ventricles which pump the blood to the
    body. Consistent 4:1–2:1 pattern of A-V block.

P-Wave Rate: "Measure out" the P waves and you will find that one occurs during
    the QRS of the 2nd, 4th, 6th, 8th, and 10th complexes. Due to the greater ampli-
    tude of the QRS, the P waves are "hidden."

Atrial Fibrillation (pages 94–95)

Rate   60   P-R Interval   undeterminable
P-Wave Rate   F waves   QRS Interval 0.06 sec — slow, irregular ventricular
                                                            response
R-Wave Rate   60   T-Wave Configuration same deflection as QRS

Atrial Standstill (pages 96–97)

Rate   60   P-R Interval   0.16 sec
              60 except
P-Wave Rate for pause   QRS Interval 0.04 sec
R-Wave Rate   60   T-Wave Configuration inverted

A-V Junctional Premature Contraction (page 97)

Rate   94   P-R Interval   0.16 sec
P-Wave Rate   94   QRS Interval 0.04 sec
R-Wave Rate   94   T-Wave Configuration slightly depressed

Premature Ventricular Contraction (pages 98–99)

Rate   60   P-R Interval   0.20 sec
P-Wave Rate   60   QRS Interval 0.14 sec
R-Wave Rate   60   T-Wave Configuration same deflection as QRS

PVC: QRS interval is 0.16 seconds due to wide, bizzare configuration of complex. T wave of opposite deflection. Nonconducted P wave (nonconducted PAC) at base of QRS in PVC.

Ventricular Tachycardia (pages 99–100)

Rate __330__   P-R Interval __undeterminable__

P-Wave Rate __undeterminable__   QRS Interval __undeterminable__

R-Wave Rate __330__   T-Wave Configuration __opposite deflection to QRS__

Rate increases toward end of strip. May soon progress into ventricular fibrillation.

Ventricular Fibrillation (pages 100–101)

Unable to distinguish any of the complexes.

Sinoatrial Block (pages 101–102)

Rate __75__   P-R Interval __0.20 sec__

P-Wave Rate __75 except for pause__   QRS Interval __0.06 sec__

R-Wave Rate __75__   T-Wave Configuration __upright__

First-Degree Block (pages 102–103)

Rate __80__   P-R Interval __0.26 sec__

P-Wave Rate __80__   QRS Interval __0.06 sec__

R-Wave Rate __80__   T-Wave Configuration __same deflection as QRS__

Second-Degree Block—Wenckebach Mobitz Type I (page 103)

Rate __50__   P-R Interval __1st complex, 0.30 sec__

P-Wave Rate __60__   __2nd complex, 0.34 sec__

R-Wave Rate __50__   __3rd complex, 0.42 sec__

QRS Interval __0.06 sec__   __4th complex, 0.46 sec__

T-Wave Configuration—__same deflection as QRS__   __5th complex, dropped QRS__

Second-Degree Block—Mobitz Type II (Page 104)

Rate __50__ (2:1)   P-R Interval __varies__

P-Wave Rate __90__   QRS Interval __0.08 sec__

R-Wave Rate __50__   T-Wave Configuration __same deflection as QRS__

Third-Degree Block (pages 104–105)

Rate __30__   P-R Interval __undeterminable__

P-Wave Rate __60__   QRS Interval __0.08 sec__

R-Wave Rate __30__   T-Wave Configuration __same deflection as QRS:__
                                          __some distorted due to superimposed P waves__

Bundle Branch Block (page 106)

Rate __80__   P-R Interval __0.20 sec__

P-Wave Rate __80__   QRS Interval __0.14 sec__

R-Wave Rate __80__   T-Wave Configuration __opposite deflection to QRS__

SERUM ELECTROLYTE ABNORMALITIES
AND THE ELECTROCARDIOGRAM

The maintenance of adequate fluid and electrolyte balance assumes high priority in the care of patients in any medical, surgical, or coronary intensive care unit. Patients being treated for renal or cardiovascular diseases are especially vulnerable to electrolyte imbalances. The cure may well be worse than the disease if electrolyte abnormalities go undetected or ignored, since they frequently are caused by the treatment rather than the disease itself. Dialysis can very quickly cause major shifts in electrolytes. Certainly the often insidious drop of serum potassium levels in the digitalized cardiac patient who receives diuretics is well known.

Potassium and calcium are probably the two most important electrolytes that are concerned with proper function of the heart. They help produce normal contraction of cardiac muscle. They are also important in the propagation of the electrical impulse in the heart. Because of the latter function of potassium and calcium, excess or insufficiency of either electrolyte frequently causes changes in the electrocardiogram. The nurse who is aware of and is able to recognize these changes may well suspect electrolyte abnormalities before clinical symptoms appear or hazardous arrhythmias occur.

Hypokalemia (hypopotassemia) is probably the most frequently encountered electrolyte abnormality. It is commonly associated with vomiting, diarrhea, prolonged diuretic and digitalis therapy, and prolonged nasogastric suctioning. The alkalotic patient may also be hypokalemic. In most laboratories normal serum potassium levels are about 3.5–5.0 mEq. per liter. The ECG which exhibits U waves should immediately alert the nurse to the possibility of hypokalemia in that patient. Although the U wave is normal for many people, it is worthwhile to obtain a serum potassium level since it may be an early sign of hypokalemia. The U wave is usually easily recognized, but may encroach on the preceding T wave and go unnoticed (Fig. 6-2.) The T wave may look notched or prolonged when it is hiding the U wave, giving the appearance of a prolonged Q-T interval. As potassium depletion increases, the U wave may become more prominent as the T wave becomes less so. The T wave becomes flattened and may even invert. The S-T segment tends to become depressed, somewhat resembling the effects of digitalis on the ECG. The above electrocardiographic changes are not particularly well correlated with the severity of hypokalemia; however, they are good indicators of this abnormality and can be recognized by the nurse who has basic knowledge of ECG complexes. Untreated hypokalemia can produce ventricular premature contractions, atrial or nodal tachycardias, and eventually ventricular tachycardia, ventricular fibrillation, and death. The severity of the arrhythmias resulting from hypokalemia certainly points out the need for early recognition of this problem.

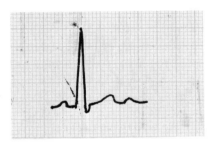

Fig. 6-2. Hypokalemia.

Hyperkalemia (hyperpotassemia) is often the result of overenthusiastic or poorly supervised treatment of hypokalemia. Sometimes early detection of hypokalemia is accomplished, treatment is instituted, and the problem is considered solved. However, if potassium supplements are not stopped or reduced when normal serum potassium levels are reached, hyperkalemia will result. Other causes of hyperkalemia include Addison's disease, acute renal failure, and acidosis. Another not infrequently seen cause of high potassium levels is the use of potassium-sparing diuretics. Triamterene (Dyrenium) is an example of this type of drug that is currently in common usage as an adjunct to the more potent diuretics. It must be remembered that these drugs not only spare potassium but also increase the potassium level of the serum.

The earliest sign of hyperkalemia on the electrocardiograph is a change in the T wave. It is usually described as narrow and "peaked" or "tenting" in appearance (Fig. 6-3). As potassium levels rise, changes occur first in the atrial portion of the ECG complex, then in the ventricular portion. The P wave flattens and becomes wider as the result of intraatrial block. Further potassium elevation causes progression to A-V nodal block and a prolonged P-R interval. The P wave may disappear entirely. With even higher potassium levels, the QRS begins to widen, indicating intraventricular block. If untreated, severe hyperkalemia will progress to increased widening of the

QRS until ventricular fibrillation occurs at serum potassium levels of 8 to 10 mEq. per liter. In terms of arrhythmias, the patient may progress from sinus bradycardia to first-degree block, through nodal rhythm, idioventricular rhythm, and ventricular tachycardia and fibrillation. Hyperkalemic changes on ECG correlate well with serum potassium levels. The T-wave changes described begin to appear at serum levels of 6–7 mEq./L.; the QRS widens at 8–9 mEq./L. Vigorous treatment must be instituted to reverse the condition at this point, as sudden death may occur at any time after these levels are reached.

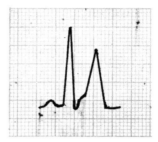

Fig 6-3. Hyperkalemia.

Calcium is the second electrolyte important to normal functioning of the heart. It is thought to have an effect on linking the electrical impulse to myocardial contraction. Calcium increases cardiac contractility and is often administered intravenously to the patient who has sustained cardiac arrest in an attempt to increase the force of cardiac contraction.

Normal serum calcium is about 9–11 mg.%. Hypercalcemia is often seen in patients with hyperparathyroidism, neoplastic diseases and acute osteoporosis. Hypocalcemia may occur in patients with renal failure, hypoparathyroidism and malabsorption syndromes.

The Q-T interval length is the most frequent ECG indicator of excess or insufficient calcium. It is somewhat shortened in hypercalcemia and lengthened in hypocalcemia (Figs. 6-4 and 6-5). Hypocalcemia may also cause lowering and inversion of the T wave.

Calcium abnormalities are not often seen in the cardiac patient unless there is an associated noncardiac disease. The more frequent cause of Q-T interval shortening or prolongation in the cardiac patient is the administration of cardiac drugs. Digitalis may cause a *shortened* Q-T interval. Quinidine frequently causes *prolongation* of the Q-T interval. Drugs should always be considered when evaluating the ECG for electrolyte abnormalities.

Arrhythmias are not commonly associated with either calcium excess or insufficiency; however, infusion of calcium salts too rapidly intravenously may result in ventricular fibrillation and sudden death. The digitalized patient who receives calcium salts seems especially prone to this for reasons not known.

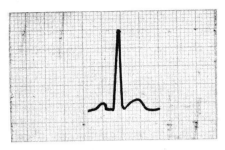

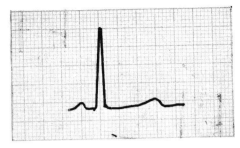

Fig. 6-4. Hypercalcemia.

Fig. 6-5. Hypocalcemia.

Just as the patient who sustains myocardial infarction may not have chest pain, the patient who has electrolyte abnormalities may not exhibit any of the ECG changes described. Conversely, a patient with normal serum electrolytes may show some of these ECG changes for other reasons. None of the ECG manifestations described here even approaches being diagnostic. They are of value primarily in alerting one to suspect electrolyte abnormalities. It is appropriate for the nurse, especially one who cares for the critically ill patient, to be alert to ECG changes and to interpret what is seen in the context of what is already known about that patient.

BIBLIOGRAPHY

Goldman, Mervin J., *Principles of Clinical Electrocardiography*. Los Altos, Calif.: Large Medical Publications, 1964.

Massie, Edward, and Thomas J. Walsh, *Clinical Vectorcardiography and Electrocardiography*. Chicago: Year Book Publishers, Inc., 1960.

Relman, Arnold S., and John A. Kastor, *Disturbances of Potassium and Calcium Balance and their Effect on the Electrocardiogram*. Rocom.

Ritota, Michael C., *Diagnostic Electrocardiography*. Philadelphia: J. B. Lippincott Company, 1969.

SERUM ENZYME STUDIES

It is sometimes argued that laboratory results are the responsibility of the physician, and that the nurse need not concern herself with them. Others argue that the role of the nurse is being expanded and that it does include this type of knowledge and responsibility. With a basic understanding of the purpose and significance of laboratory values, the nurse can exercise judgment in their interpretation in relation to other information she has about the patient. Her ability to exercise this kind of judgment in regard to certain laboratory tests may well affect the clinical course or prognosis of the patient. Serum enzyme studies certainly fall into this category.

Enzymes are proteins that are found in all living cells. Different enzymes are found in different kinds of cells and in varying concentrations. The function of an enzyme is to serve as an accelerating agent or catalyst for chemical reactions. It does this by temporarily combining with one substance to form another, which then breaks down to form the end products of this chemical reaction. When the enzyme has completed this task, it is liberated to continue its function as a chemical reaction catalyst.

Enzymes are produced in the cells and are released into the plasma. Over-active, diseased, or injured cells increase the release of their particular enzymes into the serum. The difference in composition and concentration of various enzymes from one kind of tissue to another (cardiac, liver, skeletal muscle, and the like) determines which serum enzyme elevations result from damage to specific tissues. Thus serum enzyme determinations can be used to detect cell damage and to suggest where the damage has occurred.

Many studies have been done in relation to the diagnostic value of serum enzyme determinations. As sometimes happens in research, the results vary and are debated by clinical diagnosticians and pathologists alike. To further cloud the issue, enzymes are determined by a variety of laboratory methods and the results are reported in a variety of measuring units. These factors result in differing sets of upper and lower normals in laboratories. The nurse must become familiar with the limits of normal for each enzyme as it is reported by the laboratory where she works.

Serum enzyme determinations have been helpful in the diagnosis of cardiac, hepatic, pancreatic, muscular, bone, and malignant diseases. Each of the above kinds of tissue releases a particular enzyme or enzymes when diseased or damaged. Each of these cells contains and releases more than one enzyme, and there is overlapping of enzymes from one tissue source to another. For this reason there is no one serum enzyme elevation that is diagnostic of any one disease.

The term "cardiac enzyme" is used in reference to those enzymes which occur and are released in proportionately larger amounts in cardiac tissue. These include creatine phosphokinase (CPK), hydroxybutyric dehydro-genase (HBD), glutamic oxalacetic transaminase (GOT), and lactic dehy-drogenase (LDH). Serum glutamic pyruvic transaminase (GPT) may show a slight increase in the presence of massive myocardial infarction, but it is more specific for liver disease. Each of these enzymes varies in its degree of spe-cificity for myocardial disease.

Total LDH is probably the least specific for cardiac disease of the "cardiac enzymes." It is abundant in kidney, cardiac, liver and muscle tissues and in red cells (Fig. 6-6). The onset of LDH elevation occurs 12–24 hours after tissue damage and peak elevation, averaging about three times upper normal, is at 72 hours. Return to normal is not complete for 7–11 days. The fact that LDH elevation is prolonged for a week or more after myocardial infarction is often helpful in late diagnosis. Some patients do not come to the hospital until several days after their initial symptoms and early blood specimens cannot be obtained.

Because LDH has widespread distribution in body tissues, its serum level is elevated in a variety of diseases. In 1957 it was found that LDH could be sub-jected to certain procedures that separate the enzyme into five components or

SGOT	CPK	LDH (ISOENZYMES)	
Heart Kidney Red cells Brain	Heart Brain	Heart Kidney Red cells Brain	*(Fast)*
   Pancreas Lung		Lymph nodes Spleen Leukocytes Pancreas Lung	*(Intermediate)*
Liver Skeletal muscle	 Skeletal muscle	Liver Skeletal muscle	*(Slow)*

Fig. 6-6. Enzyme distribution in cells.

isoenzymes which demonstrate five zones of activity of the enzyme. Since enzyme activity is measured by its rate of acceleration of chemical reactions, these five zones range from fastest-acting to slowest-acting. The two fastest-acting isoenzymes are found in cardiac muscle, the renal cortex, erythrocytes, and the cerebrum and reflect disease or damage in these tissues. Thus if these isoenzymes are elevated in the serum of a patient who presents with chest pain but has no evidence of kidney, hemolytic, or cerebral disease, myocardial infarction is the likely diagnosis. The two slowest-acting LDH isoenzymes are found in the liver, skeletal muscle, and skin. These reflect acute liver disease or hepatic congestion, muscle injuries, and dermatological disease or trauma. The intermediate isoenzyme is found in lymph nodes, spleen, leukocytes, pancreas, and lung tissues. It in turn reflects disease or damage to these tissues. These five isoenzymes, also called fractions of LDH, are numbered one through five. However, some laboratories report LDH_1 and LDH_2 as the faster isoenzymes and LDH_4 and LDH_5 as the slower, while others report them in reverse order. Here again the nurse must be aware of how these are reported in her hospital laboratory.

The introduction of isoenzyme separation has made the LDH isoenzymes one of the most specific tests for the diagnosis of myocardial infarction. LDH_1 and LDH_2 have been found in the serum up to two weeks or more after infarction even though total LDH has returned to normal.

When blood specimens for LDH determinations are collected, it is essential to avoid hemolysis of the sample. Since LDH is found in erythrocytes, even slightly hemolyzed blood will show an elevation of the serum LDH.

The enzyme HBD may possibly be the same as the fast-moving cardiac isoenzyme of LDH. It correlates with the LDH fractions and therefore is frequently omitted from the commonly used series of enzymes. HBD activity is always associated with LDH activity. The serum evaluation of both enzymes after myocardial infarction is about the same, both in quantity and in duration of elevation, with only a slight time lag in HBD. In laboratories that do not have the necessary equipment for fractionating LDH isoenzymes, HBD determination can serve as an alternate for this study, although it is felt to be less specific.

CPK is the fastest-rising and fastest-falling of all the "cardiac enzymes." Onset of serum elevation is about 3–5 hours after infarction, with a peak elevation of five to twelve times normal or more by 24–36 hours. Serum levels may return to normal by the second or third day. This transient nature of CPK elevation following myocardial infarction can be a distinct aid to diagnosis if the patient is reached early in the acute episode. However, this frequently is not the case; the CPK rise may be missed entirely by the time the patient enters the hospital, is seen by a physician, and a tentative diagnosis is made. About 90 percent of patients with myocardial infarction show the early rise in serum CPK.

The CPK enzyme is second only to LDH isoenzymes in specificity for cardiac damage. CPK is found in skeletal and cardiac muscle and in brain tissue. Since red cells contain almost no CPK, slight hemolysis does not interfere with the accuracy of its determination. It is of particular value in diagnosing cardiac disease because it is not found in liver tissue as are LDH and SGOT. Hepatic congestion or disease which frequently accompanies cardiac disease will therefore not affect CPK values. CPK determination is also helpful in differentiating myocardial infarction from pulmonary embolism, which often present very similar clinical pictures. Because of the proportionately smaller amount of CPK in lung tissue, any rise with pulmonary embolism will be much smaller than the very high elevation associated with myocardial infarction. CPK values are normal in pericarditis, but an elevation occurs in myocarditis because of the cardiac muscle involvement. Recall that overactivity as well as disease or damage of tissue cells will cause release of enzymes into the serum. This should be kept in mind when CPK elevation is found in the patient who collapsed on the golf course or while skiing. Severe or prolonged exercise of the untrained "social athlete" can result in CPK elevation for up to 48 hours. Other conditions causing a rise in CPK levels include acute cerebrovascular disease and muscle trauma. Slight elevations are sometimes found following peripheral arterial embolism, repeated intramuscular injections and operative procedures.

SGOT is the last of the most frequently used "cardiac enzymes" to be discussed. Its tissue distribution is quite widespread, with large SGOT concentrations in red cells, cardiac, liver, skeletal muscle, and renal tissue. Lesser amounts are found in brain, pancreas, and lung tissue. Its widespread distribution makes it one of the least specific enzymes, second only to total LDH. Over 95 percent of patients with myocardial infarction have SGOT elevation; as little as 5 percent infarction can cause a serum rise. It falls between CPK and LDH in both degree and duration of elevation. SGOT rise begins about 6–8 hours after onset of an acute myocardial episode, reaches its peak in 18–36 hours, and returns to normal at the end of 4–6 days. Average elevation following myocardial infarction is five times normal, but may go much higher with an extensive infarct.

As mentioned previously, the SGPT enzyme is more specific for liver disease and does not usually rise with cardiac damage. However, both SGOT and SGPT will rise if myocardial infarction is accompanied by prolonged or profound shock or severe congestive heart failure which results in liver congestion or damage. SGOT evaluation may be of particular value in the early diagnosis of reinfarction. A second infarction often cannot be read on ECG because of the changes already incurred by the first infarction in this situation. A rise in serum GOT within 6–8 hours after an episode of chest pain will help to make the diagnosis. The enzyme is rarely elevated in pulmonary infarction unless there is severe and prolonged shock, in which case SGPT will also rise, again because of liver congestion.

One can almost always be assured that myocardial infarction has not occurred if serum enzyme levels remain normal for 36–48 hours after onset of symptoms. If infarct has occurred, all the enzymes should be elevated between 24 and 48 hours after symptom occurrence (Fig. 6-7). In comparing enzyme elevations, CPK rises first and highest and falls to normal first, followed by SGOT, with LDH rising last. LDH has the least amount of elevation but is the most prolonged. In comparing the specificity of each enzyme as an indicator of myocardial necrosis, LDH isoenzymes are most specific, followed by CPK, SGOT, and total LDH as least specific. In general it can be said that the size of the infarct correlates with the height of the enzyme peaks and the duration of enzyme elevation, as well as with patient mortality.

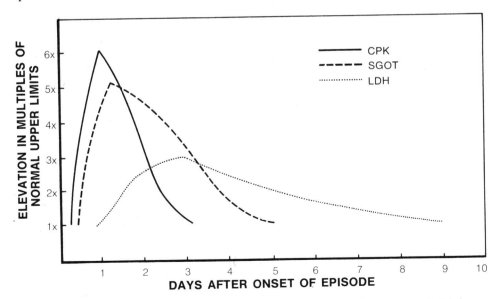

Fig. 6-7. Peak elevation and duration of serum enzymes after myocardial injury.

There are a number of "red herrings" to be kept in mind when evaluating elevated serum enzymes. Severe or prolonged exercise has been mentioned. Repeated defibrillation or defibrillation with large amounts of voltage may cause enzymes to rise because of the sudden severe contraction of all muscle tissue. Even one defibrillation with 400-watt-seconds may result in enough enzyme rise to mimic myocardial infarction. HBD, which is thought to be much like the cardiac isoenzymes of LDH, sometimes rises with liver disease. The extent of surgical trauma during operative procedures should be considered when evaluating enzyme elevations postoperatively. Tissue damage from frequent intramuscular injections must also be remembered as the source of slight enzyme rises. It is also possible to produce elevation of SGOT and SGPT with administration of salicylates, coumadin, and other drugs that are detoxified in the liver.

It is apparent from the discussion of these four enzyme studies used in diagnosing myocardial infarction that none of them are actually diagnostic. No enzyme or enzyme fraction has yet been found to exist in cardiac muscle alone. There are still many areas unclear or unknown about enzymes, and researchers continue to strive to improve the value of serum enzymes as a diagnostic aid. Recently serum pyruvate kinase has been recognized as a specific diagnostic enzyme for myocardial infarction, but as yet is not commonly used. Other enzymes have been found to rise with myocardial necrosis, but they are either no more specific than the ones currently used, or are technically difficult and time-consuming to measure.

As yet enzyme determinations can serve only as an adjunct to diagnosis by ECG and the patient's clinical picture. In order to be of most value they should be ordered with discretion. Consideration must be given to the length of time that has passed since the onset of symptoms, as each enzyme rises and returns to normal at different time intervals. One often finds an order for "stat" enzymes upon admission of the patient with suspected myocardial infarction to the critical care unit. The results will be useless if only an hour or two has passed since the onset of symptoms. If the patient suffered only moderate symptoms and did not come to the hospital until several days later, CPK determination is useless because it will already have returned to normal. Usually two enzyme determinations are considered more valid than one, but the gamut of enzyme tests may not be necessary.

Enzyme determinations have been of greatest value in the patient whose ECG and clinical picture are equivocal for diagnosis of myocardial infarction. Enzyme elevation may well confirm a suspected diagnosis in this case. Sometimes it is difficult or impossible to interpret infarction on ECG because of previous infarction changes, the effects of certain drugs or electrolyte imbalances, conduction defects such as bundle branch block or Wolff-Parkinson-White syndrome, arrhythmias, or a functioning pacemaker. Enzyme determination may be a distinct advantage here. If a definite diagnosis can be made by ECG, there may be no need for enzyme tests, except for academic interest.

It must be stressed that serum elevations are nonspecific in the diagnosis of myocardial infarction and they must be considered in view of the total clinical picture. We are in a highly technical age of nursing and must not forget to look at and listen to the patient before making judgments and decisions.

BIBLIOGRAPHY

Cohen, Louis, "Contributions of Serum Enzymes and Isoenzymes to the Diagnosis of Myocardial Injury," *Modern Concepts of Cardiovascular Disease,* August 1967.

Conrad, Fred G., "Transaminase," *New England Journal of Medicine,* March 28, 1957.

Dade Reagents, Inc., *Diagnostic Enzymology,* 1970.

Gesink, Melvin H., "Enzymes in the Diagnosis of Myocardial Infarction," unpublished paper, 1971.

Shaft, Franklin R., Robert W. Ban, and Hedy Imfeld, "Serum Pyruvate Kinase in Acute Myocardial Infarction," *American Journal of Cardiology,* Vol. 26 (1970), pp. 143–150.

Wilkinson, J. Henry, "The Diagnostic Value of LDH Isoenzymes in Clinical Medicine," *Clinical Profile,* Beckman Instruments, Inc., Vol. 1 (1968).

THE SIGNIFICANCE OF AUSCULTATION OF THE HEART

Nurses throughout the country have done well in terminating and preventing lethal arrhythmias. With the development of electrocardiographic monitoring and the education of nurses in interpreting arrhythmias and initiating emergency treatment, the mortality incidence among patients with myocardial infarction has decreased. However, nurses need to improve their care of patients who develop heart failure. Of the patients who develop blatantly obvious left ventricular failure, an estimated 40 percent die.[1]

One of the earliest and frequently the only cardiac sign of congestive heart failure in the adult is the development of a third heart sound. If nurses are taught to detect the third heart sound and are aware of its clinical significance, it is possible that they could decrease the incidence of heart failure in their patients.

The Characteristics of Sound

Sound is a series of disturbances in matter to which the human ear is sensitive. Sound is a wave motion which has four characteristics—intensity, pitch, duration, and timbre. *Intensity* is the force of the amplitude of the vibrations. It is a physical aspect of sound, whereas loudness is a subjective aspect dependent upon (1) intensity of the sound, and (2) sensitivity of the ear. *Pitch* is the frequency of the vibrations per unit of time. The human ear is most sensitive to vibrations of 500–5,000/second. Vibrations less than 20/second or greater than 20,000/second cannot be heard by the human ear. *Duration* is the third characteristic of sound. It is the length of time that the sound persists. *Timbre* is a quality dependent upon overtones that accompany the fundamental tone. In other words, most fundamental vibrations have higher frequency vibrations called *overtones*. Overtones account for the difference in sound between the same note played on a piano and on a flute.[2,3]

Sound waves are initiated by vibrations. The heart sounds are produced by vascular walls, flowing blood, heart muscle, and heart valves. Sudden changes in intra-arterial pressures cause the vascular walls to vibrate, resulting in sound production. Turbulence of blood flow is produced when rapidly moving blood passes through chambers of irregular size, such as the chambers of the heart and the great vessels. When the heart muscles contract, sound waves are initiated by the contracting fibers. Sound waves are produced when the heart valves open as the blood flows through or when they close, especially with a sudden snapping of the chordae tendineae. Of the previously mentioned causes of heart sounds, the closing of the heart valves accounts for most of the sound production. [4,5]

Systole is defined as the time during which the ventricles contract. Systole begins with the beginning of the first heart sound and ends with the beginning of the second heart sound. *Diastole* is defined as the time during which the ventricles relax. Diastole begins with the beginning of the second heart sound and ends with the beginning of the next first heart sound. The cardiac cycle is determined by the cycle of the ventricles. In other words, cardiac systole and ventricular systole are synonymous.

The transmission of the heart sounds is dependent upon the position of the heart, the nature of the surrounding structures, and the position of the stethoscope in relation to the origin of the sound.[6] The stethoscope is a tool used to transmit sounds produced by the body to the ear. Sound waves that travel a shorter distance are of greater intensity; likewise, the shorter the distance the less the possibility for distortion to occur. It then follows that the shorter the tube of the stethoscope the better the transmission of sound. Convenience and comfort as well as maximum sound production must be considered.

In order to facilitate accurate auscultation, the patient should be comfortable, in a quiet room, and in a recumbent position. The bell of the stethoscope transmits low-pitched sounds best when there is an airtight seal and when the instrument is applied lightly to the chest wall. An airtight seal helps to occlude extraneous sounds. The diaphragm of the stethoscope best transmits the high-pitched sounds when it is applied with firm pressure to the chest wall.

The First Heart Sound

The first heart sound is produced by the asynchronous closure of the mitral and tricuspid valves. Mitral closure precedes tricuspid closure by 0.02–0.03 second. Such narrow splitting is generally not audible. The first heart sound is therefore composed of two separate components. The first component of the first heart sound is the closure of the mitral valve. The second component of the first heart sound is the closure of the tricuspid valve. The first heart sound is generally best heard at the apex. It represents the beginning of ventricular systole.[7]

The Second Heart Sound

The second heart sound is produced by the vibrations initiated by the closure of the aortic and pulmonic semilunar valves. The second heart sound, like the first heart sound, is composed of two separate components. The first component of the second heart sound is closure of the aortic valve. The second component of the second heart sound is the closure of the pulmonic valve. With inspiration, systole of the right ventricle is slightly prolonged due to increased filling of the right ventricle. With increased right ventricular filling, the pulmonary valve closes later than the aortic valve. Aortic valve sounds are generally best heard in the second intercostal space to the right of the sternum, whereas the sound produced by the pulmonic valve is generally best heard in the second left intercostal space. Splitting of the second heart sound is best heard upon inspiration with the stethoscope placed in the second intercostal space to the left of the sternum. The second heart sound represents the beginning of ventricular diastole.[8,9] See Figure 6-8 for a graphic representation of the normal first and second heart sounds.

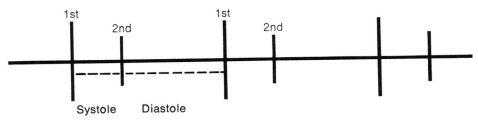

Fig. 6-8. Normal heart sounds.

Comparison between Electrocardiogram and Phonocardiogram

To facilitate understanding of the phonocardiogram, it will be compared with the electrocardiogram. The electrocardiogram is a graphic representation of the electrical activity of the heart, whereas the phonocardiogram is a recording of the sound vibrations produced by the heart.

When the sinoauricular node fires, the electrical current travels through the atrial muscle to the atrioventricular node. The P wave is then written on the electrocardiogram. The electrical current then travels down the common bundle of His, right and left bundle branches, Purkinje fibers, and throughout the ventricular muscle. Following electrical stimulation of the ventricles, the latter contract. Early in ventricular systole the mitral and tricuspid valves close. This is the reason the first heart sound occurs during or following ventricular depolarization, which is represented on the electrocardiogram by the QRS complex (Fig. 6-9).

During ventricular systole, the blood is forced from the right and left ventricles into the pulmonic and aortic arteries. When the ventricles relax,

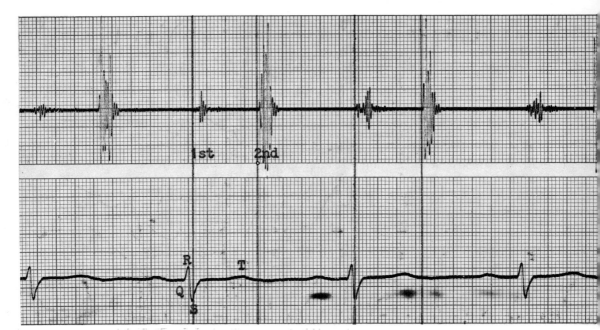

Fig. 6-9. Simultaneous recording of a phonocardiogram and an electrocardiogram.

the aortic and pulmonic semilunar valves close. The second heart sound represents the beginning of ventricular diastole. The second heart sound occurs after the repolarization of the ventricular muscle, which is represented by the T wave on the electrocardiogram.

The Third Heart Sound

A third heart sound represents pathology in the adult. The third heart sound is believed to be produced by the rapid inrush of blood into a nonpliable ventricle. During ventricular diastole, the apex extends downward and the mitral valve extends upward. As the ventricle fills, the chordae tendineae become tense and partially close the mitral valve. This, along with the increasing resistance of diastole, causes a sudden decrease in blood flow. The cardiac muscle, chordae tendineae, heart valves, and blood are set into motion and are responsible for the production of sound. The third heart sound is heard after the closure of the semilunar valves, early in diastole, and best at the apex. Most third heart sounds are of relatively low pitch, between 25 and 35 vibrations per second. They are best heard with the bell of the stethoscope applied lightly to the chest wall[10,11] (Fig. 6-10).

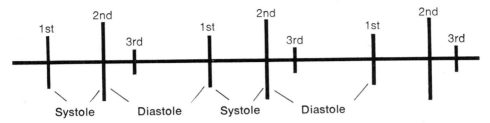

Fig. 6-10. Third heart sound.

The Fourth Heart Sound

The fourth heart sound, also called an atrial sound, is believed to be produced by atrial contraction that is more forceful than normal. At the end of atrial contraction, more blood is forced from the atria into the ventricle which causes a sudden increase in ventricular pressure. This increased pressure produces vibrations which cause the fourth heart sound. The fourth heart sound is therefore believed to be produced by atrial contraction and the consequent impact of the rapid inflow of blood on the ventricle. The fourth heart sound is of low pitch, heard best at the lower end of the sternum and sometimes at the apex. It has a short duration and a low frequency. It is best heard with the bell of the stethoscope.[12] Figure 6-11 shows the timing of the fourth heart sound.

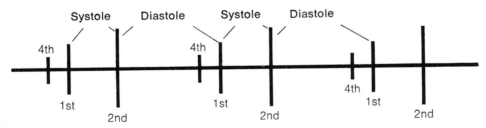

Fig. 6-11. Fourth heart sound.

Gallop Rhythms

Gallop rhythm is the name given to the heart sounds when they are grouped so as to mimic the cadence of galloping horses. There are three types of gallop rhythms. The protodiastolic or early diastolic gallop rhythm, also known as the ventricular gallop rhythm, is believed to be due to an exaggerated third heart sound. This rhythm is commonly heard in congestive heart failure. It is frequently the earliest sign of heart failure. Controversy still exists regarding the significance of the third sound. The ventricular gallop is generally believed to result from the rapid inflow of blood into a dilated ventricle early in diastole. The third heart sound occurs between 0.12–0.18 second after the second heart sound. It is of low pitch and heard best at the apex with the bell of the stethoscope.[13,14]

A presystolic gallop rhythm exists when the gallop sound occurs late in diastole or immediately preceding systole. The sound occurs with atrial systole and is believed to represent an accentuated atrial sound. It occurs with systolic overloading notably in hypertension, myocardial infarction, aortic stenosis, pulmonary hypertension, pulmonary stenosis, and various cardio-myopathies. It is often unaccompanied by heart failure. The presystolic or atrial gallop rhythm is low-pitched and is heard best with the bell of the stethoscope. A left atrial sound is heard best on expiration at the apex, whereas a right atrial sound is best heard on inspiration at the left border of the sternum.[15]

A summation gallop occurs because of a tachycardia so rapid that the third and fourth heart sounds combine and are heard as one[16] (Fig. 6-12).

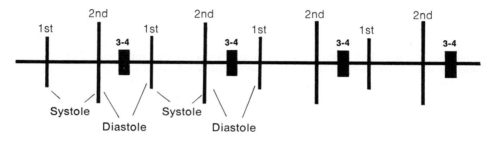

Fig. 6-12. Summation gallop.

Mechanisms of Heart Murmurs

In order to understand the heart murmurs it is vital to understand the mechanism responsible for the sound production. To fully understand murmur formation it is important to understand the principles of turbulence of blood flow. Blood flows most rapidly in the center of a vessel, less rapidly nearer the wall, and least rapidly immediately along the internal surface of the vessel. In other words, as blood flows through a vessel the friction along the wall of the vessel tends to slow the rate of blood flow nearest the wall. The smoother the internal surface of the vessel the less turbulence in blood flow. The slower the rate of blood flow the less chance there is for turbulence. Any irregularity in the inner surface of the vessel or change in the size of the lumen results in turbulence of blood flow and sound production. The nar-rower the opening the more rapid the rate of blood flow and the greater the possibility for turbulence and murmur formation.[17]

The murmurs of mitral stenosis, mitral insufficiency, aortic stenosis, and aortic insufficiency will be discussed. With the knowledge of the mechanisms which produce these murmurs, the nurse will be able to deduce the mechanisms responsible for the other murmurs not discussed. The mechanisms responsible for the murmurs of mitral stenosis and mitral insufficiency are also responsible for the murmurs of tricuspid stenosis and tricuspid insufficiency. The only difference is that the latter murmurs occur on the right side of the heart. Likewise, the mechanisms responsible for the murmurs of aortic stenosis and aortic insufficiency are also responsible for the murmurs of pulmonary stenosis and pulmonary insufficiency. The difference is that the latter murmurs occur on the right side of the heart.

The Murmur of Mitral Stenosis

In mitral stenosis the mitral orifice can be narrowed by inflammation and/or fibrosis of the mitral valve because of rheumatic heart disease or arteriosclerosis. A stenotic mitral valve causes an increased left atrial pressure during ventricular diastole. In ventricular diastole the left atrium contracts forcing blood through the narrowed opening. This produces turbulence of blood flow and the production of a diastolic murmur. The murmur is low-pitched and rumbling.[18]

The murmur of mitral stenosis may be a crescendo or decrescendo in configuration. It may be a crescendo in shape because the left atrium contracts progressively, the rate of blood flow increases, and the mitral valve becomes narrower. It may be a decrescendo in shape because as the ventricle fills, the left atrium empties, and the amount of blood passing through the stenotic valve decreases. The murmur therefore decreases in intensity and is a decrescendo in shape[19] (Fig. 6-13).

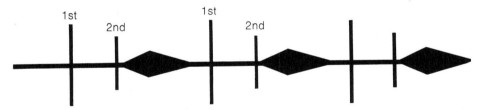

1st

2nd

1st

2nd

Fig. 6-13. Murmur of mitral stenosis.

The Murmur of Mitral Insufficiency

The murmur of mitral insufficiency is heard in systole. Mitral insufficiency occurs when the mitral valve is incompetent, and the valve leaflets fail to approximate. During ventricular systole the intraventricular pressure exceeds intra-atrial pressure. With an incompetent mitral valve, the blood regurgitates through the valve opening into the left atrium. This results in turbulence of blood flow and a high-pitched, blowing murmur. The murmur is systolic, heard best at the apex, and is transmitted laterally to the axillary

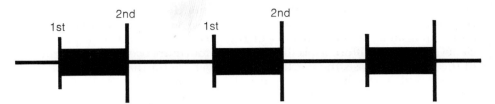

Fig. 6-14. Murmur of mitral insufficiency.

line when the heart is enlarged. As a rule, a murmur is transmitted in the direction of the blood flow that is responsible for the turbulence. The murmur of mitral insufficiency is generally pansystolic or holosystolic[20,21] (lasting all of systole) (Fig. 6-14).

The murmur of mitral insufficiency is the murmur of myocardial infarction. In myocardial infarction, dilatation of the left ventricle occurs because of ischemia and/or necrosis. When the left ventricle is dilated, the papillary muscle tends to move away from the valve leaflets. The chordae tendineae are unable to lengthen, and the mitral leaflets are held open, preventing complete approximation. With dilatation of the left ventricle, the mitral ring dilates. The leaflets remain the same size and are unable to close the enlarged opening. When the left ventricle dilates, it loses its ability to contract and there is an associated papillary muscle dysfunction.[22]

The Murmur of Aortic Stenosis

The murmur of aortic stenosis is heard during systole. Aortic stenosis is the result of narrowing of the aortic cusps. During ventricular systole, the pressure within the ventricle exceeds the pressure of the aorta and the blood flows out of the ventricle into the aorta. If there is thickening of the aortic cusps or narrowing of the aortic valve, the rapidly flowing blood passes through the constricted valve and causes turbulence of blood flow. The murmur is of medium pitch and has a rough or harsh sound. It is heard best over the aortic valve area, the second right intercostal space. The murmur of aortic stenosis is transmitted into the arteries of the neck, since the blood flow responsible for the turbulence is moving in that direction. It can also be transmitted to the apex, where it may be confused with the murmur of

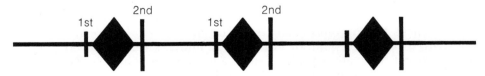

Fig. 6-15. Murmur of aortic stenosis.

mitral insufficiency—also a systolic murmur. The murmur of aortic stenosis occurs in systole, and it is a diamond shape. It is composed of a crescendo and a decrescendo[23,24] (Fig. 6-15).

The Murmur of Aortic Insufficiency

The murmur of aortic insufficiency is diastolic in time. In ventricular diastole, the intraventricular pressure is lower than the intra-aortic pressure. The aortic cusps fail to support the blood and it regurgitates into the ventricle. Turbulence of blood flow results in the formation of a high-pitched, blowing murmur. It is usually best heard in the third left intercostal space. As the pressure in the ventricle increases and the aortic pressure decreases, the turbulence of blood flow decreases. The murmur is therefore a decrescendo in shape[25,26] (Fig. 6-16).

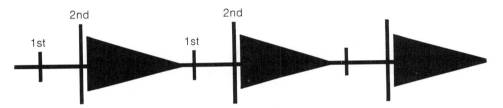

Fig. 6-16. Murmur of aortic insufficiency.

Nurses need not distinguish the specific heart murmur; however, it is important for nurses to recognize the difference between the extra heart sounds and the murmurs. The key diagnostic sign of early congestive heart failure is the development of the third heart sound. Nurses can and should become adept at auscultating the heart. This knowledge and skill should be an integral part of the nursing assessment.

REFERENCES

1. Lawrence E. Meltzer, Faye G. Abdellah, and J. Roderick Kitchell, *Concepts and Practices of Intensive Care for Nurse Specialists* (Philadelphia: Charles Press Publishers, Inc., 1969), p. 52.
2. Abe Ravin, *Ausculatation of the Heart* (Chicago: Year Book Medical Publishers, Inc., 1967), pp. 15–17.
3. George E. Burch, *A Primer of Cardiology* (Philadelphia: Lea & Febiger, 1955), p. 97.
4. Aubrey Leatham, "Auscultation of the Heart," *The Lancet* (Oct. 4, 1958), p. 703.
5. Burch, *op. cit.*, p. 98.
6. *Ibid.*
7. Leatham, *op. cit.*, pp. 703–704.
8. *Ibid.*, pp. 49–52.

9. Leatham, *op. cit.,* pp. 704–706.
10. Ravin, *op. cit.,* pp. 80–83.
11. Burch, *op. cit.,* p. 108.
12. Ravin, *op. cit.,* pp. 64–67.
13. Harrison, *loc. cit.*
14. Ravin, *op. cit.,* pp. 64–68.
15. *Ibid.,* pp. 65–66.
16. *Ibid.,* pp. 84–87.
17. Burch, *op. cit.,* pp. 122–124.
18. Ravin, *op. cit.,* pp. 123–125.
19. Burch, *op. cit.,* pp. 125–127.
20. *Ibid.,* pp. 133–134.
21. Ravin, *op. cit.,* pp. 102–105.
22. *Ibid.,* p. 104.
23. *Ibid.,* pp. 111–115.
24. Burch, *op. cit.,* pp. 138–140.
25. *Ibid.,* pp. 140–143.
26. Ravin, *op. cit.,* pp. 131–134.

BIBLIOGRAPHY

Burch, George E., *A Primer of Cardiology.* Philadelphia: Lea & Febiger, 1955.
Freeman, Ira M., *Physics: Principles and Insights.* New York: McGraw-Hill Book Company, 1968.
Harriston, T. R., et al., *Principles of Internal Medicine.* New York: McGraw-Hill Book Company, 1966.
Leatham, Aubrey, "Auscultation of the Heart," *The Lancet,* Oct. 4, 1958, pp. 703–708.
Marshall, Robert M., Gilbert Blount, and Edward Genton, "Acute Myocardial Infarction," *Archives of Internal Medicine,* Vol. 122 (December 1968), pp. 472–475.
Meltzer, Lawrence E., Faye G. Abdellah, and Roderick J. Kitchell, *Concepts and Practices of Intensive Care for Nurse Specialists.* Philadelphia: Charles Press Publishers, Inc., 1969.

CENTRAL VENOUS PRESSURE

Central venous pressure refers to the pressure of blood in the right atrium or vena cava. It actually provides information about three parameters—blood volume, the effectiveness of the heart as a pump, and vascular tone. CVP is to be differentiated from a peripheral venous pressure, which may only reflect a local pressure.

Central venous pressure is measured in centimeters or millimeters of water pressure, and considerable variation exists in the range of normal values cited. Usually pressure in the right atrium is 0–4 cm. H_2O, while pressure in the vena cava is approximately 6–12 cm. H_2O. More important, it is the trend of the readings that is most significant regardless of the baseline value. The upward or downward trend of the central venous pressure, combined with clinical assessment of the patient, will determine appropriate interventions. For example, a patient's CVP may gradually rise from 6 cm. H_2O to 8 cm. then to 10 cm. While this may still be in the range of "normal," other parameters may indicate ensuing complications. Ausculation of breath sounds may reveal basilar roles, a third heart sound may be audible, or the pulse and respiratory rate may be increasing insidiously. In this context the trend of a gradual rise in CVP is more significant than the actual isolated value. When the nurse interprets CVP data in conjunction with her other clinical observations, she has a better understanding of their significance for that particular patient and recognizes the outcome to which her interventions must be geared. In this instance she is aware that too much fluid administration would further compromise the patient's circulatory status and would act accordingly to reduce this risk.

Sometimes rate of fluid administration is titrated according to the patient's CVP and urinary output. So long as the urinary output remains adequate and the CVP does not change significantly, this is an indication that the heart can accommodate the amount of fluid being administered. If the CVP begins to rise and the urine output drops, indicating a decreased cardiac output to perfuse the kidneys, circulatory overload must be suspected and either ruled out or validated in view of other clinical symptomatology.

The patient who is started on a vasopressor agent will show a rise in CVP due to the vasoconstriction produced. In this situation the blood volume is unchanged but the vascular bed has become smaller. Again, this change must be interpreted in conjunction with other information the nurse assesses about the patient. Alone a CVP value can be meaningless, but used in conjunction with other clinical data it is a valuable aid in managing and predicting the patient's clinical course.

For central venous pressure recordings a long intravenous catheter is

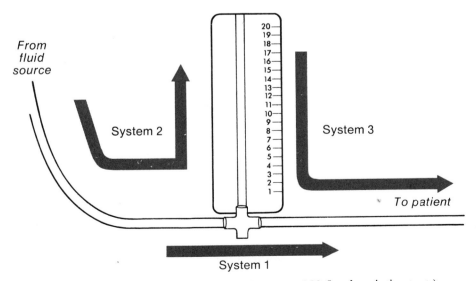

Fig. 6-17. Central venous pressure. (See page 130 for descriptive text.)

inserted into an arm or leg vein or the subclavian vein and threaded into position in the vena cava close to the right atrium. Occasionally the catheter may be advanced into the right atrium as indicated by rhythmic fluctuations in the pressure manometer corresponding to the patient's heartbeat. In this situation the catheter may simply be withdrawn to the point at which the pulsations cease.

Figure 6-17 illustrates a typical setup for measuring the central venous pressure. A manometer with a three-way stopcock is introduced between the fluid source and the patient's intravenous catheter. In this way three separate systems can be created by manipulating the stopcock. System 1 connects the fluid source with the patient and can be utilized for routine administration of I.V. fluids or as an avenue to keep the system patent. System 2 runs from the fluid source to the CVP manometer and is opened in order to raise the fluid column in the manometer prior to measuring the venous pressure. System 3 connects the patient's intravenous catheter with the manometer and it is this pathway which must be open to record the central venous pressure. Pressure in the vena cava displaces or equilibrates with the pressure exerted by the column of fluid in the manometer and the point at which the fluid level settles is recorded as the central venous pressure.

To obtain an accurate measurement, the patient should be flat, with the zero point of the manometer at the same level as the right atrium. This level corresponds to the midaxillary line of the patient or can be determined by measuring approximately 5 cm. below the sternum. However, consistency is the important detail, and all readings should be taken with the patient in the same position and the zero point calculated in the same manner. If deviations from the routine procedure must be made, as when the patient cannot tolerate being flat and the reading must be taken with the patient in a semi-Fowler's position, it is valuable to note this on the patient's chart or care plan to provide for consistency in future readings. A patent system is assured when the fluid column falls freely and slight fluctuation of the fluid column is apparent. This fluctuation follows the patient's respiratory pattern and will fall on inspiration and rise on expiration due to changes in inter-pulmonic pressure. If the patient is being ventilated on a respirator, a false high reading will result. If possible, the respirator should be discontinued momentarily for maximum accuracy. If the patient cannot tolerate being off the respirator for even this short period, significant trends in the CVP can still be determined if consistency in taking the readings is followed.

As noted earlier, changes in central venous pressure must be interpreted in terms of the clinical picture of the patient. There are however, some situations which commonly produce an elevated CVP. These include congestive heart failure when the heart can no longer effectively handle the venous return, cardiac tamponade, a vasoconstrictive state, or states of increased blood volume such as overtransfusion or overhydration.

A low central venous pressure usually accompanies a hypovolemic state due to blood or fluid loss or drug-induced vasodilatation. Increasing the rate of fluid administration or replacing blood loss is indicated in this situation.

7

Anatomy, Physiology, and Pathophysiology of the Respiratory System

MARGARET ANN BERRY, R.N., M.A., M.S.
JOSEPH O. BROUGHTON, M.D.

NORMAL FUNCTION OF THE RESPIRATORY SYSTEM

Introduction

All reactions in higher living organisms which release energy to the overall system are combustion reactions. That is, the reaction requires oxygen in some step along the way to eventually break down certain chemical compounds to give energy, carbon dioxide, and water. Organisms living in an aquatic environment extract oxygen from the water, while other organisms, including man, must have some method of removing oxygen from the air and transporting it to the cells where it is used. At the same time man must also transport carbon dioxide, an end product of the combustion reactions, back to the atmosphere. Man has the ability to store energy compounds but must have a constant source of oxygen to maintain life. Perhaps the most basic of all human needs is the need for air, and one of the most critical subsystems of the organism is the respiratory system. Because of the respiratory system's dependency upon the cardiovascular system, the latter also occupies a position of extreme critical importance. At times it is most difficult to establish priorities between these two subsystems, and it is probably more accurate to consider them as being equally critical to the dynamic stability of the human organism.

Respiration means literally the movement of oxygen from the atmosphere to the cells and the return of carbon dioxide from the cells to the environment. As such, then, the total process can be divided into four major phases.[1]
   1. Pulmonary ventilation—actual flow of air in and out between the atmosphere and the alveoli of the lung.
   2. Diffusion of oxygen and carbon dioxide between the alveoli and the blood.
   3. Transport of oxygen and carbon dioxide in the blood and body fluids to and from the cells.
   4. Regulation of ventilation by control mechanisms of the body with regard to rate, rhythm, and depth.

Functional Anatomy of the Respiratory System

The basic components of the respiratory system are the nose and the nasal cavity, the mouth and the pharyngeal cavity, the nasapharynx, the trachea, the primary and secondary bronchi, the bronchioles, the alveolar ducts, the alveolus, and the functional respiratory membrane in the alveolar sack. For further detail it is recommended that the reader review the anatomical characteristics of these various structures by using standard textbooks and audio visual materials.

Mechanics of Respiration

The downward and upward movement of the diaphragm which lengthens and shortens the chest cavity, combined with elevation and depression of the ribs, which increases and decreases the anteroposterior diameter of the cavity, combine to cause the expansion and contraction of the lungs. It is estimated that about 70 percent of the expansion and contraction of the lungs is accomplished by the change in anteroposterior measurement and about 30 percent by the change in length due to movement of the diaphragm.

Respiratory Pressures

The lungs—two air-filled spongy structures—are attached to the body only at their hila and thus the outer surfaces have no attachment. However, the membrane lining the interpleural space constantly absorbs fluid or gas which enters this area creating a partial vacuum. This phenomenon holds the visceral pleura of the lungs tightly against the parietal pleura of the chest wall. As the volume of the chest cavity is increased by the muscles of inspiration the lungs also enlarge and as it is decreased during expiration, they likewise become smaller. The two pleura slide over one another with each inspiration and expiration, lubricated by the few millimeters of tissue fluid containing proteins in the intrapleural space.

Because of the foregoing reasons, with each normal inspiration the pressure within the alveolar sacs, the intra-alveolar pressure, becomes slightly negative (−3 mm. Hg) with regard to the atmosphere. This slightly negative pressure sucks air into the alveolar sacs through the respiratory passage. During normal expiration and resultant compression of the lungs, the intra-alveolar pressure builds to about +3 mm. Hg and forces air out of the respiratory passages. During maximum respiratory efforts, the intra-alveolar pressure can vary from −80 mm. Hg during inspiration to +100 mm. Hg during expiration.

The lungs continually tend to collapse. Two factors are responsible for this phenomenon. First of all there are many elastic fibers contained within the lung tissue itself which are constantly attempting to shorten. The second and more important factor contributing to this tendency to collapse is the high surface tension of the fluid lining, the alveoli. A lipoprotein substance call "surfactant" is constantly secreted by the epithelial alveolar lining which decreases the surface tension of the fluids of the respiratory passages seven- to fourteenfold. The absence of the ability to secrete surfactant in the newborn is called *hyaline membrane disease* or *respiratory distress syndrome.*

No single factor or phenomenon is responsible for the body's ability to maintain inflated functional lungs; rather it is the combination of all of these factors that gets the job done.

Compliance of the Lungs and Thorax

As can be seen from the preceding discussion, both the lungs and the thorax itself have elastic characteristics and thus exhibit expansibility. This expansibility of the lungs and thorax is called *compliance,* and is expressed as the volume increase in the lung for each unit increase in intra-alveolar pressure. Normal total pulmonary compliance, i.e., both lungs and thorax, is 0.13 liter per centimeter of water pressure. Or every time alveolar pressure is increased by an amount necessary to raise a column of water one centimeter in height, the lungs expand 130 ml. in volume.

Conditions or situations which destroy lung tissue cause it to become fibrotic, produce pulmonary edema, block alveoli, or in any way impede lung expansion and expansibility of the thoracic cage reduce pulmonary compliance and decrease the efficiency of meeting the need for oxygen to carry on the necessary functional activities of the total organism.

It is extremely important to emphasize that when lungs are expanded and contracted through the action of the respiratory muscles, energy is required for the muscular activity involved.

In addition to this "work," energy is also required to overcome two other factors which tend to prevent expansion of the lungs. They are (1) nonelastic tissue resistance, and (2) airway resistance, meaning that energy is required to rearrange the large molecules of viscous tissues of the lung itself so that they slip past one another during respiratory movements. In the presence of tissue edema, the lungs lose much of their elastic qualities, and increased viscosity of the tissues and fluids increases the nonelastic resistance. Thus the "work" of breathing is increased and the energy expended to accomplish the task is also greatly increased.

Under normal conditions the airway resistance is low and the energy required to move air along the passages is only slight. When the airway becomes obstructed, such as in obstructive emphysema, asthma, or diphtheria, then airway resistance is greatly increased and the energy required simply to move air in and out is greatly increased.

Pulmonary Volumes and Capacities

The preceding sections have discussed the factors that contribute to pulmonary ventilation, but have said nothing about the volume of air moved with each respiratory cycle. Under certain conditions such as exercise or forced expiration or inspiration, the actual volume of air will vary and the events of pulmonary ventilation become difficult to describe. Consequently, to facilitate the discussion of the events of pulmonary ventilation, the air in the lung has been defined in terms of four volumes and capacities.[2]

The four respiratory volumes when added together result in the maximum volume to which the lung can be expanded. There is a difference between males and females in all pulmonary volumes and capacities. They are approximately 20–25 percent lower in females. Obviously, general body size and the amount of physical development also affect these measurements.

The volume of air moved in and out with each normal respiration is called *tidal volume* and is about 500 ml. in normal young males. If the individual forces inspiration over and beyond tidal volume, it amounts to about 3,000 ml. and is called the *inspiratory reserve volume*. Conversely, the *expiratory reserve volume* is the volume of a forced expiration following the normal tidal expiration and amounts to about 1,100 ml. The *residual volume* is the volume of air remaining following forced expiration. This volume can only be measured by indirect spirometry while the others can be measured directly.

When one studies the actual moment-to-moment events of the pulmonary cycle, it is sometimes more convenient to consider some volumes in combination with others. These various combinations are known as the *four pulmonary capacities*. The first we will consider is the *inspiratory capacity,* which is equal to the tidal volume plus the inspiratory reserve volume. This is about 3,500 ml. and is that amount of air which when starting from normal expiratory level, the individual can forcibly inspire. The second capacity, the *functional residual capacity* is the sum of the expiratory reserve volume and the residual volume. It is the amount of air remaining in the lungs at the end of normal expiration or about 2,300 ml.

The *vital capacity* is the summation of the inspiratory reserve volume, the tidal volume and expiratory reserve volume. Stated another way, this is the maximum amount of air that can be forcibly expired following a forced maximal inspiration. This volume is about 4,000 ml. in a normal male.

The last capacity is that of *total lung capacity*. This is equal to the volume to which lungs can be expanded with greatest inspiratory effort. The volume of the capacity is about 5,800 ml.

Two major factors determine the amounts of the above-mentioned volumes. They are *body size* and *position when measured.* Collectively, the various volumes and capacities give a picture of respiratory efficiency and pulmonary compliance.

A very important factor of respiratory function is the rate of alveolar air renewed with each cycle or *alveolar ventilation.* Obviously, per minute alveolar ventilation is less than the minute respiratory volume (tidal volume × respiratory rate) because a large amount of the air inspired goes to fill respiratory passages whose membranes are essentially incapable of gaseous exchange with the blood. This dead-space volume is about 150 ml. in young adult males and is effected by activity and the physiological state of the individual. In normal individuals it is all the space except the alveoli. In individuals with nonfunctional alveoli, abnormal pulmonary ventilation, or abnormal pulmonary circulation, the dead space increases and pulmonary efficiency is reduced.

About 2,300 ml. of air remains in the lung at the end of expiration. With each new breath about 350 ml. of new air is brought into the alveoli and mixed with the volume remaining from the last cycle, thus only about one-seventh the total volume. The normal alveolar ventilation rate is about 4,300 ml. per minute. At this rate the alveolar gases are replaced by new air about every 23 seconds. The slow turnover rate prevents rapid fluctuations in concentration in the alveolus with each breath.

Diffusion of Gases through the Pulmonary Membrane

The pulmonary membrane in humans is made up of all the surfaces in the respiratory wall that are thin enough to permit the exchange of gases between the lungs and the blood. The total area of this membrane in the average normal adult male is about 60 square meters, or about the size of a moderate-sized classroom. It is 0.2 to 0.4 micron thick, or less than the thickness of the average red blood cell. These two outstanding features combine to allow large quantities of gases to diffuse across the pulmonary membrane in a very short pteriod of time.

The air that is taken into the respiratory passages is a mixture of primarily nitrogen and oxygen, (99.5 percent) and a small amount of carbon dioxide and water vapor. (0.5 percent) The molecules of the various gases behave as in solution and exhibit Brownian movement. Thus a mixture of gases such as air has all molecular species evenly distributed throughout the given volume. Because of this constant molecular bombardment the volume of gases exerts pressure against the walls of the container. This pressure can be defined as the force with which a gas or mixture of gases attempts to move from the confines of the present environment. Therefore each of the species in a mixture such as air will account for part of the total pressure of the entire mixture. Consequently, if we take 100 volumes of air and place them in a container under 1 atmosphere of pressure (760 mm. Hg), by analysis we would find that nitrogen makes up 79 of the 100 volumes and oxygen makes up 21 volumes, or 79 and 21 percent concentration respectively.

Both these gases are contained at 760 mm. Hg pressure in this container. If now we take the same volume of nitrogen and move it to a container of the same volume and allow to expand until it completely filled all of the volume (100 percent) we will observe that the pressure in the second container drops from 760 to 600 mm. Hg. If we do the same thing with the 21 volumes of oxygen and allow them to expand to 100 percent of the volume, we observe that the pressure in the third container drops from 760 to 160 mm. Hg. One concludes then that in the original container that *part* of the total pressure due to nitrogen was 600 mm. Hg and that *part* due to oxygen was 160 mm. Hg. This pressure of nitrogen is called the *partial pressure* of nitrogen (pN_2) and that of oxygen the *partial pressure* of oxygen (pO_2). As stated earlier, the partial pressure of a gas in a given volume is the force it exerts against the walls of the container. If the walls of the container are permeable, like the pulmonary membrane, then the penetrating or diffusing power of a gas is directly proportional to its partial pressure.

It is extremely important to point out that atmospheric air differs from alveolar air in partial pressures of the components. The comparative concentrations of each are as follows:

GAS	ATMOSPHERIC AIR, PERCENT	ALVEOLAR AIR, PERCENT
N_2	78.62	74.9
O_2	20.84	13.6
CO_2	0.04	5.3
H_2	0.50	6.2
	100.00	100.00

The difference between atmospheric air and alveolar air is in the increased concentration of carbon dioxide and water in alveolar air. The reasons for these differences are twofold. First, the air is humidified as it is inspired by the moisture of the epithelial lining of the respiratory tract. At normal body temperature water vapor has a partial pressure of 47 mm. Hg and mixes with and dilutes the other gases decreasing their partial pressures.

Secondly, molecules in a given volume of gas behave like molecules in a solution and diffuse from an area of high concentration to one of lower concentration.

The factors that govern the rate of diffusion of the gases through the pulmonary membrane are as follows. First the greater the pressure difference on either side of the membrane the faster the rate of diffusion. Second, the larger the area of the pulmonary membrane the larger the quantity of gas that can diffuse across the membrane in a given period of time. The thinner the membrane the more rapidly do gases diffuse through it to the compartment on the opposite side. Lastly, the diffusion coefficient is directly proportional to the solubility of the gas in the fluid of the pulmonary membrane inversely proportional to molecular size. Therefore, small molecules that are highly soluble diffuse more rapidly than do large molecular gases that are less soluble. The diffusion coefficients are as follows:

Oxygen	1
Carbon dioxide	20.3
Nitrogen	0.53

These three gases are very similar to each other with regard to molecular size but have quite different solubilities in the fluids of the pulmonary membrane. It is these differences that account for the difference in the rate of diffusion of the gases through the pulmonary membrane.

Transport of Oxygen and Carbon Dioxide through the Tissues

As oxygen diffuses from the lungs to the blood, a small portion of it becomes dissolved in the plasma and cell fluids but more than 60 times as much combines immediately with hemoglobin and is carried to the tissues. Here the oxygen is used by the cells and carbon dioxide is formed. As the carbon dioxide diffuses into the interstitial fluids, about 5 percent is dissolved in the blood and the remainder diffuses into the red blood cells where one of two things occur: (1) carbon dioxide either combines with water to form carbonic acid and then reacts with the acid base buffer and is transported as the bicarbonate ion, or (2) a small portion of the carbon dioxide combines with hemoglobin at a different bonding site than oxygen and is transported as carbamenohemoglobin.

Nitrogen diffuses from the alveolus into the blood, but because there is no carrier mechanism and under standard conditions nitrogen has only slight solubility in tissue fluid, it quickly establishes an equilibrium state on either side of the membrane and thus is essentially inert.

The relative partial pressure (mm. of Hg) in the various compartments is as summarized below.

GAS	ATMOSPHERIC AIR	ALVEOLAR AIR	VENOUS BLOOD	ARTERIAL BLOOD
pO_2	159	104	40	100
pCO_2	0.15	40	45	40
pN_2	597	569	569	569

It can readily be seen that concentration gradients are established that then foster the diffusion of these gases in the direction which is physiologically advantageous. Figure 7-1 drawings summarize the events of gaseous diffusion through pulmonary membrane and transport to and from the tissues.

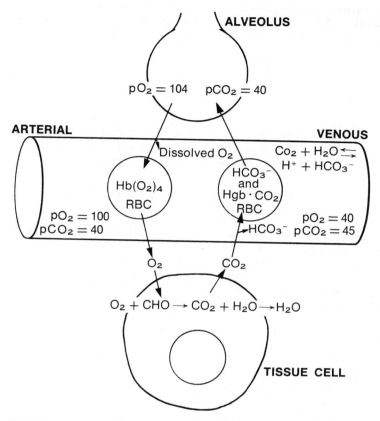

Fig. 7-1. Gaseous diffusion through pulmonary membrane in respiration.

Regulation of Respiration

The basic rhythm of respiration is controlled by the interaction of inspiratory and expiratory neurons of the respiratory center in the brain stem. This center receives stimuli from spinal cord, cortical, and midbrain areas of the brain and from the vagus and glossopharyngeal nerves which cause reflex excitation or depression of the respiratory center. It sends motor impulses to the spinal cord and nerves that serve these muscles and via the phrenic nerve—a special nerve innervating the diaphragm. Located throughout the lung tissue itself are many nerve endings which when the lungs are distended send inhibitory impulse via the vagus nerve to the inspiratory neurons of the respiratory center. This response to lung distention is called the *Hering-Breuer reflex*. Its function is to prevent overinflation and aid the respiratory center in maintaining the basic rhythm of respiration.

Regardless of the continuity of the basic respiratory rhythm, the rate and depth of respiration vary tremendously in response to physiologic demands in the body. Four factors serve to affect the rate and depth of respiration: carbon dioxide concentrations, hydrogen-ion concentration, oxygen concentration, and exercise.

The most powerful stimulus for the respiration center is the carbon dioxide content of the blood and tissue fluids of the body. When the carbon dioxide level rises above normal both inspiratory and expiratory neurons are stimulated and thus both rate and depth of respiration are increased. Approximately one-half the carbon dioxide effect on respiration is due to the direct effect of this substance on the respiratory neurons themselves. The other half is due to the indirect effect of carbon dioxide in the cerebrospinal fluid. As carbon dioxide diffuses into the cerebrospinal fluid, it combines with water to form carbonic acid which then dissociates to hydrogen bicarbonate ions. This familiar reaction is represented by the following equation:

$$CO_2 + H_2O \rightleftarrows H_2CO_3 \rightleftarrows H^+ + HCO_3{-}$$

The increased hydrogen-ion concentration directly stimulates the neurons of the respiratory center as the fluid bathes the sides of the brain stem.

The respiratory system's response to carbon dioxide concentrations is extremely important because it is the main pathway for regulating carbon dioxide levels in body fluids. Should carbon dioxide accumulate in the tissues and fluids of the body, all chemical reactions of the body are essentially inhibited. If the carbon dioxide level drops too low, alkalosis develops which is also incompatible with life.

Hydrogen-ion concentration, as implied by the previous section, is the second most powerful influence on alveolar ventilation. Referring back to the equation showing carbon dioxide combining with water in body fluids, it is noted that the reactions are reversible. Therefore, if there is an accumulation of hydrogen-ion concentration (a low pH and tending toward acidosis), the center neurons respond, increasing the rate rhythm of respiration, which drives the reaction to the left and lowers the hydrogen-ion concentration. If the hydrogen-ion concentration is low (pH high and tending toward alkalosis) alveolar ventilation is depressed and the reaction is driven to the left. This response of the respiratory system in conjunction with the kidney to a large extent controls the acid-base balance of the body.

Although normally hemoglobin is almost completely saturated with oxygen, the body does have chemoreceptors located in the carotid bodies in the neck and in the aortic arch which monitors blood oxygen levels. These receptors are sensitive to oxygen diffusion, and the respiratory center is stimulated via the vagus and glossopharyngeal nerves. The chemoreceptor mechanism is not as powerful a respiratory stimulus as either carbon dioxide or hydrogen-ion concentration.

The rate and depth of respiration are directly proportional to the amount of work done during exercise. It is not the chemical factors that appear to cause increased rate and depth of respiration during exercise, except secondarily. The primary cause of increased respiration during exercise is the presence of simultaneous stimulation by the cerebral cortex as it innervates the muscle exercised and the simultaneous stimulation of the sensory pathway from the cord that stimulates the respiratory center.

PATHOPHYSIOLOGY OF THE RESPIRATORY SYSTEM

A broad definition of the function of the respiratory system is (1) to provide adequate oxygenation to all body tissues, and (2) to eliminate excess CO_2 gas produced by the tissues. Performance of these functions requires not only normally functioning lungs and thorax, but also a normally functioning medullary respiratory center and cardiovascular system, normally functioning aortic and carotid chemoreceptors, and a normal amount of functioning hemoglobin. Malfunction of any of these components can cause respiratory failure—inadequate oxygenation of the tissues, inadequate elimination of CO_2 gas, or both. Since hypoxemia and hypercapnea are the essence of respiratory failure, they deserve special attention.

Normal function of the lungs and thorax may be impaired by various disease processes. These pulmonary diseases are often placed in two main categories: (1) airway obstructions, and (2) restrictive defects. The obstructive diseases seen most commonly are chronic bronchitis, asthma, and emphysema. Frequent subjection to irritants, allergens, and infections can cause gradual but definite tissue changes. In chronic bronchitis and asthma the airways may be obstructed by mucosal edema, increased mucus in the lumen, and presumably by spasms of the muscle encircling the bronchi and bronchioles. In chronic bronchitis there may also be an increased number of mucus glands, and in emphysema there may be loss of support for the walls of the airways so that they collapse rapidly on expiration, like a wet straw.

Rarer causes of airway obstructions are aspirated foreign bodies (most often in children), bronchial or tracheal stenosis from scarring (often from a previous tracheostomy), intrabronchial tumors, occasionally silicosis, tuberculosis, and other granulomatous diseases and sometimes the frothy, bubbly secretions of severe pulmonary edema. Upper-airway obstruction from large tonsils and adenoids has on occasion been the cause of respiratory failure in children.

On pulmonary function tests, obstructive diseases are manifested by slowing of expiratory flow ratio; i.e., reduced FEV_1, FEV/VC ratio of less than 75 percent, and reduced FEF 25–75 percent (MMEF). If severe, obstructive diseases usually cause hypoxemia and hypercapnea.

Although many conditions can cause restrictive pulmonary problems, obstructive problems are more common. Restrictive refers to any situation which makes it difficult to expand the lungs. Diffuse interstitial pulmonary fibrosis, either idiopathic or associated with sarcoid, causes fibrosis inside the lung. The stiffness or noncompliance of the tissue restricts lung expansion. Fibrosis outside the lung as in pleural thickening or fibrosis can also make it difficult to expand the lungs, and is therefore a restrictive process.

Abdominal distention and/or abdominal pain can limit movement of the diaphragm, thereby restricting lung expansion. Failure of the left ventricle results in pulmonary vascular congestion, another restrictive process. Skeletal abnormalities such as hypkoscolisis and ankylizing spondylitis as well as neuromuscular disorders such as Guillain-Barré syndrome also restrict chest expansion.

On pulmonary function tests, restrictive problems are reflected by low vital capacity and reductions in all other lung volumes. They do not often cause blood gas abnormalities unless they are associated with another abnormality; i.e., diffusion (gas transport) problems. When restriction to lung expansion is caused by interstitial fibrosis there is usually interference with transport of oxygen from the alveoli into the bloodstream, and this is reflected by a low pO_2. If the diffusion problem is severe there may be hypoxemia at rest but if the condition is mild or moderate, the pO_2 at rest is usually normal and exercise is required to demonstrate the hypoxemia. With exercise, blood flows through the lung faster than at rest, so blood may not remain in the pulmonary capillaries long enough to pick up oxygen if the oxygen is delayed in getting into the capillaries because of a diffusion problem.

Pulmonary edema is another cause of diffusion problems. It may take longer for oxygen to diffuse from the alveoli through alveolar edema, through the interstitial edema and into the capillary. In other conditions such as emphysema there may be a diffusion abnormality because of a lack of alveoli and/or pulmonary capillaries, thus less opportunity for gas transport.

If the pO_2 is normal, 97 percent of the oxygen-carrying capacity of hemoglobin is used. Even though the pO_2 may rise as high as five times normal when a person breathes 100 percent oxygen, the hemoglobin can carry only 3 percent more oxygen.

There are certain disease states in which the hemoglobin is abnormal and carries either more or less oxygen for a given pO_2 than does normal hemoglobin. When a type hemoglobin carries less oxygen than normal at a given pO_2, it is the same as having the oxyhemoglobin dissociation curve shifted to the right.

When hemoglobin does not carry its full amount of oxygen, it assumes a blue or dark color. Generally cyanosis is recognized when there are 5 gm. or more of hemoglobin this is not saturated with oxygen. [Occasionally because of hypoxemia the body may make too many red blood cells (RBC) and too much hemoglobin.] When there is more than the usual amount of hemoglobin and when the circulation moves the RBC slowly more unsaturated hemoglobin is present, so that cyanosis is more apparent. Sometimes, then, cyanosis may be present—particularly in the extremities—when the arterial oxygen concentration is normal, if there is an excess of hemoglobin or reduction in blood flow. Much more common is the opposite situation in which arterial oxygen concentration is low but no cyanosis is recognizable. If one relies on cyanosis to diagnose significant hypoxemia, many instances of hypoxemia will be missed completely and others will be discovered late. Cyanosis is especially hard to diagnose in anemic patients. In spite of the unreliability of cyanosis as an early indicator of hypoxia, many nevertheless continue to rely on the absence of cyanosis to indicate adequate oxygenation, to the detriment of the patient. Hypoxia may be caused by hypoventilation, diffusion problems, living at high altitudes, right-to-left shunts, and ventilation/perfusion mismatching.

Conditions which cause just hypoxemia may be even less obvious than those associated with hypoxemia and with hypercapnea. A pulmonary embolus may cause or may intensify hypoxemia. Other causes of chest pain, such as fractured ribs, may cause decreased expansion of part of the lung and lead to hypoxemia. Probably the most common cause of hypoxemia is ventilation/perfusion inequality ($\dot{V}/\dot{Q}$ problems) or more simply stated, mismatching of ventilation and perfusion. If any area of the lung is underventilated, for instance because its bronchus is partially obstructed by a mucus plug with that part of the lung still receiving its normal blood supply, then there is relatively too little ventilation for the amount of perfusion (blood flow); this situation might be represented as $\dot{v}/\dot{Q}$ as compared to the normal $\dot{V}/\dot{Q}$. The blood to this part of the lung does not have the opportunity to pick up its full quota of oxygen because of the reduction in ventilation. If the bronchus to an area of the lung were completely obstructed yet with the perfusion remaining normal, it would represent a right-to-left shunt; i.e., unsaturated venous blood would flow from the right ventricle through the lungs without picking up any oxygen, would mix with blood from other parts of the lungs, then be pumped by the left ventricle into the systemic circulation.

Incidentally, just the opposite type of $\dot{V}/\dot{Q}$ problem may occur yet may not cause hypoxemia. For instance, the pulmonary artery to part of the lung might be occluded but the ventilation to that part of the lung might be maintained and there would therefore be excessive ventilation in respect to perfusion which could be represented as $\dot{V}/\dot{q}$. This is called *wasted ventilation*. This condition does not necessarily cause serious problems but often is associated with excessive work of breathing.

Usually the lung reflexly reduces ventilation to match reduced perfusion, and vice versa. However, in some disease states these reflex changes do not occur. For instance, in patients who have severe pathology in the upper abdomen such as pancreatitis, or who have just undergone gastric surgery or cholecystectomy, pain or tight bandages may prevent the diaphragm from descending normally with inspiration, thereby reducing ventilation in the lung bases. Sometimes the chest X-ray shows atelectasis or sometimes just a high diaphragm, but underventilation may occur without noticeable X-ray changes. If perfusion remains normal, some blood flows through underventilated bases without getting oxygenated so that the systemic arterial blood shows hypoxemia. As mentioned above, this type of reduced ventilation in relation to perfusion in some lung areas can occur in many different diseases and is probably the most common cause of hypoxemia. It occurs in many ill patients who would not be expected to have respiratory failure—patients with shock, GI bleeding, heart failure—in fact, almost in any patient sick enough to be in ICU or CCU.

Diffusion problems usually occur with interstitial lung disease such as diffuse interstitial pulmonary fibrosis and metastic carcinoma spreading through the lymphatics of the lung in the interstitial spaces (between alveoli). Diffusion problems also may occur in pulmonary edema in which edema fluid is found in the interstitial space, and often in the alveoli as well. With diffusion problems the pO_2 may be normal at rest, but with exercise the pO_2 falls; in more severe diffusion problems the pO_2 may be low even at rest. Generally the patient with a diffusion problem hyperventilates in an effort to move adequate amounts of oxygen from the alveoli through the widened interstitial space into the capillary blood. In doing this hyperventilation, the pCO_2 is lowered. Usually in diffussion problems there is no difficulty in getting air through the airways. In severe pulmonary edema, however, because of the frothy, bubble secretions occluding the airways, there may be enough obstruction to airflow to cause a rise in pCO_2. In summary, diffusion problems first show hypoxemia only with exercise and later hypoxemia even at rest. The hyperventilation necessary to keep pO_2 up causes a low pCO_2. Only in severe problems such as severe pulmonary edema is the pCO_2 elevated.

Living at high altitudes, even with normal ventilation, is associated with hypoxemia because the inspired oxygen concentration is low. The hypoxemia usually leads to hyperventilation in an effort by the body to raise the pO_2, and the hyperventilation causes a low pCO_2. For instance, the normal pCO_2 in Denver is 36 mm. Hg as compared to the normal at sea level of 40 mm. Hg.

Right-to-left shunts which may occur with ventricular septal defects, for example, are associated with hypoxemia because part of the blood from the right heart which is destined to be oxygenated in the lungs bypasses the lungs and is shunted directly into the systemic arterial circulation. The resulting systemic arterial hypoxemia may lead to hyperventilation and therefore low pCO_2. Occasionally right-to-left shunting occurs through abnormal vascular channels in the lung.

Hypoventilation from any cause leads to hypoxemia *and hypercapnea.* The hypoventilation is most frequently associated with airway obstruction such as emphysema or chronic bronchitis, or even the obstruction due to the frothy secretions which occur in severe pulmonary edema. Hypoventilation also may occur with a variety of neurological problems such as myasthenia gravis, Guillain-Barré syndrome, or polio. Hypoventilation may occur with some head injuries or with oversedation. Rarely hypoventilation may be caused by restrictive pulmonary problems such as large pleural effusion, immobile chest with ankylosing spondylitis, and so forth.

The hypoventilation that occurs with airway obstruction may be due to retained secretions, airways narrowing due to edema or swelling of the mucosal lining, bronchospasm, or airway collapse. Increase in secretions is due to increase in output of the goblet cells and submucosal glands. The submucosal glands are stimulated to produce mucus by the vagus nerve and local irritants in the tracheobronchial tree; the goblet cells are stimulated to produce mucus mainly by local irritants.

In many diseases of the respiratory tract such as asthma and bronchitis there is edema of the mucosal lining. Treating bronchospasm without treating the associated mucosal edema is treating only half of the problem, so we should usually combine an inhaled vasoconstrictor with an inhaled bronchodilator. In conditions such as emphysema there is often a rapid collapse of the trachea and bronchi during expiration which causes airway obstruction during expiration.

Hypoxemia caused by hypoventilation is accompanied by hypercapnia, but hypoxemia due to any of the other causes is usually associated with hyperventilation and therefore low pCP_2.

Therefore when hypoxemia is associated with a high pCO_2 it generally means that hypoxemia is due to hypoventilation. When hypoxemia is associated with a low or normal pCO_2 it may be cause by diffusion problems, $\dot{V}/\dot{Q}$ mismatching, right-to-left shunting, or living at high altitude. The latter is obvious. Diffusion problems usually respond by a return of arterial oxygen concentrations to normal with low-to-moderate amounts of supplemental oxygen, while $\dot{V}/\dot{Q}$ mismatching and shunts usually require high levels of O_2 to bring the arterial oxygen concentrations to normal, and even then the arterial oxygen sometimes does not return to normal.

Hypercapnea (also called *hypercarbia*) is easier to explain. It always means alveolar hypoventilation. The most common causes of hypoventilation are mentioned above. Hypoventilation (and therefore hypercapnea) of limited degree may also be due to compensation of nonrespiratory alkalosis. With more significant hypoventilation, however, there is hypoxemia which is a strong stimulus to ventilation. This hypoxemia, then, increases ventilation and therefore prevents severe hypoventilation from occurring in compensation for nonrespiratory alkalosis.

There is only one cause of hypercapnea—hypoventilation. There are several causes of hypoxemia, one of which is hypoventilation. Therefore hypercapnea is a better reflector of hypoventilation than hypoxemia.

The work of breathing is often increased in diseases in which the lungs fail, and this increased work of breathing may be due to reduced compliance, increased airway resistance, or both. Reduced compliance occurs in restrictive conditions such as diffuse interstitial pulmonary fibrosis or conditions in which there is reduced surfactant—adult and newborn respiratory distress syndromes. Increased airway resistance occurs with anything that causes airway obstruction as listed above. In both increased airway resistance and reduced compliance, increased pressure is required to deliver a normal tidal volume. This is easily recognized in patients on ventilators. Increased airway resistance is noted by an initial high pressure which then falls to a lower level and increase in compliance is noted by a sustained high pressure.

Respiratory Failure

Arbitrary values for defining when respiratory failure is present have been proposed. Respiratory failure is said to be present when the pO_2 falls below 50 mm. Hg (O_2 saturation below 85 percent) or when pCO_2 rises above 50 mm. Hg. Numbers, though, are not the perfect way to diagnose a complicated situation like respiratory failure. Some persons are in mild respiratory failure even before the pO_2 falls below 50 mm. Hg or before the pCO_2 rises above 50 mm. Hg. There are other persons who have increased pCO_2 and/or decreased pO_2 who are in a stable state, often still working, because they have adapted to the abnormal blood gases. In spite of these exceptions, *blood gases* are by far the best means of detecting respiratory failure.

It is easy to understand how respiratory failure occurs in one of the airway obstructive diseases—i.e., emphysema, chronic bronchitis, or asthma. A very important fact is that these diseases account for fewer than half of the cases of respiratory failure that occur in a general hospital.

It is most important to be able to diagnose respiratory failure at an early stage when treatment is most likely to be successful. Even more desirable is the recognition of *impending* respiratory failure. This can be accomplished by (1) knowing the setting in which respiratory failure is most likely to occur, (2) being aware that there are many nonspecific signs and symptoms which are indicators of early or impending respiratory failure, and (3) being inquisitive enough to obtain *arterial blood gases* when the question of respiratory failure enters your mind. (See Chapter 10, Blood Gases.)

Settings

Drugs such as sedatives, tranquilizers, sleeping pills, or analgesics—and rarely, alcohol—may cause depression of respiratory drive and may allow the pCO_2 to rise significantly while the patient is under the influence of the drug. Once the effect of the drug is gone, the remaining elevation of pCO_2 is often enough to cause continuing respiratory depression. It is important to remember that a small rise in pCO_2 is a large stimulus to breathing, but that larger rises in pCO_2 can cause depression of the respiratory center resulting in hypoventilation. Other brain functions may also be depressed. If the pCO_2 is already elevated enough to cause respiratory depression, the carotid chemoreceptors may sense hypoxemia and respond to this last remaining stimulus to breathing. If oxygen is administered because the patient is cyanotic or appears to have labored breathing, the final stimulus to respiration, hypoxemia, may be removed, causing the patient to have even less ventilation. Such a patient who has respiratory center depression due to drugs, a significantly elevated pCO_2, or both, when given enough O_2 to reduce his respiratory drive may no longer appear cyanotic and as he ventilates less he may no longer appear to be laboring to breathe. In fact, he may become quieter and go to sleep. It is extremely important to recognize the set of circumstances mentioned above, for it happens daily in chronic airway obstruction patients in hospitals across the country.

Often respiratory failure is misdiagnosed as congestive heart failure, as a stroke, or as "pneumonia occurring in a patient with a lousy personality." Usually the personality improves as the pneumonia clears, yet the diagnosis of respiratory failure was never made.

The patient who is semiconscious and flaccid in all extremities may be said to have a "stroke" when in reality there is no localizing finding of a cerebral thrombosis or hemorrhage, and instead hypoxia and hypercapnea cause the impaired consciousness and impaired motor function. Unless someone has a high degree of suspicion, the patient may die of respiratory failure masquerading as a stroke. On the other hand, it is certainly possible for a patient with a typical stroke to retain enough secretions in his respiratory tract to develop respiratory failure.

Most common are the patients with obvious right-sided congestive heart failure. The cause of right-sided congestive heart failure — lung failure — often goes unrecognized. Fortunately, many of these patients improve just with treatment of the heart failure, but they would improve more if respiratory failure and its cause were recognized and treated.

It is easy to recognize the respiratory distress present in a patient with asthma, but it is often difficult to tell when the patient is in real danger. The physical exam can be misleading. Occasionally, in asthma, little or no wheezing is heard because there is virtually no air exchange. He may appear to be making normal respiratory movements, though labored, yet in fact be exchanging very little air. The earliest blood gas abnormality in an asthmatic is hypoxemia. The hypoxemia may be worsened by treatment with the usual bronchochilators, even though the wheezing is decreasing. The worsening hypoxemia is probably due to changing $\dot{V}/\dot{Q}$ relationships. The hypoxemia causes hyperventilation which in turn causes hypocapnea. In spite of attempts at hyperventilation, if the asthma becomes more severe with increasing airway obstruction, the pCO_2 rises to normal. As the situation worsens even mild elevations of pCO_2 combined with the hypoxemia (if the patient has not been treated with O_2) signify severe asthma. In asthma slight elevation of pCO_2 signifies impending crisis, while similar elevations of pCO_2 in chronic bronchitis or emphysema have much less significance. As in other respiratory problems, the best indicator is arterial blood gases, but the interpretation of blood gases must be related to the clinical situation.

Usually some additional insult occurs in patients with chronic airway obstruction (CAO) which either (1) increases airway obstruction or (2) reduces respiratory drive. Both of these cause hypoventilation and result in an increase in pCO_2 and a decrease in pO_2.

Often the patient with CAO is getting by with only marginal lung function, and even minor insults tip him over into frank respiratory failure. Such an insult may be an infectious process leading to bronchial mucosa edema, leading to increased mucus production, leading to bronchospasm leading to increased airway obstruction leading to worsening hypercapnea and hypoxemia.

Nonspecific Signs and Symptoms

There are also a number of situations in which anyone can recognize respiratory failure; i.e., patient with cardiac arrest, with drug overdose or head injury who stops breathing, and patients with cyanosis and labored breathing. However, in many patients the presence of respiratory failure may not be so obvious. The signs and symptoms may be nonspecific and manifested as lethargy, irritability, headaches, confusion (sometimes intermittent), vagueness, facetiousness, jerky motions, and asterrhexis (flapping tremor of hand). Other less specific manifestations may be sweating, mydriasis, tachycardia, hypotension, anorexia, impaired motor function, impaired judgment, and coma.

Respiratory failure occurs in a variety of clinical settings and is associated with a variety of signs and symptoms. One must be exceedingly astute to recognize respiratory failure every time it occurs, and perhaps all that can be expected is that one should learn to develop a high index of suspicion regarding the existence of respiratory failure and be eager to obtain arterial blood gases when a suspicion of respiratory failure exists.

The treatment of respiratory failure is designed to raise the pO_2 to normal and/or reduce the pCO_2 to normal. Usually this can be accomplished by initially supplying supplemented oxygen and treating the factors which are causing the altered physiology; for example, bronchospasm, infection, mucosal edema, and retained secretions are treated. This treatment if instituted early enough, usually allows the patient to increase his own ventilation so that in most cases of respiratory failure ventilators are not required. It is most important for the patient to receive adequate oxygen—just enough to raise his pO_2 to about 60 mm. Hg while the other treatment is being instituted. Raising the pO_2 to 60 will help to prevent secondary problems such as the development of heart failure or worsening coma. Hypoxemia can cause death in minutes, but it takes hours or days for hypercapnea to become marked enough to cause death.

REFERENCES

1. Arthur C. Guyton, *Textbook of Medical Physiology*, 4th ed. W. B. Saunders, (Philadelphia; 1971), pp. 545-603.
2. *Ibid*, pp. 550.

8

Management Modalities

BOYD BIGELOW, M.D.
JANET KERKMAN, R.N., A.R.I.T.
THELMA L. LOHR, R.N., M.S.

RESPIRATORY INSUFFICIENCY—FAILURE MANAGEMENT MODALITIES

The increasing knowledge surrounding the conditions known as "respiratory problems" has caused an upsurge of inhalation therapy departments and/or respiratory care units in hospitals throughout our country. Many hospitals have the "hardware" but lack adequately trained personnel.

The nurse may find herself a member of a respiratory team or she may be the sole member with the physician. Either way, the nurse has specific responsibilities that need to be accepted.

1. *Keen observation*—to recognize the subtle, suggestive signs and symptoms as well as the obvious ones. A listing of the less obvious indicators of impending respiratory failure can be found in the chapter "Respiratory Pathophysiology." Treatment of impending respiratory failure is usually more effective and offers less stress for the patient.

2. *Initiative*—to institute those measures which are nursing functions; i.e., suctioning, breathing exercises, obtaining blood gases. If these are not considered to be independent nursing functions, guided by the physician, the patient's condition may worsen seriously before adequate orders or consultation can be obtained.

3. *Skillful care*—to continue practice of those skills which are effective and to modify and/or change those which are ineffectual and, perhaps, more harmful than helpful. Two important factors that form the basis for skillful care are knowledge and attitude. It is vital to continue seeking knowledge which will expand the nursing concepts of respiratory failure and respiratory

care. It is also vital to recognize one's own attitudes toward the nursing functions of this care. A question you might answer for yourself is: "Will you suction, *without* an order, an alert yet restless patient with labored breathing because of secretions he is unable to raise, or will you suction, *without* an order, only those patients in more acute crisis such as respiratory arrest?"

4. *Negotiation*—to negotiate written policies with governing medical and nursing services before crises arise. The nursing staff can then be free to give full attention to the patient's needs without question as to their own status. This negotiation is not enough, however. It is important for personnel to seek out educational programs, either formal or informal, which will assist in developing respiratory care skills.

The therapy for patients with respiratory problems must be aggressive and aimed at the underlying cause. It is necessary to life that the patient resume his own respiratory work as soon as possible. This chapter has six sections: Respirators/Ventilators, Bronchial Hygiene, Postural Drainage, Breathing Exercises, Maintenance of Ventilation in Cardiopulmonary Emergencies, and Intubation. Each section includes the accompanying physiology of the therapy, and suggested guidelines for skillful care. It is not a chapter on the mechanics of specific equipment. The reader is referred to the manufacturer's literature for this.

RESPIRATORS/VENTILATORS

During the past decade many types and models of ventilators/respirators have appeared on the market. Generally they can be categorized as *positive-pressure respirators* and *volume respirators*. The primary characteristic of positive pressure machines is the pressure, while the volume of air delivered is secondary. Just the reverse is true of volume respirators. Their primary characteristic is the volume of air delivered, and their secondary characteristic is pressure.

The intermittent positive-pressure ventilators (IPPB) are widely used and still much in demand. Examples are the Bennett and Bird. These machines deliver a volume of air at a set rate and at a set pressure. As the patient begins his inspiration, the machine is triggered and forces a volume of air under positive pressure into the lungs. When the pressure is released, the machine closes off and the patient exhales passively.

The volume respirators (Morch, Emerson, Ohio) are preset to deliver a specific volume of air and the pressure needed may vary from patient to patient. Advantages of the volume respirators are:

1. It delivers a prescribed volume of air regardless of the pressure needed.
2. It delivers a constant volume of air regardless of a changing status in lung compliance and airway resistance.
3. It allows for estimations of total lung resistive changes by noting pressure-volume relationships.
4. It allows for management of special problems—i.e., frail chest.
5. It is capable of high pressures.

To understand the dynamics between the ventilators and the lungs, Heironimus[1] suggests the following analogy. Consider the healthy lung as an old balloon—it takes very little pressure to blow in enough air and stretch it out to full size. Consider the noncompliant lung as a new, stiff balloon—it takes greater pressure to blow in enough air to stretch it to partial size. The distinctions between pressure and volume respirators becomes crucial in patients who have decreased in lung compliance.

The most frequent situations for the utilization of respirators are to maintain the patient with complete respiratory failure, to correct acidosis or alkalosis, to increase alveolar gas distribution, and to increase tidal volume while decreasing the work of breathing.

Physiological Effects of Respirators

Gravity and the respiratory muscles normally cause the periphery and the bases of the lungs to receive greater ventilation than the central bronchial parts. The respirator negates these two means of moving air and so the central parts have increased ventilation while the bases and periphery have decreased ventilation. This can lead to areas of atelectasis and decreased gas exchange. In the nondiseased lung, the "sigh" mechanism of the respirator can be utilized to increase the depth of the respiration and thus inflate the hypoventilated areas. (Normally, people sigh several times an hour, accomplishing the same task.) In diseased lungs, edema, secretions and narrowed air passages cause the airflow to be turbulent. If the inspiratory flow rate is too high or the sigh mechanism is utilized, the flow of air can become more turbulent, resistance may increase, and areas of atelectasis may spread. It is important to keep the air flow as low as possible and yet properly ventilate the patient. Frequent suctioning to remove secretions and plugs will also aid in decreasing the turbulence.

The patient may "fight the respirator." Many times the patient is attempting to receive more air from the machine than he is getting. This can be the result of slow rate, low air flow, and/or anxiety. The first measure to assist the patient in synchronizing his respirations with the respirator is to remove the respirator, ventilate the patient several times with an ambu-bag, and then put the respirator on again. If synchronization is difficult, drugs such as narcotics (morphine) and muscle relaxants (curare, barbituates) may be administered.

Intrathoracic pressures are negative (below atmospheric pressure) in spontaneous respirations with venous return more favored in inspiration. The positive-pressure machine reverses the negative intrathoracic pressure to positive. The high pressure in the alveoli causes high pressure in the intrapleural space, thus compressing the intrathoracic veins. Venous blood is held back, unable to enter the right heart, so that cardiac output is decreased. If expiratory time is sufficient for equalization of intrathoracic pressures, venous return is facilitated and the cardiac output will not be significantly reduced. The increase in intra-alveolar pressure many times is helpful in reversing pulmonary edema by limiting transudation across the alveolar-capillary membranes.

The increase in alveolar ventilation enhances gas exchange and if the inspiratory rate is adequate, pO_2 will rise and pCO_2 will lower to within normal limits. If respiratory acidosis is corrected too rapidly, it may cause convulsions and ventricular fibrillation.

All patients who are placed on a respirator need constant observation for proper operation and maximum effectiveness. The alert patient needs guidance and support. If the equipment fails he is in little or no danger; the comatose patient, however, is in grave danger. Complications may occur not only from equipment failure but also from prolonged utilization of artificial respiration. Diffuse atelectasis may occur when smaller than normal tidal volumes are used. Postural drainage, suctioning, frequent turning, and aeresol medication are useful. Gastrointestinal dilatation may occur causing pressure on the vena cava and reduction in cardiac output. A nasogastric tube should be inserted to remove the gastric contents. Alveolar-capillary block may occur when insufficient humidification is used and the alveolar-capillary membranes are destroyed due to dehydration.

Infections may arise for any patient if the equipment is not cared for properly.

Drugs

Drugs which may be administered to reverse conditions causing respiratory failure are Isuprel, tedral, amesec, aminophylline.

Sympathonimetics: Bronchodilators and decongestants (1) relax circumferential smooth muscle in airway, (2) relax smooth muscle fibers that extend into alveolar ducts and alveoli, and (3) shrink mucosa and effect secretory activity.

Side effects are mostly through the cardiovascular and central nervous systems.

Arrhythmias—tachycardias and premature beats.

Nervousness.

Insomnia.

Convulsions—seen with high doses of aminophylline.

BRONCHIAL HYGIENE

Bronchial hygiene can be defined as any measure that clears the air passages and lungs of irritants and secretions. A major nursing activity directed toward this end is suctioning.

Selection of Equipment

The selection of a catheter should be one big enough to obtain secretions, but not so large that it occludes the air passage. The catheter is attached to one side of an upper Y connector so that pressure can be controlled by the nurse. To prevent infections, clean and/or sterile disposable catheters are used, and the hand is gloved.

Oral Suctioning through Patient's Natural Airway

The patient should first be instructed to blow his nose. Then cleanse the mouth by inserting a catheter upside down, and when in the mouth apply pressure and turn for suctioning. If the patient is receiving O_2, it should be increased 3 L's during the procedure. Place the patient in an upright position with neck hyperextended.

A second catheter is recommended for endotracheal suctioning. Ask the patient to extend his tongue so that the nurse can apply gentle traction, causing the glottis opening to move in line with the trachea. The patient should then be instructed to pant or gently cough repeatedly, after which the catheter is inserted into the trachea. Test to determine if the catheter is in the trachea and not the esophagus: the patient will cough, and he cannot speak. 5-10 cc. of normal saline can be introduced if secretions are thick. Suction is then applied and the catheter completely drawn in a twirling motion. To avoid hypoxia, suctioning should not be extended beyond 15 seconds.

Since suctioning will remove the air from the "dead spaces" of the air passages, it is important to have the patient take several deep breaths upon withdrawal of the catheter. To determine the effectiveness of the suctioning, "listen" to the patient's breath sounds (see Auscultation, Physical Diagnosis, in Chapter 9). If the chest is not clear, the procedure may be repeated. Care must be taken not to traumatize the tracheal mucosal with repeated and/or forceful suctioning.

Suctioning through Endotracheal and Tracheal Tubes

If the patient is on his side, it is wise to suction in that position first for he has been draining the opposite side.

This procedure demands two nurses—one responsible for ventilating the patient when he is off the respirator and the second responsible for the suctioning. When each is ready, the respirator is removed and the patient is ventilated with the ambu-bag, which may or may not be connected to oxygen, depending upon the patients' status. The nurse can deliver a volume of 800 cc. with one hand and 1,000 cc. with two hands. The ambu-bag is then removed for the insertion of the normal saline. The amount necessary may vary from 10–50 cc. The patient is then "ambu-bagged" again to force the solution and to help loosen secretion. Suctioning is accomplished as previously stated. The normal saline may be absorbed by the tissues if they are dehydrated, or by the mucus if it is thick. It should thin the secretions, facilitating their removal the next time. Again, between each suctioning the patient must be "bagged" to prevent hypoxia. The patient, especially with elevated pCO$_2$'s who have had their oxygen removed, are more likely to have arrhythmias and/or arrest. Suctioning can also stimulate the vagus and cause arrhythmias. Take the apical pulse and listen for irregularities in rhythms.

Upon completion, listen to the chest to evaluate the effectiveness of the procedure.

Cuffed Tracheal and Endoctracheal Tubes

The cuffed tubes provide a better opportunity to maintain a closed system while the patient is on the respirator. The cuff may be an integral part of the tube, or it may be attached to the side. The cuff is inflated by injecting through its special tubing 7–10 cc. of air or the amount necessary to first occlude the space between the trachea and the outside of the tubing. Too much air will put additional pressure on the tracheal mucosa, causing injury and necrosis. Too little air will allow air to escape along the outside of the tube, causing inadequate ventilation. It will also produce a "hissing" sound. Additional air must be injected, but only enough to stop the escape sounds. The cuffs are deflated for at least 15 minutes every 2 hours, allowing increased circulation to the surrounding tissues. In new tracheostomies, the cuff remains inflated for the first 24–36 hours. The pharnyx must be suctioned before the cuff is deflated to prevent secretions from sliding down into the trachea.

When using tubes which have the cuffs attached to the side, the nurse must be alert not to overinflate the cuff. Frequently it causes the cuff to herniate over the internal opening and obstructs the airway. The patient will have difficulty breathing if this is the case. A simple test is to deflate the cuff again and see if his breathing improves. If so, the tube must be replaced immediately before the cuff slides totally off the tube and is aspirated further.

Humidification

Humidification of airflow is essential for all patients who have been intubated, received tracheostomies, and who are on respirators. The nurse must consider three factors when providing humidification; (1) the size of the droplet, (2) the temperature of the mist, and (3) the pathology.

The size of the droplet. Droplets are measured in microns. They range from 0.4 to over 40 microns in size. The larger droplets are deposited in the upper portions of the bronchi and the small droplets, 1–2 microns, travel further into the lower bronchioles and more particles are deposited. The tiny droplets, below 1 micron, are so small that they are blown off in exhalation.

Temperature of the mist. The temperature of the mist determines the amount of moisture which can be held. If one thinks about the weather temperatures and humidity, it is easily understood. If the air contains 50 percent of moisture, humidity will be higher with cold temperatures and less with warm temperatures. Warm or hot air is expandable and can hold more moisture without an increase in the humidity. So the humidity of cold steam will decrease when warmed to the body's temperature to 98°F, while the humidity of hot steam will increase when cooled to the body temperature.

Pathology. The type of secretions, not the amount, determines the amount of moisture necessary. Thick, tenacious mucus and dried plugs absorb larger amounts before they become thin and watery. Hydration of the tissues is another indicator. If the tissues are dehydrated, they will absorb the fluid.

One usually thinks of the respiratory system as having an "insensible" loss of fluid. However, with high humidification, a patient can absorb as much as 300–400 cc. of water. Edema can be detected on the back, for one will see creases in the skin from the sheets. Heat of the water and oral fluid intake should be decreased.

Thin secretions require more suctioning. If secretions bubble out over the end of the tube, it is an indication for deeper suctioning. For deep suctioning of the left bronchus, rotate the patient's head to the right and his chest to the left and elevate his chin. The opposite position will allow entry into the right bronchus.

Time to suction. In the beginning, the patient should be suctioned whenever the nurse's observations so indicate; i.e., changes in the sounds of the respirator or changes in patient's respiratory patterns, elevated temperature, and pulse rate. Unfortunately the latter symptoms are frequently overlooked as indicators. In other instances the nurse may inject normal saline into the trachea and upon suctioning find no returns. Thinking the patient is clear, she reduces the numbers of times the patient is suctioned. Most likely the saline was absorbed by the tissue and/or mucus. For more conclusive evidence, she must listen to the various lung areas and ascertain if they are being well ventilated. Also an analysis of arterial blood gases would be indicated.

As the patient improves he will need less suctioning. Appropriate times for suctioning then would be before meals, so he can enjoy his food; before rest and sleep periods, so his rest is undisturbed; and before exercise, so he has adequate oxygen for the work of his muscles.

POSTURAL DRAINAGE—CLAPPING AND VIBRATION

Postural drainage with clapping and vibration is extremely helpful in moving secretions from small airways into the main bronchi. The bronchi then can assist in moving the secretions. The bronchi widen and lengthen on inspiration, allowing air to pass into lower structures without driving the secretions deeper. On expiration, they narrow and shorten, and with the aid of the cilia movements, cause the secretion to move upward. Coughing may then be an adequate force to eject the secretions or suctioning may be necessary.

The areas to be drained can be determined by auscultation, percussion and X-ray. The patient is then placed in a position to utilize gravity as the major force to move secretions. The five positions shown in Fig. 8-1 are adequate to drain all lobes of patients in crisis. Depending on the patient's status and tolerance, the nurse may alter these, affording the patient more comfort.

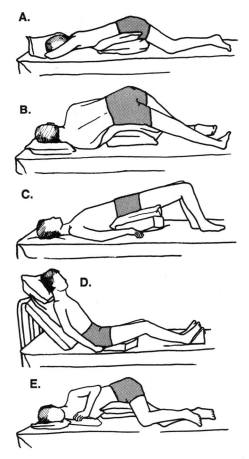

Fig. 8-1. Positions used in lung drainage. A. Face-lying—hips elevated 16–18 inches on pillows, making a 30–45 degree angle. Purpose: to drain the posterior lower lobes. B. Lying on the left side—hips elevated 16–18 inches on pillows. Purpose: to drain the right lateral lower lung segments. C. Back lying—hips elevated 16–18 inches on pillows. Purpose: to drain the anterior lower lung segments. D. Sitting upright or semireclining—to drain the upper lung field and allow more forceful coughing. E. Lying on the right side—hips elevated on pillows forming a 30–45 degree angle. Purpose: to drain the left lower lobes.

Before positioning, all restrictive clothing should be removed to facilitate thorac movement. The patient should then be instructed to cough. Coughing deeply, put tongue forward between teeth, inhale deeply and then eject air forcefully, using the abdominal muscles and/or, inhale deeply and follow with three consecutive coughs, ejecting as much air as possible with each cough. It usually takes more than one deep cough to move up secretions. If the patient is unable to cough, stroking the trachea will stimulate coughing.

The position that facilitates drainage of the affected lobe is then assumed. A towel is used to cover the patient's skin to prevent stinging when clapping. Clapping is accomplished by cupping the hands and gently clapping the chest wall over the area to be drained. This action should dislodge mucus plugs secretions. The treatment should last at least 5 minutes and not more than 30 minutes, the duration based upon the production of secretions and the tolerance of the patient.

If additional positions are to be assumed, select one that allows for drainage of the mainstem bronchus first, thus preventing cross drainage from side to side.

Clapping is not advised for patients on steroid therapy or those with osteoporosis.

Vibration can also enhance drainage and is done only on the expiratory phase. The nurse places both hands over the affected area or one on each side of the chest wall. Instruct the patient to use his abdominal muscles, to take a deep breath through his nose, and to exhale through his mouth. On exhalation, the nurse tenses and contracts her shoulder muscles. This will produce a vibratory movement from her shoulders, through the arms and hands and to the patients' chest wall. Use the amount of pressure that will produce secretions; however, do not "push" when vibrating. Vibration is very useful for patients with painful chests who cannot tolerate percussion.

Postural drainage should be performed at least three times a day until the lung is cleared. The positions cause abdominal organs to press forward; therefore the procedure should wait until 45 minutes to an hour following meals. This will eliminate the feeling of nausea so often associated with it. Since the work of breathing has been increased, rest periods are recommended following each procedure.

BREATHING EXERCISES

Patients with decreased muscle tone and impaired breathing can increase respiratory muscle tone and/or strengthened the auxillary muscles—the diaphragm and abdominal muscles. Inspiration is not the problem—expiration through narrowed bronchi is. Most exercises are focused on assisting the patient to have more expiratory time, thereby releasing trapped air and lowering pCO_2 levels.

Pursed-lip breathing is a method for prolonging the expiratory phase. Once it becomes a pattern of breathing, the patient is more relaxed and has the capability of more exercise. The patient is encouraged to purse his lips and to blow out slowly increasing the time to approximately twice the length of inspiration.

Abdominal and diaphragmal breathing increases ventilation of the lower portions of the lung. The patient lies flat on his back with knees flexed, allowing for full excursion of the chest. He then is instructed to breathe quietly through his nose while pushing out his abdomen. Expiration is through pursed lips, slowly, while he sucks in his abdomen. Pressure may be applied to assist the patient's beginning efforts. Later he may use a small object (book) to produce the same effect. As his muscle tone increases he is encouraged to assume new positions and continue his practice.

Therapy for respiratory failure usually includes one or more of the above modalities. The nurse must be able to initiate and skillfully perform them if the patient is to resume his own work of breathing.

REFERENCE

1. Terring W. Heironimus, III, *Mechanical Artificial Ventilation*, 2nd ed. (Springfield, Ill.: Charles C Thomas, 1970), p. 11.

BIBLIOGRAPHY

Egan, Donald F., *Fundamentals of Inhalation Therapy*. St. Louis: C. V. Mosby Company, 1969, p. 11.

Secor, Jane, *Patient Care in Respiratory Problems*. Philadelphia: W. B. Saunders Company, 1969.

Petty, Thomas and Louise Nett, *For Those Who Live and Breathe with Emphysema and Chronic Bronchitis*. Springfield, Ill.: Charles C. Thomas, 1967.

Thacher, Edith W., *Postural Drainage and Respiratory Control*, 2nd ed. London: Lloyd-Luke, 1959.

MAINTENANCE OF VENTILATION IN CARDIOPULMONARY EMERGENCIES

The maintenance of ventilation is a critical factor in cardiac resuscitation. Furthermore, the need for ventilatory support occurs in a wide variety of other clinical situations, especially in the critical care unit.

This outline, for critical care nurses, is designed to review briefly the function of the lungs, the management of respiratory emergencies, the need for blood gas monitoring of patients, and oxygen therapy.

The function of the lung is to arterialize venous blood (add oxygen to unsaturated venous blood) and to eliminate carbon dioxide. This is the goal of external or mechanical ventilation during cardiac resuscitation. The functions of the lung are achieved by three mechanisms which must occur concomitantly: (1) ventilation, i.e., movement of air in and out of the lungs, (2) diffusion of gases across the alveolar-capillary membrane, and (3) circulation of blood through the pulmonary capillary bed.

To emphasize the need for ventilatory support in a variety of respiratory emergencies examples have been outlined in Table 8-1. In some of these emergencies only the respiratory system is involved. On the other hand, a number of these situations may be present in a single patient, having resulted as a complication of cardiac arrest. Another possibility is that a respiratory emergency may result from one of the causes listed, and because of resultant hypoxia a cardiac arrhythmia or arrest may ensue. One must never fail to remember that, the interdependent associations of the cardiac and pulmonary systems frequently causes an emergency affecting hypoxia to affect arrhythmia.

Table 8-1 draws attention to the problem of obstruction of major and minor airways which may impair ventilation. Often attempts at assisted ventilation are ineffective because of obstruction of the upper airways with foreign bodies such as food, vomitus, or dentures. Laryngospasm and laryngoedema can occur as a result of food or drug allergy and can be life-threatening. Severe bronchospasm secondary to anaphylaxis may also occur.

Respiratory center depression can occur from a variety of drugs and anesthetic agents. The apnea that occurs during cardiac arrest is most likely the result of hypoxia of the respiratory center. The use of oxygen in a high-flow, uncontrolled manner can also suppress respiration. This will be discussed in more detail below under Oxygen Therapy.

Neuromuscular defects which affect the "bellows action" of the respiratory muscles should be mentioned. It is important to bring attention to the idiosyncrasies of several drugs—Colistin, Kanamycin, Streptomycin and Neomycin—which have caused transient respiratory paralysis. The exact mechanism by which this occurs is unknown.

Decreased lung and thorax expansion can cause failure of the respiratory apparatus. It is now appreciated that ascites, peritonitis, and abdominal surgery may precipitate respiratory failure because of poor diaphragmatic motion. This may occur in patients who have no prior lung disease.

Under acute diffusion problems, the one of importance with regard to the present discussion is acute pulmonary edema. This is an ever-present danger in cardiac patients.

The problems of respiratory failure in chronic lung disease have been omitted from this discussion purposely. However, the principles for supporting ventilation are essentially the same as outlined for the other entities.

Management of the Respiratory Emergency

Table 8-2 outlines the important aspects for maintaining ventilatory support. The airways must be patent. This can usually be accomplished with an oral-pharyngeal airway for the immediate establishment of ventilation. The placement of an endotracheal tube should be done by an experienced person. Too often valuable time is lost in the attempt by an inexperienced individual to perform this critical function. During placement the patient is not ventilated. Most generally, at least initially, adequate ventilation can be accomplished with a face mask, an oral-pharyngeal airway, and a self-inflating resuscitation bag.

A tracheostomy is rarely an emergency procedure in the respiratory emergency. In the majority of cases an endotracheal or nasotracheal tube can be placed. After an endotracheal tube is in place and the emergency situation under control, then, if necessary, a tracheostomy can be performed over the endotracheal tube.

If an endotracheal tube cannot be placed because of severe upper airway obstruction, then a tracheostomy or an opening through the cricothyroid membrane (cricothyroidotomy) must be performed immediately. Tracheotomes and other such "gadgets" should not be used.

Ventilation must be provided. This can be started at once by the mouth-to-mouth method if a self-inflating resuscitation bag is not available. However, the self-resuscitation bag should be a part of *every* emergency tray along with endotracheal tubes, oral-pharyngeal airways, and a laryngoscope. Such emergency equipment *should be* in every critical care unit, ward, and emergency room. A mechanical respiratory (IPPB) should *never* be used for emergency ventilatory support or during external cardiac massage. Once the emergency situation is controlled and if the patient still requires ventilatory support, then time can be taken to attach and adjust a respirator. If a respirator (IPPB) apparatus should fail on a patient requiring assisted or controlled ventilation, it should be disconnected at once and ventilation continued with the self-inflating resuscitation bag until help arrives.

In ventilating patients with a resuscitation bag, a slow rate (10–12/minute) with deep breaths provides the best gas exchange. If the self-inflating bag holds approximately 1,000–1,200 cc., 10 breaths per minute will provide a minute ventilation of 10–12 L./minute. This is hyperventilation, but it is undoubtedly the best approach during the emergency phase. Adjustments can be made later as dictated by blood gas analysis.

Additional oxygen should be provided when using the resuscitation bag, which can be administered from a tank or wall service.

During respiratory emergencies general cardiovascular support must also be provided. Obviously, adequate perfusion of the pulmonary capillary bed and the peripheral tissues must be maintained.

It is well recognized that metabolic acidosis develops within minutes whenever the tissues are poorly perfused and hypoxia develops. Anaerobic metabolism causes the production of lactic acid which can create profound acidemia (increased H^+ and a drop in pH). Consequently, during cardiac arrest sodium bicarbonate is always given intravenously. Acidemia will hinder the restoration of normal cardiac rhythm and aggravate peripheral vascular collapse. The monitoring of the arterial blood pH is important in determining the amount of bicarbonate necessary to return the pH to normal (pH 7.35–7.45). Usually 2–6 ampules of sodium bicarbonate (44 mEq./ampule) are needed.

Blood Gas Monitoring

Modern laboratory equipment makes it possible to obtain rapid, accurate determinations of the arterial blood oxygen saturation, PCO_2 (partial pressure of carbon dioxide) and pH. Monitoring patients who require mechanical ventilation with arterial blood gas analyses is the only reliable method of determining the effect of such support. Bedside impressions regarding the presence or absence of cyanosis has been proven to be an unreliable index of estimating arterial oxygen saturation. Samples of arterial blood are easily and safely obtained.

Oxygen Therapy

It has now become well recognized that arterial oxygen unsaturation (hypoxemia) can occur in a variety of clinical situations in patients *without* chronic lung disease such as emphysema or chronic bronchitis. This hypoxemia is further aggravated by the decreased partial pressure of oxygen in the air at Denver.

When a patient has chronic lung disease or congestive heart failure severe hypoxemia may be present. Severe hypoxemia may be present *without cyanosis*. Subtle and early signs of hypoxemia may be restlessness or any change in mental behavior. A tachycardia or change in blood pressure may also signal arterial oxygen unsaturation.

Therefore in the cardiac patient the use of additional oxygen appears very important. It has been found that the nasal prongs (double nasal cannula) is an ideal way to supply a small amount of additional oxygen (contrary to what has been reported in a recent nursing journal). The nasal prongs allow the patient to eat, drink, and converse while receiving constant oxygen.

The goal of this type of oxygen therapy is *not* to supply 100 percent oxygen, but to make certain that the arterial oxygen is maintained in the normal range. This is practically always achieved with low flow, controlled oxygen, usually 3L./minute. Oxygen wall gauges are frequently in error and should be checked.

The concern with oxygen administration in patient with chronic bronchitis and emphysema has always been the removal of the hypoxic drive of respiration. This has undoubtedly been overly exaggerated. Studies at the University of Colorado Medical Center have shown that only a minority of patients with emphysema or chronic bronchitis will retain carbon dioxide if oxygen is used at *low flows*. High flow, uncontrolled, unmonitored oxygen can be dangerous and should not be used.

The fear of respiratory depression should not cause oxygen to be withheld. The minority of patients who do retain carbon dioxide need assisted or controlled ventilation. Hypoxemia must be corrected.

Once oxygen has been ordered, even though it is only at 3L./minute, it should never be stopped without a doctor's order. Allowing the oxygen to be discontinued may cause sudden drop in arterial oxygen saturation with catastrophic effects on the cardiovascular system.

Summary

The need for ventilatory support is always present during cardiac resuscitation. However, respiratory emergencies can occur in many clinical situations, and these possibilities must be appreciated by the critical care nurse.

Managing the respiratory emergency entails maintaining an open airway and providing ventilation, ideally with the self-inflating resuscitation bag. A mechanical respirator (IPPB) machine is not the emergency equipment to be used.

Blood gas analysis is important in monitoring the efficiency of ventilatory support and the acid-base status.

The use of low-flow, controlled oxygen therapy is important in the cardiac patient due to the hypoxemia which frequently exists.

TABLE 8-1
ACUTE RESPIRATORY EMERGENCIES

I. Impaired Ventilation
    A. Obstructed Major and Minor Airways
        1. Foreign bodies: food, vomitus, teeth, tongue, blood, fluid, etc.
        2. Laryngospasm, laryngoedema, epiglottitis
        3. Bronchospasm (anaphylaxis), acute status asthmaticus
    B. Respiratory Center Damage or Depression
        1. Narcotics, barbiturates, hypnotics, tranquilizers, sedatives, etc.
        2. Anesthetics
        3. Cerebral infarction or trauma
        4. Cardiac arrest
        5. High-flow, uncontrolled oxygen therapy
    C. Neuromuscular Defects
        1. Myasthenia gravis, "cholinergic crisis"
        2. Guillain-Barré syndrome, multiple sclerosis, polio
        3. Drug toxicity: colistin, kanamycin, streptomycin, neomycin
        4. Parathion poisoning (acetyl cholinesterase inhibitor)
        5. High spinal anesthesia
    D. Decreased Lung and Thorax Expansion
        1. Pneumothorax
        2. Hemothorax
        3. Costal trauma
        4. Ascites, peritonitis, abdominal surgery
II. Acute Diffusion Problems
    A. Acute pulmonary edema
    B. Smoke inhalation
    C. Chlorine, mustard, phosgene, SO_2, NO, NO_2 inhalation
III. Miscellaneous
    A. Lung hemorrhage
    B. Drownings
    C. CO poisoning

TABLE 8-2
MANAGEMENT OF RESPIRATORY EMERGENCIES

I. Open Airway
    A. Oral pharyngeal airway
    B. Endotracheal tube
    C. Tracheostomy
    D. Cricothyroidotomy

II.   Ventilate
    A. Mouth-to-mouth
    B. Self-inflating resuscitation bag
    C. Respirator (not emergency equipment)
III. Oxygenate
IV. Provide general cardiovascular support
V.   Be aware of possible complicating acidosis

INTUBATION: A NEW ROLE FOR NURSE SPECIALISTS IN CARDIOPULMONARY EMERGENCIES

Introduction

The prompt use of endotracheal intubation in treating a cardiac arrest or pulmonary emergency is thought by some to improve the chances of survival. Others feel that the establishment of ventilatory support with intubation is not necessary in cardiopulmonary resuscitation.

Intubation during cardiopulmonary emergencies from whatever cause provides an open airway allowing controlled ventilation with a self-inflating bag supplied with oxygen. Aspiration of vomitus often occurs when the stomach becomes distended with air while ventilating with a resuscitation bag and mask alone for a prolonged interval. Endotracheal intubation isolates the trachea from the gastrointestinal tract, thus preventing the catastrophe of aspiration. This treatise is written in support of the use of endotracheal intubation in these cases.

When the critical patient is first seen he should receive a few breaths with oropharyngeal airway, mask, and self-inflating bag connected to oxygen. Then, when further resuscitation is still needed, rapid and skillful intubation should be performed. However, care should be taken not to waste time in unsuccessful attempts at intubation by inexperienced personnel. Care must also be exercised in avoiding use of oropharyngeal airways that are too long and may stimulate vomiting in patients with full stomachs.

Need for Experienced Personnel

The ideal method for handling cardiopulmonary emergencies in a general hospital is to have a physician skilled in endotracheal intubation and well versed in the physiology and pharmocology of cardiopulmonary emergencies available for 24 hours a day, 7 days a week. In most hospitals this is essentially impossible.

This fact has lead to the creation of a new role for nurses. Well-motivated, intelligent nurses can be trained to provide respiratory support in cardiopulmonary emergencies on a 24-hour basis during the absence of a well-qualified physician. This plan extends the new concept of the critical care nurse who has learned to take responsibility for observation and interpretation of signs and symptoms of impending cardiopulmonary emergencies.

Now the carefully trained Nurse Specialist can participate in the continuous delivery of critical care, not only in the recognition of cardiopulmonary emergencies but also in its management in the absence of a physician.

An Approach to Cardiopulmonary Emergencies

All too frequently chaos develops when a cardiopulmonary emergency occurs. This problem has been solved in one community hospital as follows:

The chief of staff appointed a committee for planning appropriate management of "Cor Zero" (the code word used to alert the hospital team of a cardiopulmonary emergency that exists) or cardiopulmonary emergencies, consisting of one physician from each specialty including internal medicine, surgery, orthopedics, and anesthesiology. The committee proposed a team approach by allied medical personnel and developed a detailed protocol for this purpose. The protocol specified objectives, identified members, and described the responsibilities of the team. Specific actions to be taken by the team were as follows.

1. Nursing specialists trained in cardiopulmonary resusitation direct the "Cor Zero." A coronary care Nurse Specialist is the team leader. The pulmonary Nurse Specialist performs pulmonary resuscitation and endotracheal intubation when indicated. When the attending physician is present, he may direct the cardiopulmonary resuscitation or he may ask the Nurse Specialist team to continue to direct and carry out the procedures. All other physicians not well versed in cardiopulmonary resuscitation are expected to leave the procedure in the hands of the Nurse Specialist team.

2. The nurse leader may ask for and supervise assistance from other allied medical personnel, for cardiac massage, the drawing of blood, the administration of drugs, the starting of I.V.'s or the acting as recorders of events.

3. The parent Cor Zero committee of physicians takes full responsibility for the actions of the cardiopulmonary resuscitation team.

4. The leader may ask for assistance from physicians who may be present.

5. The team continues resuscitation until directed to stop by the attending physician, by a member of the Cor Zero committee, or by any qualified physician who is at the scene.

6. All nursing specialists assigned to the cardiopulmonary resuscitation team are required to meet once a month for a critical review of their performance by physicians especially qualified in the management of cardiopulmonary disease.

7. Any criticisms of the cardiopulmonary team must be submitted in writing to the parent committee.

Three matters of paramount importance deserve special comment.

A. In most hospitals, especially those with limited house staff or none at all, physicians trained and experienced in cardiopulmonary resuscitation are not available during many hours of each day. Many specialized and otherwise well-qualified physicians have had only an occasional exposure to cardio-pulmonary emergencies. When physicians not familiar with cardiopulmonary emergencies answer a Cor Zero without previous plan or organization, chaos is common. To have modern coronary care and critical care units without a plan to provide effective cardiopulmonary resuscitation on a 24-hour basis tends to defeat the purpose of such units.

B. The concept had to be developed that Nurse Specialists could act on the orders of physicians and be under their supervision without their physical presence. This concept and protocol was approved by the Colorado State Board of Medical Examiners as not in conflict with the Colorado Medical Practice Act.

C. Cardiopulmonary resuscitation, including endotracheal intubation, performed by the Nurse Specialist *in the absence of a physician* is highly justified and logical when the gravity of the situation is considered. For the patient who has suffered a cardiopulmonary catastrophe, death is imminent, if not inevitable. Immediate and precise efforts at resuscitation including cardiac massage, defibrillation, endotracheal intubation, respiratory support, and intravenous drugs are potentially lifesaving.

Recognizing and Managing Cardiopulmonary Emergencies

Cardiopulmonary emergencies often arise in a variety of clinical situations without previous warning. The nurse must be aware of these many and varied clinical situations in which such catastrophic events frequently occur.

In the coronary care unit the patient who develops complications such as arrhythmias, hypotension, and congestive heart failure, or has a recurrence of the chest pain, is the most likely candidate for a cardiopulmonary catastrophe. Similar situations may occur with patients in the emergency room, intensive care unit, recovery room, or even on a general medical or surgical ward. Cardiopulmonary emergencies and the need for intubation often occur without warning and are abruptly announced by apnea. In other situations the need for intubation and assisted and/or controlled ventilation may be recognized only by arterial blood gas analysis—sometimes the sole means of recognizing serious life-threatening hypercarbia or hypoxemia.

The nurse should be aware that hypercarbia and hypoxemia have many *non*specific manifestations such as restlessness, confusion, irritability, and somnolence. She should be alert to the patient's clinical appearance, noting the degree of respiratory distress, level of consciousness, excursion of the thorax and abdomen, skin color, and temperature along with the classical vital signs.

An understanding with the attending physician regarding the nurse's use of arterial blood gas analysis in evaluating seriously ill patients is of paramount importance. Permission to collect arterial blood in seriously ill patients is usually quite easy to obtain if the physician realizes that the nursing personnel have been trained in recognizing the clinical indications of impending respiratory failure, in the technique of arterial puncture, and in the interpretation of the arterial blood gas analysis.

Training for Endotracheal Intubation

Endotracheal intubation is a skill that can be accomplished by physicians or paramedical personnel who posses proper knowledge of the anatomy, have received expert instruction, and are given an opportunity to practice the new-found skill. A limiting factor for a nurse to maintain her skill of endotracheal intubation, once it has been perfected, is having enough opportunities to use the technique.

It is not the purpose of this chapter to discuss the specific technique of endotracheal intubation, which has been described completely elsewhere. The Nurse Specialist who is assigned the responsibility of emergency endotracheal intubation must have expert instruction, accomplished through training with an experienced anesthesiologist who must believe that training of the Nurse Specialist is of vital importance. The nurse, under the supervision of an anesthesiologist, goes to the operating room and gains experience in endotracheal intubation on anesthetized, relaxed patients who are in need of such management. Only after mastering the technique under these ideal conditions is she ready to begin handling emergency situations. To maintain this skill the nurse needs to have opportunities to use her techniques frequently, or she must return to the operating suite at regular intervals to improve her proficiency under a physician's supervision. The use of cadavers and/or dummy models provide only limited and inadequate experience for training in endotracheal intubation.

With such training as described above a group of nurse specialists have achieved a greater than 85 percent success rate in emergency endotracheal intubations.

Equipment

The availability of proper equipment and an understanding of its purpose is essential. A standardized set of intubation equipment should be instantly available at all times. Attaché cases can be easily adapted using pegboard and rubber tubing to secure the equipment for convenient checking and rapid use (Fig. 8-2 and 8-3).

Laryngoscopes must be available in various sizes and have either straight or curved blades. Individual preference seems to be the basis for choice between the straight blade which picks up the epiglottis directly and the curved blade which inserts into the glossoepiglottic groove (above the epiglottis) and indirectly lifts the epiglottis from the laryngeal opening. Some experts consider the curved blade of greater benefit in avoiding trauma to the subepiglottic mucosa and providing more room for insertion of the tube. A #3 or #4 curved blade is adequate for most medium to large adults. A #1 or #2 curved blade is adequate for children from age three months to age 9; smaller straight blades are available for newborn and premature infants. Both straight and curved blades in adult and pediatric sizes should be a part of each emergency intubation setup. Fresh batteries to insure brightly lighted laryngoscopic bulbs are a crucial requirement.

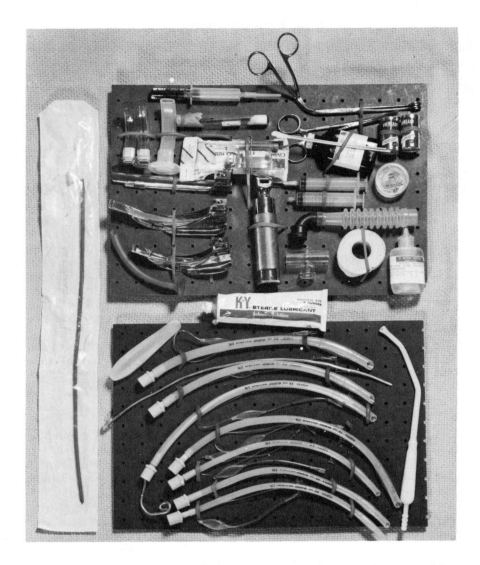

Fig. 8-2. Two sections of pegboard are cut to fit inside an attache case. Rubber tubing is utilized to secure standardized intubation equipment to the pegboard.

Various types of intubation tubes are available. The portex polyvinyl chloride disposable tubes with the large cylindrical cuff are excellent. These cuffs are reliable since they are used only once. The firmness of this tube is a desirable aide in intubation. Multiple use rubber tubes are also available in French sizes. Standardized 15-mm. adaptors allowing a tube of any kind to

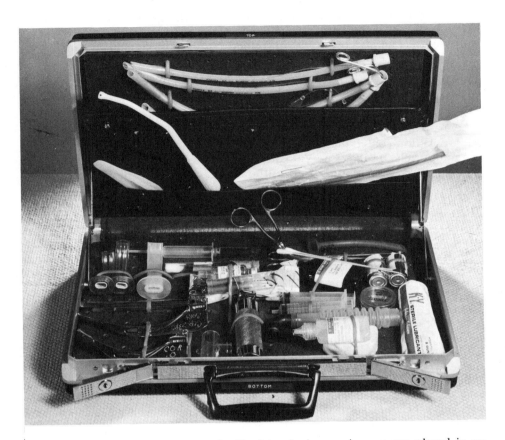

Fig. 8-3. Pegboards holding standardized intubation equipment are placed in an attache case. The middle divider in the case separates the intubation tubes from the other equipment.

be attached to a self-inflating bag unit or respirator is mandatory. French gauge tubes between sizes F32 and F36 for adult females and between sizes F34 and F40 for adult males will be utilized most frequently. In our experience, Portex tubes between sizes 6 mm. ID. and 7 mm. ID. for adult males will be utilized most frequently.

A good rule of thumb for children is as follows: The age of the child in years + 18 equals the French size required. Experienced anesthesiologists state that a tube which fits through the nares will most likely pass through the vocal cords. Preparation of two tubes, one of the estimated size and one of size smaller, is a good procedure to follow.

Stylets are often placed inside tubes as an aide to insertion. Stylets should be firm, curved at one end, and long enough to bend easily over the adaptor end of the endotracheal tube. Inserting the stylets and curving the endotracheal tube often aids in guiding the tube to the glottic opening. The upward curve of the tube aids in entering the glottic opening rather than the esophagus. The stylets should be pulled back approximately ½ inch from the end of the tube to prevent trauma. Bending the proximal end of the stylets over the adaptor on the endotracheal tube stabilizes the position of the stylets and aids in removal. A stylet may easily perforate the trachea if not stabilized in this manner.

Suction catheters must be immediately available and should be of two types. The Yankauer pharyngeal suction tip is handy for cleaning the oropharynx, while a Teflon-coated plastic catheter is used for evacuation of secretions from the endotracheal tube. The Yankauer suction tip is rigid, allowing it to be easily introduced and manipulated in the oral cavity. The Teflon-coated plastic suction catheter does not stick to the endotracheal tube and is of adequate length for deep suctioning. Other equipment included in the attaché cases are anesthetic water-soluble jelly for lubrication of the endotracheal tube, a 10-cc. syringe for inflation of the tracheal cuff, a rubber-sheathed forceps to prevent air leak from the cuff, one-inch tape, and tincture of benzoin.

Immediate evaluation of tube placement is achieved by observing equal chest expansion and by auscultation of both sides of the chest for equal breath sounds, indicating equal ventilation of both lungs. Decreased breath sounds on the left usually indicate intubation of the right main stem bronchus and inadequate ventilation of the left lung. Intubation of the right main stem bronchus is a common error and occurs easily because it is more vertical in position. A chest X-ray should be obtained to accurately define the placement of the tube as soon as the patient's condition permits. This is ordered by the nurse according to protocol.

Securing the tube in proper position is mandatory for adequate ventilation and to prevent accidental extubation. Not infrequently, as patients arouse, they may become combative and wrist restraints as well as sedation with drugs such as Valium may become necessary. Applying tincture of benzoin to each cheek and to the upper lip insures good adhesion of the tape. Secure the tube by using one-inch tape beginning on the skin beneath the ear lobe encircling the tube, crossing the upper lip, and continuing down beneath the opposite ear lobe. Lower jaw motion and/or secretions do not loosen the tube when it is taped in this manner.

An oral-pharyngeal airway is inserted into the oral cavity. It can be taped to the endotracheal tube to secure good positioning. The oral-pharyngeal airway prevents the patient from biting on the endotracheal tube and obstructing his ventilation. It also provides a route for oral suctioning.

The self-inflating bag connected to oxygen is the ideal way to ventilate the patient via an endotracheal tube during the initial phase of cardiopulmonary resuscitation until he can be moved to a critical care unit where a mechanical respirator can be applied for continued ventilatory support. Using the self-inflating bag, one can match the patient's respirations breath for breath, easily coordinate respirations with cardiac massage, and provide whatever volume is needed to ventilate the patient.

Important points to remember when utilizing the self-inflating bag attached to the endotracheal tube are the following:

1. If the patient has spontaneous efforts, it may be wise to follow and assist these at certain times. At other times the patient's rate and pattern may be inappropriate and controlled ventilation must be accomplished.
2. Hyperventilation in patients with chronic airway obstruction having a pCO_2 above 50 should be avoided. Excessive ventilation may lower the pCO_2 too rapidly, causing seizures, hypotension, and/or cardiac arrythmias.
3. Care must be taken in adding oxygen to the self-inflating bag. The valves on some bags may lock in the inspiratory position with oxygen flow rates of as low as 5–10 L./min. The locked valve prevents patient exhalation. A locked valve should be suspected when each inspiration requires greater pressure on the bag. The bag should be immediately removed from the endotracheal tube to allow the patient to exhale the trapped air.

Inserting a nasogastric tube after intubation is valuable in evacuating air and other stomach contents. Subsequent abdominal distention and possible vomiting with aspiration are thus avoided.

Attitude

A discussion of such a new and controversial responsibility as intubation by the Nurse Specialist deserves some comment. Troublesome attitudes regarding these new responsibilities and functions of the nurse originate both from other nurses and from physicians.

Taking responsibility for techniques that deal with life-and-death situations is a new concept for nurses. We are in the early stages of developing such concepts. Consequently, many nurses are hesitant to take on duties which involve such responsibilities. Proper support from supervising physicians and hospital administration is necessary for the nurse to have enough confidence to proceed with her training. Having physicians who are eager and willing to train nurses in these skills is also important. A positive attitude by the nurse with regard to her new role in performing intubation during cardiopulmonary emergencies is a prime requirement for success. Subjective feelings concerning the patient, his condition, his family, and her own state of self-confidence are very real experiences. The nurse will have to recognize and explore such feelings before facing these tasks. The ability to become objective during cardiopulmonary emergencies and to utilize the knowledge she does possess is necessary for a successful intubation. She will also have to face up to and deal with failure.

Attitude is important in the training situation as well. This type of training is new for nurses. For the first time she may be using cadavers who have not survived cardiopulmonary resuscitation. Nurses who are not used to such an experience may feel that this is "practicing" on a patient and depriving him of his final dignity. Receiving instruction from a physician in a technique which has been the responsibility only of physicians is another new experience. Approaching these new challenges with a positive attitude is the only way the nurse can achieve success.

As the nurse is asked to take on more responsibility, especially to assume roles that heretofore have been handled by physicians, she should expect to meet resistance. The nurse must remember that anyone who has pioneered in the field of medicine has always met resistance. Only when these new programs gain wider acceptance will she find that physicians, administration, and allied medical personnel will acknowledge the value of such programs. Consequently, while the Nurse Specialist concept is in its infancy, the nurse must be prepared to face skepticism, criticism, and resistance from many sectors of the health care team. As with any new project, the nurse must proceed with a positive attitude, physician supervision and direction, and close adherence to principle and protocol.

Summary

This section was designed to describe one new facet of the Nurse Specialist in cardiopulmonary resuscitation. Since cardiopulmonary emergencies occur in a wide variety of clinical settings, the need for immediate cardiopulmonary resuscitation is imperative at all times in any hospital. In community hospitals physicians expert in endotracheal intubation are often not available when needed. To manage cardiopulmonary resuscitation properly it has naturally evolved that a Nurse Specialist can and should be expert in pulmonary resuscitation and be able to intubate when indicated. Through physician supervision and guidance by a protocol with expert training by anesthesiologists, Nurse Specialists have successfully acquired this new technique.

A description of the manner in which one community hospital approached these problems has been described along with discussions of how the pulmonary Nurse Specialist must plan and organize for cardiopulmonary emergencies.

BIBLIOGRAPHY

Fillmore, S. J., M. Shapiro, and T. Killip, "Serial Blood Gas Studies During Cardiopulmonary Resuscitation," *Annals of Medicine,* Vol. 72, (1970), p. 465.

Talmage, E. A., "House Officer Training for Cardiovascular Resuscitation," *Guthrie Clinical Bulletin,* Vol. 41, (1971), p. 40.

Milstein, B. B., *Cardiac Arrest and Resuscitation.* Chicago: Year Book Medical Publishers, 1963, pp. 121–128.

Lissauer, W. S., and D. B. Bigelow, Cardiopulmonary Resuscitation, A New Role for Nurses. To be published.

Grace, W. J., "Intensive Care—What Are We Talking About?" *Heart and Lung,* Vol. 1, (1972), p. 187.

Bigelow, D. B., R. L. Petty, D. G. Ashbaugh, B. E. Levine, M. Nett, and S. Tyler, "Acute Respiratory Failure (Experiences of a Respiratory Care Unit)," *Medical Clinics of North America,* Vol. 51, No. 2 (March 1967), p. 323.

Sitzman, J. E., "Nursing Management of the Acutely Ill Respiratory Patient," *Heart and Lung,* Vol. 1, No. 2 (March–April 1972), p. 207.

Safar, P., and D. F. Proctor, *Respiratory Therapy.* Philadelphia: F. A. Davis Company, 1965, pp. 29–92.

Garvin, J. P., W. B. Neptune, L. W. Pratt, and P. Safar, "Saving the Asphyxiating Patient," *Patient Care,* June 15, 1971, p. 22.

Votteri, B. A., "Hand-Operated Emergency Ventilation Devices," *Heart and Lung,* Vol. 1, No. 2 (March–April, 1972), p. 277.

9

Assessment Skills for the Nurse

JOSEPH O. BROUGHTON, M.D.

UNDERSTANDING BLOOD GASES

Blood gases are obtained in a variety of clinical situations, but they are obtained for two major reasons: (1) to determine if the patient is well oxygenated, and (2) to determine the acid base status of the patient, concentrating on either the respiratory component, the metabolic (nonrespiratory) component, or most often, both respiratory and metabolic components of a patient's acid base status. In the following discussion, the term *nonrespiratory* will be used interchangeable with the term *metabolic*.

Most often blood gases are measured on arterial blood rather than venous blood for two reasons.

1. Studying arterial blood is a good way to sample a mixture of blood that has come from various parts of the body. Blood obtained from a vein in an extremity gives information mostly about that extremity and can be quite misleading if the metabolism in the extremity differs from the metabolism of the body as a whole, as it often does. This difference is accentuated if the extremity is cold or underperfused as in a patient in shock, or if the patient has done local exercise with the extremity such as opening and closing his fist, or if there is local infection in the extremity, etc. Sometimes blood is sampled through a central venous catheter (CVP catheter) in hopes of getting mixed venous blood, but even in the superior vena cava or right atrium where a CVP catheter ends there is usually incomplete mixing of venous blood from various parts of the body. For complete mixing of the blood, one would have to obtain a blood sample from the right ventricle or pulmonary artery, and even then one would not get information about how well the lungs are oxygenating the blood.

2. The second reason for selecting *arterial* blood is that it gives the added

information of how well the lungs are oxygenating the blood. Oxygen measurements of CVP blood can tell if the tissues are getting oxygenated, but cannot separate the contribution of the heart from that of the lungs. In other words, if the CVP oxygen is low it means that either heart or lungs or both are at fault. So if CVP blood has a low oxygen concentration, it means either (a) that the lungs have not oxygenated the arterial blood well and that when the tissues extract their usual amount of oxygen from arterial blood, the resulting venous blood has a low oxygen concentration, or (b) that the heart is not circulating the blood well so that it is taking blood a long time to circulate through the tissues. The tissues, therefore, must extract more than the usual amount of oxygen from each cardiac cycle since the blood is flowing slowly. This produces a low venous O_2 concentration. If it is known that the arterial oxygen concentration is normal (indicating that the lungs are doing their job), but the mixed venous oxygen concentration is low, then one can infer that the heart and circulation are failing.

One advantage of using mixed venous blood instead of arterial blood is that if the oxygen concentration in mixed venous blood is normal, one can infer that the tissues are receiving enough oxygen—that is both ventilation and circulation are adequate.

Oxygen

There are three ways to measure oxygen in blood: (1) the number of ml. of oxygen carried by 100 ml. of blood, (2) the pO_2 or pressure exerted by oxygen dissolved in the plasma, and (3) the oxygen saturation of hemoglobin which is a measure of the percentage of oxygen that hemoglobin is carrying related to the total amount the hemoglobin could carry, or

$$O_2 \text{ Sat} = \frac{\text{Amount of oxygen that hemoglobin is carrying}}{\text{Maximum amount of oxygen that hemoglobin can carry}} \times 100$$

The first of these three methods is the easiest to understand but the most difficult to measure, so it is not used routinely. The latter two methods which are used routinely are more understandable when compared to the first method in the table below. Each gram of hemoglobin in 100 ml. of blood can carry a maximum of 1.34 ml. of oxygen, so if a patient has 15 gm. Hgb./100 ml. blood, then each 100 ml. of blood can carry 15×1.34 cc. or 20.1 cc. of oxygen. If hemoglobin is only 97 percent saturated (carrying 97 percent of the total it is able to carry), then it carries 97 percent of 20.1 ml. or 19.5 ml.

TABLE 9-1
HOW OXYGEN IS CARRIED IN BLOOD

Dissolved in plasma .... 0.3 ml./100 ml. blood ....Reflected by pO_2 90 mm. Hg
Combined with Hgb. ......19.5 ml./100 ml. blood ....Reflected by O_2 Sat Hgb. 97%
Total in whole blood......19.8 ml./100 ml. blood

The table reminds us that the majority of oxygen carried by the blood is carried by hemoglobin, and that a very small amount is dissolved in plasma. The percent saturation of hemoglobin with oxygen, then, gives a close estimate of the total amount of oxygen carried in blood. The pO_2 measurement, however, tells only of the pressure exerted by the small amount of oxygen that is dissolved in plasma. pO_2 is widely used and is valuable because the relationship between pO_2 (pressure of oxygen dissolved in plasma) and O_2 Sat of Hgb. (which is closely related to the total oxygen content of whole blood) are related to each other in a definite fashion and the relationship has been charted — the oxyhemoglobin dissociation curve. (See Table 9-1.) When the pO_2 in plasma is high, Hgb. carries much oxygen. When the pO_2 is low, Hgb. carries less oxygen. Once this relation is known, pO_2 is just as valuable as a measurement of total O_2 content or the percentage of oxygen that hemoglobin is carrying. The relationship between pO_2 and O_2 saturation of hemoglobin is not a linear one, so that as for a given rise or fall in pO_2 there is not always the same amount of rise or fall in O_2 saturation of hemoglobin. Instead, for very low pO_2 a rise in pO_2 is associated with more rapid rise in O_2 saturation and for pO_2 in the normal range or higher, a rise in pO_2 is associated with a very small rise in O_2 saturation. This relationship is much easier to understand if one looks at the oxygen dissociation curve for hemoglobin. In simple terms, the dissociation curve indicates that environments where the pO_2 is high, such as the capillaries of the lungs, hemoglobin combines with and carries a high percentage of the total oxygen it could carry; in environments where the pO_2 is low, such as the capillaries in the tissues, hemoglobin carries a lower percentage of the total oxygen it could carry, having given up the difference in oxygen for use by the tissues.

The dissociation curve presented applies only to normal conditions. In the presence of acidosis or fever, the entire dissociation curve is shifted to the right, so that for a given oxygen saturation the pO_2 is greater than usual, and more oxygen is available for the tissues. In the presence of alkalosis, hemoglobin is more stingy and for a given oxygen solution, the pO_2 is lower than usual. Certain abnormal types of hemoglobin may shift the dissociation curve to the right or the left and the presence of certain compounds such as 2,3 diphosphoglycerate (2,3 DPG) may also shift the dissociation curve. 2,3 DPG in excess amounts shifts the curve to the right, thereby making more oxygen available to the tissues for a given O_2 Sat of Hgb.

One should always relate the oxygen content of blood to the FIO_2 the fractional percentage of oxygen in the inspired air. For instance, an O_2 saturation of Hgb. of 96 percent is normal if the patient is breathing room air which has an FIO_2 of 21, but is quite abnormal if the FIO_2 is 40, for instance. Some hospitals formally measure the A-a oxygen gradient, (the difference between pO_2 in alveolar air and pO_2 in arterial blood) but much the same information can be obtained if one compares the paO_2 or O_2 Sat of Hgb. to the FIO_2.

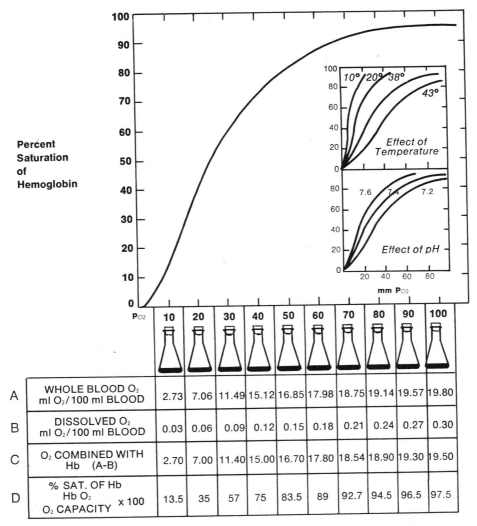

		10	20	30	40	50	60	70	80	90	100
A	WHOLE BLOOD O₂ ml O₂/100 ml BLOOD	2.73	7.06	11.49	15.12	16.85	17.98	18.75	19.14	19.57	19.80
B	DISSOLVED O₂ ml O₂/100 ml BLOOD	0.03	0.06	0.09	0.12	0.15	0.18	0.21	0.24	0.27	0.30
C	O₂ COMBINED WITH Hb (A-B)	2.70	7.00	11.40	15.00	16.70	17.80	18.54	18.90	19.30	19.50
D	% SAT. OF Hb Hb O₂ / O₂ CAPACITY × 100	13.5	35	57	75	83.5	89	92.7	94.5	96.5	97.5

Fig. 9-1. HbO_2 dissociation curves. The large graph shows a single dissociation curve, applicable when the pH of the blood is 7.40 and temperature 38° C. The blood O_2 tension and saturation of patients with CO_2 retention, acidosis, alkalosis, fever, or hypothermia will not fit this curve because the curve shifts to the right when temperature, pH, or pCO₂ is changed. Effects on the HbO₂ dissociation curve of change in temperature and in pH are shown in the smaller graphs. [From: Julius H. Comroe, Jr., *Physiology of Respiration* (Chicago: Year Book Medical Publishers).]

Normal values for blood gases are given in Table 9-2. Following this the main emphasis will concern acid-base interpretation.

TABLE 9-2
NORMAL BLOOD GAS VALUES

	ARTERIAL BLOOD	MIXED VENOUS BLOOD
pH	7.40 (7.35–7.45)	7.36 (7.31–7.41)
pO_2	80–100 mm. Hg	35–40 mm. Hg
O_2 Sat	95% or greater	70–75%
pCO_2	35–45 mm. Hg	41–51 mm. Hg
HCO_3	22–26 mEq./L.	22–26 mEq./L.
Base excess (B.E.)	−2–+2	−2–+2

The normal values for blood gas parameters are given in Table 9-2. Note that only three of these—pO_2, O_2 saturation, and pCO_2—are actually measurements of gases. However, all should be determined in blood gas analyses. It is imperative that a measure of the nonrespiratory (or metabolic) component be included, and actual HCO_3 and base excess are the most useful. Many other terms may be given on a blood gas report, but you need to be concerned only with the ones listed in Table 9-2.

Older persons have values for pO_2 and O_2 saturation near the lower part of the normal range, and younger people tend to have high normal values.

Normal values for mixed venous blood are more variable than for arterial blood but representative normals are given in Table 9-2. There is not enough difference in normal values HCO_3 and base excess between arterial and mixed venous blood to warrant remembering a different set of values for venous blood.

TABLE 9-3
DEFINITIONS

Acid: A substance that can donate hydrogen ions, H^+. Example:

$$H_2CO_3 \longrightarrow H^+ + HCO_3$$
(acid)

Base: A substance that can accept hydrogen ions, H^+.
All bases are alkaline substances. Example:

$$OH^- + H^+ \longrightarrow H_2O$$
$$HCO_3^- + H^+ \longrightarrow H_2CO_3$$
(bases)

An acid is any substance that can donate a hydrogen ion, H^+. H^+ can be thought of as the most important part of an acid substance.

Many substances may include H in their chemical structure, but some cannot donate the H because it is too tightly bound. Only those substances that can give up their H^+ are acids.

Bases are substances that can accept or combine with H^+. The terms *base* and *alkali* are used interchangeably.

Each of the acid-base parameters will now be discussed in more detail.

TABLE 9-4
ACID-BASE PARAMETERS

pH measurement = Only way to tell if body is too acid or too alkaline
Acidemia = Acid condition of the blood – pH < 7.35
Alkalemia = Alkaline condition of the blood – pH > 7.45
Acidosis = Process causing acidemia
Alkalosis = Process causing alkalemia

The pH measurement is the only way to tell if the body is too acid or too alkaline. Low pH numbers (below 7.35) – indicate an acid state, and high pH numbers (above 7.45) – indicate an alkaline state.

If the numbers are lower than 7.35 there is acidemia, and if higher than 7.45, an alkalemia. Acid*emia* refers to a condition in which the *blood* is too acid. Acid*osis* refers to the *process* in the patient which causes the acidemia, and the adjective for the process would be acid*otic*. Alkalosis refers to the *process* in the patient which causes the alkal*emia,* and the adjective for this process is alkal*otic*.

This much time has been spent in defining the terms because later it will be seen that in a patient there may be more than one process occurring at a time. For instance, if both an acidosis and an alkalosis are occurring at once, then the pH will tell us which is the stronger of the two processes. The pH will be below 7.35 if the acidosis is the stronger, above 7.45 if the alkalosis is the stronger and between 7.35 and 7.45 if the acidosis and alkalosis are of nearly equal strength. So the pH values of blood represents an average of the acidoses and alkaloses which may be occurring. This will be explained in more detail later in the chapter.

TABLE 9-5
pCO_2, THE RESPIRATORY PARAMETER

pCO_2 = Pressure (tension) of dissolved CO_2 gas in blood
pCO_2 – Influenced only by respiratory causes

$$Food \xrightarrow[\text{by body}]{\text{converted}} H_2O + CO_2 + energy$$

$$CO_2 + H_2O \rightleftarrows H_2CO_3 \rightleftarrows HCO_3 + H$$

Normal pCO_2 = normal ventilation
High pCO_2 = hypoventilation
Low pCO_2 × hyperventilation

The Respiratory Parameter: pCO_2

The pCO_2 refers to the pressure or tension exerted by dissolved CO_2 gas in the blood. The pCO_2 is influenced *only* by respiratory causes. This is an over-simplification, but still you must remember that pCO_2 *is influenced only by the lungs.*

Where does the CO_2 come from? It is present only in very tiny amounts in the air we breathe. It comes indirectly from foods we eat. As a result of metabolism for the production of energy, foods are converted by the body tissues to water and CO_2 gas. When the pressure of CO_2 in the cells exceeds 40 mm. Hg (the normal arterial value), the CO_2 spills over from the cells into the plasma. In plasma, CO_2 may combine with H_2O to form H_2CO_3 (carbonic acid), but there is actually 800 times as much CO_2 in dissolved gas in plasma as is converted to H_2CO_3.

YOU SHOULD CONSIDER CO_2 GAS AN ACID SUBSTANCE because when it combines with water, an acid is formed—carbonic acid, H_2CO_3.

H_2CO_3 dissociates into hydrogen ion, H^+ and bicarbonate HCO_3^-. Much of the H^+ forms a loose association with the plasma proteins (is buffered), thus reducing the free H^+. The body has to get rid of the waste product, CO_2, and can do so in two ways:

1. The least important way is by converting the CO_2 gas to carbonic acid, H_2CO_3, which dissociates to H^+ and HCO_3^-. The H^+ can be excreted by the kidney mainly in the form of NH_4^+, and HCO_3^- can also be excreted by the kidneys.
2. A much more important way is to have the lungs get rid of the CO_2.

Getting rid of CO_2 gas, then, is one of the main functions of the lungs and a very important relationship exists between the amount of ventilation and the amount of pCO_2 in blood. If the pCO_2 in blood (i.e., the dissolved CO_2 gas in blood) is too high, it means that the lungs are not providing enough ventilation. This is called *hypoventilation.* Hypoventilation can thus be detected by finding high levels of pCO_2 in the blood. If the pCO_2 is too low, there is excessive ventilation by the lungs, or *hyperventilation,* and if the pCO_2 is normal, there is exactly the right amount of ventilation. This relationship between pCO_2 in blood and amount of ventilation is very important, pCO_2 being much more important than pO_2 in judging whether there is normal ventilation, hyperventilation, or hypoventilation.

TABLE 9-6
RESPIRATORY ABNORMALITIES

PARAMETER	CONDITION	MECHANISM
↑ pCO_2	Respiratory acidosis	Elimination by lungs of CO_2 gas
↓ pCO_2	Respiratory alkalosis	Elimination by lungs of CO_2 gas

As seen in Table 9-6, there are only two abnormal conditions associated with abnormalities in pCO_2; respiratory acidosis (high pCO_2) and respiratory alkalosis (low pCO_2).

TABLE 9-7
CAUSES OF RESPIRATORY ACIDOSIS (↑ pCO_2)

1. Obstructive lung disease
2. Oversedation and other causes of reduced function of the respiratory center (even with normal lungs)
3. Neuromuscular disorders
4. Hypoventilation with mechanical ventilator

The causes of respiratory acidosis (high pCO_2) are (1) obstructive lung disease (mainly chronic bronchitis, emphysema and occasionally asthma), (2) oversedation, head trauma, anesthesia, and other causes of reduced function of the respiratory center, (3) neuromuscular disorders such as myosthenia gravis or the Guillain Barré syndrome, (4) hypoventilation with a mechanical ventilator, and (5) other rarer causes of hypoventilation (such as the Pickwickian syndrome). It should be noted that *respiratory* acidosis may occur even with normal lungs if the respiratory center is depressed.

The term *respiratory acidosis* means elevated pCO_2 due to hypoventilation.

TABLE 9-8
CAUSES OF RESPIRATORY ALKALOSIS (↓ pCO_2)

1. Hypoxia
2. Nervousness and anxiety
3. Pulmonary embolus, fibrosis, etc.
4. Pregnancy
5. Hyperventilation with mechanical ventilator
6. Other causes of hyperventilation

The causes of respiratory alkalosis (low pCO_2) are hypoxia, nervousness, anxiety, pulmonary emboli, pulmonary fibrosis, pregnancy, hyperventilation with mechanical ventilator, and other causes of hyperventilation.

The term *respiratory alkalosis* means low pCO_2 due to hyperventilation.

The Nonrespiratory Parameters: HCO_3^- and Base Excess

Bicarbonate and base excess are influenced *only* by metabolic causes, not by respiratory causes. Again, this is a simplification, but a very important fact to remember—BICARBONATE AND BASE EXCESS ARE INFLUENCED ONLY BY METABOLIC PROCESSES. We can define a *metabolic process* for our purposes as anything other than respiratory causes that affects the patient's acid-base status. Examples of common metabolic (nonrespiratory) processes would be diabetic acidosis and uremia. When a metabolic process leads to the accumulation of acids in the body or losses of bicarbonate, bicarbonate values drop below the normal range and base excess values become negative. On the other hand, when a metabolic process causes loss of acid or accumulation of excess bicarbonate, bicarbonate values rise above normal and base excess values become positive. Base excess may be thought of as representing an excess of bicarbonate or other base. Bicarbonate, then, is base—or in other words, an alkaline substance. The term *base excess* refers principally to bicarbonate but also to the other bases in blood (mainly plasma proteins and hemoglobin).

TABLE 9-9
NONRESPIRATORY ABNORMALITIES

PARAMETER	CONDITION	MECHANISM
↑ HCO_3 or ↑ B.E.	Nonrespiratory (metabolic) alkalosis	1. Nonvolatile acid is lost, or 2. HCO_3^- is gained
↓ HCO_3^- or ↓ B.E.	Nonrespiratory (metabolic) acidosis	1. Nonvolatile acid is added (using up HCO_3^-) or 2. HCO_3^- is lost

As seen in Table 9-9, there are only two abnormal conditions associated with abnormalities in HCO_3^- or base excess; nonrespiratory alkalosis and nonrespiratory acidosis. (Nonvolatile acid is any acid other than $pCO_2 - H_2CO_3$.)

TABLE 9-10
CAUSES OF NONRESPIRATORY (METABOLIC)
ALKALOSIS (↑ HCO_3^-)

1. Diuretic Rx-mercurial, Edecrin, Lasix, thiazides
2. Cushing's disease
3. Rx with corticosteroids (prednisone, cortisone, etc.)
4. Aldosteronism
5. Fluid losses from upper GI tract— vomiting or N-G tube, loss of acid

Augmented renal excretion of $H^{\pm}$, K^+, and Cl

The causes of nonrespiratory (metabolic) alkalosis (increased HCO_3^-) are: (1) diuretic therapy with mercurial diuretics, ethacrynic acid, Lasix, and thiazide diuretics, (2) Cushing's disease, (3) treatment with corticosteriods for example, prednisone or cortisone, (4) aldosteronism, and (5) loss of acid-containing fluid from the upper GI tract as, by nasogastric suction or vomiting. This loss of acid from the stomach leaves the body with a relative excess of alkali.

The first four causes listed are due to excessive acid and potassium and chloride excretion by the kidneys. Usually, replacing potassium and chloride allows the kidneys to stop excreting acid, thus correcting the metabolic alkalosis. Treatment with two other diuretics, aldactone and dyrenium, does not cause metabolic alkalosis.

The following is an explanation of the relationship between hypokalemia (low K^+), hypochloremia (low Cl^-) and metabolic alkalosis. Normally in the kidney Na^+ and Cl^- pass from the blood into the urine at the glomerulus. Further along in the tubules of the kidney this Na^+, which is in the urine, must be reabsorbed from the urine into the kidney tubule cells and then into the blood.

Because Na^+ has a positive charge (+), when it is reabsorbed into the cells, the Na^+ must either:

1. Be reabsorbed with something that has a negative charge (−) like Cl^- or

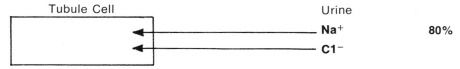

2. Enter the tubule cell in exchange for something else that has a positive charge, like K^+ of H^+ (which passes from the tubule cell to the urine).

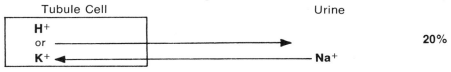

Fig. 9-2. Low Cl^- and low K^+ can cause metabolic alkalosis.

Normally, 80 percent of the Na^+ is reabsorbed while accompanied by Cl^- and 20 percent is exchanged for K^+ or H^+.

When there is hypochloremia (↓ Cl^-), the amount of Na^+ that is reabsorbed in the company of Cl^- is reduced and more Na^+ must be exchanged for K^+ or H^+. When Na^+ is exchanged for K^+ and H^+, the loss of H^+ represents a loss of acid leaving the patient alkalotic—therefore a hypochloremia alkalosis.

When Na^+ is exchanged for K^+ and H^+, only a small amount of K^+ is available, and when this is used up the patient becomes hypokalemic and H^+ is lost. The loss of H^+ is a loss of acid, leaving the patient with an alkalosis—hypokalemia alkalosis. (*Hypokalemia* means low K^+.)

TABLE 9-11
CAUSES OF NONRESPIRATORY (METABOLIC)
ACIDOSIS (HCO_3^-)

IN MEASURABLE ANIONS	IN UNMEASURABLE ANIONS
Diabetic ketoacidosis	Diarrhea
Poisonings	Drainage of pancreatic
Salicylate	juice
Ethylene glycol	Ureterosigmoidotomy
Methyl alcohol	
Paraldehyde	Rx with Diamox
Lactic acidosis	Rx with NH_4Cl
Renal failure	Renal tubular acidosis

The causes of nonrespiratory (metabolic) acidosis (low HCO_3^-) can be divided into those causes in which there is an increase in the unmeasurable anions and those causes in which there is no such increase. Unmeasurable anions are acids that accumulate in certain diseases or poisonings. If one subtracts the sum of HCO_3^- and Cl^- concentration from Na^+ concentration and finds a difference greater than 15, there is said to be an increase in unmeasurable anions. Conditions causing this are diabetic ketoacidosis, poisonings (salicylate, ethylene glycol, methyl alcohol, paraldehyde), lactic acidosis, and renal failure. In these cases there is accumulation of or ingestion of an unusual acid. Conditions that cause a metabolic acidosis without an increase in unmeasurable anions are diarrhea, drainage of pancreatic juice, ureterosigmoidotomy, treatment with Diamox, renal tubular acidosis, and treatment with ammonium chloride. In most of these latter conditions there is a deficit of bicarbonate, leaving relatively too much acid.

In all of the conditions in the left-hand column there is an accumulation of an abnormal acid substance in blood which then reacts with and uses up some of the usual amount of bicarbonate, leaving the patient with reduced levels of bicarbonate and also of base excess.

One of the most important causes of nonrespiratory acidosis is lactic acidosis. Whenever body tissues do not have enough oxygen they lose their ability to metabolize lactic acid and lactic acid accumulates in the blood. This lactic acid then combines with some of the normal amount of bicarbonate, using up the bicarbonate. In a cardiac arrest, we customarily administer bicarbonate, about 1 ample (44 mEq.) every 5 minutes, to resupply the bicarbonate which is used up by combining with lactic acid. Other conditions beside cardiac arrest which may be associated with lactic acidosis are shock, severe heart failure and severe arterial hypoxemia.

TABLE 9-12

pCO_2 — Respiratory Parameter
   Gas
   Acid
   Regulated by the lungs
HCO_3^- or Base Excess — Nonrespiratory Parameter
   Solution
   Base
   Regulated mainly by the kidneys

To review (Table 9-12), pCO_2 is the respiratory parameter, is a gas, an acid, and is regulated by the lungs. HCO_3^- and base excess are nonrespiratory parameters, occur in solution, are bases (alkaline substances), and are regulated mainly by the kidneys (not by the lungs).

Where does the CO_2 content fit in this scheme? Determination of electrolytes consists of Na^+, K^+, CO_2, and Cl^-. In this case CO_2 is an abbreviation for CO_2 content; if the term CO_2 CONTENT were used it would improve understanding. Note that in conversation CO_2 is sometimes used to mean CO_2 content (mainly bicarbonate) and sometimes to mean CO_2 GAS. This double use of the term CO_2 is one of the main reasons understanding acid base problems is hard. Use the terms CO_2 CONTENT and CO_2 GAS to avoid confusion.

TABLE 9-13

HCO_3^-	24 mEq./L.
Dissolved CO_2 gas	1.2 mEq./L. $= 40$ mm. Hg pCO_2
CO_2 content	25.2 mEq./L.

Table 9-13 shows that CO_2 content is made up mainly of bicarbonate (HCO_3^-) and to a lesser extent, dissolved CO_2 gas. The normal value of CO_2 content 25.2 mEq./L. consists of 24 mEq./L. of HCO_3^- and 1.2 mEq./L. of dissolved CO_2 gas. The 1.2 mEq./L. of dissolved CO_2 gas is expressed in different terminology, so pCO_2 of 40 mm. Hg equals 1.2 mEq./L. To convert from mm. Hg to mEq./L., the conversion factor is 0.03, so 40 mm. Hg $\times$ 0.03 = 1.2 mEq./L.

TABLE 9-14

$$\frac{HCO_3^- \text{ (base)}}{pCO_2 \text{ (acid)}} = \frac{24 \text{ mEq./L.}}{1.2 \text{ mEq./L.}} = \frac{20}{1}$$

In Table 9-14 you will note that the ratio of HCO_3^- to pCO_2 is 24:1.2 or 20:1. The body always tries to keep this ratio of HCO_3^- to pCO_2 stable at 20:1. That is, the ratio of alkali (HCO_3) to acid (pCO_2) is normally 20:1. As long as the ratio remains 20:1, the pH remains normal. If bicarbonate (HCO_3^-) or base excess increases, there is alkalosis causing the pH to rise. If HCO_3^- or base excess falls, there is acidosis and the pH falls. IF THE pH CHANGE IS DUE MAINLY TO CHANGE IN BICARBONATE (OR BASE EXCESS) IT IS SAID TO BE DUE TO METABOLIC (NONRESPIRATORY) CAUSES.

Just the opposite happens with pCO_2 which, remember, is an acid substance. If the pCO_2 rises, there is an acidosis causing the pH to fall. If the pCO_2 falls, there is an alkalosis and the pH rises. IF THE pH CHANGE IS DUE MAINLY TO CHANGES IN pCO_2 IT IS SAID TO BE DUE TO RESPIRATORY CAUSES.

TABLE 9-15

TYPES		PRIMARY ABNORMALITY
Alkalemia (high pH)	Nonrespiratory (metabolic)	$\uparrow HCO_3^-$
	Respiratory	$\downarrow pCO_2$
Acidemia (low pH)	Nonrespiratory (metabolic)	$\downarrow HCO_3^-$
	Respiratory	$\uparrow pCO_2$

As seen in Table 9-15, acid base abnormalities can be separated into just four categories to make understanding them easier. First they are divided by pH into either alkalemia or acidemia. Next they are subdivided into either nonrespiratory (metabolic) or respiratory causes. This is the procedure one uses in interpreting acid base abnormalities.

For example, if pH is high there is an alkalemia. There may be two types of alkalemia: (1) nonrespiratory, in which the primary abnormality is due to an increase in bicarbonate (example, a person who has taken too much bicarbonate or baking soda), and (2) the second type of alkalemia is respiratory, in which the primary abnormality is hyperventilation with loss of CO_2 gas. CO_2 gas is an acid substance; when CO_2 gas is lost (due to hyperventilation) an alkalosis occurs. (An example would be a nervous person having a hyperventilation attack.)

If the pH is low there is an acidemia, and there are just two types of acidemia: (1) nonrespiratory, in which the primary abnormality is loss of HCO_3^-, usually due to reaction with excessive metabolic acids. (An example of this is diabetic acidosis in which ketoacids accumulate; these acids then react with the normal amount of HCO_3^-, using up HCO_3^- and leaving HCO_3^- and base excess levels low.) (2) The second type of acidemia is respiratory, in which there is an accumulation of CO_2 gas (high pCO_2) which, you remember, is an acid substance. (An example is a patient with acute respiratory failure who *hypo*ventilates because his airways are obstructed by mucus) In respiratory acidosis there is an accumulation of volatile acid—CO_2 gas, but in nonrespiratory acidosis the acids which accumulate are not gases.

TABLE 9-16
COMPENSATION VS. CORRECTION OF ACID-BASE ABNORMALITIES

In both:	Abnormal pH is returned toward normal.
Compensation:	Abnormal pH is returned toward normal BY ALTERING THE COMPONENT NOT PRIMARILY AFFECTED, i.e., if pCO_2 is high. HCO_3^- is retained to compensate.
Correction:	Abnormal pH is returned toward normal BY ALTERING THE COMPONENT PRIMARILY AFFECTED, i.e., if pCO_2 is high, pCO_2 is lowered, correcting the abnormality.

There are two ways in which an abnormal pH may be returned toward normal: (1) compensation, and (2) correction. In *compensation,* the system not primarily affected is responsible for returning the pH toward normal. For example, if there is respiratory acidosis (high pCO_2) the kidneys *compensate* by retaining bicarbonate to return the ratio of HCO_3^- to pCO_2 to 20:1, for when the ratio is 20:1, the pH is normal.

In *correction,* the system primarily affected is repaired, returning the pH toward normal. For example, if there is respiratory acidosis (high pCO_2) vigorous bronchial hygiene may improve ventilation and lower pCO_2 returning the pH toward normal. In most cases, we as physicians, nurses, and paramedical persons are more interested in correcting the abnormality than in ing the pH toward normal. In most cases, we as physicians, nurses, and paramedical persons are more interested in correcting the abnormality than in helping the body to compensate. In both compensation and correction the pH is returned toward normal. The body tries hard to maintain a normal pH, for the various enzyme systems in all organs function correctly only when the pH is normal.

Next we will discuss how the body compensates for the various acid-base abnormalities. Remember, the body compensates for abnormalities by trying to return the ratio of HCO_3^- to pCO_2 to 20:1, for if this ratio is 20:1, the pH is normal. If the primary process is respiratory, then the compensating system is metabolic, and vice versa. When the lungs compensate for a nonrespiratory abnormality, compensation occurs in hours, but the kidneys take 2–4 days to compensate for a respiratory abnormality.

In the following four examples the first column lists normal values for the parameters listed in the second column. The uncompensated state is listed in the third column, and the last column demonstrates how compensation takes place. The primary abnormality is enclosed in a box.

TABLE 9-17
COMPENSATION FOR RESPIRATORY ACIDOSIS

NORMAL		ABNORMAL	COMPENSATED
24	HCO_3^-, mEq./L.	24	36
1.2	pCO_2, mEq./L.	1.8	1.8
40	pCO_2, mm. Hg	60	60
20:1	ratio	13:1	20:1
7.40	pH	7.23	7.40

In primary respiratory acidosis, characterized by elevated levels of pCO_2 (an acid) the system at fault is the respiratory system, and compensation occurs through metabolic process. To compensate, the kidneys excrete more acid and excrete less HCO_3^-, thus allowing levels of HCO_3^- to rise, returning the ratio of HCO_3^- to pCO_2 toward 20:1 and therefore returning pH toward normal.

If the pCO_2 is high (respiratory acidosis) but the pH is normal it means that the kidneys have had time to retain HCO_3^- to compensate for the elevated pCO_2 and that the process is not acute (has been present at least a few days to give the kidneys time to compensate).

TABLE 9-18
COMPENSATION FOR RESPIRATORY ALKALOSIS

NORMAL		ABNORMAL	COMPENSATED
0	B.E.	+2.5	−5
24	HCO_3^-, mEq./L.	24	18
1.2	pCO_2, mEq./L.	0.9	0.9
40	pCO_2, mm. Hg	30	30
20:1	ratio	27:1	20:1
7.40	pH	7.52	7.40

In primary respiratory alkalosis, characterized by low pCO_2, compensation occurs through metabolic means. The kidneys compensate by excreting GCO_3^- thus returning the ratio of HCO_3^- to pCO_2 back toward 20:1, and this compensation by the kidneys takes 2–3 days.

TABLE 9-19
COMPENSATION FOR NONRESPIRATORY ACIDOSIS

NORMAL		ABNORMAL	COMPENSATED
0	B.E.	-17	-10
24	HCO_3^-, mEq./L.	12	12
1.2	pCO_2, mEq./L.	1.2	0.6
40	pCO_2, mm. Hg	40	20
20:1	ratio	10:1	20:1
7.40	pH	7.11	7.40

In primary nonrespiratory acidosis, the major abnormality is low HCO_3^- or base excess. In most cases excess acids such as ketoacids in diabetic keto acidosis have reacted with the normal amounts of HCO_3^- using up some of the HCO_3^- and leaving a low level of HCO_3^-. The body compensates by hyperventilating, thus lowering the pCO_2 so that the ratio of HCO_3^- to pCO_2 returns toward 20:1. Because the compensating system is the lungs, compensation can occur in hours.

TABLE 9-20
COMPENSATION FOR NONRESPIRATORY ALKALOSIS

NORMAL		ABNORMAL	COMPENSATED
0	B.E.	$+13$	$+9$
24	HCO_3^-, mEq./L.	36	36
1.2	pCO_2, mEq./L.	1.2	1.8
40	pCO_2, mm. Hg	40	60
20:1	ratio	30:1	20:1
7.40	pH	7.57	7.40

If the primary disturbance is nonrespiratory alkalosis (i.e., presence of excess HCO_3^-), the body compensates with the respiratory system by hypoventilating so that pCO_2 rises and the ratio of HCO_3^- to pCO_2 is returned toward the normal of 20:1, therefore, returning the pH to normal.

In this instance respiratory compensation is by hypoventilation, and this occurs over one or several hours. Hypoventilation allows pCO_2 to rise only to a maximum of 50–60 mm. Hg before other simuli of ventilation such as hypoxia take over to prevent further hypoventilation. In compensating for one abnormality, high HCO_3^-, the body creates another abnormality, high

pCO_2, but in doing so brings the ratio of HCO_3^- to pCO_2 to 20:1, allowing the pH to return to normal in spite of two abnormalities. These two abnormalities balance each other.

It is important to realize that in each of these situations the body's compensation is only an effort to return the pH to normal, and the primary abnormality is not corrected. The physician's definitive treatment is aimed at correcting the primary abnormality.

For instance, if the primary problem is excess HCO_3^- (nonrespiratory alkalosis), treatment is directed toward getting rid of excess HCO_3^- rather than just allowing pCO_2 to rise and normalize the ratio. Excess HCO_3^- can be corrected by giving the patient Diamox to make his kidneys excrete more HCO_3^-, or more commonly by giving KCl to allow the kidneys to excrete K^+ and Cl^- rather than acids. Sometimes ammonium chloride (NH_4Cl), arginine monohydrochloride or even hydrochloric acid (HCl) are given to react with the excessive HCO_3^-, thereby correcting the metabolic alkalosis.

Respiratory alkalosis (low pCO_2) is treated by getting the patient to stop hypoventilating.

Nonrespiratory acidosis, where excess acids have used up HCO_3^- or HCO_3^- has been lost, is treated by supplying HCO_3^- in the form $NaHCO_3^-$ orally or intravenously while also treating the cause of acid accumulation or HCO_3^- loss. Multiplying the body weight (in kilograms) by the deficiency of HCO_3^- (in mEq./L.) by 0.3 gives a rough guide to the amount of $NaHCO_3^-$ (in mEq.) that should be administered. Thus a 100-Kg patient with a HCO_3^- of 14 would be given 300 mEq. of $NaHCO_3^-$, or

$$(24 - 14 = 10 \times .3 \times 100 = 300)$$

Respiratory acidosis (high pCO_2) is treated by increasing ventilation enabling the lungs to get rid of the CO_2. Although *overtreatment* may occur, *overcompensation* by the body usually does not occur. In fact, complete compensation seldom occurs, so that instead of the ratio returning to 20:1 it returns to nearly 20:1 and pH instead of returning to 7.40 returns almost to this point.

It is the fact that the pH usually does not return completely to 7.40 that allows us in many cases to decide just from blood gas values which is the primary process and which is the compensating process. We first look at the pH to see which side of 7.40 it is on. Even though it is in the normal range, pH is usually either above or below 7.40. If above 7.40, the primary process is alkalosis. For example:

pH   7.42
pCO_2 52 mm. Hg.............Respiratory acidosis
HCO_3^- 33 mEq./L................Metabolic acidosis

Which is the primary process, respiratory acidosis or metabolic alkalosis? Since the pH, though normal, is tending towards alkalemia, the primary process is probably alkalemia. So this is a metabolic alkalosis with nearly complete compensation. Often it is clinically obvious which is the primary abnormality, but sometimes this is not clinically apparent.

It must be pointed out that there may be more than one *primary* acid base abnormality; so, if there is both a respiratory and nonrespiratory acid base abnormality, instead of one compensating for the other, both may be acidoses or both alkaloses in which case the pH abnormality is more marked than if either of the abnormalities were present alone.

Here is an example of blood gases to interpret:

pH	7.24
pCO_2	38 mm. Hg
HCO_3^-	15.5 mEq./L.
B.E.	−11

Coronary care nurses deciphering an arrhythmia are taught to first find the P wave, and in trying to interpret an acid base abnormality, one must look first at the pH to see if there is an alkalemia or an acidemia. Here we have an acidemia for the pH is low. Next look at the pCO_2 to see if there is a respiratory abnormality. Here there is no abnormality, for the pCO_2 is normal. Next, look at either HCO_3^- or base excess to see if there is a metabolic abnormality. Here the HCO_3^- and the base excess are low indicating a metabolic acidosis. So we have an acidemia caused by a metabolic acidosis.

Next is a tougher example:

pH	7.20
pCO_2	55 mm. Hg
HCO_3^-	20.5 mEq./L.
B.E.	−8

First, look at the pH to see if there is an alkalemia or acidemia. Here the pH is low indicating an acidemia. Does the pCO_2 indicate a respiratory abnormality? Yes, pCO_2 is high, indicating respiratory acidosis. Does the HCO_3^- or B.E. indicate a nonrespiratory abnormality? Yes, HCO_3^- and base excess are low, indicating nonrespiratory (metabolic) acidosis. Therefore, this is an acidemia caused by combined respiratory and metabolic acidoses.

Refinements and Use of Nomogram

The foregoing is all that is necessary to solve most acid-base problems. Some experts feel that the use of confidence limits is a big help or even a necessity in solving acid-base problems. This concept will be discussed below and may help to explain some of the intricacies of acid-base problems. The use of a nomogram will also be presented.

Some of the statements made above are true most of the time but not all of the time. For instance because of the equation, $CO_2 + H_2O \rightleftarrows HCO_3^- + H^+$ it can be seen that elevations of pCO_2 will raise the HCO_3^- just because of the chemical reaction. Later—several days later—the HCO_3^- is elevated further because the kidneys excrete less HCO_3^- in an effort to compensate.

Ninety-five percent confidence limits have been compiled so that if the primary problem is respiratory acidosis (hypercapnia), for instance, one can look up the level of HCO_3^- that would be expected in 95 percent of the cases of chronic hypercapnia.

Consider the example where the pH is 7.1, pCO_2 80 mm. Hg, and HCO_3^- is 24 mEq./L. One might first say there is a respiratory acidosis and no non-respiratory problem, but if one looks at the nomogram showing the confidence limits, one learns that in acute hypercapnia of this degree the HCO_3^- should be higher than 24 mEq./L. and in chronic hypercapnia the HCO_3^- should be much higher; therefore, a concomitant nonrespiratory acidosis must be present in addition to the respiratory acidosis, and this nonrespiratory acidosis has lowered the HCO_3 below what would otherwise be expected. Without using the 95 percent confidence limits or without consulting the nomogram, one may occasionally miss the less obvious of combined acid base problems.

The area labeled A in Figure 9-3 represents the 95 percent confidence limits for normal men exposed to various levels of CO_2 gas for 30–90 minutes. The area labeled B represents the 95 percent confidence limits for patients with chronic elevations of pCO_2 stable for at least 1 week and presumably representing maximum compensation. The region between area A and B represents respiratory acidosis with the area A showing least compensation and the area B showing maximum compensation.

Ninety-five percent confidence limits for acute and chronic hypocapnia—i.e., uncompensated and maximally compensated respiratory alkalosis—are

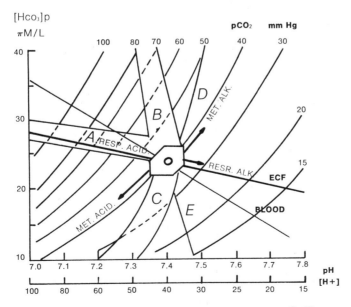

Fig. 9-3. pH—[HCO_3^-]$_p$ diagram. (Courtesy of *Chest: The Journal of Circulation, Respiration and Related Systems.*)

not available, but the area representing acute (uncompensated) hypocapnia (respiratory alkalosis) and line E represents the maximum compensation in a group of patients with chronic hypocapnia (respiratory alkalosis).

The area labeled C represents 95 percent confidence limits for completely compensated metabolic (nonrespiratory) acidosis. The area to the left of C represents less than completely compensated nonrespiratory acidosis.

The line D represents maximal compensation for chronic metabolic (nonrespiratory) alkalosis and less than full compensation is represented by the area to the right of line D.

Further use of the pH–HCO_3 diagram is explained in the article or reference by Collier. (See bibliography.) Again it must be emphasized that most acid base problems can be solved without use of the nomogram or confidence limits, but some feel that the nomogram makes understanding acid base problems easier and that the use of 95 percent confidence limits are essential in recognizing all aspects of the acid base problems.

PROCEDURE FOR DRAWING BLOOD
FOR ARTERIAL BLOOD GAS ANALYSIS

A. Equipment
   1. 10-cc. glass syringe
   2. 10-cc. bottle of heparin, 1000 units/cc. (reusable)
   3. #20 or #21 needle (disposable)
   4. Cork
   5. Alcohol swab
   6. Container of ice (emesis basis or cardboard milkshake cup)
   7. Request slip on which to write patient's clinical status, etc. including name, date, time, whether receiving O_2, and if so how much and by what route, whether in shock, recent bicarbonate Rx, etc. If on continuous ventilation: tidal volume, respiratory frequency, and inspired concentration (FIO_2).

B. Technique:
   1. Call the lab to notify them you plan to draw a blood gas sample so that they can be calibrating equipment for 15–30 minutes.
   2. Patients should be in steady state for at least 15 minutes (no recent IPPB, change in inspired O_2, exercise, etc.).
   3. Brachial artery generally best though radial or femoral are sometimes used.
   4. Elbow is hyperextended and arm is externally rotated (very important to have elbow *completely straight* — usually a folded towel or pillow under the elbow accomplishes this).
   5. 1 cc. of heparin is aspirated into the syringe, barrel of the syringe is wet with heparin, and then the excess heparin is discarded through the needle, being careful that the hub of the needle is left full of heparin and there are no bubbles.
   6. Brachial artery is located by palpation with index and long fingers, and point of maximum impulse is found.

7. Needle is inserted into the area of maximum pulsation with the syringe and needle approximately perpendicular to the skin.

8. Often the needle goes completely through both sides of the artery and only upon slowly withdrawing the needle does the blood gush up into the syringe.

9. The only way to be certain that arterial blood is obtained is the fact that the blood pumps up into the syringe under its own power. (If one has to aspirate blood by pulling on the plunger of syringe — as is required with a tighter fitting plastic syringe — it is impossible to be positive that blood is arterial.) *The blood gas results do not allow one to determine whether blood is arterial or venous.* If one suspects that blood may be venous, then draw another sample of obviously venous blood and compare the two samples. If the two samples are similar, then the first sample also was venous, but if the pO_2 and O_2 saturation on the second (obviously venous) sample are significantly lower than the first sample, then the first sample is probably arterial.

10. After 8–10 cc. of blood are obtained, the needle is withdrawn and the assistant puts constant pressure on site of arterial puncture for at least 5 minutes. (If the patient is anticoagulated, longer period of pressure may be required.) Even if attempt is unsuccessful, pressure must be applied.

11. Any air bubbles should be squirted out of the syringe and needle immediately, for these can change the blood gas values. The needle is then stuck into a cork, and the syringe is shaken to ensure that the blood mixes with the heparin.

12. Corked syringe and needle are labeled and placed immediately into ice or ice water, then taken to the lab.

13. Minimal analyses required are (a) pH; (b) pCO_2 (by direct electrode or astrup tonometer technique); (c) pO_2; and (d) Hgb. Base excess and actual bicarbonate should be calculated (standard bicarbonate may be substituted for actual bicarbonate). Other calculated values such as buffer base should not be reported, for they just tend to be confusing.

14. *Other:* (a) If O_2 saturation is also measured, this provides a cross-check for accuracy of the pO_2 (use pO_2 and pH to calculate O_2 saturation on blood gas slide rule and see if this calculated O_2 saturation agrees with the measured O_2 saturation; (b) If CO_2 content is also measured, this provides a cross-check for accuracy of pCO_2. (Use pCO_2 and pH to calculate CO_2 content on blood gas slide rule and see if this calculated CO_2 content agrees with the measured CO_2 content.)

15. Results should be reported back to the ward on the same request slip that includes the patient's status as listed in A-7 above so that results of blood gases can be related to clinical condition. (If all information is not on the same slip, it becomes impossible to interpret data hours, days or weeks later.)

16. The technician performing analysis should report any suspicion that results are not reliable. For instance:

1. If syringe comes to her with air bubbles in it.
2. If she introduces air into the sample inadvertently.
3. If calculated O_2 saturation and measured O_2 saturation do not agree.
4. If calculated CO_2 content and measured CO_2 content do not agree.
5. If equipment does not appear to be functioning correctly.

OXYGEN

The normal values for oxygen in arterial blood in Denver or any other place above sea level are lower than those at sea level because there is progressively lower pO_2 in the ambient air as one ascends.

TABLE 9-21
ARTERIAL BLOOD O_2

	DENVER	SEA LEVEL
Oxygen content	18.9 cc. O_2/100 cc. of blood	20.3
pO_2...............................	70 mm. Hg (range 65–75)	> 80 mm. Hg
O_2 Saturation of Hgb.........	93% (range 92–94%)	> 95%

In mixed venous blood the normal values for oxygen are more variable and there are smaller differences between the normal values for Denver and those at sea level, so one set of values suffices for both altitudes.

TABLE 9-22
MIXED VENOUS BLOOD O_2

Oxygen content .... 14–16 cc. O_2/100 cc. of blood
pO_2............................... 35–40 mm. Hg
O_2 Saturation of Hgb........ 70–75%

Oxygen content refers to the total amount of oxygen that is present in blood in any form. Oxygen is carried in blood just two ways, (1) dissolved in the plasma, and (2) combined with hemoglobin. By far the larger amount of oxygen is carried in combination with hemoglobin, and a very small amount is dissolved in plasma. Oxygen is not very soluble in plasma or water, so only a very small amount can dissolve in plasma. Oxygen content and O_2 saturation of hemoglobin are indicators of the *amount* of oxygen in blood or in the red blood cells respectively.

TABLE 9-23
HOW OXYGEN IS CARRIED IN BLOOD (DENVER)

	ARTERIAL	MIXED VENOUS
Dissolved in plasma	0.2 cc. O_2/100 cc. blood	0.1 cc. O_2/100 cc. blood
Combined with Hgb.	18.7 cc. O_2/100 cc. blood	14.0 cc. O_2/100 cc. blood
Total oxygen content	18.9 cc. O_2/100 cc. blood	14.1 cc. O_2/100 cc. blood

TABLE 9-24
HOW OXYGEN IS CARRIED IN BLOOD (SEA LEVEL)

	ARTERIAL	MIXED VENOUS
Dissolved in plasma	0.3 cc. O_2/100 cc. blood	0.1 cc. O_2/100 cc. blood
Combined with Hgb.	19.5 cc. O_2/100 cc. blood	15.4 cc. O_2/100 cc. blood
Total oxygen content	19.8 cc. O_2/100 cc. blood	15.5 cc. O_2/100 cc. blood

The oxygen that is combined with hemoglobin exerts no pressure, but the oxygen that is dissolved in plasma exerts a pressure or tension. The pressure or tension of O_2 dissolved in plasma can be readily measured and is known as pO_2. We shall soon see that there is a close relationship between the pressure exerted by dissolved O_2 and the amount of oxygen carried by hemoglobin. It should be made quite clear, though, that pO_2 is a measure of the pressure or tension exerted by dissolved oxygen, and pO_2 is not a measure of the *amount* of oxygen in blood.

An explanation of pO_2 must start with an explanation of barometric pressure. Barometric pressure may be thought of as the weight of the atmosphere or the pressure exerted by the atmosphere. We are not conscious of the weight or pressure exerted on us by the atmosphere, partly because the atmosphere is made up of gases. If we dive into water we are much more aware of the weight or pressure exerted on us by the water, and this pressure increases as we dive deeper because there is progressively more water above us. Just as in water, the deeper we are in the atmosphere the lower the barometric pressure. So, at the top of Pike's Peak (elevation 14,110 feet above sea level) we are near the top of the atmosphere and the barometric pressure is higher—760 mm. Hg. Denver and the cities of Colorado and Wyoming are between these two extremes; the average barometric pressure in Denver is 625 mm. Hg. (Of course, as weather fronts approach, the barometric pressure may fluctuate slightly even though the elevation is constant.)

With high-pressure weather fronts, the barometric pressure may increase by 10–15 mm. Hg, and with low-pressure fronts the barometric pressure may fall by 10–15 mm. Hg. In blood gas laboratories a barometer is necessary for determining the barometric pressure each day.

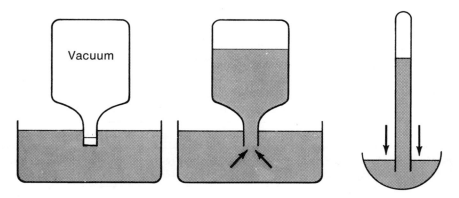

Fig. 9-4. Effects of barometric pressure.

If one takes a bottle in which a vacuum has been created and inverts this bottle in a pan of water, when the cork is removed from the bottle the water in the pan will rise in the bottle (Fig. 9-4). The force that makes the water rise in the bottle is the difference between the barometric pressure exerted on the pan and the absence of barometric pressure in the vacuum bottle.

If we substitute a long tube for the bottle, create a vacuum in the tube, and invert the tube in a container of mercury instead of a pan of water, we have a barometer. Since the vacuum in the tube remains constant, the only factor influencing how high mercury rises in the tube is the barometric pressure (or weight of the atmosphere) pressing down on the mercury in the container.

The following is a simplified explanation of why the arterial pO_2 in Denver is about 70 mm. Hg and at sea level about 95 mm. Hg.

It should be pointed out that the percent of O_2 in the atmosphere is 21 percent (actually 20.93) everywhere in the atmosphere and that changes in pO_2 with altitude are due to changes in barometric pressure with altitude and not due to changes in percentage of oxygen present.

The percent saturation of hemoglobin is defined as the amount of O_2 that hemoglobin *is* carrying compared to the amount of O_2 that hemoglobin *can* carry, expressed as a percent:

$$\text{Percent } O_2 \text{ saturation of Hgb.} = \frac{\text{Amount } O_2 \text{ Hgb. is carrying}}{\text{Amount } O_2 \text{ Hgb. can carry}} \times 100$$

TABLE 9-25

AT SEA LEVEL	AT DENVER	REMARKS
760 − 47	625 mm. Hg − 45 mm. Hg	Average barometric pressure Water vapor pressure at body temperature (subtracted because in the body this pressure is exerted by water vapor)
713	578 mm. Hg	Corrected barometric pressure (in body or completely humidified air at body temperature
× 21%	× 21%	Percent of Oxygen in the atmosphere
150 mm. Hg − 40	121 mm. Hg − 36	pO_2 in air that is completely humidified pCO_2—pressure exerted by CO_2 in alveolus
110 mm. Hg − 10 mm. Hg	85 mm. Hg − 10 mm. Hg	pO_2 in alveolus Gradient for diffusion of O_2 from alveolus into capillary
100 mm. Hg − 5 mm. Hg	75 mm. Hg − 5 mm. Hg	pO_2 in capillary blood in lungs Due to venous shunting
95 mm. Hg	70 mm. Hg	pO_2 in arterial blood

Since the amount of O_2 that Hgb. can carry is a constant,

$$\frac{1.34 \text{ cc. of } O_2}{\text{per Gm. of Hgb.}} - \% \text{ saturation of Hgb.} = \text{cc. of } O_2 \text{ that Hgb. is carrying}$$

(It should be noted that there are rare abnormal types of hemoglobin that cannot carry 1.34 cc. of O_2 per Gm. There are also rare situations in which normal Hgb. has been poisoned so that it cannot carry 1.34 of O_2 per gram—sulfhemoglobin or methemoglobin, for example.)

In 100 cc. of blood } 1 Gm. of Hgb. can carry 1.34 cc. of O_2
15 Gm. of Hgb. can carry 15 × 1.34 cc. of O_2

In arterial blood in Denver if O_2 saturation of Hgb. is 93 percent (i.e., Hgb. *is* carrying 93 percent of the total amount of O_2 it *can* carry), then 93 percent of 20.1 cc. equals 18.7 cc. of O_2 carried by Hgb. in Denver. At sea level, arterial O_2 saturation of Hgb. is 97 percent, so Hgb. is carrying 97 percent of 20.1 cc. or 19.5 cc. of oxygen.

The major factor which determines how much O_2 Hgb. *is* carrying is the pO_2 that the Hgb. is exposed to. At high pO_2 Hgb. carries more O_2; at low pO$_2$ Hgb. carries less O$_2$. The exact relationship between the amount of O$_2$ that Hgb. is carrying and the pO$_2$ is shown by the oxyhemoglobin dissociation curve, Fig. 9-5.

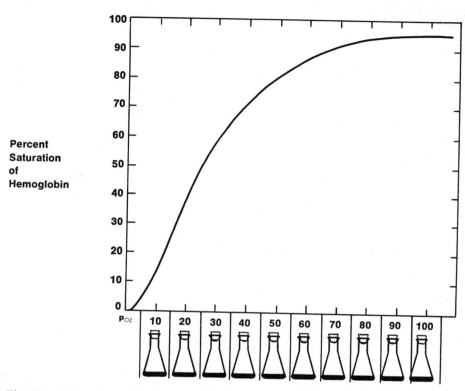

Fig. 9-5. HbO$_2$ dissociation curve. (Adapted from Julius H. Camroe, Jr., *Physiology of Respiration.*)

There are four pulmonary reasons why arterial blood may not be carrying the normal amount of oxygen (Fig. 9-5).

1. Alveolar hypoventilation—associated with high pCO$_2$
2. Diffusion defect (alveolar-capillary block)
3. Right-to-left shunt (in lung or chest)
4. Mismatching of ventilation and blood flow in the lungs. (Blood goes by alveoli that are not ventilated or underventilated. This blood, as it passes through the lungs, picks up little or no oxygen. This blood then returns to the heart and is pumped out in the arteries to the body, therefore causing arterial blood to have less than the normal amount of oxygen.)

associated with low or normal pCO$_2$

The amount of oxygen that is transported to the tissues is more important than the pO_2. The pO_2 is a measure of intensity or pressure due to oxygen, and oxygen content is a measure of amount of oxygen.

Oxygen transport to the tissues = Arterial O_2 content $\times$ Cardiac output

The oxygen transported to the tissues depends on (1) the amount of oxygen in arterial blood (arterial O_2 content), and (2) the ability of the heart to pump this blood containing oxygen around to the tissues.

The arterial O_2 content depends in turn on (1) how well the lungs are able to get oxygen from air into the blood, and (2) a normal amount of functioning hemoglobin to carry the oxygen.

In summary,

| Oxygenation of the tissue | depends on: | I. Arterial O_2 content depends on 1. Lungs' ability to get O_2 into blood 2. Ability of hemo- globin to hold onto enough O_2 | and | II. Cardiac output (circulation) |

The pulmonary causes of tissue hypoxia have already been mentioned.

The nonpulmonary causes of tissue hypoxia are (1) reduced blood flow to the tissues (reduced cardiac output); (2) anemia—not enough hemoglobin to carry O_2; (3) nonfunctioning hemoglobin—enough hemoglobin but hemoglobin that exists cannot carry O_2 because it has been "poisoned"; and (4) right to left cardiac shunts—most frequently seen in cyanotic congenital heart disease.

1. Reduced blood flow to the tissues (reduced cardiac output) might be caused by:
   (a) Myocardial infarction
   (b) Abnormal cardiac rhythm
   (c) Reduced cardiac function (other causes) congestive heart failure, dilatation of heart, valvular heart lesion, etc.
   (d) Hypovolemia (intimately related to anemia)
2. Anemia: If 1 Gm. of Hgb. carries 1.34 cc. O_2 and normally there are 15 Gm. of Hgb. to carry 15×1.34 cc. O_2 or 20.1 cc. of O_2. If there is anemia so that only 7.5 Gm. of Hgb. are present, then 7.5×1.34 cc. $O_2 = 10$ cc. of O_2 are all that can be carried; if anemia is milder (between 7.5 and 15 Gm. Hgb.) more O_2 can be carried; if anemia is more severe (less than 7.5 Gm. of Hgb.) even less O_2 can be carried. Usually the body compensates for anemia by having the heart circulate faster the lesser amount of hemoglobin that is present.
3. Nonfunctioning hemoglobin: A few rare conditions exist in which there might be a normal amount of hemoglobin, but even this normal amount

cannot function because it has been poisoned. Some examples of this are:
(a) Carbon monoxide poisoning
(b) Methemoglobinemia
(c) Sulfhemoglobinemia
    In each of these situations something (carbon monoxide, for example) has combined with hemoglobin, making it hard for oxygen to combine with and be carried by this hemoglobin.
4. In right-to-left cardiac shunts, oxygen gets through the lungs normally into the blood stream, there is enough functioning hemoglobin to carry the oxygen, and the heart is strong enough to circulate the oxygenated blood. However, some venous blood that never passes through the lungs is *shunted* into the systemic arterial system, and the combination of oxygenated blood plus mixed venous unoxygenated blood is carried through the arteries to the tissues, supplying them with less oxygen than they need.

The patient who is hypoxemic compensates for hypoxia in the following ways: (1) tachypnea (rapid breathing), (2) tachycardia (rapid heartbeat), and (3) erythrocytosis (high hemoglobin and hematrocrit-polycythemia). The tachypnea and tachycardia represent extra energy expenditure by the patient. Erythrocytosis simply means increased production of red blood cells by the hypoxic patient's bone marrow in an attempt to get more O_2 to the tissues. If the fault is lack of enough red blood cells, this is useful. But if the fault is in getting enough O_2 through the lungs, increasing the number of red blood cells helps little or nothing. The hypoxemic patient tries all the various means above of compensating for hypoxemia and often all of these together are inadequate. Hypoxia often leads to pulmonary hypertension (high blood pressure in the arteries of the lungs), and this can lead to strain or failure of the right side of the heart.

If oxygen is administered to the patient to treat his hypoxemia, tachypnea and tachycardia do not occur, no erythrocytosis occurs, and pulmonary hypertension usually goes away. Complete compensation is possible with oxygen treatment, but sometimes is not possible with patient compensation. It can be seen that supplemental oxygen is rational treatment for the patient with hypoxemia, but long-term continuous oxygen is usually reserved for the patient who when completely stable has a pO_2 below 50 mm. Hg (O_2 saturation below 85 percent) and who also has one or more of the following: (1) right heart failure which is difficult to manage with digitalis and diuretics, (2) significant secondary erythrocytosis, and (3) a progressive downhill course with weight loss and progressive muscle wasting.

Often such a patient responds to nocturnal oxygen (oxygen for 8 hours at night), or if the patient is living at a high altitude a move to a lower altitude may make supplemental oxygen unnecessary.

Oxygen treatment may lead to CO_2 retention if the O_2 is not carefully controlled.

There are two major reflex stimuli to breathing: (1) CO_2 retention (hypercapneic stimulus to breathe), and (2) low pO_2 (hypoxic stimulus to breathe).

Small elevations of pCO_2 are a major stimulus to breathing. Increasing the pCO_2 by 4 mm. Hg can cause a 100 percent increase in ventilation. Large elevations in pCO_2 reduce the amount of ventilation. In patients with significant elevation of pCO_2, hypoxemia may be their most important stimulus to breathe. If a patient who no longer has his hypercapneic stimulus to breathing is treated with oxygen, thereby eliminating his hypoxic stimulus to breathe, he may breathe even less, significantly worsening his condition. It has become apparent that giving a controlled amount of oxygen—just enough to raise the arterial pO_2 to approximately 60 mm. Hg—allows the patient to benefit from the oxygen and usually does not reduce ventilation.

It should be clear that oxygen therapy, though often given in a haphazard fashion, requires just as much understanding and precision in dosage as any other form of drug therapy.

BIBLIOGRAPHY

Collier, Clarence R., Jack D. Hackney, and John G. Mohler, "Use of Extracellular Base Excess in Diagnosis of Acid-Base Disorders; A Conceptual Approach," *Chest*, Vol. 61 (February 1972), pp. 65–105.

Comroe, Julius H., Jr., *Physiology of Respiration*. Chicago: Year Book Medical Publishers, 1965.

Filley, Giles, *Acid Base and Blood Gas Regulation*. Philadelphia: Lea & Febiger, 1971.

Schwartz, William B., "Disturbances of Acid-Base Equilibrium," in Paul B. Beeson and Walsh McDermott, eds., *Cecil-Loeb Textbook of Medicine*, 13th ed. Philadelphia: W. B. Saunders Company, 1971, pp. 1628–1636.

Winters, Robert W., Knud Engel, and Ralph B. Dell, *Acid-Base Physiology in Medicine*, 2nd ed. Cleveland: The London Company of Cleveland and the Radiometer A/S of Copenhagen, 1969.

CHEST PHYSICAL DIAGNOSIS

There is increasing recognition that nurses can contribute significantly to the care of patients with respiratory problems by performing chest physical examinations on these patients. This examination allows her an opportunity to establish a "baseline" of information and provides a framework to detect some of the rapid changes in their condition. Since the nurse is with the patient more frequently than the physician, it makes sense for the nurse to detect the patient's changing condition rather than the physician, who visits the patient only once or twice a day, or even daily chest X-rays.

Sometimes a chest examination by the nurse is the quickest and most reliable assessment of the situation. In the following example, the patient, a 69-year-old hypertensive man fainted in the shower and fell, breaking five ribs on the left side. When he recovered consciousness it was clear that he had had a CVA (cerebrovascular accident) with left-side hemiparesis. He did well until the third day of hospitalization, when he developed respiratory distress. The working diagnosis was congestive heart failure, but the nurse was able to convince those in attendance that the breath sounds and thoracic move-ment on the left side—which everyone agreed was depressed due to rib fractures—were more depressed than they had been previously. A chest X-ray, showing atelectasis of the entire left lung, confirmed her observations. The X-ray showed the lung returned to normal the next day after trache-ostomy, vigorous bronchial hygiene, and tracheal suction. This is just one example of many in which the nurses' ability to do a competent chest physical examination led to improve patient care.

Physical diagnosis of the chest includes four examinations: (1) inspection, or looking at the patient (Fig. 9-6), (2) palpation, or feeling the patient, (3) percussion, or thumping on the patient, and (4) auscultation, or listening to the patient's chest with a stethoscope.

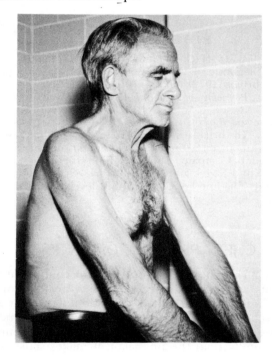

Fig. 9-6 Frequently observe the patient's overall aspect.

Inspection

In inspecting the patient, one of the factors we are most interested in is the presence or absence of cyanosis. Cyanosis is notoriously hard to detect when the patient is anemic, and the patient who is polycythemic may have cyanosis in his extremities even when he has a normal oxygen tension. We generally differentiate between *peripheral* and *central* cyanosis; peripheral cyanosis occurs in the extremities or on the tip of the nose or ears, even with normal oxygen tensions, when there is diminished blood flow to these areas, particularly if they are cold (Fig 9-7). Central cyanosis, as noted on the tongue or lips (Fig. 9-8), has a much greater significance; it means the patient actually

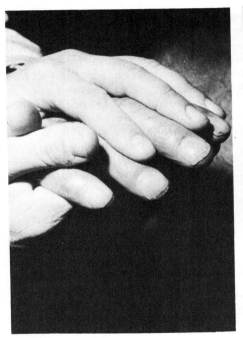

Fig. 9-7. Feel the patient's extremities and assess their temperature.

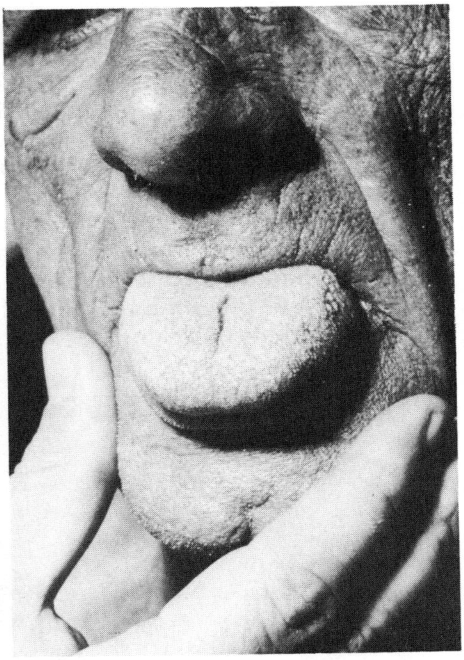

Fig. 9-8. Examine the tongue and lips for cyanosis.

has a low oxygen tension. The presence or absence of labored breathing is an obvious sign that we look for; we are particularly interested in knowing if the patient is using the accessory muscles or respiration. Sometimes the number of words a patient can say before having to gasp for another breath is a good measure of the amount of labored breathing. In looking at the patient we are interested in determining whether there is an increase in the AP (anteroposterior) diameter of the chest—i.e., an increase in the size of the chest from front to back. This is often due to overexpansion of the lungs from obstructive lung disease, but an increase in AP diameter may also be present in a patient who has kyphosis or is a hunchback. Chest deformities and scars are important in helping us to determine the reason for respiratory distress. For instance, a scar may be our first indication that the patient has had part of his lung removed. A chest deformity such as kyphoscoliosis may indicate why the patient has respiratory distress. It is also quite important to notice the patient's posture, for patients with obstructive lung disease often sit and prop themselves up on outstretched arms, or lean forward with their elbows on a desk in an effort to elevate their clavicles, thereby giving them a slightly greater ability to expand their chests.

In inspecting the patient, we are interested in the position of the trachea (Fig. 9-9). Is the trachea in the midline as it should be, or deviated to one side or the other? A pleural effusion or a tension pneumothorax usually deviates the trachea away from the diseased side. On the other hand, atelectasis often pulls the trachea toward the diseased side. The respiratory rate is an important parameter to follow; it should be counted over at least a 15-second period, rather than just estimated. Often the respiratory rate is recorded as 20 breaths/minute, which frequently means the rate was estimated rather than counted. The depth of respiration is often as meaningful as is the respiratory rate. For instance, if a patient were breathing 40 times/minute, one might think he had severe respiratory problems, but if he was breathing quite deeply 40 times/minute, it might mean that he had Kussmaul respirations due to diabetic acidosis or other acidosis. However, if the respirations

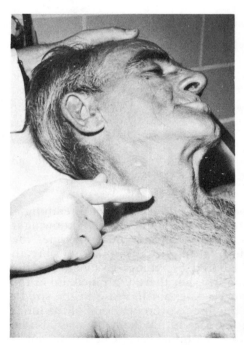 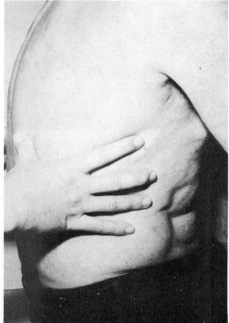

Fig. 9-9. Note the position of the trachea.   **Fig. 9-10.** Note the general chest expansion.

were shallow at a rate of 40 times/minute, it might mean he had severe respiratory distress from obstructive lung disease, restrictive lung disease, or other pulmonary problems. The duration of inspiration versus the duration of expiration is important in determining whether or not there is airway obstruction. In patients with any of the obstructive lung diseases, inspiration is prolonged, requiring more than one and one-half times as long for expiration as for inspiration.

We are quite interested in general chest expansion in examining a patient; normally we expect about a 3-inch expansion from maximum expiration to maximum inspiration (Fig. 9-10). Ankylosing spondylitis, or Marie-Strumpell arthritis, is one condition in which general chest expansion is limited. We compare the expansion of the upper chest to that of the lower chest and use of the diaphragm to see if the patient with obstructive lung disease is concentrating on expanding his lower chest and using his diaphragm properly. We look at the expansion of one side of the chest versus the other side, realizing that atelectasis, especially atelectasis caused by a mucous plug, may cause unilateral diminished chest expansion. A pulmonary embolus, pneumonia, pleural effusion, pneumothorax, or any other cause of chest pain, such as fractured ribs, may lead to diminished chest expansion. An endotracheal or nasotracheal tube inserted too far, so that it extends beyond the trachea into one of the mainstem bronchi (usually the right), is a serious and frequent cause of diminished expansion of one side of the chest. When the tube slips into the right mainstem bronchus the left lung is not expanded, and the patient usually develops hypoxemia and atelectasis on the left side. Fortunately the nurse who is aware of this problem usually recognizes it. The presence of intercostal retractions, i.e., sucking in of the muscles and skin between the ribs during inspiration, usually means that the patient is making a larger effort at inspiration than normal. Usually this signifies that the lungs are less compliant (stiffer) than usual. The effectiveness and frequency of a patient's cough are important to note, as are sputum characteristics such as amount, color, and consistency.

Palpation

Palpation of the chest is done with the heel of the hand flat against the patient's chest (Fig. 9-11). Often we are determining whether tactile fremitus is present. We do this by having the patient speak, particularly asking him to say "ninety-nine." Normally, when a patient speaks, or says a word such as "ninety-nine," a vibration is felt by the hand on the outside of the chest. This is similar to the vibration one feels when he puts his hand on the chest of a cat when the cat is purring. In many normal patients tactile fremitis is present. It may be diminished or absent when there is something which comes between the patient's lung and the hand on the chest wall. For instance, when there is a pleural effusion, thickened pleura, or pneumothorax, either it is impossible to feel this vibration or the vibration is diminished. When the

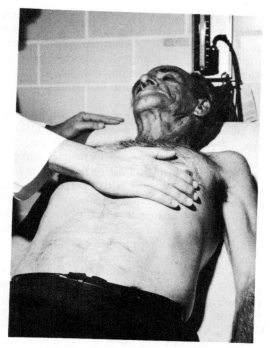

Fig. 9-11. In palpation, place the heel of your hand flat against the patient's chest.

patient has atelectasis due to an occluded airway, the vibration also cannot be felt. Tactile fremitus is slightly increased in conditions of consolidation, but detection of this slight increase may be difficult. Just palpating over the patient's chest with quiet breathing, one may sometimes feel palpable rhonchi which are due to mucus moving in large airways.

Percussion

In percussing a patient's chest or back (Fig. 9-12), one must use a finger which is pressed flat against the patient's chest; this finger is struck over the knuckle by the end of a finger from the opposite hand. Normally the chest has a resonant or hollow percussion note. In diseases in which there is increased air in the chest or lungs, such as pneumothorax or emphysema, there may be a hyperresonant (even more drumlike) percussion notes. Hyperresonant percussion notes, however, are sometimes hard to detect. More important is a dull or flat percussion note such as is heard when one percusses over a part of the body which contains no air. A dull or flat percussion note is heard when the lung underneath the examining hand has atelectasis, pneumonia,

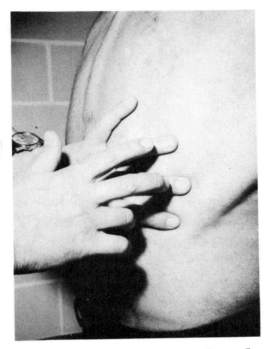

Fig. 9-12. In percussion, press a finger flat against the patient's chest or back and strike this finger over the knuckle with the end of a finger from the opposite hand.

pleural effusion, thickened pleura, or a mass lesion. A dull or flat percussion note is also heard when percussing over the heart.

Auscultation

In auscultation, one generally uses the diaphragm of the stethoscope and presses this firmly against the chest wall (Fig. 9-13A) or the back (Fig. 9-13B). It is important to listen to the intensity or loudness of breath sounds, and to realize that normally there is a fourfold increase in loudness of breath sounds when a patient takes a maximum deep breath as opposed to quiet breathing. The intensity of the breath sounds may be diminished due to decreased airflow through the airways or due to increased insulation between the lungs and the examining stethoscope. In airway obstruction, such as chronic obstructive pulmonary disease or atelectasis, the breath sound intensity is diminished. With shallow breathing there is diminished air movement through the airways and the breath sounds are also not as loud. With

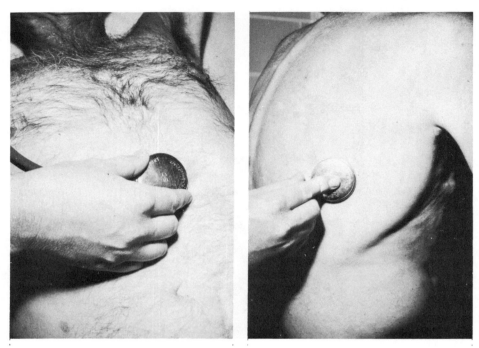

Fig. 9-13. In auscultation press the stethoscope firmly against the chest wall (A) or the back (B).

restricted movement of the thorax or diaphragm, there may be diminished breath sounds in the area of restricted movement. In pleural thickening, pleural effusion, pneumothorax, and obesity there is an abnormal substance (fibrous tissue, fluid, air, or fat) between the stethoscope and the underlying lung; this substance insulates the breath sounds from the stethoscope, making the breath sounds seem less loud. Generally, there are three types of sounds which are heard in the normal chest: (1) vesicular breath sounds which are heard in the periphery of the normal lung, (2) bronchial breath sounds which are heard over the trachea, and (3) bronchovesicular breath sounds which are heard in most areas of the lung near the major airways. Bronchial breath sounds are high-pitched, seem to be close to the ear, are loud, and there is a pause between inspiration and expiration. *Vesicular breath sounds* are of lower pitch, having a rustling quality, and there is no noticeable pause between inspiration and expiration. *Bronchovesicular breath sounds* represent a sound halfway between the other two types of breath sounds. Bronchial breathing, in addition to being heard over the trachea of the normal person, is also heard in any situation where there is consolidation—for instance, pneumonia. *Bronchial breathing* is also heard above a pleural effusion where the normal lung is compressed. Wherever there is bronchial breathing, there may also be two other associated changes: (1) "E to A" changes, and (2) whispered pectoriloquy. An E to A change merely means that when one listens with a stethoscope and the patient says "E," what one hears is actually an A sound rather than an E sound. This occurs where there is consolidation. *Whispered pectoriloquy* is the presence of a loud volume as heard through the stethoscope when the patient whispers. For bronchial breathing and these two associated changes to be present there must be either: (1) an open airway and compressed alveoli, or (2) alveoli in which the air has been replaced by fluid.

Extra sounds which are heard with auscultation include rales, rhonchi, wheezes, and rubs. *Rales* are divided into three categories: fine, medium, and coarse. Fine rales are also called *crepitant rales,* and are produced in the small airways in patients with diseases such as pneumonia or heart failure. Medium rales are sounds produced in the medium airways and occur later in pneumonia, heart failure, and pulmonary edema. Coarse rales, also called *rhonchi,* are continuous, bubbling, gurgling, or rattling sounds, often musical and usually coming from the large airways. Extra sounds such as wheezing mean there is airway narrowing. This may be caused by asthma, foreign bodies, mucus in the airways, stenosis, etc. If the wheeze is heard only in expiration it is called a *wheeze;* if the wheezing sound occurs in both inspiration and expiration, it is usually due to retained secretions and is best called a *rhonchus.* A *friction rub* is heard when there is pleural disease such as a pulmonary embolus, peripheral pneumonia, or pleurisy, and is often difficult to tell from a rhonchus. If the abnormal noise clears when the patient coughs, it usually means that it was a rhonchus rather than a friction rub.

Certainly, critical care nurses and respiratory nurse therapists and, hopefully, ward nurses and inhalation therapy technicians should learn to participate in chest physical diagnosis so that they can detect changes in the patient's condition as soon as they occur, rather than waiting for the physician's visit once or twice a day, or depending on a daily chest X-ray.

CHECK LIST OF FINDINGS

In this section the abnormal physical findings which might be seen in a variety of diseases are presented.

Bronchitis
  Occasional increased respiratory rate
  Occasional use of accessory muscles
  Occasional intercostal retraction
  Prolonged expiratory phase (often)
  Increased AP diameter of the chest (often)
  Decreased motion of the diaphragm (often)
  Decreased intensity of breath sounds
  Fine, medium, and coarse rales (rhonchi)

Wheezes (often)
Often coarse rales (rhonchi) and wheezes clear after cough
Pneumothorax
  Increased respiratory rate
  Trachea deviated to side of pneumothorax
  Occasional cyanosis
  Decreased movement of chest on side of pneumothorax (splinting)
  Hyperresonance (unreliable sign)
  Decreased breath sounds
  Decreased tactile fremitus and decreased vocal fremitus the
    most reliable signs
  Decreased vocal fremitus
Emphysema
  Increased respiratory rate (often)
  Use of accessory muscles (neck)
  Intercostal retractions
  Propped up on outstretched arms
  Prolonged expiratory phase
  Increased AP diameter
  Decreased chest expansion
  Decreased motion of diaphragm
  Hyperresonance to percussion
  Decreased intensity (loudness) of breath sounds
  Little or no increase in loudness of breath sounds with deep breath
  Fine rales at bases (often)
  Occasional wheeze
Pneumonia
  Increased respiratory rate
  Occasional cyanosis
  Decreased expansion (splinting) (often)
  Increased fremitus (tactile and vocal)
  Occasional palpable rhonchi—usually are removed by coughing
    or suctioning
  Dullness to percussion
  Bronchial breathing, whispered pectoriloquy, and E to A changes
    (usual if consolidation is extensive)
  Fine or medium rales
  Occasional coarse rales (rhonchi)—clear with cough or
    suctioning, usually
  Occasional pleural friction rub
Atelectasis
  Increased respiratory rate
  Increased pulse
  Cyanosis (often)
  Trachea deviated to side of atelectasis

Decreased chest expansion on side of atelectasis (splinting)
Decreased fremitus (tactile and vocal)
Dull or flat percussion note
Decreased breath sounds
Occasional rales
Pleural effusion
Occasional increase in respiratory rate
Trachea deviated away from side of effusion
Decreased fremitus (tactile and vocal)
Decreased breath sounds
Above effusion (compressed lung open airway)
Bronchial breathing
E to A changes
Whispered pectoriloquy
Friction rub—after fluid is removed and visceral pleura
  rubs against parietal pleura
Large mass lesion (tumor)
Dullness over tumor
Fine rales (often)
Decreased breath sounds if airway is occluded
Bronchial breathing, E to A changes, and whispered
  pectoriloquy if airway is open
Occasional pleural friction rub
Subcutaneous emphysema
Crackling sounds similar to rales that come from air outside
  the chest in the soft tissue
Pulmonary edema (congestive heart failure)
Increased respiratory rate
Cyanosis (often)
Use of accessory muscles (usually)
Apprehensive
Sitting upright (often)
Increased fremitus (due to interstitial edema)
Dull percussion (due to interstitial edema)
Bronchovesicular sounds (due to interstitial edema often
  obscured later by rales)
Fine rales → medium rales later
Occasional coarse rales (rhonchi)
Occasional wheezing
Pulmonary interstitial fibrosis
Increased respiratory rate (often)
Intercostal retractions
Cyanosis (late)
High-pitched, fine, and medium rales
Occasional bronchovesicular breathing

10

Normal Structure and Function of the Renal System

MARGARET ANN BERRY, R.N., M.A., M.S.

NORMAL FUNCTION OF THE KIDNEY

The regulation and concentration of solutes in the extracellular fluid of the body is the primary function of the kidney. This is accomplished by removing waste products of metabolism and excess concentrations of constituents and by conserving these substances which are present in normal or low quantities. Figure 10-1 is a schematic representation of the general macro- and microscopic structure of the kidney.

Urine, the end product of kidney function, is formed from the blood by the *nephron* and flows from the nephrons through *collecting tubules* to the *pelvis* of the kidney. From here it leaves the kidney itself via the *ureters* and flows into the *urinary bladder*. Each kidney in humans contains about one million nephrons, all of which function identically, and thus kidney function can be explained by describing the function of one nephron.

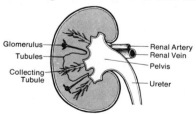

Fig. 10-1. General characteristics of kidney structure. Note that the glomerulus is in the cortex of the kidney while the proximal, distal, and collecting tubules are in the medulla.

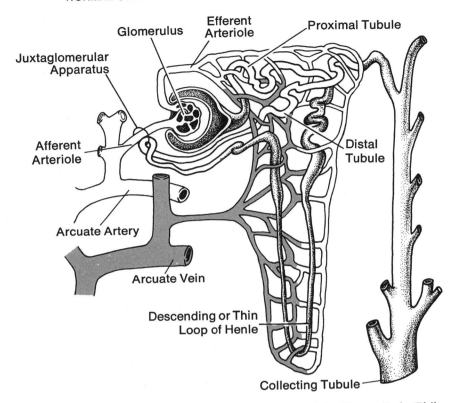

Fig. 10-2. The nephron. [From A. C. Guyton, *Functions of the Human Body* (Philadelphia: Saunders, 1969), p. 196.]

Figure 10-2 is a composite drawing of a functional nephron. Each nephron is made up of two major components; the *glomerulus* where water and solutes are filtered from the blood, and the *tubules* which reabsorb essential materials from the filtrate and permit waste substances and unneeded materials to remain in the filtrate and flow into the renal pelvis as urine.

For purposes of further describing these two major divisions of the nephron a more schematic diagram appears in Fig. 10-3.

The *glomerulus* consists of a tuft of capillaries fed by the *afferent arteriole,* and drained by the *efferent arteriole,* and surrounded by *Bowman's capsule.* Fluid which is filtered from the capillaries into this capsule then flows into the tubular system. The first section is called the *proximal tubule;* the second, the *loop of Henle;* the third, the *distal tubule,* and last, the *collecting tubule.*

Most of the water and electrolytes are reabsorbed into the blood in the *peritubular capillaries* and the *vasa recta* while the end products of metabolism pass into the urine.

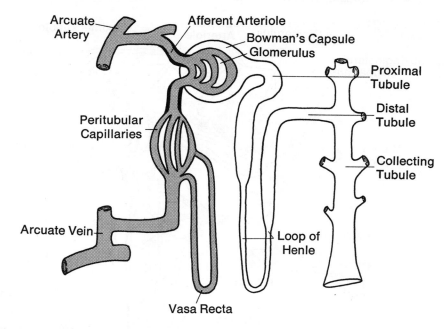

Fig. 10-3. Schematic representation of the nephron. [From A. C. Guyton, *Functions of the Human Body* (Philadelphia: Saunders, 1969).]

The Glomerular Membrane and Filtration Pressure

The *glomerular membrane* is composed of all the membranes of the tuft capillaries. Like other capillary membranes it is essentially impermeable to plasma protein. The difference in permeability lies in its increased permeability to water and small molecular solutes. However, the glomerular membrane follows the same principles of fluid dynamics that are applicable to any other capillary membranes. That is, the effective movements of materials out of the capillary and into the capsule is a function of the difference in fluid and osmotic pressure on either side of the membrane. Another distinguishing characteristic of the glomerulus is the increased fluid pressure (70 mm. Hg) in the tuft as compared to low fluid pressure (10–20 mm. Hg) found in other capillaries. This high fluid pressure (e.g., blood pressure) causes fluid to constantly leak out of tuft and into Bowman's capsule. Figure 10-4 illustrates these principles.

The reader will recall from his past experiences that the effective filtration pressure in the glomerular membrane is the result of the net difference in pressure on either side of the membrane. That is, if the pressure tending to push material out of the capillary is 70 mm. Hg and the osmotic pressure of the blood holding fluid in the capillary is 32 mm. Hg, the total force push-

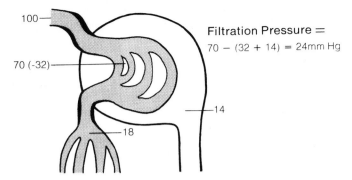

Filtration Pressure =
70 − (32 + 14) = 24mm Hg

Fig. 10-4. Normal fluid pressures at various points in the nephron. [From: A. C. Guyton, *Functions of the Human Body* (Philadelphia: Saunders, 1969), p. 197.]

ing fluid out is 38 mm. Hg. At the same time, the filtrate formed exerts fluid pressure against the membrane attempting to push fluid back into the capillary. In the normally functioning nephron, this is about 14 mm. Hg. Thus the net filtration pressure is 24 mm. Hg.

Glomerular Filtration Rate

The rate at which fluid flows from the glomerulus into Bowman's capsule is called the *glomerular filtration rate*. This rate is directly proportional to the net filtration pressure, which means that any factor effecting a change in any one of the pressures on either side of the membrane will affect the glomerular filtration rate. For example, an increase in blood pressure in the afferent arteriole, a decrease in osmotic pressure in the blood, or a decrease in fluid pressure in Bowman's capsule would all result in an *increased* glomerular filtration rate. It is easily seen how the formation rate of glomerular filtrate acts as a regulatory mechanism for blood pressure. An increased blood pressure causes an increase in filtrate formation, decreasing the fluid volume of the blood which then lowers arterial blood pressure. As a result of low arterial pressure, the nephron decreases its function, thus permitting blood fluid volume to build up until it exceeds normal values again and initiates the whole process again.

The Glomerular Filtrate

Glomerular filtrate, produced in Bowman's capsule, is an ultrafiltrate of plasma. That is, it contains all but the protein fraction of the plasma. A very small amount of plasma proteins (ca. 0.03 percent) does enter the glomerular filtrate, but is extremely small when compared to their concentration in the plasma (ca. 7 percent). The kidneys form about 125 ml. of glomerular filtrate per minute. This results in about 180 L. of filtrate per day, about 4.5 times the total amount of fluid in the entire body. A quick glance at these statistics illustrates the tremendous effectiveness of the kidneys in maintaining normal body fluids and their constitutents.

The glomerular filtrate produced in Bowman's capsule of the nephron enters the tubular system where nearly all but one liter of the 180 liters formed is reabsorbed into the blood. As seen in Fig. 10-3, the peritubular capillaries are found in close proximity to the tubules as they loop into the medullary portion of the kidney. In tubular reabsorption substances in the tubular fluid are first moved from the tubule lumen into the interstitial fluid and then into the peritubular capillaries. Reabsorption of materials across the tubular epithelium is accomplished by *active reabsorption, diffusion,* and *osmosis.*

Active Reabsorption

Active reabsorption is very similar to active transport of materials across cell membranes. It means the transport of materials through the epithelial cells of the kidney tubule and into the interstitial spaces, by the involvement of special chemical carriers and the expenditure of energy. From the intercellular space the materials diffuse into the peritubular capillary. Materials reabsorbed in this fashion include glucose, amino acids, proteins uric acid, and most of the electrolytes (e.g., Na^+, K^+, Mg^{++}, Ca^{++}, HCO_3^-, Cl^-). Active processes for glucose, amino acids, and proteins are extremely efficient so that nearly all of these substances are reabsorbed in the proximal tubules and the urine is virtually devoid of any of them. The reabsorption of electrolytes, however, is variable according to the concentration required in the extracellular fluid of the body and are regulated by a special mechanism. Therefore, when an electrolyte is present in excessive amounts in the extracellular fluid of the body, very little of it is absorbed from the tubules. When there is a depleted amount in the extracellular fluid, nearly all will be reabsorbed. This *selective* reabsorption of essential materials is the mechanism by which the kidney controls the concentration of electrolytes in the body.

The electrolyte that is actively reabsorbed to the greatest extent is sodium. Approximately 1,200 Gm. of this substance is reabsorbed daily. This represents nearly three fourths of the active reabsorption of all materials from the glomerular filtrate. Therefore, sodium serves as a good example of the mechanism of active reabsorption. Figure 10-5 demonstrates the mechanism of the active reabsorption of sodium.

The tubular cells of the proximal tubules are serrated on the luminal side and the cell membrane of this *brush border* is extremely permeable to the sodium ion. Because of this, the sodium ion rapidly diffuses down its concentration gradient. The membranes facing the interstitial spaces are impermeable to sodium, and it is actively pumped out of the cell and into the peritubular space. The active transport at the base membrane is most likely

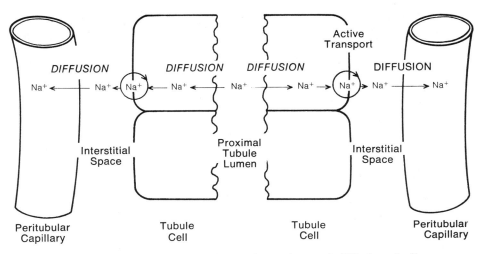

Fig. 10-5. Movement of Na$^+$ by active reabsorption and diffusion. Sodium moves from the proximal tubule into the tubular cell by diffusion. From there it moves by active transport to the interstitial space, where it diffuses into the peritubular capillary; thereafter it flows back into the general circulation.

similar to that proposed for active transport in any cell membrane. That is, the sodium ion becomes chemically bound to a carrier dissolved in the cell membrane. The combination of sodium and its carrier diffuses across the membrane where the carrier releases the sodium into the peritubular fluid in the interstitial space. The high-energy compound adenosine triphosphate (ATP), which is transformed to adenosine diphosphate, supplies the energy for the carrier. The necessary enzymes for the reaction are also located in the base membrane.

As stated earlier, the active reabsorption of other substances occurs in the the same manner, each having its own specific carrier and enzymes which catalize the reactions. The importance of the active reabsorption mechanism lies in the fact that it regulates the absorption of materials even when the concentration gradient favors no removal of materials from the tubular filtrate. Because of this the metabolism of the tubular cells is commensurate with the energy requirements needed for transforming the potential energy of nutrient's into chemical energy for reabsorption.

Diffusion and Osmosis

Diffusion and osmosis also play an important role in the reabsorption of other materials from the glomerular filtrate, especially water. *Diffusion* is the random movement of molecules in a liquid or gas and is caused by the kinetic movement of all molecules in the liquid or gas. Since there are pores in the epithelial membranes of the tubules, certain materials such as water can diffuse through them and into the renal interstitial spaces following their concentration gradients.

The principal method of reabsorption of water, however, is by osmosis. *Osmosis* is the net diffusion in one direction of permeable substances, caused by the presence of larger concentrations of nonpermeants on one side of the membrane than on the other. Thus the active transport of relatively impermeant (i.e., nondiffusable) substances, such as electrolytes, glucose, and amino acids, decreases their concentrations in the tubular filtrate, which increases them in the peritubular interstitial spaces. As this continues, an osmotic gradient for water develops and the water diffuses through the membrane. As a result, the initial phenomenon is one of active reabsorption of osmotically active substances with osmotic reabsorption of water simply following in its wake.

Some materials, such as the end products of metabolism like urea, are undesirable in body fluids. Urea diffuses through the pores at a much slower rate than water. In fact, it diffuses several hundred times less easily. As a consequence only about 50 percent of the urea in the tubular filtrate diffuses into the interstitial spaces and the remainder is excreted in the urine. Sulphates, phosphates, creatinine, nitrates, and phenols—all end products of metabolism—are removed in the same manner. If these substances are permitted to accumulate, they produce toxic effects on cells of the body and slow down essential metabolic reactions.

A certain few substances are actively secreted from the tubular capillaries into the tubules. This phenomenon, presumed to be the reverse of active reabsorption, requires energy and a carrier mechanism. Penicillin, diodrast, and phenolsulfophthalein are removed in this fashion; however, normally only potassium and hydrogen ion regulation is maintained by this method.

Clearance

From the foregoing discussion a very important concept in renal function emerges—that of *clearance*. Each time that a small fraction of plasma filters through the glomerular membrane, the resulting filtrate passes down the tubules and reabsorption occurs, a large proportion of unwanted metabolic end products are left behind in the urine. The blood is "cleared" of these substances. Indeed, of each 125 ml. of glomerular filtrate formed per minute, 60 ml. leaves its urea behind in the fluid within the tubules. Stated another way, 60 ml. of plasma is cleared of urea each minute in normally functioning kidneys. In the same way 125 ml. of plasma is cleared of creatinine, 12 ml. of uric acid, 12 ml. of potassium, 25 ml. of sulfate, 25 ml. of phosphate, etc., each minute. It is possible to calculate renal clearance by simultaneously sampling urine and plasma. By dividing the quantity of substance found in each millimeter of plasma into the quantity found in the urine, the milliliters cleared per minute can be calculated. This method is used as one means of testing kidney function.

Regulatory Mechanisms

From the foregoing discussion it is apparent that kidney function is impor-tant in the regulation of (1) electrolyte concentration, (2) osmotic pressure, and (3) both the pH and the volume of the extracellular fluids (i.e., blood and interstitial fluid) of the body. As pointed out in the section on respiration, the kidney functions in conjunction with the respiratory system in the regula-tion of pH. The mechanisms by which materials are filtered, reabsorbed, and secreted have also just been discussed. It is important now to look at the special mechanisms which regulate these processes for certain molecules.

Nearly 90 percent of all positively charged ions in the extracellular fluids of the body are sodium. Only moderate changes in concentration of this ion can affect transmission of nerve impulses, strength of cardiac contraction, endocrine and exocrine secretory processes, and secretory processes and

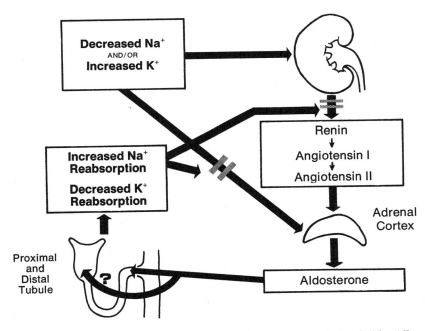

Fig. 10-6. Regulation of Na^+ and K^+ concentrations in extracellular fluids. All condi-tions in boxes occur in extracellular fluid. "//" equals negative feedback mechanism with ↑ Na^+ and ↓ K^+. When sodium reaches normal levels in the extracellular fluid, negative feedback occurs. Aldosterone is no longer stimulated by the low sodium level. Renin is no longer released by the kidney, and therefore Angiotensin II is not available to stimulate the adrenal cortex to produce aldosterone. Because of these negative feedback mechanisms, the level of aldosterone falls and as a result Na^+ is no longer being reabsorbed in exchange for K^+ in the distal tubule. [From: A. C. Guyton, *Functions of the Human Body* (Philadelphia: Saunders, 1969).]

function of the brain. Consequently the extracellular concentration is finely regulated so as to not vary more than ± 5 mEq. around a mean of 142 mEq. per liter. Figure 10-6 summarizes the overall mechanism for sodium ion regulation and the main secondary effect of regulating potassium concentration as well.

In the face of decreased extracellular concentration of sodium, the kidney releases *renin,* an enzyme which converts a plasma protein in the blood to *angiotensin I.* A converting enzyme found in pulmonary tissue changes angiotensin I to *angiotensin II.* Angiotensin II increases the secretion of *aldosterone,* a hormone of the adrenal cortex. The decreased extracellular Na^+ concentration is believed to cause the increase of aldosterone directly. In addition to causing increased aldosterone secretion, angiotensin II is also a potent vasopressor and thus also increases glomerular filtration. Aldosterone increases the rate of reabsorption of sodium in the tubules, exchanging a sodium for a potassium. This occurs primarily in the distal convoluted tubules, thereby finely regulating the extracellular levels of both sodium and potassium.

A backup mechanism for potassium regulation is also found in renal function. If there are high levels of potassium in the face of normal sodium levels, the distal tubules and collecting ducts actively secrete (reverse of active reabsorption) potassium back into the urine. Similar specific reabsorption mechanisms appear to exist for divalent ions such as calcium, magnesium, and phosphates.

The regulation of the monovalent anions, chloride and bicarbonate, is secondary to sodium-ion regulation. As the positively charged cation, sodium is reabsorbed, a negatively charged ion follows to maintain electroneutrality. Whether the negative ion is bicarbonate or chloride is dependent upon the regulation of pH in conjunction with the respiratory system.

The regulation of fluid volume by the kidney resides in the mechanisms for concentrating and diluting urine. The *countercurrent mechanism* is responsible for the kidney's ability to concentrate urine. Anatomically the kidney can be divided into two major regions, the *cortex,* where the glomeruli and the proximal and distal tubules are located, and the *medulla.* The loop of Henle extends deep into the medulla, and the collecting tubules pass through it before emptying into the renal pelvis. Referring to Figs. 10-2 and 10-3, notice that the peritubular capillaries extend into the medulla forming long loops called *vasa recta* which empty into the renal veins in the cortex. As discussed earlier, sodium is actively reabsorbed from the filtrate into the interstitial spaces. It finally reaches concentrations that are three to four times normal. The reduced rate of flow as well as the anatomical arrangement of the vasa recta, prevent the blood from carrying away large amounts of sodium. This is accomplished in the following manner: Blood flows downward in the vasa recta and sodium diffuses rapidly into the blood from the interstitial fluid until it reaches the bottom of the loop where the concentration reaches levels that are approximately three times normal. As the blood flows back up toward the cortex, sodium diffuses back into the peritubular fluid, conserving sodium. As the filtrate flows through the loop, it becomes very dilute and is hypotonic by the time it enters the collecting tubule. The epithelium of the collecting duct alters its permeability to water in response to the posterior pituitary antidiuretic hormone (ADH).

When ADH is released, most of the water is reabsorbed from the urine in the collecting tubules and the urine is concentrated. The release of ADH is effected by special neural osmoreceptors located in the suproptic nuclei near the hypothalamus in the brain. When extracellular fluid is too concentrated these neurons stimulate the release of ADH from the posterior pituitary. In the presence of dilute extracellular fluid ADH is not released and a dilute urine is produced, decreasing extracellular fluid volume.

Summary of Renal Function

The total blood flow into the nephrons of both kidneys is estimated to be about 1,200 ml. per minute. Of this total amount, about 650 ml. is plasma. Approximately one-fifth of the plasma filters through the glomerular membranes into the Bowman's capsules, forming 125 ml. glomerular filtrate per minute. This filtrate is essentially plasma minus proteins. The pH of glomerular filtrate is equal to that of plasma, or 7.4. As the glomerular filtrate passes through the proximal tubules, nearly 80 percent of the water and electrolytes, all of the glucose proteins and most of the amino acids are reabsorbed. The glomerular filtrate passes on through remaining tubules where water and electrolytes are reabsorbed, depending upon need of body fluids and the effectiveness of the regulatory mechanism responsible for maintaining their normal levels. The pH of the forming urine may rise or fall, depending upon the relative amount of acidic and basic ions which are reabsorbed by the tubule walls. The osmotic pressure of the tubular fluid will depend upon the amounts of electrolytes and water that are reabsorbed. Because of those factors, urine pH may vary from 4.5 to 8.2 and osmotic pressure may vary from one-fourth that of plasma to approximately 4 times plasma pressure. The amount of urine delivered to the renal pelvis is usually about $1/125$ the amount of glomerular filtrate produced or about 1 ml. per minute. This 1 ml. of urine will contain nearly one-half the urea contained in the original 125 ml. of glomerular filtrate, all of the creatinine, and large proportions of uric acid, phosphate, potassium, sulfates, nitrates, and phenols. It should be pointed out that even though all glucose and proteins, nearly all amino acids, and large amounts of water and sodium in the original glomerular filtrate are reabsorbed, a very large proportion of the waste products are never reabsorbed and are found in the urine in highly concentrated form.

11

Renal Failure: Pathophysiology and Management

ALLEN C. ALFREY, M.D.
DONALD E. BUTKUS, M.D.

PATHOPHYSIOLOGY OF RENAL FAILURE

The adverse effect of reduced renal perfusion on renal function, as a consequence of various shock states, has been recognized for over a hundred years. However, it was during and following World War II that most of the knowledge in regard to understanding the pathogenesis, physiology, and management of renal ischemia was obtained. Since about 1950 evidence has been accumulated to suggest that early diagnosis of renal failure in association with aggressive treatment of the shock state can reverse functional abnormalities and prevent acute tubular necrosis.

Because of the large amount of renal blood flow required to maintain normal renal function, changes in urinary composition occur early in the shock state when renal perfusion is decreased. Normally the kidneys receive 20–25 percent of the cardiac output (approximately 1,200 ml./minute). Almost 90 percent of the blood flow to the kidney is concerned with cortical distribution and in turn, glomerular filtration. The kidney has an intrinsic ability to regulate blood flow (autoregulation) so that the glomerular filtration rate is maintained constant over a blood pressure range of 80 to 180 mm,/Hg. This is accomplished by variations in the tone of pre- and postglomerular arterioles.

However, when renal blood flow is severely compromised either as a result of reduction in effective blood volume, a fall in cardiac output or a decrease in blood pressure below 80 mm./Hg, characteristic changes occur in renal function. Thus the capacity for complete autoregulation is exceeded. The glomerular filtration rate falls. The amount of tubular fluid is reduced and the fluid travels through the tubule more slowly. This results in increased sodium and water reabsorption. Because of the reduced renal circulation the solutes reabsorbed from the tubular fluid are removed more slowly than normal from the interstitium of the renal medulla. This results in increased medullary tonicity, which in turn further augments water reabsorption from the tubular fluid. Therefore, the urinary changes are typical in the shock state. The urinary volume is reduced to less than 400 ml./day (17 ml./hour), urinary specific gravity is increased, and urinary sodium concentration is low (usually less than 5 mEq./L.).

In addition, substances such as creatinine and urea which are normally filtered but poorly reabsorbed from the renal tubule are present in high concentration in the urine as a result of the increased water reabsorption. Because of the characteristic changes associated with renal underperfusion, measurement of urinary volume and specific gravity are simple methods of determining the effect of shock management on renal perfusion. An increase in systemic blood pressure does not necessarily imply improvement in renal perfusion. This may be especially evident when drugs such as norepinephrine (Levophed) are used to correct the hypotension associated with states of volume depletion. These drugs may be associated with further reduction in renal blood flow as a consequence of constriction of renal arteries. This is manifested by a further fall in urinary volume and rise in specific gravity. In turn, if the shock state is more appropriately and specifically treated by replacing volume, improving cardiac output, correcting arrhythmias, or by giving isoproterenol (Isuprel), the improved renal perfusion will be manifested as an increased urinary volume and a fall in specific gravity of the urine.

Management of Acute Reversible Renal Failure

Primary management of renal function impairment is directed at the adequate and specific management of the shock state. The three most common causes for reduced renal perfusion are decreased cardiac output, altered peripheral vascular resistance, and hypovolemia.

Decreased Cardiac Output

Factors such as cardiac arrhythmias, acute myocardial infarction, and acute pericardial tamponade, all of which decrease cardiac output, may be associated with a reduction in renal blood flow. The reversibility of the renal failure is thus dependent on the ability to improve cardiac function. The specific management has been discussed in earlier chapters.

With the above conditions cardiac output is usually acutely and severely compromised. However, when cardiac output is impaired to a lesser extent over a more chronic period of time, features of congestive heart failure occur. Again there is reduced renal perfusion, although to a lesser extent.

The major feature of this state, from the renal aspect, is avid sodium reabsorption, which results in increased extracellular fluid volume, elevation of central venous pressure and edema.

Several mechanisms are responsible for the increased tubular reabsorption of sodium. First, there is a greater reduction in renal blood flow than in glomerular filtration, bringing into play the mechanisms discussed earlier. Second, it has been suggested that blood flow to the superficial cortex is reduced while blood flow to the inner cortical area is increased. It is also thought that the nephrons in the inner cortical region reabsorb a greater percent of the filtered sodium than the nephrons in the outer cortex of the kidney. Other factors include increased proximal and distal tubule sodium reabsorption. The mechanisms responsible for the increased proximal tubule sodium reabsorption are poorly understood; however, aldosterone is largely responsible for the increased distal tubule sodium reabsorption. It can be seen that numerous mechanisms are responsible for the increased tubular reabsorption of sodium in congestive heart failure.

Therapy is largely directed at increasing urinary sodium excretion. At times this can be accomplished by improving cardiac output which in turn increases renal perfusion. This is not always possible, however. Diuretics are frequently used to increase sodium excretion. These agents directly inhibit sodium reabsorption in the renal tubule. The potency of a diuretic is primarily determined by the site in the renal tubule where sodium reabsorption is blocked. The two most potent diuretics presently available are furosemide (Lasix) and ethacrynic acid (Edecrin). These agents block sodium reabsorption in the ascending limb of the loop of Henle and in the distal tubule. It is still unclear whether they have an effect in the proximal tubule as well. The thiazide diuretics have their major site of action in the distal tubule and are therefore somewhat less potent than the above agents. Another diuretic commonly used is spironolactone (Aldactone) which increases urinary sodium by blocking the renal tubular effect of aldosterone.

Altered Peripheral Vascular Resistance

Renal perfusion is compromised in these states as a result of increased size of the intravascular compartment and redistribution of blood volume. This may be a consequence of gram-negative septicemia, certain drug overdoses, anaphylactic reactions, and electrolyte disturbances such as acidosis. Management is primarily directed at treating the basic disturbance with appropriate specific therapy plus fluid, electrolyte, and colloid replacement. The controversy in regard to the use of steroids and various pressor agents in gram-negative sepsis is beyond the scope of this discussion.

Hypovolemia

Restoration of extracellular fluid and blood volume is of major importance in the management of any shock state. Evidence for extracellular volume depletion is usually obtained from the history and physical examination. Historically the patient may give evidence of external sodium and water loss as a result of vomiting, diarrhea, excessive sweating, or surgical procedures. Blood volume may also be compromised as a result of fluid redistribution as seen both with burns and with inflammatory processes in the abdomen, such as pancreatitis or peritonitis. The physical findings associated with extracellular volume depletion are sunken eyes, dry mouth, loss of skin turgor and tachycardia. Postural hypotension may also be noted. Therapy is directed at sodium and water replacement. Response to treatment can be judged by changes in urinary volume, specific gravity, central venous pressure and the above physical findings.

Maintenance of Urinary Flow

At times in spite of adequate treatment of the shock state, urinary volume remains low. This may be a result of either continuing functional impairment in the postshock period or parenchymal renal damage suffered as a consequence of the shock state. Not only is it necessary to differentiate these two states from each other, but a number of authors also feel that prolonged oliguria, if allowed to persist, may eventually lead to acute tubular necrosis. Mannitol and furosemide have been used in this setting both for diagnosis and maintenance of urinary function.

Mannitol is the reduced form of the six-carbon sugar mannose. It is distributed in the extracellular fluid and is essentially not metabolized. It is freely filtered at the glomerulus and not reabsorbed by the tubule. Because of its small molecular size (180) it exerts a significant osmotic effect and in turn increases urinary flow. Mannitol is usually infused rather rapidly. The more rapid the infusion the higher the blood level and in turn the filtered load. Urine flow is dependent on the amount of mannitol filtered, and if the infusion is too slow, changes in urinary flow rate will be delayed and less apparent.

The usual test done of mannitol is 12.5 Gm. given intravenously as a 25 percent solution over 3–5 minutes. If urine flow increases to greater than 40 ml./hour the patient is felt to have reversible renal failure and his urine volume is then maintained at 100 ml./hour with additional mannitol.

More recently furosemide and ethacrynic acid have largely replaced mannitol in the diagnosis of reversible renal failure. A number of patients who fail to develop a diuresis following mannitol will have an acceptable increase in urinary volume following furosemide or ethacrynic acid. Furosemide in dosages of 200 to 1,000 mg. is given intravenously. The peak diuresis usually occurs within two hours of its administration. If furosemide is effective in increasing urinary volume, it is then repeated at 4–6 hour intervals to maintain the urinary flow rate. In patients failing to respond to furosemide a diagnosis of acute tubular necrosis is seriously entertained. In patients who respond to furosemide and mannitol it is important to realize that sodium and water depletion will occur if losses are not replaced. Usually urine volume is replaced by half-strength normal saline. In addition potassium replacement also is frequently required.

Acute Tubular Necrosis

Although approximately 30 percent of the cases of acute tubular necrosis occur without a specific etiology being found, some of the more common causes for the development of this syndrome include shock, nephrotoxic agents and acute renal failure associated with myoglobinuria and hemoglobinuria.

There is little doubt that the severity and duration of traumatic shock plays a major role in predisposing to the development of acute tubular necrosis. Over 40 percent of a large number of combat casualties in World War II developed acute tubular necrosis. In contrast, acute tubular necrosis has been uncommon in Vietnam casualties. This reduced incidence has been attributed to early air evacuation and rapid treatment of shock.

A large number of chemicals and drugs have been found to be nephrotoxic. In the hospital patient probably the most common group of nephrotoxic agents are the antibiotics. These include gentamicin, cephaloridine, colistin, kanamycin, and polymyxin. Because of the frequency with which acute tubular necrosis occurs in patients receiving these agents, renal function should be routinely evaluated before and during treatment with these drugs.

A third major category of acute tubular necrosis are those associated with abnormal release of body pigments (myoglobin and hemoglobin). Characteristically the urine is dark in color and positive for hemoglobin. Patients with states associated with intravascular hemolysis such as transfusion reactions, malaria, arsine intoxication, etc., may develop acute tubular necrosis. In addition, acute renal failure commonly occurs in patients with myoglobinuria of a variety of etiologies.

Numerous investigations have been carried out to define the mechanisms by which nephrotoxic agents and shock induce acute tubular necrosis and oliguria, but to date these have not been clearly defined. Renal blood flow has been found to be reduced to approximately one third of normal in acute tubular necrosis, whereas the glomerular filtration rate is almost completely suppressed. This is in contrast to other states in which a similar reduction in renal blood flow is accompanied by much better maintenance of glomerular filtration and renal function.

A number of animal studies have suggested that intratubular obstruction from casts and cellular debris may be involved in the suppression of glomerular filtration. If this obstruction is relieved, renal function returns. Other studies have suggested that there is disruption of the tubule epithelium with excessive back flow of the filtrate out of the tubule lumen, thus explaining the lack of urine formation in the face of continuing, although reduced, renal blood flow.

More recently Hollenberg and his colleagues have put forth evidence that cortical blood flow is severely compromised in acute tubular necrosis resulting from ischemia as well as nephrotoxic agents.[1] The mechanism responsible for the decreased superficial cortical blood flow in the kidney with acute tubular necrosis has not been defined. However, the recent demonstration of converting enzyme being present in the kidney suggests that renin-angiotensin may play a role in this phenomenon.

Classically patients have oliguria in association with acute tubular necrosis; however this is not invariably so. A group of patients present with acute nonoliguric (partially reversible) renal failure. This state is especially common in patients receiving nephrotoxic antibiotics. If antibiotics are discontinued before renal function is markedly reduced, the patient frequently sustains moderate functional impairment for 7–10 days with gradual return to normal. Similarly, mannitol and furosemide may halt deterioration of renal function during shock and convert an irreversible renal failure into a nonoliguric acute tubular necrosis. In general, patients with nonoliguric acute renal failure have few symptoms and the disease is much less serious than the oliguric form of acute tubular necrosis.

The more classical or oliguric form of acute tubular necrosis begins with an acute precipitating event immediately followed by oliguria (urine volume less than 400 ml./day). The mean duration of oliguria is around 12 days although it may last only 2–3 days or as long as 30 days. This is accompanied by a usual rise in BUN of 25–30 mg./100 ml./day and creatinine of 1.5–2 mg./100 ml./day. The most common complication in this period is overhydration with resulting cardiac failure, pulmonary edema, and death. In addition the patient may develop acidosis, hyperkalemia, and symptoms of uremia.

The oliguric phase is followed by gradual return of renal function as manifested by a stepwise increase in urine volume (the diuretic stage). The degree of diuresis is primarily determined by the state of hydration at the time the patient enters the diuretic stage. If the patient is markedly overloaded, urinary volume may eventually exceed 4–5 L./day. This may result in marked sodium wasting, with death resulting from electrolyte depletion. Because of the slow return of renal function during the diuretic phase the degree of azotemia may increase during the early part of the diuretic period and the patient will have similar complications as noted in the oliguric phase. A period of several months is required for full recovery of renal function after the end of the diuretic period.

Differentiating Acute Tubular Necrosis From Decreased Renal Perfusion

During the immediate postshock period the differentiation between continuing decreased renal perfusion and acute tubular necrosis has to be made. The routine urine analysis is usually of little help in differentiating these two states in that the changes are nonspecific. In both conditions there may be mild proteinuria in association with a moderate number of red blood cells, white blood cells, and granular casts. The major features of the two states are shown in Table 11-1.

TABLE 11-1
USE OF LAB VALUES IN DIFFERENTIATING ACUTE TUBULAR
NECROSIS FROM DECREASED RENAL PROFUSION

TEST	ACUTE TUBULAR NECROSIS	REDUCED RENAL BLOOD FLOW
Urine		
Volume	Less than 400 ml./24 hr.	Less than 400 ml./24 hr.
Sodium	Between 40–100 mEq./L.	Less than 5 mEq./L.
Specific gravity	1.010	Usually greater than 1.020
Osmolality	250–350 mOsm/L.	Usually greater than 500 mOsm/L.
Urea	200–300 mg./100 ml.	Usually greater than 600 mg./100 ml.
Creatinine	Less than 60 mg./100 ml.	Usually greater than 150 mg./100 ml.
Blood		
BUN:Cr	10:1	Usually greater than 20:1
Response to		
Mannitol	None	None or flow increases to greater than 40 ml./hr.
Furosemide	None	Flow increases to greater than 40 ml./hr.

The urinary changes present in patients with acute tubular necrosis are largely a consequence of loss of tubule function. Hypertension is uncommon in patients with acute tubular necrosis and when present suggests fluid and sodium excess.

When the patient presents to the hospital with oliguric renal failure other causes of acute renal insufficiency must be considered such as lupus glomerulonephritis, periarteritis, rapidly progressive glomerulonephritis, poststreptococcal glomerulonephritis, etc. In addition, the possibility of chronic parenchymal renal disease exists.

Rarely does the patient with acute tubular necrosis have total anuria. This is an important point in helping to differentiate acute tubular necrosis from obstructive uropathy. However, retrograde urography is frequently necessary to exclude obstruction.

Management

The primary consideration in any patient with acute tubular necrosis is maintenance of fluid and electrolyte balance. During the oliguric phase urinary volume is usually less than 300 ml./day. Insensible losses average 800–1,000 ml./day and are virtually free of electrolytes. In general, fluid replacement should be approximately 500 ml./day. Additional water will be obtained from the water present in foods plus the water of oxidation from metabolism. Because of the utilization of body proteins and fats, the patient ideally should lose around 1 pound a day in order to maintain water balance. The danger of fluid overload with resulting congestive heart failure and pulmonary edema exists throughout the oliguric period. In contrast, during the diuretic phase of acute tubular necrosis there may be extensive sodium wasting in association with the increased urinary volumes. It is thus necessary to keep accurate intake and output records as well as daily weights during both phases. This is especially important when there are other avenues of fluid and electrolyte losses such as with vomiting, diarrhea, nasogastric suction, and drainages from fistulae. In general, losses occurring as a result of the above should be replaced in full.

Outside of adequate fluid and electrolyte replacement, intake is directed

TABLE 11-2
RECOMMENDED DOSAGE FOR ANTIBIOTICS

GROUP	ANTIBIOTIC	RECOMMENDED DOSE	
		SERUM CREATININE 4–10 mg. percent	SERUM CREATININE 10 mg. percent
1. Marked reduction in dosage	Tetracycline Oxytetracycline Kanamycin Streptomycin Colimycin Polymyxin	Loading dose followed by standard doses at intervals of 1 to 2 days.	Loading dose followed by standard dose at intervals of 3 to 4 days.
2. Modest reduction in dosage	Penicillin G Lincomycin Cephalothin	Loading dose followed by: Standard doses at 4- to 5-hr. intervals. Standard doses at 6-hr. intervals. Standard doses at 12-hr. intervals.	Loading dose followed by: Standard doses at 8- to 10-hr. intervals. Standard doses at 12-hr. intervals. Standard doses at 24-hr. intervals.
3. No reduction in dosage	Chloramphenicol Erythromycin Methicillin Oxacillin Novobiocin	Same as in the normal.	Same as in the normal.

From W. B. Schwartz and J. P. Kassirer, *American Journal of Medicine*, Vol. 44 (1968), p. 796.

at supplying the patient with calories in the form of carbohydrates and fats to decrease the rate of breakdown of body protein. Since one gram of urea is formed from every six grams of protein metabolized, protein intake is usually restricted in order to prevent the BUN from rising at too fast a rate.

Certain drugs should be avoided or dosage reduced in any patient with markedly impaired renal function. Because of the possibility of magnesium intoxication, antacids containing magnesium should be avoided. Because of the reduced renal function digitalis excretion may be reduced. Dosage should be altered to avoid excessively high blood levels. In addition, certain antibiotics should be given in much smaller dosages than usually employed. (See Table 11-2.)

Before administering a drug to a patient with renal failure, it is wise to review the following questions:
1. Does the drug depend on the kidney for secretion?
2. Does an excess blood level affect the kidney?
3. Does the drug add chemically to the pool of urea nitrogen?
4. Does the effect of the drug alter electrolyte imbalance?
5. Is the patient more susceptible to the drug because of kidney disease?

Acidosis

Metabolic acidosis of moderate severity is usually present in patients with renal failure. This results from the inability of the kidneys to excrete fixed acids (e.g., H_2PO_4) produced from normal metabolic processes. The acidosis can usually be easily controlled by giving the patient 30–60 mEq. of sodium bicarbonate daily.

Hyperkalemia

Hyperkalemia commonly occurs in patients with acute tubular necrosis. This is a consequence both of the reduced ability of the kidneys to excrete potassium and the release of intracellular potassium because of acidosis. The acidosis results in movement of the hydrogen ion into the cell, thus displacing potassium into the extracellular fluid. This maintains electrical neutrality but increases the hyperkalemic state. Hyperkalemia is manifested clinically by cardiac and neuromuscular changes. Both cardiac conduction disturbances and acute flaccid quadraplegia are life-threatening complications. These hyperkalemic changes are rapidly reversed by giving intravenous calcium gluconate which has a direct antagonist effect on the action of potassium. Reduction of the serum potassium can be accomplished by treating the acidosis with intravenous sodium bicarbonate. In addition, glucose and insulin are frequently used as an additional method of shifting extracellular potassium to intracellular pools. Hyperkalemia is usually preventable by avoiding potassium supplements, giving chronic therapy for acidosis and using sodium polystyrene sulfonate resin (Kayexalate) when serum potassium is even slightly elevated.

During the oliguric phase sodium retention may occur. However, with the onset of the diuretic period urinary volume and sodium excretion may markedly increase. Urinary volume is largely determined by the state of hydration at the onset of the diuretic period. Since urinary sodium concentration is relatively fixed, sodium losses are largely determined by urinary volume. Therefore, if the patient is markedly overhydrated at the onset of the diuretic phase, sodium losses may be severe. Clinically sodium depletion is characterized by either extracellular volume depletion as manifested by tachycardia

TABLE 11-3
COMMON FLUID AND ELECTROLYTE IMBALANCES

ELECTROLYTE DISTURBANCE	MAJOR SYMPTOMS	MAJOR PHYSICAL FINDINGS	ETIOLOGY
Increased sodium and water	Dyspnea	Edema, anasarca, rales, increased JVP.	Congestive failure, renal disease, liver disease.
Decreased sodium and water	Thirst Weakness	Tachycardia, postural hypotension, sunken eyes, dry mouth, decreased skin turgor.	Excessive sweating, vomiting, diarrhea, Addison's disease, renal disease, diuretics without replacement.
Decreased sodium normal water	Headaches Psychological disorder	Hyperreflexia, pathological reflexes, convulsions, coma.	Water without sodium replacement in above states. Excess ADH.
Normal sodium and decreased water	Thirst	Often no findings or those found in decreased sodium and water.	Lack of water intake, diabetes insipidus, excessive sweating, fever.
Hyperkalemia	Weakness	Paralysis, ECG changes: Spiked T waves.	Renal disease, excess potassium replacement.
Hypokalemia	Weakness	Paralysis, patalytic ileus, hypoventilation, ECG changes: T waves and prominent U waves.	Diuretics, renal diseases, diarrhea, vomiting, excess laxatives.
Acidosis	Weakness	Kussmaul respiration.	Renal disease, diabetic acidosis, certain intoxications.
Hypermagnesemia	Weakness	Muscle weakness, hypoventilation, hypotension, flushing.	Antacids with renal disease.

and postural hypotension or water intoxication when sodium losses exceed water losses. This latter syndrome is characterised by markedly reduced serum sodium concentrations in association with personality changes, convulsions, coma, and death if allowed to progress untreated. With acute water intoxication, treatment is directed at raising the serum sodium concentration. This can usually be accomplished by giving hypertonic (3–5 percent) sodium chloride intravenously. Table 11-3 lists common fluid and electrolyte imbalances.

In addition to the above specific electrolyte disturbances, the patient may develop symptoms associated with any uremic state. Early the patient has nausea, anorexia, and vomiting. Later this progresses to stupor, convulsions, and coma. In addition, the patient may develop bleeding abnormalities, uremic pneumonitis, pericarditis, pleuritis, etc. Dialysis is indicated prior to the development of clinical symptoms of uremia. With the availability of hemodialysis or peritoneal dialysis in most hospitals, there is little reason for the clinical features of uremia to occur in patients with acute tubular necrosis. Most patients having oliguria for more than 4–5 days will require dialysis sometime during the course of their acute tubular necrosis. There is little doubt that dialysis has improved survival in patients with acute tubular necrosis. During World War II, when dialysis was not available, mortality rate was 90 percent in battle casualties developing renal failure. Mortality rate was reduced to 50 percent with hemodialysis in casualties with renal failure during the Korean War.

Prognosis is largely determined by the primary event that led to the development of acute tubular necrosis. Medical causes of acute tubular necrosis such as transfusion reactions, myoglobinuria, nephrotoxic agents, and simple volume depletion are accomplished by a mortality rate of around 25 percent, whereas cases resulting from trauma and severe surgical complications have a mortality rate of 70–80 percent. Death usually results as a complication of poor wound healing and sepsis. In view of the continuing high mortality rate associated with acute tubular necrosis, every effort should be directed toward the prevention of this complication when the patient is seen early during the course of his shock state.

REFERENCE

1. N. K. Hollenberg, D. F. Adams, D. E. Oken, H. L. Abrams, and J. P. Merrill, "Acute Renal Failure Due to Nephrotoxins," *New England Journal of Medicine*, Vol. 282 (1970), p. 1329.

SELECTED RENAL FUNCTION TESTS CREATININE CLEARANCE, SPECIFIC GRAVITY, AND OSMOLALITY

The patient whose condition is serious enough to warrant observation in the critical care unit will frequently manifest abnormalities of renal function, either as the result of impaired ability to excrete nitrogenous waste products or because of an inability to handle water loads efficiently, or both. It is therefore mandatory that certain aspects of renal function be monitored, either on an intermittent or continuing basis, in order that these complications can be detected early and appropriate therapy instituted. In most circumstances the parameters followed will include the urine output, the urine solute concentration (frequently in relation to the plasma solute concentration), and some parameter of the kidneys' ability to excrete nitrogenous waste products.

The most commonly used test of renal excretory function is the creatinine clearance. Creatinine is formed as a byproduct of normal muscle metabolism and is excreted in the urine primarily as the result of glomerular filtration, with a small percentage secreted into the urine by the kidney tubules. It is therefore a useful indicator of the glomerular filtration rate. The amount of creatinine excreted in the urine of any given individual is related to his muscle mass and will remain quite constant unless muscle wasting occurs. The actual creatinine clearance is calculated by the formula:

$$\text{Clearance creatinine} = \frac{UV}{P}$$

where U is the urine creatinine concentration, V the urine volume, and P the plasma creatinine concentration. The most important technical aspect of this test is the accuracy of the urine collection, as it is important to know the exact time it took to form the sample and the exact amount of creatinine present. The expression UV tells how much creatinine appears in the urine during the period of collection, and this can be readily converted to mg./minute which is the standard reference point. Dividing this by the plasma creatinine concentration (which has to be converted from mg./100 ml. to mg./ml.) tells the minimum number of milliliters of plasma which must have been filtered by the glomeruli in order to produce the measured amount of creatinine in the urine. The final result is expressed in ml./min. and the range in normals varies between 80–120 ml./minute, depending on the individual's size and age. If the kidneys are damaged by some disease process the creatinine clearance will decrease and the serum creatinine concentration will rise. The urine creatinine excretion will initially decrease until the blood level rises to a point at which the amount of creatinine appearing in the urine is again equal to the amount being produced by the body. For example, a normal individual with a serum creatinine concentration of 1.0 mg./percent and a creatinine excretion of 1.0 mg./minute has a creatinine clearance of 100 ml./minute. If the individual develops renal disease with 50 percent loss of renal function his serum creatinine will rise to 2.0 mg./percent and he will continue to excrete 1.0 mg. of creatinine in his urine per minute. In many situations where the patient has rapidly changing renal function and oliguria, as in acute tubular necrosis, the creatinine clearance becomes less reliable until the situation becomes more stable. It is therefore useful to follow the serum creatinine concentration as an indicator of the rate and direction of change until stability occurs.

The specific gravity of the urine is the time-honored test of the kidneys' ability to concentrate and dilute the urine. The specific gravity measures the buoyancy of a solution compared to water and depends upon the number of particles in solution as well as their size and weight. Two methods have been used to obtain this measurement in clinical practice, the *hydrometer* and the *refractometer* (or TS meter, as it is frequently called). The hydrometer has been in clinical use for many years and is the less preferred of the two methods because it requires a much larger volume of urine, results are less reproducible, and it requires a greater amount of time. The refractometer is highly reproducible and requires only a drop of urine for the measurement. In addition, this instrument can be used to measure the total solids of plasma (thus the name TS meter) which is a good indicator of the plasma protein concentration and a useful indicator of the state of a patient's fluid balance, especially when serial determinations are made. The refractometer because of the above advantages should replace the hydrometer for specific gravity determinations and should be used in the critical care unit.

The normal kidney has the capacity to dilute the urine to a specific gravity of 1.001 and to concentrate the urine to at least 1.022 (higher values are not unusual). Normally the individual's water balance will determine whether the urine is concentrated or dilute, a dilute urine being an indicator of water excess and a concentrated urine an indicator of a water deficit. In many renal diseases the ability of the kidneys to form a concentrated urine is lost and the specific gravity becomes "fixed" at 1.010, a finding which might be seen in acute tubular necrosis and acute nephritis.

As with many simple laboratory tests there are limitations in the accuracy of the specific gravity determination. The specific gravity is not always the most accurate indicator of the ability of the kidneys to concentrate the urine because the concentrating ability is a reflection of the concentration of particles in the urine. In addition to the concentration of particles, the specific gravity is also in part dependent upon the size and weight of the particles in solution. Therefore, a falsely high specific gravity determination will be found when high-molecular-weight substances such as protein, glucose, mannitol, and radiographic contrast material are present in the urine. A greater degree of accuracy can be obtained with urine osmolality determinations.

The *osmolality* of a solution is an expression of the total number (concentration) of particles in solution and is independent of the size, molecular weight, or electrical charge of the molecules. All substances in solution contribute to the osmolality to a certain degree. For example, a mol (gram molecular weight) of sodium chloride dissociates incompletely into Na^+ and Cl^- ions and produces 1.86 osmols when dissolved in a kilogram of solvent (such as plasma). A mol of nonionic solute (such as glucose or urea) produces only one osmol when dissolved in a kilogram of solvent. The total concentration of particles in a solution is the osmolality and is reported in units of osmols/kg. of solvent. In clinical situations, because we are dealing with much smaller concentrations, the osmolality is reported in milliosmols (thousandth of an osmol, abbreviated mOsm) per kilogram of solvent (plasma or serum).

The osmolality is determined in the laboratory by measuring the freezing point of the solution, the freezing point being directly related to the number of particles in solution. The normal serum osmolality is made up primarily of sodium and its accompanying anions, with urea and glucose contributing about 5 mOsm each. Therefore, knowing the serum sodium, urea and glucose concentrations we can calculate the osmolality of plasma by the formula

$$\text{Osmolality} = 2\,\text{Na} + \frac{\text{BUN}}{2.6} + \frac{\text{glucose}}{18}$$

The calculated osmolality will normally be within 10 mOsm of the measured osmolality, which normally averages 290 ± 5 mOsm/kg. The plasma osmolality in normal individuals is quite constant from day to day.

Because water permeates freely between the blood, interstitial fluid and tissues, a change in the osmolality of one body compartment will produce a shift in body fluids so that the osmolality of the plasma is always the same as that of the other body compartments, except in the most rapidly changing conditions, where a slight lag may occur.

The significance of the osmolality lies in the fact that the plasma osmolality is the main regulator of the release of antidiuretic hormone (ADH). When sufficient water is not being taken in the osmolality will rise stimulating the release of ADH which signals the kidneys to conserve water and produce a more concentrated urine. When excessive amounts of water are ingested the osmolality decreases, ADH release is inhibited and the urine becomes more dilute. Under maximum ADH stimulation the kidneys can concentrate the urine to approximately 1,200 mOsm/kg., and with maximum ADH suppression (water load) the kidneys can dilute the urine to approximately 50 mOsm/kg. Thus there is no single normal urine osmolality but rather a range in which predicted values might be expected, depending upon the clinical setting. Also, unlike the plasma, the urine osmolality is less dependent on the urine sodium concentration, and other substances such as urea play a more important role. In renal disease one of the first renal functions to be lost is the ability to concentrate urine. As a reflection of this, the urine osmolality becomes fixed within 50 mOsm of the simultaneously determined serum osmolality. Therefore the osmolality is a useful parameter of renal function.

The serum and urine osmolality are of use in combination in a number of other circumstances. In the patient with diabetes insipidus, as a result of neurologic disease or injury the urine volume would be increased with a low urine osmolality (50–100 mOsm) and the serum osmolality would be increased (310 mOsm or greater) unless the fluid loss had been replaced. On the other hand, the patient with carcinoma of the lung, porphyria, or CNS disease might have an excess production of ADH, or an ADH-like material, and have the opposite picture, with a low serum osmolality and a disproportionately high urine osmolality.

As already indicated, the serum osmolality may be increased or decreased in various states. A decrease in the serum osmolality can only occur when the serum sodium is decreased. An increase in the serum osmolality can occur whenever the serum sodium, urea, or glucose are elevated or when there are abnormal compounds present in the blood, such as drugs or poisons or metabolic waste products which are not usually measured, such as lactic acid. Symptoms due to increased osmolality usually occur when the osmolality is greater than 350 mOsm, and coma occurs when the osmolality is in the 400 range or above.

The usual close correlation between the measured and calculated osmolality has been mentioned. In certain circumstances the measured serum osmolality might be significantly higher than the calculated osmolality when substances of unusual nature are present in the blood. Many drugs and toxins such as aspirin and alcohol raise the serum osmolality. In a comatose patient a discrepancy between the measured and calculated serum osmolalities might lead to the appropriate drug screen to provide the correct diagnosis. In patients with heart failure, hepatic disease, or shock a discrepancy between the measured and calculated osmolalities, due to unknown metabolities of 40 or more mOsm, has been correlated with a mortality of 95 percent or greater. The knowledgeable use and interpretation of the laboratory determinations described in the preceding paragraphs are of major importance in the assessment of the renal complications of the seriously ill patient. Their value lies in the prevention as well as the diagnosis of these complications. They are not cited to the exclusion of the usual parameters of close and accurate fluid and electrolyte balance, which are equally important to the understanding of the renal status of the patient.

12

Assessment Skills for the Nurse
and
Management Modalities

ANNE T. BOBAL, R.N., B.S.

MONITORING FLUID BALANCE

Body fluid equilibrium is based on intake and output—the amount of fluid taken in and the volume excreted. Water is lost through the kidneys, gastrointestinal tract, skin and lungs and is replaced by water from fluids, solid foods (which are 60–90 percent water), and from the oxidation of food and body tissues. Under normal circumstances and in the presence of adequate renal function, the losses equal the intake and the net balance is zero. Table 12-1 summarizes water gains and losses.

A review of the variables that interfere with normal fluid balance may assist the nurse in evaluating fluid problems in the clinical setting. Fluid imbalances may be the result of inadequate intake, excessive losses without adequate replacement, and impaired renal function.

Inadequate Intake

Inadequate fluid intake in the conscious patient may be the result of anorexia, apathy, lethargy, and difficulty in swallowing. Weak and feeble patients and infants are especially vulnerable simply because they cannot make their need for water known. In central nervous system disturbances the sense of thirst may be impaired, while in unconscious states the patient is entirely dependent on nursing personnel for fluid administration.

TABLE 12-1
WAYS IN WHICH WATER AND
ELECTROLYTES BALANCE EACH OTHER IN HEALTH

GAINS	RANGE IN ML.	LOSSES	RANGE IN ML.
Water from fluids	500–1,700	Water vapor loss through lungs & skin	850-1,200
Water from solid food	800–1,000	Water loss through urine	600–1,600
Water from oxidation of food and body tissues	200–300	Water loss through feces	
Total	1,500–3,000	Total	1,500–3,000

The chief sources of fluid gain in health are...
  • water present in liquids
  • water present in solid food and
  • water derived from oxidation

These gains equal the losses caused by...
  • water lost via insensible perspiration
  • water lost through urine and
  • water lost through feces

Travenol Laboratories, Inc.

Excessive Losses

Circumstances which increase losses include the following.
  A. Fever and increased respiratory rate. A patient with a temperature of 104°F and a respiratory rate of 30–40/minute can lose as much as 2500 ml. in a 24 hour period.
  B. Environment—hot and dry climates.
  C. Activity—increased metabolic rate.
  D. Hyperventilation.
  E. Tracheostomy.
  F. Increased gastrointestinal losses due to vomiting, diarrhea, gastric suction, fistulas, and ileostomies.
  G. Burns—fluid loss through the skin may amount to 1,000 to 2,000 ml./day.

H. Perspiration—with mild sweating a patient may lose up to 500 ml./day, with profuse sweating up to 1,000 ml./day.
I. Diuretic phase of acute tubular necrosis (see Chapter 11).

Decreased Renal Function

The kidneys play an essential role in regulating water and electrolyte balance. Providing renal function is normal, a minimum of 400 ml. of fluid must be excreted as urine to prevent the accumulation of metabolic wastes. However, this minimum urinary volume is markedly influenced by the osmotic load excreted. In certain states such as hyperalimentation the increased urea production will necessitate a larger urinary volume. This also occurs in uncontrolled diabetes where marked glycosuria requires increased excretion.

Nursing Assessment

The nurse's role in the evaluation, correction, and maintenance of fluid balance includes accurate recording of intake-output, weight, and vital signs. The most sensitive indices of changes in body water content are serial weights and intake-output patterns, while trends in vital signs provide important supporting data. Assessment of fluid imbalance is based on observation and recognition of pertinent symptoms, and nursing action involves replacement or restriction of fluids.

Intake and Output

An accurate intake-output record will provide valuable data in evaluating and treating fluid imbalances. It is important that all nursing personnel, the patient, and his visitors are involved and instructed. Circumstances will dictate how exact the record should be and what data will be included. For example, in an uncomplicated postsurgical situation, fluid replacement may be projected on estimated and actual losses for a 24-hour period. All measurable intake and output are recorded and totaled at the end of every shift. However, in the presence of excessive losses and/or deteriorating cardiac and renal function more detailed recording of every source of fluid intake and output is necessary. Calculations are often done on a q 1–4 hour basis. Intake includes not only pure liquids such as water and juices, but also those foods which are high in water such as oranges, grapefruit, and those which become liquid at room temperature such as Jello and ice cream. Ice chips and cubes must also be measured. It is useful to keep a list of fluid equivalents for fruits, ice cubes, and other sources of fluids. In severe electrolyte and fluid imbalances the time and type of fluid intake and the time and amount of each voiding should be recorded. This becomes important as it may be useful baseline data during tests for renal function.

A record of losses should also include emeses, stools, and drainages. When dressings are saturated with drainage, they should be weighed before and after changing. Other data such as temperature, pulse, respiratory rate and degree of perspiration should be available for estimating insensible losses.

Weight

Rapid daily gains and losses in weight are usually related to changes in fluid volume. Because of the difficulties in obtaining accurate figures for intake and output records, serial weights are often more reliable. In addition, weight changes will usually pick up imbalances before symptoms are apparent. As with intake and output records the weighing procedure should be consistent. The patient should be weighed on the same scale with the same attire, preferably in the morning before breakfast and after voiding. Variations in the procedure should be noted and made known to the physician. A kilogram scale provides for greater accuracy since drug, fluid, and diet calculations utilize the metric system and conversion from pounds to kilograms may lead to discrepancies.

Normally, a patient with a balanced nutritional intake will maintain his weight. A patient whose protein intake is limited or who is catabolic will lose about a pound a day. A weight gain of more than 1 lb./day suggests fluid retention. A generally accepted guide is that a quart of fluid is reflected in one-half kilogram of weight gained.

Assessment of Hypovolemia and Hypervolemia

The diagnosis of extracellular volume depletion or overload is seldom made on the basis of one parameter. The first clue to the nurse may be the patient's general appearance, after which more specific observations are noted. Symptoms will vary with the degree of imbalance some symptoms being seen early in imbalance states and others not being evident until severe imbalances are reached. The following chart lists the physical assessment and symptoms of fluid imbalance, and can be used as a guide for nursing assessment.

Other guidelines used to evaluate fluid states are hematocrit, central venous pressure, urine specific gravity, osmolality, and chest X-rays. Specific gravity and CVP readings have been discussed in Chapters 6 and 11. In fluid overload, a chest X-ray may show the following changes: prominent vascular markings, increased heart size, pleural effusion, infiltrates, or frank pulmonary congestion. The hematocrit may be elevated in depletion states and decreased in overload, but other factors must be considered. For example, the hematocrit with hypovolemia may be low when significant blood loss has taken place. All data should be evaluated in the light of other influences. Trends are usually more significant than isolated values. For example, when the nurse notes a decrease in urine output, a systematic assessment should

TABLE 12-2
PHYSICAL ASSESSMENT
AND SYMPTOMS OF IMBALANCE

ASSESSMENT OF	HYPOVOLEMIA	HYPERVOLEMIA
Skin and subcutaneous tissues	Dry, loss of elasticity	Warm, moist, pitting edema over bony prominences, wrinkled skin from pressure of clothing
Face	Sunken eyes (late symptom)	Periorbital edema
Tongue	Dry, coated (early symptom), fissured (late symptom)	Moist
Saliva	Thick, scanty	Excessive, frothy
Thirst	Present	May not be significant
Temperature	May be elevated	May not be significant
Pulse	Rapid, weak thready	Rapid
Respirations	Rapid, shallow	Rapid dyspnea, moist rales
Blood Pressure	Low, orthostatic hypotension, small pulse pressure	Normal to high
Weight	Loss	Gain

follow in order to determine why this is happening and what nursing interventions are most appropriate. Any system of assessment will work when it is consistent and thorough. After reviewing the intake and output records for both the current and the previous day and assessing the symptoms and parameters just discussed, a decision to increase or decrease fluid intake can be made. In the absence of symptoms of fluid retention, when intravenous fluids are behind schedule and intake is inadequate for the patient's condition, missed fluids should be given. The patient's fluid status, especially his urine output, should be watched closely for the next few hours to evaluate whether or not the increase in fluid intake corrected the patient's fluid balance. If, however, urine output is zero or diminished in the presence of adequate fluid intake, no further fluids are given and the physician is called immediately. If a patient presents any of the symptoms of fluid overload discussed earlier all fluid intake is restricted and the physician is notified immediately.

As stated previously, fluid replacement may be calculated for any given period of time, depending on the severity of the situation. For example, a 24-hour calculation of intake for a patient who is oliguric with normal insensible losses could be:

Previous 24-hour urine output	100 cc.
Insensible loss replacement	500 cc.
Total 24-hour fluid allowance	600 cc.

While the physician will specify the total amount and kind of fluid replacement, the details of distribution are often decided by the nurse. Priority is given to requirements for administration of drugs, both intravenous and oral. Distribution of the remaining fluid is then made according to patient preference. The nurse guides the patient in his selection to avoid having his entire day's allowance gone early in the day. Because sodium and potassium may be restricted in the patient with renal failure, fluids such as ginger ale, 7-Up, and Kool Aid which are low in sodium and potassium are given.

HEMODIALYSIS

Principles of Operation

Dialysis refers to the diffusion of dissolved particles from one fluid compartment to another across a semipermeable membrane. In hemodialysis, the blood is one fluid compartment and the dialysate is the other. The semipermeable membrane is a thin, porous cellophane. The pore size of the membrane permits the passage of low-molecular-weight substances such as urea, creatinine, and uric acid to diffuse through the pores of the membrane. Water molecules are also very small and move freely through the membrane. Most plasma proteins, bacteria, and blood cells are too large to pass through the pores of the membrane. The difference in the concentration of the substances in the two compartments is called the *concentration gradient*. The blood, which contains waste products such as urea and creatinine, flows into the dialyzer or artificial kidney where it comes into contact with the dialysate containing no urea and creatinine. A maximum gradient is established so that movement of these substances is from the blood to the dialysate. Repeated passages of the blood through the dialyzer over a period of time (6–10 hours) reduces the level of these waste products to a near normal state. Hemodialysis is indicated in acute and chronic renal failure, drug and chemical intoxications, severe fluid and electrolyte imbalances, and hepato-renal syndrome.

The functions of the artificial kidney system are summarized as follows.

1. Removes the byproducts of protein metabolism such as urea, creatinine, and uric acid.
2. Removes excess water (ultrafiltration) by changing osmotic pressure. This is done by adding a high concentration of dextrose to the dialysate, or effecting a pressure differential between the blood and fluid compartments by mechanical means.
3. Maintains or restores the body buffer system.
4. Maintains or restores the level of electrolytes in the body.

Major Components of the Artificial Kidney System

A. The dialyzer or artificial kidney which supports the cellophane compartments. Dialyzers vary in size, physical structure and efficiency. The efficiency of a dialyzer refers to its ability to remove water and waste products. There are advantages and disadvantages to each dialyzer that must be considered in dialyzer selection. Whether the dialyzer will be used primarily for acute or chronic dialysis is an important consideration. A highly efficient, shorter-run dialyzer may be more appropriate for use in drug intoxications or in acutely ill patients where a long dialysis is undesirable. On the other hand, the more rapid fluid and electrolyte changes, characteristic of an efficient dialyzer, are often avoided in the chronic patient. A low-blood-volume dialyzer is advantageous in dialyzing children and small adults. Economy of cost may dictate the selection of a shorter-run dialyzer to prevent higher personnel costs. Sometimes the final selection depends solely on the training and philosophy of personnel in charge of the unit.

B. Dialysate or Dialyzing Solution
The dialysate or "bath" is a solution composed of water and the major electrolytes of normal serum. It is made in a clean system with filtered tap water and chemicals. It is not a sterile system, but since bacteria are too large to pass through the membrane, contamination from this source is not a major problem. Dialysate concentrates are usually provided by commercial manufacturers. A "standard" bath is generally used in chronic units but variations may be made to meet specific patient needs.

C. Dialysate Delivery System
A single delivery unit provides dialysate for one patient; the multiple delivery system may supply up to twenty units. Two systems are commonly used for preparing dialysate. In the batch system the dialysate is prepared in a large 100-300-L. tank. In the proportioning system water and dialysate concentrate are automatically delivered in preset amounts to a mix tank. Metering and monitoring devices assure precise control of the water-concentrate ratio.

D. Accessory equipment includes a blood pump, infusion pumps for heparin and protamine delivery, and monitoring devices to detect unsafe temperature concentration, pressure leaks, and blood leaks.

E. The Human Component

Expertise in the use of highly technical equipment is accomplished through theoretical and practical training in the clinical setting. The operation and monitoring of dialysis equipment will differ, however. Reference to the manufacturer's instruction manuals will give the nurse guidelines for the safe operation of equipment. Although the technical aspects of hemodialysis may at first seem overwhelming, they can be learned fairly rapidly. A more critical aspect and one that takes long to achieve is the understanding and knowledge that the nurse will utilize in her care of the patients during dialysis. Because hemodialysis is a dynamic changing process, alterations in blood chemistries and fluid balance can occur. The nurse's observation skills, assessment of symptoms, and appropriate actions can make the difference between a smooth dialysis with a minimum of problems and one fraught with a series of crises for the patient and the nurse.

Predialysis Assessment

The degree and complexity of problems arising during hemodialysis will vary from patient to patient and will depend on many factors. Important variables are the patient's diagnosis, stage of illness, age, other medical problems, fluid and electrolyte balance, and emotional state.

An essential first step in the hemodialysis procedure is a review of the patient's history, the clinical records, laboratory reports, and finally the nurse's observation of the patient.

The patient's emotional state should be included in this initial evaluation. The anxiety and apprehension, especially during a first dialysis, may contribute to change in blood pressure, restlessness, and gastrointestinal upsets. The security provided by the presence of a nurse during the first dialysis is probably more desirable than giving the patient a drug that might precipitate changes in vital signs.

Risk Factors: Prevention, Assessment, and Nursing Intervention

FLUID IMBALANCES

Evaluation of fluid balance is desirable prior to dialysis so that corrective measures may be initiated early in the procedure. Parameters such as blood pressure, pulse, weight, intake and output, and the presence of certain symptoms will assist the nurse in estimating fluid overload or depletion.

The term "dry" or "ideal" weight is used to depict the weight at which a patient's blood pressure is in a normal range for him and he is free of the symptoms of fluid imbalance. The figure is not an absolute one, but it gives the nurse a guideline for fluid removal or replacement, especially in patients with chronic renal failure. It requires frequent review and revision, especially in the newly dialyzed patient in whom frequent changes in weight are taking place due to fluid removal or accumulation and to tissue gains or losses.

HYPERVOLEMIA

The presence of some or all of the following may suggest fluid overload: blood-pressure elevation, increased pulse and respiratory rate, dyspnea, moist rales, cough, edema, excessive weight gain since last dialysis, and a history or record of excessive fluid intake in the absence of adequate losses.

A chest X-ray to assess heart size and/or pulmonary congestion may confirm the diagnosis of fluid overload, but may not be essential in the presence of overt symptoms. Increase in abdominal girth will suggest accumulation of fluid in the abdominal cavity. If ascites is present, measuring the abdominal girth will provide another useful tool in estimating correction of the problem.

Treatment of fluid overload during dialysis is directed toward the removal of the excess water. Care must be taken to avoid too rapid volume depletion during dialysis. Excessive fluid removal may lead to hypotension, and little is gained if intravenous fluids are given to correct the problem. Thus it is better to reduce the volume overload over a period of two or three dialyses. An analysis of the causes of the fluid overload is necessary to prevent re-occurrences. The intake and output record may provide a clue. For example, the patient may have been given excessive I.V. fluids in a "keep open" I.V. or fluids used as a vehicle for I.V. medications may not have been calculated in the intake. The patient may not have adhered to his fluid restriction or may have had a decrease in his fluid losses. For example, gastric suction may have been discontinued. Often, after the institution of chronic dialysis, urinary output decreases. If the patient continues his normal fluid intake he will become fluid-overloaded. In the chronic hemodialysis patient fluid overload may be related to the intake of high sodium foods. Moderate restriction is necessary for all patients to prevent extracellular fluid overload. Change in weight provides an indication of water load and an acceptable weight gain is 0.5 kg. for each 24-hour between dialyses.

HYPOVOLEMIA

Assessment of hypovolemia is also made on the evaluation of trends in vital signs and symptoms. Clues to hypovolemia include falling blood pressure, increasing pulse and respiration rates, loss of skin turgor, dry mouth, a falling CVP, and a decreasing urine output. A history of excessive fluid loss through profuse perspiration, vomiting, diarrhea, and gastric suctioning with resulting weight loss, will further substantiate the diagnosis. Treatment is directed toward the replacement of previous losses and the prevention of further losses during dialysis.

It is usual practice to plebotomize the patient at the onset of dialysis. The patient's blood is pumped through the dialyzer, displacing the priming normal saline solution. In the hypovolemic patient the nurse can connect the venous return blood line immediately and infuse the normal saline into the patient. This 200 ml. of solution might be sufficient to restore balance or at least prevent further hypotension. Ultrafiltration will be avoided in the hypovolemic patient and he may even require additional fluids. Normal saline is the solution used most frequently to replace volume depletion during dialysis because small volumes usually produce the desired effect. Replacement in increments of 50 ml. are suggested, with frequent monitoring of blood pressure. Blood-volume expanders such as albumin are sometimes used in patients with a low serum protein. The treatment is expensive when the underlying cause of the hypoproteinemia is not corrected and repeated infusions become necessary.

HYPOTENSION

Hypotension during dialysis may be caused by preexisting hypovolemia, excessive ultrafiltration, loss of blood into the dialyzer, and antihypertensive drug therapy. Hypotension at the beginning of dialysis may occur in patients with a small blood volume such as children and small women. Using a small-volume dialyzer or starting dialysis at a slower blood flow rate may avoid or minimize problems.

Hypotension later in dialysis is usually due to excessive ultrafiltration. This may be confirmed by weighing the patient and estimating fluid loss. Keeping the patient in a horizontal position, reducing the blood-flow rate, and discontinuing ultrafiltration may return the blood pressure to normal. If hypotension persists, saline or other plasma expanders may be administered. I.V. fluids should be kept to a minimum and discontinued as soon as the patient is normotensive. Salty liquids or food may be given, but their effect is slower than intravenous administration.

Blood loss due to technical problems such as membrane leaks and line separations may lead to hypotension. The use of blood leak detectors and other monitoring devices has reduced the risk of excessive blood loss due to these causes, but they do occur. If separation of blood lines occurs, clamping the arterial blood line and stopping the blood pump immediately will minimize further blood loss. In a membrane leak the dialysis is discontinued and the dialyzer replaced. Although small leaks may seal over, they may progress to gross leaks and dialysate may cross the membrane into the blood compartment. In this situation, the blood may be returned to the patient, but he should be observed for pyrogenic reactions. If the patient's hematocrit is low, the risk of blood loss may be greater than the possiblity of dialysate contamination. Some units have standing policies to cover this contingency; however, decisions may be made on individual circumstances.

The use of antihypertensive drugs in the dialysis patient may precipitate hypotension during dialysis. To avoid this, it is standard practice in many units to omit antihypertensive drugs 4–6 hours before dialysis. Fluids and sodium restrictions are more desirable controls for hypertension. Sedatives and tranquilizers may also cause hypotension and should be avoided if possible.

HYPERTENSION

The most frequent causes of hypertension during dialysis are fluid overload, disequilibrium syndrome, and anxiety.

Hypertension during dialysis is usually caused by sodium and water excesses. This can be confirmed by comparing the patient's present weight to his ideal or dry weight. If fluid overload is the cause of hypertension, ultrafiltration will usually bring about a reduction in the blood pressure.

Some patients who may be normotensive before dialysis become hypertensive during dialysis. The rise may occur either gradually or abruptly. The cause is not well understood, but may be the result of increased cardiac output as fluid overload is corrected.

Hypertension is a common finding in dialysis disequilibrium syndrome and will usually respond to correction of that condition. If the diastolic blood pressure is over 120 or the patient has symptoms, small doses of Apresoline may be given intravenously into the venous blood line. An initial dose of 10 mg. may bring about a favorable response. Apresoline is preferred to Aldomet because its effect is more rapid. Blood pressure is monitored at frequent intervals following the administration of antihypertensive drugs.

Anxiety, fear, and apprehension, especially during the first dialysis, may cause transient and erratic hypertension. Sedatives may be necessary, but confidence in the staff and a smooth, problem-free dialysis will help reduce anxiety during subsequent treatments.

DIALYSIS DISEQUILIBRIUM SYNDROME

Dialysis disequilibrium syndrome is manifested by a group of symptoms suggestive of cerebral dysfunction. Symptoms range in severity from mild nausea, vomiting, headache, and hypertension to agitation, twitching, mental confusion, and convulsions. It is thought that rapid efficient dialysis results in shifts in water, pH, and osmolality between cerebrospinal fluid and blood, causing the symptoms.

Disequilibrium syndrome in the acutely uremic patient may be avoided by dialyzing the patient slowly for short periods daily for two or three treatments. Dilantin is sometimes used prior to and during dialysis in the new patient to reduce the risk of CNS symptoms.

Restlessness, confusion, twitching, nausea, and vomiting may suggest early disequilibrium. Reduction of the blood flow rate and administration of sedatives may prevent more severe symptoms, but it may be necessary to discontinue dialysis if symptoms persist or worsen.

ELECTROLYTE IMBALANCE

With the trend toward early and adequate dialysis the severe extremes of electrolyte imbalances are not seen with the same frequency as before the widespread use of hemodialysis. However, critical electrolyte changes and their management have been discussed earlier in the pathophysiology section.

Maintenance and restoration of electrolyte balance in the dialysis patient is accomplished primarily with dialysis and to a lesser degree with dietary controls. With the exception of potassium, very few changes in the standard concentration of electrolytes in the dialysate are necessary.

Laboratory tests to evaluate electrolyte status are done before and after each dialysis in acute renal failure. The nurse's role includes knowledge of normal values, recognizing symptoms of imbalance, and evaluating the probable causes. In many institutions nursing intervention also includes taking the necessary corrective measures as defined by the policies of the critical care unit. For example, a patient complains of extreme muscle weakness. The nurse notes excessive amounts of gastric drainage during the previous 24-hour period. The situation suggests hypokalemia and the nurse orders a stat serum K^+ level. If the result is low, the nurse increases the potassium level in the dialysate from the standard 2.0 mEq./L. to 3.5 mEq./L. She also monitors the patient for possible cardiac arrhythmias during the procedure.

The electrolytes of main concern in dialysis and which are normally corrected during the procedure are sodium, potassium, bicarbonate, calcium, phosphorus, and magnesium.

A. Serum Sodium Serum sodium concentration normally varies between 135 mEq./L. and 145 mEq./L. and is a reflection of water volume. A low serum sodium usually indicates water intake in excess of sodium and is characterized by an increase in body weight. A high serum sodium usually indicates water loss in excess of sodium and is reflected in weight loss. Serum sodium extremes do not, as a rule, become a problem unless the values fall below 120 mEq. or rise above 160 mEq./L. The rate of change is probably more important than the absolute value.

Although serum sodium extremes are not usually seen in the adequately dialyzed patient, nevertheless thrist may indicate sodium excess. The patient who is thirsty because of excessive sodium intake will drink excessive amounts of water, which can lead to hypertension and fluid overload. Evaluation of sodium intake should be made in the patient who gains excessive amounts of fluid between dialyses. Again, the recommended weight gain is approximately one pound for each day between dialysis. Shifts in sodium and water during hemodialysis may lead to muscle cramping. This can be alleviated by reducing the flow rate and ultrafiltration.

B. Potassium Both hypo- and hyperkalemia occur in renal failure. Normal serum concentration is between 3.5 and 5.0 mEq./L. Levels below 3.0 mEq. and above 7.0 mEq./L. may lead to generalized muscle weakness and cardiac arrhythmias (see Chapter 6). Extremes in the serum potassium level are seen more frequently in the acute patient and may result from either the disease or the therapy. Crushing injuries with extensive tissue destruction, blood transfusions, potassium drugs, and acidosis all contribute to hyperkalemia. Vomiting, diarrhea, and gastric suction may lead to hypokalemia. Rapid correction of serum potassium in either direction should be avoided. Therefore, with serum potassium levels of 7–8 mEq./L. the patient should be dialyzed against a 5–6 mEq. potassium bath for an hour or two before proceeding to the standard K^+ bath. Patients on digitalis are of special concern because a low serum potassium potentiates the affects of digitalis. Therefore, rapid lowering of the potassium level during dialysis can lead to hypokalemia, increased effects of digitalis and possibly to serious and sometimes fatal arrhythmias (see Chapter 6). The potassium level in this situation is kept at 3.5 mEq./L. Patients with overt or potential problems should be monitored for cardiac function during dialysis.

C. Bicarbonate   Bicarbonate protects the body from excessive acid loads. Normal concentration varies between 25 and 30 mEq./L. In uremia, the bicarbonate is depleted because it has been used to buffer the acidosis resulting from the inability of the kidneys to excrete acids. Acidosis in the uremic patient who has not been started on dialysis is corrected by giving sodium bicarbonate. During dialysis, acidosis is corrected by adding acetate to the dialysate. Acetate diffuses into the blood where it is metabolized to form bicarbonate.

D. Calcium   Normal serum calcium levels range between 9–11 mg. percent. Disturbances in calcium metabolism which result in hypocalcemia occur in renal failure and are thought to result from impaired absorption of dietary calcium and resistance to the action of vitamin D. The dialysate calcium is kept at 3 mEq./L. to prevent the loss of calcium from the blood to the dialysate. Dialysis, however, does not seem to correct the bone problems which occur in the chronic patient as a result of calcium-phosphorus imbalances.

E. Phosphorus   In chronic renal failure antacids are used to bind phosphorus in the intestinal tract and prevent its absorption. The lowered serum phosphorus reduces the risk of soft-tissue calcifications. Antacids are usually given during or after meals, however, because of the medication's unpleasant taste and consistency, patients often omit taking antacids. A high serum phosphorus is an indication to the nurse that the patient is not adhering to the prescribed dose. Some patients save their meager amounts of fluids to wash away the unpleasant taste. Rinsing the mouth with water or a mouthwash may also help.

F. Magnesium   The normal plasma level of magnesium is 1.5–1.7 mEq./L. Magnesium accumulates in the serum, bone, and muscle in the presence of renal failure. It is thought to be involved, along with calcium and phosphorus, in the bone problems accompanying chronic renal failure. Although magnesium is removed by the artificial kidney, high levels remain in the bone. It is also difficult to reduce magnesium intake in the diet, but the regular use of magnesium drugs should be avoided. This applies particularly to antacids which are taken regularly by patients on chronic dialysis. Acceptable non-magnesium antacids include aluminum hydroxide (Amphojel), dihydroxy-aluminum aminoacetate (Robalate), and basic aluminum carbonate gel (Basaljel).

Infection The uremic patient has a lowered resistance to infection, which is thought to be due to a decreased immunological response. Therefore, all possible foci of infection should be eliminated. Indwelling urinary catheters and intracaths should be removed as soon as possible, or their use should be avoided altogether. Strict aseptic technique is essential in catheterizations, venipunctures, wound dressings, and tracheal suctioning.

Pulmonary infections are a leading cause of death in the acute uremic patient. Contributing factors include depression of the cough reflex and respiratory effort due to central nervous system disturbances, increased viscosity of pulmonary secretions due to dehydration and mouth breathing, especially in the unresponsive patient, and pulmonary congestion due to fluid overload. Fluid in the lungs not only acts as a media for growing bacteria but also impedes respiratory excursion. Nursing techniques which prevent or minimize pulmonary complications cannot be overlooked during the hemodialysis procedure. They include frequent turning, deep breathing and coughing, early ambulation, adequate humidification, and hydration, tracheal aspiration, use of intermittent positive-pressure machines, and oxygen therapy. Oral hygiene is important because bleeding from the oral mucous membrane and the accumulation of dry secretions promote growth of bacteria in the mouth which can lead to a pneumonia.

BLEEDING AND HEPARINIZATION

Bleeding during dialysis may be due to an underlying medical condition such as an ulcer or gastritis, or may be the result of excessive anticoagulation. Blood in the extra corporeal system, such as the dialyzer and blood lines, clots rapidly unless some method of anticoagulation is used. Heparin is the drug of choice because it is simple to administer, increases clotting time rapidly, is easily monitored, and may be reversed with Protamine.

Specific heparinization procedures vary. Two methods are commonly used —intermittent and constant infusion. In both cases an initial priming dose of heparin is given, followed by smaller doses either at intervals or at a constant rate by an infusion pump. The resulting effect is *systemic heparinization,* in which the clotting time of the patient and the dialyzer are essentially the same. Normal clotting time of 6–10 minutes is increased to 30–90 minutes. As a general guide, 30–60 minutes in the Twin Coil and 60–90 minutes for the Kiil will prevent clotting. Because the Dow Hollow Fiber Artificial Kidney has a propensity for clotting, the range is increased from 90–120 minutes. The effect of heparin is monitored by the modified Lee White method, which measures the length of time it takes for 1 cc. of blood to form a solid clot in a clean standard Lee White tube.

It is difficult to prescribe a heparin dose that will insure optimal anticoagulation for each patient and dialyzer. Initially, doses are decided on the basis of weight, and the clotting time is the regulator of the dose. During the first dialysis clotting times are monitored as frequently as every 30–60 minutes and the heparin dose adjusted accordingly. After that, heparin requirements will remain fairly constant.

Systemic heparinization usually presents no risk to the patient unless he has overt bleeding such as G.I. bleeding, epistaxis, or hemoptysis, is 3–7 days postsurgery, or has uremic pericarditis. In these situations, *regional heparinization* is employed. In this technique the patients clotting time is kept normal while that of the dialyzer is increased. This is accomplished by infusing heparin at a constant rate into the dialyzer and simultaneously neutralizing its effects with protamine sulfate before the blood returns to the patient. As with systemic heparinization there is no standard heparin-protamine ratio. Frequent monitoring of the clotting times is the best way to achieve effective regional heparinization. It may be necessary to switch from systemic to regional heparinization during dialysis. Severe bleeding may develop from something as simple as a nosebleed. Here again guidelines are limited. A neutralizing dose of protamine is given to reduce the patient's clotting time to normal. Protamine in large doses has an anticoagulant effect, and therefore dosage should not exceed 50 mg. in any 10-minute period. Instead, small doses of 5–10 mg. are given with frequent monitoring of clotting time.

Bleeding problems occasionally occur because of accidental heparin overdose. This may be caused by infusion pump malfunction or carelessness in setting the delivery rate. Because of the hazards, careful, frequent monitoring of heparin delivery cannot be overemphasized.

PROBLEMS WITH EQUIPMENT

One of the major objectives of a dialysis unit is the prevention of complications resulting from the treatment itself. Hemodialysis involves the use of highly technical equipment. The efficiency of the dialysis, as well as the patient's comfort and safety, is compromised if both the patient and the equipment are not adequately monitored. Mechanical monitors provide a margin of safety, but should not replace the observations and actions of the nurse.

Monitoring devices are designed to monitor many parameters, the most important of which are the flow, concentration, and temperature of the dialysate, and flow and leakage of blood. The design and operation of dialysis equipment and monitoring devices vary greatly, however, they all have a common purpose.

A. Dialysate Flow   Inadequate dialysate flow will not harm the patient, but it will compromise dialysis efficiency. Flow is maintained at the rate recommended for each particular dialyzer. The nurse usually checks the flow at least every hour and makes adjustments as necessary.

B. Dialysate Concentrate   Sudden or rapid changes in dialysate concentrate may result in red blood cell hemolysis and cerebral disturbances. Mild symptoms include nausea, vomiting, and headache. In severe cases, convulsions, coma, and death may ensue. If several patients in a unit develop similar symptoms simultaneously, dialysate concentrate imbalance should be thought of immediately. If a patient is accidentally dialyzed against water, the first symptom may be sudden severe pain in the returning vein. Because of hemolysis, blood will immediately turn dark brown to black. Dialysis is discontinued at once.

In a single delivery, proportioning system, monitoring devices are built into the system and the concentrate is monitored continuously. If the concentrate exceeds the predetermined limits, dialysate automatically bypasses the dialyzer until the problem is corrected. The problem may have been caused by an interruption in the water or concentrate delivery. Inflow lines should be checked for kinking and the concentrate container checked for quantity.

In a Central Delivery System the electrolyte concentration is also checked continuously by a meter which measures the electrical conductivity of the solution. If the solution exceeds the limits, the transfer valve between the mix tank and the supply tank is automatically closed so that no solution in unsafe concentrations is delivered to the supply tank. The solution is discarded and another batch is mixed and rechecked. A system of visual and audible alarms alerts dialysis personnel to problems.

In a batch system, the bath may be checked in a number of ways. The test for chloride ion is commonly used. It is done before dialysis commences and any time the bath is changed.

C. Temperature   Most dialysate delivery systems use a heating element to maintain dialysate temperature at optimal levels (98–101°F). Some systems include alarms, others require visual observation of the temperature gauge. Cool temperatures may cause chilling and vessel spasm. Sometimes chilling in the patient is the first indication of a drop in dialysate temperature. High temperatures (over 101°F) may produce fever and discomfort in the patient, while extremely high temperatures (of 110°F) will cause hemolysis. Corrections should be made as soon as the temperature reaches 101°F.

D. Blood Flow   Monitoring adequate blood flow rate throughout dialysis is essential to dialysis efficiency. Factors that influence blood flow rate are blood pressure, shunt and fistula function, and the extracorporeal circuit. A manometer connected to the drip chamber is used to measure the pressure in the blood lines. Changes in blood line pressures are transmitted to the drip chamber and register on the manometer as high or low-pressure alarms. A high-pressure alarm indicates a problem in the venous blood line, vessel spasm, or a clotted vein. Vessel spasm is seen in new shunts or with chilling and a heating pad over the shunt may help to relax the vessel. If a clot is suspected, the vein is irrigated with a heparinized saline solution. A low-pressure alarm reflects an obstruction to blood flow from the patient. Arterial spasm, clotting, displacement of a fistula needle, and a drop in blood pressure are possible causes. Correction is again directed to the cause.

E. Blood Leaks   A blood leak detector is invaluable when outflow dialysate is not visible, as in a single-pass delivery system. One type of blood leak detector is a color-sensitive photocell which picks up color variations in the outflow dialysate. Any foreign material such as blood will be detected and an alarm set off. Since false alarms are sometimes set off by air bubbles, the nurse will check the dialysate visually for a gross leak and with a hemostix for smaller leaks. Dialysis is usually discontinued immediately with a goss leak. Whether or not the blood is returned to the patient is either a matter of unit policy or an individual determination. If the patient is severely anemic, the risk of losing the blood in the dialyzer may outweigh the risk of a reaction to dialysate contaminated blood. Sometimes minor leaks, in which there is no visible blood in the dialysate and only a small hemostix reaction, seal over and dialysis is continued.

Access to Circulation

Successful repeated hemodialysis depends on access to the patient's circulation. Three methods commonly used are the arterial venous shunt, the arterial venous fistula. and the femoral vein catheter; the latter is usually a temporary method used before either of the above is available.

ARTERIAL VENOUS SHUNT

The A-V shunt consists of two soft plastic (Silastic) cannulas, one of which is inserted into an artery and the other into a vein. Between dialyses, the cannulas are joined by a hard, plastic (Teflon) connector and blood flows freely between the two vessels. At the time of dialysis the two cannulas are separated and attached to the blood tubing of the dialyzer. Cannulation is a surgical procedure performed in the operating room under local anesthesia. The cannula is usually inserted in the forearm of the nondominant arm, although circumstances may dictate placement in other extremities. Pre-surgical care should include avoiding venipunctures, intravenous administrations, tourniquets, and blood-pressure cuffs in the affected limb. Nursing care is directed at maintenance of good function and prevention of clotting and infection beginning in the immediate postsurgical period. General recommendations for promoting shunt life are
1. Limiting Activity in the Postoperative Period
   Shunt functioning can be promoted by elevating the affected extremity for two to three days to reduce swelling and discomfort, and avoiding weight bearing in a leg shunt for at least a week.
2. Cleanliness
   The shunt site should be kept clean and dry. Good aseptic technique is essential in dressing changes and handling of the shunt. Daily dressing changes are not recommended unless infection with drainage is present. Cleansing at the time of dialysis is usually sufficient and should be done from the exit sites outward. Separate gauze and applicators are used for each exit to prevent cross-contamination. Picking at crusts should be avoided.
3. Proper Alignment
   Misalignment may occur if the cannulas are twisted during either the hookup procedure or the reconnection at the end of dialysis. Distortions should be corrected immediately as tension at the exits may lead to small tears in the epithelium which in turn contribute to clotting and

infection. An outer dressing such as Kling, which conforms to the contours of the extremity, is recommended because it prevents the shunt and other dressings from slipping around with normal motions.

4. Gentleness

Careful, gentle handling of shunt parts is important in extending shunt life. Therefore, jerking and pulling on the cannulas during dialysis procedures should be avoided.

5. Frequent Observation

Early detection and attention to symptoms may lead to the prevention of more serious problems. Clotting and infection are the two major complications.

6. Preventing Clotting

A clue to good blood flow through the shunt is a sound or burst heard with a stethoscope. The sound has been likened to the sound of rushing water. Sometimes the bruit is so strong it can be palpated with the fingers. This is called a "thrill." If the bruit is faint or absent, the dressing is removed in order to observe the shunt. The color of the blood should be uniformly red and the shunt warm to touch. If the shunt is clotted, the blood is quite dark and the red cells and serum may have already separated. Declotting may or may not be successful, depending on the length of time that has elapsed between clotting and detection. The routine declotting procedure consists of evacuating the clots by irrigating each cannula with a weak heparinized saline solution. Aseptic technique is again emphasized. Once flow has been reestablished, the shunt is reconnected and observed closely. It has been the experience of dialysis personnel that once clotting occurs, it will recur unless the cause has been determined and corrective measures taken. A history of trauma, obstruction to flow caused by sleeping with a limb bent or crossing legs, hypotension, and infections is often found. The patient, however, may have an intrinsic clotting problem which may necessitate the use of an anticoagulant such as Coumadin. This will necessitate the usual observations and precautions taken with anticoagulation therapy. The patient will also need a readjustment in his heparin during dialysis.

7. Preventing Infection

The shunt is routinely inspected at the time of dialysis. It is also inspected when the patient develops any unusual symptoms such as pain or bleeding at exits, between dialyses. Any of the signs of inflammation, such as redness, swelling, tenderness, and drainage are cause for concern and require prompt attention. Cultures are routinely done by the nurse if drainage is noted. Each exit site is cultured separately. Some physicians will treat the infection without cultures, assuming that most shunts are infected with *Staphylococcus aureus*. However, *Pseudomonas* and *Escherichia coli* are sometimes cultured out. Aside from the possibility of further shunt surgery, the most serious complication of a shunt infection is septicemia. To forestall this possibility, some physicians choose to remove an extremely infected shunt immediately. Whether this is done or not, the patient should be observed closely especially during the hemodialysis procedure when contamination of the blood stream from an infected shunt is a strong possibility. The development of chills, fever, and hypotension in a patient with an infected shunt should be regarded as a serious sign. Blood cultures should be drawn immediately and the physician notified promptly.

ARTERIAL VENOUS FISTULA

The arterial venous fistula technique was developed in response to the frequent complications encountered with the arteriovenous shunt.

In this procedure the surgeon anastomoses an artery and a vein, creating a fistula or artificial opening between them. Arterial blood flowing into the venous systems results in marked dilatation of the veins which are then easily punctured with a large bore 14-gauge needle. Two venipunctures are made at the time of dialysis, one for a blood source and one for a return. The "arterial" needle is inserted toward the fistula to obtain the best blood flow, but the tip should not be placed closer than 1–1½ inches from the fistula. A traumatic puncture might lead to damage and closure of the fistula. The venous needle is directed away from the fistula in the direction of normal venous flow. It may be placed in either the same vessel, another vein in the same arm, or even in another extremity. If both needles are inserted into the same vessel, the tips should be at least 8-10 cm. apart to avoid mixing of the blood which would result in inadequate dialysis. If it is necessary to place the needles close to each other, a tourniquet is applied between the two needles.

Care of the arterialvenous fistula is less complicated than with the arteriovenous shunt. Normal showering or bathing with soap provides adequate skin cleansing. Traumatic venipunctures or repetition in the same site should be avoided as these lead to excessive bleeding, hematoma and scar formation. Excessive manipulation and adjustment of the needles should also be avoided for the same reasons. Postdialysis care includes adequate pressure on the puncture sites after the needles are removed.

FEMORAL CATHETERS

Femoral catheters (also called Shaldon catheters) are used for hemodialysis when other mean of access to the blood stream are not available. This method is used primarily in acute dialysis, but may also be used for chronic dialysis patients because of shunt or fistula failure. It should be considered a temporary measure. The procedure involves inserting one or two Teflon catheters into the femoral vein. If an arm vein can be used for blood return, only one catheter is used. When two catheters are needed, the lower one is used for the blood supply, the higher one for the return. Femoral catheterization trays are standard equipment in dialysis units and in critical care units which perform acute dialysis.

The femoral catheters must be secured to the leg to prevent accidental slipping, and observed frequently for bleeding during hemodialysis. The catheters are usually removed after dialysis, but may be left in place if the patient is scheduled for another dialysis within 24 hours. Leaving femoral catheters in place over 24 hours may lead to infection. Catheters left in place are irrigated periodically with a weak heparinized saline solution to prevent clotting. The usual dilution is 1000 units of heparin to 30 cc. of normal saline, and 4–5 cc. are instilled into the catheter q 2–4 hours. If the catheters are removed at the end of dialysis, pressure is applied to the puncture sites until complete clotting occurs. The site is checked for several hours thereafter to detect any renewal of bleeding.

PERITONEAL DIALYSIS

Peritoneal dialysis accomplishes the same functions and operates on the same principles of diffusion and osmosis as hemodialysis. In this instance, however, the peritoneum is the semipermeable membrane.

Peritoneal dialysis is an effective alternate treatment when hemodialysis is either not available or when access to the blood stream is not possible. It is sometimes utilized as an initial treatment for renal failure while the patient is being evaluated for a hemodialysis program. The advantages of peritoneal over hemodialysis include use of less complicated technical equipment, less need for highly skilled personnel, availability of supplies and equipment, and minimizing adverse symptoms of the more efficient hemodialysis. This may be important in patients who cannot tolerate rapid hemodynamic changes.

On the other hand, peritoneal dialysis requires more time to adequately remove metabolic wastes and to restore electrolyte and fluid balance. In addition, repeated treatments may lead to peritonitis, while long periods of immobility may lead to such complications as pulmonary congestion and venous stasis. Because fluid is introduced into the peritoneal cavity, peritoneal dialysis is contraindicated in existing peritonitis, recent or extensive abdominal surgery, the presence of abdominal adhesions, and in impending kidney transplantation.

Materials Used in Peritoneal Dialysis

1. Solutions

    As in hemodialyses, peritoneal dialysis solutions contain "ideal" concentrations of electrolytes, but lack urea, creatinine, and other substances which are to be removed. Unlike dialysate used in hemodialyses, solutions must be sterile. Solutions vary in dextrose concentrations. A 1.5 percent dextrose solution is usually used for drug intoxications and acute renal failure if excessive fluid removal is not necessary. A 7 percent dextrose solution is used with patients who are severely fluid overloaded. Since this concentration of dextrose may lead to excessive fluid removal with hypotension, it is sometimes used only for several exchanges. If hyperkalemia is not a problem, 4 mEq. of potassium chloride is added to each liter.

2. Dialysis administration set
3. Peritoneal dialysis catheter set
   The set usually includes the catheter, a connecting tube for connecting the catheter to the administration set, and a metal stylet. The stylet is used for dislodging fibrin clots which may form and collect in the catheter.
4. Trocar set
   Commercially prepared materials have the advantage of being pre-packaged and sterile.
5. Ancillary drugs
   (a) Local anesthetic solution — 2 percent lidocaine (Xylocaine)
   (b) Aqueous heparin — 1,000 units/cc.
   (c) Potassium chloride
   (d) Broad-spectrum antibiotics

Preliminary Procedures

(a) The bladder should be emptied just prior to the procedure to avoid accidental puncture with the trocar.
(b) The abdomen is shaved, prepped, and draped as for a surgical procedure.
(c) The dialyzing fluid is warmed to body temperature or slightly warmer.
(d) Baseline vital signs, such as temperature, pulse, respirations and weight are recorded. If possible, an in-bed scale is ideal as the patient's weight can be monitored frequently. Moving a lethargic or disoriented patient to a scale may create problems such as catheter displacement.
(e) Specific orders regarding fluid removal, replacement and drug administration should be written by the physician prior to the procedure.

Procedure

Under sterile conditions, a small midline incision is made just below the umbilicus. A trocar is inserted through the incision into the peritoneal cavity. The obturator is removed and the catheter secured. The dialyses solution flows into the abdominal cavity by gravity as rapidly as possible (5–10 minutes). If it flows in too slowly, the catheter may need repositioning. When the solution is infused, the tubing is clamped and the solution remains in the abdominal cavity for 30 – 45 minutes. Then the solution bottles are placed on the floor and the fluid is drained out of the peritoneal cavity by gravity. If the system is patent and the catheter well placed, the fluid will drain in a steady forceful stream. Drainage should take no more than 10 minutes. This cycle is repeated continuously for the prescribed number of hours which varies from 12 to 36 hours, depending on the purpose of the treatment, the patient's condition, and the proper functioning of the system.

Essential Features of Nursing Care

1. Accurate intake and output records to assess volume depletion or overload.
2. Frequent monitoring of the patient's vital signs, weight, and general condition.
3. Correction of technical difficulties before they result in physiological problems.
4. Prevention of the complications of immobility.
5. Providing an environment which will assist the patient in accepting a long and potentially tiring treatment.

Complications of Peritoneal Dialysis and Nursing Intervention

TECHNICAL COMPLICATIONS

1. Incomplete recovery of fluid with each exchange. The fluid removed should at least equal or exceed that of the amount inserted. If less fluid is removed or drains very slowly, the catheter tip may be buried in the omentum or clogged with fibrin. Turning the patient from side to side, elevating the head of the bed, and gently massaging the abdomen may facilitate drainage. If clots are suspected, introducing the stylet into the catheter may reopen it. Adding heparin to the solution may prevent the formation of fibrinous clots in the catheter. The specific dose is ordered by the physician but will be in a range of 500 to 1,000 units per liter.
2. Leakage or bleeding. Superficial leaking and bleeding may occur with the first exchange. These may be controlled by a purse-string suture. Since persistent leakage around the incision site will act as a media for bacterial contamination, the problem should be solved early. Blood tinged drainage due to the trauma of insertion may be noted in the first few passes. Gross bleeding at any time is an indication of a more serious problem and should be investigated immediately.

PHYSIOLOGICAL COMPLICATIONS

1. Hypotension may occur if excessive fluid is removed. Vital signs are monitored frequently, especially if a hypertonic solution is used. A progressive drop in blood pressure and weight should alert the nurse to potential problems.
2. Hypertension and fluid overload may occur if all the fluid is not removed in each cycle. The exact amount in the bottles should be noted. Some manufacturers add 1,050 ml. to a 1,000-ml. bottle; over a period of hours this can make a considerable difference. The patient is observed for signs of respiratory distress which may indicate pulmonary congestion. In the absence of other symptoms of fluid overload, hypertension

may be the result of anxiety and apprehension. Reassuring the patient and promptly correcting problems are preferable to the administration of sedative and tranquilizers.

Pain   Mild abdominal discomfort may be experienced at any time during the procedure and is probably related to the constant distention or chemical irritation of the peritoneum. If a mild analgesic doesn't provide relief, inserting 5 cc. of 2 percent lidocaine (Xylocaine) directly into the catheter may help. The patient may be less uncomfortable if nourishment is given in small amounts, when the fluid is draining out rather than when the abdominal cavity is distended.

Severe pain may indicate more serious problems of infection or paralytic ileus. Infection is not likely in the first twenty-four hours. Aseptic technique and the use of prophylactic antibiotics minimize the risk of infection. Periodic cultures of the outflowing fluid will assist in the early detection of pathogenic organisms.

PULMONARY COMPLICATIONS

Immobility may lead to hypostatic pneumonia, especially in the debilitated or elderly patient. Deep breathing, turning, and coughing should be encouraged during the procedure. Leg exercises and the use of elastic stockings may prevent the development of venous thrombi and emboli.

Further nursing measures are directed at making the patient as comfortable as possible during the lengthy procedure. Diversions such as having visitors, reading, or watching TV should be encouraged.

BIBLIOGRAPHY

Abbott Laboratories, *Fluid and Electrolytes.* North Chicago, Ill., 1970.

Baxter, Don, Inc., *Peritoneal Dialyses—Instructions for Use.* Glendale, Calif., 1965.

Black, D. A. K., *Essentials of Fluid Balance.* Oxford: Blackwell Scientific Publications, 1964.

Goldberg Emmanuel, *A Primer of Water Electrolyte and Acid-Base Syndromes.* Philadelphia: Lea & Febiger, 1970.

Gutch, C. F., and Martha H. Stoner, *Review of Hemodialysis for Nurses and Dialysis Personnel.* St. Louis: C. V. Mosby Company, 1971.

Pendras, Jerry P., and Gerald W. Stenson, *The Hemodialysis Manual.* Seattle, Wash.: Seattle Artificial Kidney Center and University of Washington, 1969.

Shoemaker, William C., and William F. Walker, *Fluid Electrolyte Therapy in Acute Illness.* Chicago: Year Book Medical Publishers, Inc., 1970.

13

Normal Structure and Function of the Nervous System

MARGARET ANN BERRY, R.N., M.A., M.S.

INTRODUCTION

The basic organization of the nervous system is similar to other systems of the body. Its basic functional unit is the *neuron* consisting of a cell body and filament outgrowths, the *nerve fibers*. These fibers are responsible for the transmission of information from one part of the nervous system to the other. Neurons in the central nervous system process incoming peripheral information and then determine what information will be sent to various parts of the body to initiate specific activities. The nervous system consists of three major divisions which perform these functions: (1) the *sensory system*, (2) the *motor system*, and (3) the *integrative system*.

Figure 13-1 is a schematic illustration of the organization of the two larger divisions, the sensory and motor divisions.

The *sensory system* is the site of origination of most nervous system activities. That is, stimuli received and processed by this system, whether sight, sound, touch, or taste, cause a response somewhere else in the nervous system. The response may be an immediate motor response, or the information may be stored in the brain and then used to determine bodily reactions later. The sensory system, in general, transmits impulses from the body surface and deep structures into the spinal cord at all levels through the spinal nerves. From here the information is sent to the basal regions of the brain which includes the medulla and the pons and to the higher brain centers, the thalamus and the cerebral cortex. These are the primary areas of the nervous system for handling sensory input; essentially all other parts secondarily receive and process sensory input.

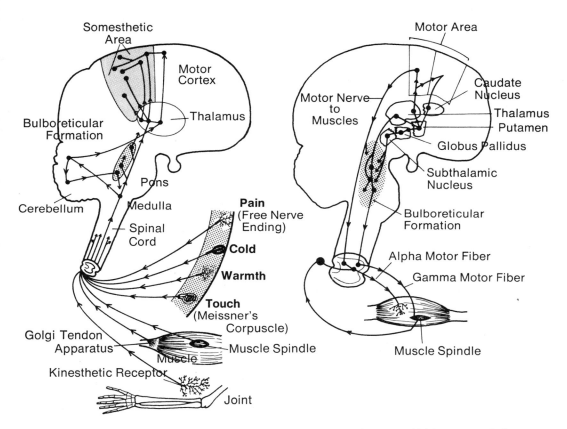

Fig. 13-1. General organization of the sensory (A) and motor divisions (B) of the nervous system. [From A. C. Guyton, 1964, *Function of the Human Body* (Philadelphia: Saunders, 1964), p. 260.]

The *motor division* of the nervous system is responsible for control of bodily functions. This is mediated through the control of the contraction of skeletal muscle, the contraction of smooth muscle of internal organs, and by the secretion of exocrine and endocrine glands. In this division the impulses arise in the motor area of the cerebral cortex, the basal regions of the brain, and in the spinal cord. Those messages arising in the basalar areas of the brain and in the spinal cord primarily are automatic responses to sensory stimuli. The higher regions are concerned with voluntary, deliberate movements associated with thought processes of the cerebrum.

The *integrative system* is concerned with processing signals to determine accurate and appropriate motor responses. It is also believed to be involved in abstract thinking. There are numerous areas in both the cord and the brain that are concerned almost exclusively with integrative activities. Lying adjacent to sensory and motor areas, these centers determine the qualities and characteristics of sensory input. Is it painful? intense? weak? Having determined this, the areas then ascertain the appropriate motor responses and transport signals to the appropriate motor area. Another extremely important function of this division is one of storing information. This activity is readily recognized as memory.

As stated earlier, the basic functional unit of the nervous system is the *neuron,* and all information and activity whether sensory, motor and/or integrative is processed by it. The precise characteristic of individual neurons is determined by their specific function. Some are extremely large and may give rise to extremely long nerve fibers. Transmission velocities in the long fibers may be as high as 100 meters per second, while smaller neurons with very small fibers demonstrate velocities of 1 meter per second. Some neurons connect to many different neurons in a "network," and still others have few connections to other cells of the nervous system.

It has been estimated that there are twelve billion neurons in the central nervous system. Three-fourths of these neurons are located in the cerebral cortex where information transmitted through the nervous system is processed. This processing as indicated above includes not only determining appropriate and effective responses, but also the storage of memory and development of associative motor and thought patterns.

The pattern of information processing is basically as follows: (1) sensory information is received, (2) this information is transmitted to the central nervous area, and (3) a motor response is determined and carried to an end organ. Many times this pattern is strictly reflexive and simple in its neuronal involvement. These instantaneous and automatic motor responses to sensory input are called *reflex* responses and involve a *receptor,* a *transmitor,* and an *effector.* A sensation such as touch, cold, or heat is detected by the receptor and transmitted by the transmitter to the central nervous system. This may be a single neuron, or several neurons in series. The effector is the end organ which receives the motor impulse, like a skeletal muscle, internal organs such as the gut or heart, or an exocrine or endocrine gland.

Many reflexes such as the withdrawal of an arm or leg from painful stimuli involve only the spinal cord, while other reflexes are much more complex and involve the integrative division. These more complex reflexes may involve information stored from earlier experiences and thus previous experience is associated with the current one. The more complex responses that involve many neurons and several areas of the nervous system are commonly called *higher functions* as opposed to the simple reflexes just described.

The above discussion has implied a basic hierarchical organization of the nervous system and indeed this is the case. There are three levels of organization: (a) the *spinal cord,* controlling many basic reflex responses; (b) the *basal regions of the brain,* controlling bodily function such as equilibrium, eating, walking, and (c) the *cerebral cortex,* controlling voluntary, discrete motor activities and thought processes.

Even though many sensory activities are responded to and carried out at spinal levels, many sensations from the body *(somasthetic sensations)* are interpreted by the brain. The interpretation of these messages enables us to determine body position, and conditions of the immediate external environment as well as conditions of the internal environment. These are called *proprioceptive, exteroceptive,* and *visceral* sensations respectively.

As indicated above, proprioceptive sensations are those sensations which describe the physical position state of the body such as tension in muscle, flexion or extension of joints, tendon tension, and deep pressure in dependent parts like the feet while standing or the buttocks while seated. Exteroceptive sensations are those that monitor the conditions on the body surface. These include temperature and pain. Visceral sensations are like exteroceptive sensations except that they originate from within and monitor pain, pressure, and fullness from internal organs.

Figure 13-1A indicates the possible pathways for processing somasthetic sensations. The fibers ending in the spinal cord initiate the cord reflexes discussed previously. Brain-stem fibers initiate reflexes such as those that position the trunk and aid in upright posture. All of these are more complex than spinal reflexes but are still subconscious. As the sensations are transmitted to higher levels they terminate in the thalamus, where the *general* origin of the sensation and the modality (type) of sensation is determined. However, the *discrete* localization and modality of the sensations are determined in the cerebral cortex where information from past experiences is involved in interpretation.

The sensory receptors for somasthetic sensations include both free nerve endings and specialized end organs. Free nerve endings are nothing more than small filamentous branches of the dendritic fibers. They detect crude sensations of touch, pain, heat, and cold. The precision is crude because there are many interconnections between the free endings of different neurons. However, they are the most profusely distributed and perform the general discriminatory functions whereas the more specialized receptors discriminate between very slight differences in degrees of touch, heat, and cold. Structurally the special exteroceptive end organs for detection of cold, warmth, and light touch differ from each other and are quite specific in their function as seen in Fig. 13-1A. The physiological basis for this specific function has not been determined but is presumed to be based upon some specific physical effect on the organ itself. There are three proprioceptive receptors. Joint kinesthetic receptors are found in the joint capsules and send messages concerning the angulation of a joint and the rate at which it is changing. Information from muscles concerning the degree of stretch is transmitted to the nervous system from the muscle spindle apparatus, while the Golgi tendon determines the overall tension applied to the tendons.

When a sensory effector is stimulated it responds with an increased frequency of firing. At first there is a burst of impulses; if the stimulus persists, the frequency of impulses transmitted begins to decrease. All sensory receptors show this phenomenon of *adaptation* to varying degrees and at different rates. Adaptation to light touch and pressure occurs in a few seconds, whereas pain and proprioceptive sensation adapt very little if at all, and at a very slow rate. The determination of the intensity of sensation is on a relative basis rather than an absolute basis and follows a logarithmic response. Therefore while the intensity of a sensation increases logarithmically the frequency of response in the nerve ending increases linearly.

Although there are structurally different receptors for detecting each type of sensation, it is the area of the brain to which the information is transmitted that determines the *modality* or type of sensation the individual feels. The thalamus, the hypothalamus, and somasthetic area of the cerebral cortex operate together to determine the various sensory qualities. As sensory input arrives at the central nervous system the different characteristics such as a pain element or touch element are determined by the cooperative effort of the areas.

The sense of pain warrants special consideration, since it plays such an important protective role for the body. At the same time there is a wide variation in individual response to pain. Whenever there is tissue damage, pain receptors are stimulated and the sensation of pain is felt. This sensation is usually felt during the time that tissue is undergoing damage, and ceases when the damage ends. This condition is due to the release of chemicals and metabolites such as histamine and bradykinen from damaged cells. Typical damaging stimuli are trauma (cutting, crushing, tearing), ischemia, intense heat or cold and chemical irritation. Most people *perceive* the pain at the same degree of tissue damage. However, there is a wide variation in the extent to which individuals *react* to pain. Differences in reactivity to pain are due to the psychic makeup of the individual and not to differences in pain-receptor sensitivity.

The nervous system responds to sensory input through motor mechanisms which control bodily function and position. As demonstrated in Fig. 13-1B, the motor division of the central nervous system is organized in a hierarchial manner like the sensory division. That is, a large number of reflexive motor functions are mediated through the spinal cord, while others operate through brain-stem centers and still others through cortical centers. The largest number of motor activities are controlled by spinal cord and brain stem, and therefore operate primarily at subconscious reflexive levels.

Simple cord reflexes include the *axon reflexes* which provide increased blood flow to damaged tissues in the skin. Proprioceptor reflexes which are processed at the spinal cord include the *stretch reflex,* which helps maintain normal muscle tone, posture, and positioning of limbs with respect to the rest of the body. Another proprioceptive reflex mediated at the spinal level is the *tendon protective reflex,* which protects the tendon and muscle against excessive stretch. The *extensor thrust reflex* aids in the support of the body against gravity.

Also included in spinal reflexes is the *withdrawal,* pain, or flexor reflex. The purpose of this reflex is obvious. Operating in association with this reflex is the *crossed extensor reflex.* When one limb flexes in withdrawal from a painful stimulus the opposite limb extends, pushing the whole body away from the source of the painful stimulus. An important feature of all reflexes is reciprocal inhibition which occurs in the antagonist muscle of the one stimulated. For example, when a flexor reflex stimulates the biceps, it also inhibits its antagonist, the triceps, and provides for more efficient performance of motor activities in the upper arm.

Spinal-cord activities also include reflex circuits which aid in the control of visceral functions of the body. Sensory input arises from visceral sensory receptors and is transmitted to the spinal cord, where reflex patterns appropriate to the sensory input are determined. The signals are then transmitted to autonomic motor neurons in the gray matter of the spinal cord which send impulses to the sympathetic nerves innervating visceral motor end organs. A most important autonomic reflex is the *peritoneal reflex.* Tissue damage in any portion of the peritoneum results in the response of this reflex, which slows or stops all motor activity in the nearby viscera. In the presence of transectional injuries at the brain stem, cord reflexes are also capable of modifying local blood flow in response to cold, pain, and heat. This vascular control by autonomic reflexes in the spinal cord operates as a backup mechanism for the usual brain stem control patterns.

Also included in the autonomic reflexes of the spinal cord are those autonomic reflexes causing the emptying of the urinary bladder and the rectum. When the bowel or bladder becomes distended, sensory signals are transmitted to the autonomic internuncial neurons of the cord. Motor signals via the parasympathetic neurons excite the main portion of the bowel or bladder, at the same time inhibiting the internal sphincters of the urethra or anus, thus causing the organ to empty. Normally these reflexes are over-ridden by cortical centers until an appropriate time and place for evacuation arises.

The lower brain stem, composed of the medulla, the pons, and the mesencephalon, contains the areas which control blood pressure, respiration, and gastrointestinal regulation. The brain stem's motor functions also include maintaining bodily support against gravity and maintaining equilibrium. Located within the brain stem is the structural area in which these latter two integrative functions occur, the bulboreticular formation. This area receives information from a variety of sources which includes all areas of the peripheral sensory receptors via the spinal cord, from the cerebellum, from the inner-ear equilibrium apparatus, the motor cortex, and from the basal ganglia. The bulboreticular area, then, is an integrative area for sensory information, motor information from the cerebral cortex, equilibrium information from the vestibular apparati, and proprioceptive information from the cerebellum: it also controls many involuntary muscular activities.

Even though most of the essential motor functions are performed by the lower levels of the central nervous system, one of the distinguishing characteristics of human beings is their ability to perform intricate, complex voluntary muscular activity such as talking and writing.

These precise, complex functions are controlled by specific areas of the cerebral cortex. There are, however, many stereotyped movements which are much more complex than postural functions of the lower brain stem but less complex than the intricate functions of the cerebral cortex. These movements are controlled by the basal ganglia, which are large conglomerates of neurons that have connections with the cerebral cortex and the thalamus. Special dampening functions for smoothing out tremors and jerkiness inherent in raw muscular activity are controlled by the cerebellum.

Another distinguishing characteristic of human beings is their ability to communicate by speech. Verbal communication is dependent upon the ability to interpret speech and the ability to translate thought into speech. Ideas are usually communicated between individuals by either spoken or written word. With the spoken word the sensory input of information is through the primary auditory cortex. In auditory association areas the sounds are interpreted as words and the words as sentences. These sentences are then interpreted by the common integrative area of the cerebral cortex as thoughts. The common integrative area also develops thoughts to be communicated. Letters seen by the eyes are associated as words, thoughts and sentences in the visual association area and integrated into thought in this area also. Operating in conjunction with facial regions of the somasthetic sensory area, the common integrative area initiates a series of impulses, each representing a syllable or word, and transmits them to the secondary motor area controlling the larynx and mouth. The speech center, in addition to controlling motor activity of the larynx and mouth, sends impulses to the respiratory center of the secondary motor cortex to provide appropriate breath patterns for the speech process.

The major portion of this discussion has dealt with sensory, motor, and integrative activities of the spinal cord, brain stem, and cerebral cortex. These activities may be unconscious, subconscious, or voluntary. Only short references have been made to the autonomic or involuntary function with regard to bowel and bladder emptying, control of blood flow, peritoneal reflex, and the like. The function of the *autonomic nervous system* is far more diffuse than this however, in the control of internal functions of the body. This system is subdivided into the *sympathetic* and *parasympathetic* division on the basis of (1) anatomical distribution of nerve fibers, (2) the antagonistic effects of the two divisions on the organs they innervate, and (3) the secretion of two different neural transmitters by the postganglionic fibers of the two divisions. Figure 13-2 shows the anatomy of the sympathetic and parasympathetic nervous systems.

As seen in Fig. 13-2, the sympathetic system is comprised of a chain of perivertebral ganglia receiving fibers from the thoracolumbar region of the spinal cord and distributing postganglionic fibers to the various organs inner-

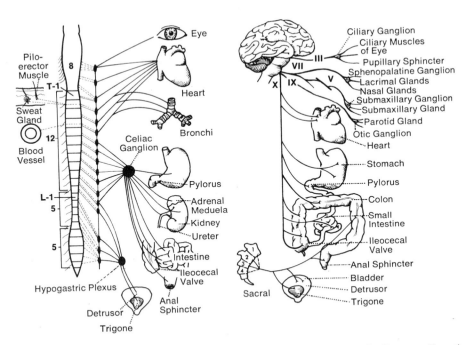

Fig. 13-2. Anatomy of the autonomic nervous system. [From A. C. Guyton, *Function of The Human Body,* 3rd ed. (Philadelphia: Saunders, 1964), pp. 333–334.]

vated. The parasympathetic system on the other hand, has rather long preganglionic fibers coming from the craniosacral area of the central nervous system which terminate in ganglia that are closely associated with the organ innervated. Short postganglionic fibers then innervate the tissues of the organs directly. A major difference between the two divisions of the autonomic nervous system is the neural transmitters secreted by the postganglionic fibers. Parasympathetic postganglionic nerve fibers secrete acetylcholine and thus are referred to as *cholinergic* fibers, whereas sympathetic postganglionic fibers are called *andrenergic* fibers, since they secrete noradrenaline (norepinephrine). The actions of these two antagonistic chemical transmitters are summarized in Table 13-1.

Impulses are transmitted continuously at a slow rate from both divisions at all times. This *tonic effect* of the individual divisions allows each to exert independently both positive and negative effects on a given organ—increasing the discharge frequently has a positive effect and decreasing the frequency a negative effect. For example, if sympathetic discharge to vasoconstrictor vessels was "on" or "off," this would result only in constriction of vessels during "on" periods. But since there is a normal resting frequency, increasing

TABLE 13-1
AUTONOMIC EFFECTS ON VARIOUS ORGANS OF THE BODY

ORGAN	EFFECT OF SYMPATHETIC STIMULATION	EFFECT OF PARASYMPATHETIC STIMULATION
Eye: Pupil	Dilated	Contracted
Ciliary muscle	None	Excited
Gastrointestinal glands	Vasoconstriction	Stimulation of thin, copious secretion containing many enzymes
Sweat glands	Copious sweating (cholinergic)	None
Heart: Muscle	Increased activity	Decreased activity
Coronaries	Vasodilated	Constricted
Systemic blood vessels:		
Abdominal	Constricted	None
Muscle	Dilated (cholinergic)	None
Skin	Constricted or dilated (cholinergic)	None
Lungs: Bronchi	Dilated	Constricted
Blood vessels	Mildly constricted	None
Gut: Lumen	Decreased peristalsis and tone	Increased peristalsis and tone
Sphincters	Increased tone	Decreased tone
Liver	Glucose released	None
Kidney	Decreased output	None
Bladder: Body	Inhibited	Excited
Sphincter	Excited	Inhibited
Male sexual act	Ejaculation	Erection
Blood glucose	Increased	None
Basal metabolism	Increased up to 50%	None
Adrenal cortical secretion	Increased	None
Mental activity	Increased	None

From A. C. Guyton, *Function of the Human Body,* 3rd ed. (Philadelphia: Saunders, 1964), pp. 335.

it causes more vasoconstriction and decreasing it results in less vasoconstriction or vasodilatation. This tonic effect persists throughout both the sympathetic and the parasympathetic divisions of the autonomic nervous system and is responsible for the high degree of effectiveness of the system in the regulation of visceral activities.

The function of the autonomic nervous system can also be regulated by stimulation of widespread areas of the bulboreticular formation of the medulla, pons, and mesencephalon. The hypothalamus also regulates many of the autonomic functions, and stimulation of certain areas of the cerebral cortex also causes both diffuse and discrete autonomic effects. Exact mechanisms for these interactions are not well known but seem to be those of integrative functions similar to that in motor and sensory integration.

14

Pathophysiology of the Central Nervous System and Management Modalities

ROBERT W. HENDEE, JR., M.D.
CAROLYN M. HUDAK, R.N., M.S.

INTRODUCTION

Nurses in a critical care unit with individuals having acute nervous system injury or illness serve as the patient's first line of defense. In order to insure superior care a multitude of routine supportive acts must be performed in repetition. Concomitantly, the nurse must carry out frequent neurological and (in cases of multiple systems injuries) other evaluations with constant vigil for subtle changes in blood pressure, pulse rate, and regularity, respiratory activity, sensorial status (level of consciousness), and motor and sensory function. Alterations when they occur may be the initial indication of impending deterioration, leading to rapid demise unless immediate action is taken to alleviate the underlying pathology.

An example may be helpful. A nineteen-year-old right-handed female was seen in the emergency room following a vehicular-induced closed head injury. During the initial neurosurgical evaluation her arousal mechanism was moderately depressed, but she responded purposefully and uniformly upon request. No focal or lateralizing signs were evident except for tendency for enlargement of the left pupil (pupillary inequality is termed *anisocoria*). One hour later, following repair of facial lacerations and with stability of her sensorial status, she was moved to the critical care unit for further observation. The patient's condition was discussed with the receiving nurse by the neurosurgical resident.

Soon thereafter the nurse noted definite, persistent anisocoria, with diminished reaction to light of the dilating pupil and more difficulty in arousing the patient. Immediately the resident was called, and in the interim mannitol was prepared for intravenous administration. This was begun upon the physician's arrival as a deteriorating situation was apparent. The patient was transferred to the operating room, by which time her respiratory condition required external assistance, both pupils had dilated, and she was unresponsive to painful stimuli. Emergency trephinations revealed an acute subdural hematoma over one cerebral hemisphere and an epidural hematoma over the opposite hemisphere.

Fortunately the young lady recovered with minimal neurologic residuals. Her life was undoubtedly spared by the awareness and prompt action of the critical care nurse.

Opportunity for the nurse to discover other interesting and extremely important findings is ever present. Serosanguinous drainage from ears, nose, or scalp wound, even when it has been debrided and repaired but incompletely explored in the emergency unit, will represent cerebrospinal fluid (CSF) leak until proven otherwise. Progressive urinary output of abnormally high levels following injury or certain types of intracranial and facial surgery may represent diabetes insipidus. Neither of the latter conditions need cause concern about the immediate demise of the patient if left undiscovered and untreated. If left unobserved too long, however, they may result in unnecessary intracranial infection or hypovolemia and severe electrolyte imbalance. These in turn will lead to new problems of care and worsened condition of the patient, possibly precluding his complete recovery or ultimately leading to his death.

Experience aids the nurse in sharpening her powers of observation to recognize the slight changes that may be the precursors of the full constellation of signs of increased intracranial pressure and/or brain herniation. The same holds for alterations in lower-extremity motor and sensory function after incomplete spinal cord injury. Experience also imparts confidence to the nurse, as does knowledge of the more common patterns of deterioration, in assisting her to determine if additional observation is warranted or whether she should seek the physician's reevaluation immediately.

Physicians rendering quality care in the treatment of critically ill patients should always allocate time to discuss with the nurse, even briefly, the particulars of each new patient upon arrival in the critical care unit. At that time the nurse must establish *precise* baseline information to her own satisfaction and seek clarification if necessary.

In these days of vehicular abuse, exposure to dangerous equipment, and utilization of complex mechanical recreational devices many of the patients in any large and active critical care unit are those with acute cranial and/or spinal injuries. Intracranial abscesses, aneurysms, arteriovenous malformations and tumors, and nontraumatic spinal cord lesions also continue to require neurosurgical care. This section will discuss some of the common problems that may arise in regard to the general neurosurgical population.

NEUROSURGICAL PROBLEMS

Increased Intracranial Pressure

Elevated intracranial pressure may be acute, subacute, or chronic, depending on the duration, severity, and rapidity with which it develops. The magnitude of the effects is determined by the extent to which the intracranial structures adapt and the time allowed for the process. It then refers to a situation wherein the normal central nervous system contents are obliged to compete for space within the bony confines of the cranium. Additional limitations are imposed by the sensitivity of the brain in general to trauma and of the cranial nerves and vessels to stretch and compression. The fibrous partitions between parts of the brain (falx cerebri, tentorium cerebelli) also act as intrinsic barriers to displacement of the cranial contents and may result in pressure against the nervous and vascular structures.

Competition with the normal intracranial contents may arise extrinsic to the brain—for example, from epidural or subdural hematomas, or tumors arising from the covering of the brain (meningiomas), all of which may exert pressure against any of the brain's surfaces. Intrinsically, hydrocephalus (due to tumors located in the posterior fossa or elsewhere, subarachnoid hemorrhage, or congential anomalies), intracerebral or intracerebellar hematomas (due, for example, to hemorrhage from aneurysms), malformations, or vessels under stress from systemic hypertension, tumors and abscesses (primary or metastatic), and cerebral edema all may create abnormal intracranial pressure.

A focal or diffuse intracranial lesion of sufficient size, regardless of the etiology or whether extracerebral or intracerebral, imparts a mass effect, the result of which is an obligatory shift of the normal contents. If the pressure is acute and the mass significantly large, dramatically rapid adverse effects will be noted, as in the case of most epidural hematomas. These are usually due to temporal bone fracture and laceration of the middle meningeal artery, implying more rapid hemorrhage than that which is venous in origin, unless large venous structures such as the major venous sinuses are involved. Such structures are the origin of major venous bleeding which may lead to early tragedy.

The ultimate result, even in the case of long-standing, slowly evolving subdural hematomas, is some degree of impingement upon the superficial cerebral substance and secondary distortion of the cranial nerves, vessels, and brain stem.

Pressure of the medial aspect (uncus) of the medially displaced temporal lobe on the superior part of the third cranial nerve (oculomotor) results in progressive pupillary dilatation on the same side because of interference with the pupilloconstrictor fibers carried by that nerve. Occasionally the opposite oculomotor nerve will be compressed against the cerebral peduncle, with false lateralization of the abnormal (enlarged) pupil.

A sign of early increased intracranial pressure may be seen in injury to the sixth cranial nerve (abducens), which is manifested by impaired abduction of the appropriate globe. The abducens transverses the greatest distance between sites of origin and function and thereby has the greatest theoretical chance of injury by compression or stretch.

Compression of the cerebral hemispheres and/or distortion of, or injury to the brain stem will result in alterations in arousal. In the latter structure the reticular activating system is involved. Interference with the cardiorespiratory centers will be evidenced by depression and perhaps irregularity of pulse rate and concomitant elevation of blood pressure, as well as abnormalities visible on the cardiac monitor suggestive of primary cardiac disease. In addition there will be abnormalities of respiratory depth, rate, and regularity. Pupillary abnormality, decreased spontaneous movement and weakness of the opposite limbs, and, where the dominant side of the brain is involved, speech dysfunction (dysphasia) will also be apparent. It should be noted, however, that lateralizing signs (hemiparesis, speech disorders, pupillary changes) may not be present initially, but rather headache, progressively severe nausea, emesis, and sensorial depression leading to obtundation will be the most striking symptoms and findings.

It is helpful for both nurse and physician to have concise understanding of the terminology used for the various pathologic levels of consciousness:

Stuporous/very lethargic—sleepy or trancelike but can still be aroused to respond with volitional, well-defined and purposeful acts, whether the acts be socially acceptable or not.

Semicomatose—does not perform volitional acts upon request but does have individual, purposeful movements (defensive withdrawal) or motor activity that is categorized as

(a) *decerebrate*—extension of lower extremities, extension and inward rotation of upper extremities.

(b) *decorticate*—extension of lower extremities, flexion and internal or external rotation of forearms.

(c) *opisthotonic*—extension of extremities and neck and forward arching of trunk.

Coma—implies no spontaneous or induced response except that noted for example, in the pulse and respiratory rate when nociceptive (painful) stimulation is utilized. It is burdensome to rely on more categories than those listed above.

Cerebral Concussion and Contusion

A cerebral concussion is the "transient stage in which consciousness is lost"[1] after a blow to the head. Implied or inherent therein is interruption of normal neural activity. The loss of consciousness is "usually reversible," according to Rowbotham.[2] Retrograde amnesia (memory of events prior to the injury, usually recent rather than remote, being lost) occurs, varying in severity depending on the degree of injury. It is obvious that severe head injuries may be sustained without cerebral concussion by the strict definition

—that is without loss of consciousness, even briefly. Moreover, injuries that consist purely of concussion should be expected to recover without any neurologic sequelae. Individuals who remain unconscious for more than one hour must be suspected of having suffered more than a simple concussion. It is worth emphasizing that loss of consciousness is not mandatory for a diagnosis of severe head injury to be made, at the same time recognizing that a certain percentage of patients with a clinical diagnosis of "simple" cerebral concussion will upon observation be found to have or develop significant injury.

This is well illustrated in the "classic" case of epidural hematoma, in which the patient is initially rendered unconscious, perhaps only for a minute or so, and appears to recover, refusing advice of medical assistance. A short time afterward the patient becomes drowsy, eventually obtunded, hemiparetic, and develops anisocoria. Unless neurosurgical intervention occurs, virtually all victims will die. This is the reason posthead-injury patients must be observed so closely in the critical care unit even though they may at the onset and, for the great percentage, later appear quite normal.

Cerebral contusion per se is usually more serious and refers to injury resulting in bruising of the brain. This may be minimal, or (unfortunately in some) a widespread, massive, and fatal nervous tissue insult. Contusions in general carry a higher risk than concussions so far as permanent damage or significant lesions. Contusion may be accompanied by brain lacerations and hematomas and may lead to depressing problems of intractable, fatal cerebral edema. Individuals with focal and/or lateralizing neurologic signs are evaluated by specific neurodiagnostic procedures (cerebral angiography) to differentiate brain contusion, a nonoperative problem, from traumatic space-occupying lesions which may be surgically remediable.

Treatment for contusion without accompanying surgical injury consists of excellent general supportive care and usually steroids to preclude or reduce concomitant cerebral edema.

Cerebral Edema

A fairly frequent and frustrating situation to deal with is that in which significant cerebral edema is present after head injury. Often no concomitant surgical lesion is present which might alleviate pressure once removed, and medical therapeutics may be to no avail. The result is that the patient succumbs.

Edema of the brain consists of swelling (excess fluid), which causes increased bulk in which the white matter is more vulnerable than the gray. It may be especially evident in the cerebral tissue surrounding tumors or abscesses, or following the removal of tumor or hematoma from the surface of the brain when significant compression with accompanying vascular stasis has occurred. Cerebral edema may be associated not only with cerebral contusions related to impact forces, but be present after thrombosis of cortical veins (in overwhelming sepsis or dehydration), hypoxia, water intoxication, vascular inflammation, exposure to cold, tin poisoning, and hormonal imbalance. This has been called "benign" intracranial hypertension or pseudotumor cerebri wherein presence of a tumor is mimicked.

Therapy directed at relief of cerebral edema consists of both medical and surgical modalities. The latter includes a technique of decompression.[3] Among the former are adequate respiratory care (airway and ventilation) to preclude or reduce hypoxia which may lead to further edema if persistent, and cerebral dehydrating agents which are hyperosmolar in nature (urea, mannitol) and serve to attract fluids into the cerebral vascular space for transport to the kidneys, acting rapidly to create diuresis. However, these agents have the propensity to create a "rebound" phenomenon unless a longer-acting agent is utilized at the same time. It is speculated that 4–5 hours after administration of urea or mannitol, plasma osmotic pressure becomes lower than tissue osmotic pressure as a result of the induced diuresis. Consequently, fluid shifts to the interstitial compartment and cerebral edema can again become a problem. Steroids such as dexamethasone (Decadron), which act to reduce swelling by action as yet not clearly understood but perhaps related to a stabilizing effect on membrane permeability, have a slower onset of action but may reduce the "rebound" effect when used in conjunction with the cerebral dehydrating agents. Other methods include relative dehydration of the body in toto by restriction of replacement fluids and use of salt-containing fluids to maintain the patient on the low or dry side of fluid maintenance; hypothermia to decrease the metabolic needs of the injured cerebral tissue; elevation of the head when feasible to promote venous return to the heart; cautious use, when deemed necessary, of intermittent positive-pressure breathing techniques, which, although beneficial to pulmonary care, may increase intracranial pressure.

Experience proves that, in general, younger patients tend to show higher rates of recovery following cerebral contusions and edema than do individuals past the second or third decade.

The signs of cerebral edema are those of any space-occupying situation if the intracranial pressure is sufficiently elevated. Severe, intractable edema may be present from the onset or appear later (by hours or days), even acutely, despite the appearance of a relatively stable course and the use of the entire spectrum of preventive or therapeutic measures.

Because of the importance of observation unaffected by outside influences, sedatives and analgesics are rarely used during periods of neurological evaluation, even in the face of other injuries (for example, femoral or other long-bone fractures). Paraldehyde seems to be most efficacious in those with head injuries, however, only when the patient is severely confused and/or combative, threatening more harm to himself by his thrashing and inability to rest. Should the patient show more depression in sensorial status at any time, squeezing the trapezius or discreet use of a safety pin in the sole will assist in determining whether arousal is possible, as from an exhausted slumber which is known to occur when a patient is exposed to a critical care unit environment for several days. If the patient is severely ill to begin with, recognition of changes indicative of deterioration becomes more difficult postoperatively or after trauma, for there is less room for physiologic change.

Cerebrospinal Fluid Fistula

Fistulae that allow leakage of cerebrospinal fluid (CSF) are dangerous in that they may predispose to meningeal infection, cerebritis, and death. They frequently follow injuries causing basilar skull fractures and meningeal tear, or depressed skull fractures where the irregular bone edge interrupts the meningeal integrity. CSF leak may occur spontaneously without antecedent trauma in situations of chronic, progressive elevated intracranial pressure. Fracture at the base involving the posterior or middle cranial fossae may allow drainage of the bloody or serosanguinous fluid via the external auditory canal. Eventually the fluid becomes xanthochromic, then clear, and if infected, may be purulent. Drainage from the nares via the paranasal sinuses or frontal sinuses is seen in basilar or low frontal fractures in the frontal fossa. Some patients who are sufficiently alert will complain of fluid trickling into the oropharynx when reclining or sitting. Often discharge via the nares is noted by a spurt or flow of fluid when the patient sits or stands and leans forward.

A specimen of the discharge should be obtained in any case for evaluation by the physician. If the fluid does not contain blood or its disintegration products, a positive glucose test (qualitative) confirms the fluid as CSF.

It is possible to be more vigilant for CSF leaks if basilar skull fracture is identified on examination of the skull radiographs, if the patient has a "Battle's sign" (ecchymosis, edema, and tenderness over the mastoid bone) or periorbital and/or nasal discoloration and edema. Suspicion should be raised promptly whenever dressings covering a scalp wound become stained with watery, usually serosanguinous, fluid. There may exist a previously undetected fracture with underlying meningeal laceration. Postoperative stainage of a craniotomy dressing will indicate inadequate meningeal closure or elevated intracranial pressure decompressing itself by CSF leak via the meningeal suture line.

In any case, it is of utmost importance that prophylactic antibiotics be administered until the fistula heals spontaneously (with the assistance of lumbar punctures to lower the CSF pressure, if necessary) or correction of wounds or operative closure is carried out. It is usual to maintain as far as possible, with appropriate right- or left-sided dependent posturing, a head-up position to allow better drainage. This lowers the intracranial CSF "pressure head" and precludes pooling of CSF in, for example, the paranasal sinuses, whereby bacterial organisms then have a better chance to congregate for access via the fistula to the intracranial fluid. In the presence of CSF leak one should not try to clear the nose by blowing, as this allows forceful retrograde displacement of organisms into the fistula.

Diabetes Insipidus

Diabetes insipidus (DI) represents a pathological state wherein abnormally great quantities of dilute urine are excreted, at times up to twenty liters per day. The kidneys have lost ability to control the amount of fluid output because of absence or deficit in antidiuretic hormone (ADH), which is produced in the supraoptic and paraventricular nuclei of the hypothalamus. The hormone is eventually released by the neurohypophysis (posterior pituitary) and appears to act on the distal renal tubules to promote reabsorption of water. Approximately 85 percent of the hypothalamic nuclei involved in production of the hormone must be impaired before insufficient ADH is available.

The excessive urinary output is matched by excessive thirst in persons alert enough to recognize it, requiring increased fluid intake. This contrasts with the situation found in psychogenic polydipsia, where excess water is consumed resulting secondarily in excess output.

Individuals with depressed arousal and inability to regulate their own intake will eventually lose enough fluid to lead to hypovolemia and death unless replacement in proper amounts is supplied for them. Replacement of water and glucose alone without appropriate electrolytes will result in water intoxication and cerebral edema, since electrolytes accompany the water lost by the kidneys.

Control of water balance is more complicated than one may be led to believe based on the preceding information alone. The entire complex mechanism is not fully understood, but incorporates not only ADH but osmoreceptors and baroreceptors and one additional hormone at least, namely aldosterone. In general however, if the water available to the body is decreased, the secretion of ADH is increased leading to water retention. In states of excess body water, ADH secretion is normally diminished, allowing for loss of the excess fluid.

Diabetes insipidus is usually expected, transiently at least, but at times it occurs in florid and permanent fashion following open procedures for pituitary and parasellar lesions (craniopharyngioma), and in transsphenoidal approaches utilizing cryotherapy for pituitary ablation. Newer transsphenoidal microsurgical techniques, where applicable, hopefully will preclude leaving a postoperative pituitary cripple and reduce the chances for diabetes insipidus.

DI may be seen also in other surgical procedures performed in the region of the hypothalamus, in head injuries with basilar fractures involving the sphenoid bone, gunshot wounds of the head, hypothalamic tumors, hydrocephalus, maxillofacial injuries with displaced fractures, nasopharyngeal tumors invasive of the base of the skull, aneurysms encroaching upon the sellar or suprasellar space, and the like. Of course, some patients without traumatic lesions may have DI among or as the sole presenting symptom.

In cases of DI it is essential that evaluation be carried out for concomitant anterior pituitary insufficiency. This is usually manifested initially as adrenal crisis with hypotension, generalized weakness, anorexia, depressed arousal, hypothermia, and psychotic symptoms.

Recognition of DI in the early postoperative period may be difficult if cerebral dehydrating agents have been used before and/or during surgery, for the diuresis created by them may continue for the first postoperative day or so. Utilization of steroids may also cause increased urinary output. If the patient is awake, however, he will complain of progressively severe thirst if DI is present. Urine output will increase and persist despite the amount of fluid intake (which is usually maintained below normal replacement levels after cranial neurosurgery), and urine specific gravity will fall or remain below about 1.007–1.008. Suspicion of the entity is confirmed by serum and urine electrolyte and osmolarity determinations. (See Chapter 11.)

Presence of persistent DI will result in exhaustion of the alert patient who is unable to rest for long because of the frequent need to micturate and replenish fluids. Replacement fluids consist of iced juices and other electrolyte-containing liquids. In this case, pitressin will eventually be required, just as in severe, continuing DI in patients unable to voluntarily replace their losses.

It should be reemphasized that patients developing florid DI may lose enormous amounts of urine in a relatively short period of time, leading to hypovolemia, unless a diagnosis is surmised or established and treatment undertaken. When the diagnosis is secure it is most efficacious to allow the patient to satisfy his replacement needs by drinking according to his thirst. It is more difficult in those requiring intravenous therapy, but especially in the latter cases, meticulous quantitation of intake and output is mandatory.

Intracranial Hemorrhage

Intracranial hemorrhage not related to trauma is encountered most frequently secondary to rupture of cerebral aneurysms. It may occur also from vascular malformation, rupture of weakened vessels under the strain of systemic hypertension, or occasionally in relation to cerebral neoplasms per se or leukemic infiltrates or aggregates. More common than generally recognized are hemorrhages during periods of anticoagulation therapy for previous myocardial infarction, because of vascular insufficiency and as prophylaxis of pulmonary embolus in phlebitis of the lower extremities. Admittedly there is usually an antecedent minor head injury or episode of severe straining in the anticoagulated patients. Massive, rapid hemorrhages also may occur in diffuse intravascular coagulopathy (DIC) whatever the basic cause. The hemorrhage may be confined to the spaces associated with the meningeal layers or involve the intracerebral substance.

In ruptured aneurysms, unless a space-occupying lesion is present necessitating emergency surgery, such as subdural and/or intracerebral hematoma, the patient is frequently too ill for immediate surgery because of severe spasm in the cerebral vessels. He generally does not become a candidate for direct attack on the aneurysm unless the neurologic situation improves markedly and repeat arteriography confirms remission of vascular spasms. This holds true despite the knowledge that a significant percentage may be expected to have a recurrent hemorrhage that could prove fatal. Headache (frequently severe), nausea, emesis, stiff and tender neck, and photophobia are common complaints if the patient is adequately alert.

Spinal Cord Injury

Trauma to the spinal cord is not uncommon in automobile, motorcycle, and mountain-climbing accidents. It also occurs from the use of trampolines. Care of the patient with complete or a significant incomplete lesion is difficult from a psychological standpoint as soon as he perceives the permanency of the neurologic deficit.

"Spinal shock" is the term used to denote complete loss of neurologic integrity on a voluntary basis distal to the level of injury. It is the *fact* of cord sectioning, not the *act*, that produces spinal shock and implies paralysis of the muscles and anesthesia of the tissue below the lesion; i.e., sensation and voluntary motion are abolished and never recover. The stretch reflexes, although lost initially, do recover and eventually become overactive several weeks after the injury. The mass-reflex response usually appears several months later with exaggerated withdrawal reflexes and spread of the reflex activity to the visceral autonomic outflow. Thus by merely stroking the sole of the foot a patient may be stimulated to perspire, withdraw extremities, and empty bladder and bowel. The mass reflex activity may be spontaneous at times.

Return of spinal reflexes is noted in the initial one to three weeks, beginning with withdrawal upon stimulation of the sole. Later in the period, anal and genital reflexes and the presence of a Babinski sign are noted. Progressively vigorous and brisk withdrawal is elicited and the zone of positive elicitation becomes larger.

Autonomic reflexes remain suppressed following injury longer than somatic reflexes. Thus the patient's skin is completely dry during the first four to eight weeks, but perspiration later may be severely intense.

Injury to the spinal cord above the cervical levels of 3 and 4 is usually not compatible with survival due to interruption of the innervation to the diaphragmatic muscles which supply respiratory function when the intercostal musculature is lost by lower cervical injuries. Higher cervical trauma may also contribute to edema, more cephalad, involving important medullary centers.

Because of the initial loss of sympathetic outflow, patients are often hypotensive as a result of loss of vascular tonus below the injury. For the same reason hypothermia may be profound because of loss of heat through the dilated vessels.

Patients with cervical injury often seem to be unstable from the standpoint of regulation of blood pressure and maintenance of respiratory activity when initially turned on their frames, especially in rotating from supine to prone positions. It is necessary to be prepared to render immediate respiratory assistance and to return the patient to supine position if significant cardiac and blood pressure irregularities occur.

REFERENCES

1. Joseph P. Evans, *Acute Head Injury* (Springfield, Ill.: Charles C Thomas, Publisher, 1963), p. 89.

2. G. F. Rowbotham, *Acute Injuries to the Head* (Baltimore: The Williams & Wilkins Company, 1964), p. 27.
3. R. N. Kjellberg and A. Priesto, "Bifrontal Decompressive Craniotomy for Massive Cerebral Edema," *Journal of Neurosurgery,* Vol. 34 (April 1971), pp. 488–493.

HYPOTHERMIA

The use of hypothermia (lowered body temperature) in clinical situations ranges from treating gastric hemorrhage to attempting to prevent irreversible cerebral damage. Decreased body temperature reduces cellular activity and consequently the oxygen requirement of tissues. Hypothermia is therefore induced in situations involving interrupted or reduced blood flow to vital areas to minimize tissue damage due to diminished oxygen delivery. This is the rationale for using hypothermia during open-heart and neurosurgical procedures.

The presence of fever (hyperthemia) in any patient produces greater cellular oxygen requirements because of the increased rate of metabolism. Each degree of temperature elevation above normal increases metabolism approximately 7 percent. This fact becomes especially significant in the patient whose vital centers may already be compromised because of cerebral edema surgically induced or resulting from another form of insult such as hypoxia from cardiac arrest. It is to provide some margin of safety in these situations until injured tissue can recover that the body temperature is lowered or maintained at normothermic levels. Current emphasis is on preventing marked elevations in body temperature as opposed to markedly lowering the temperature. Physiological responses to cold remain the same, and there are occasions when actual hypothermia is desirable.

Since the critical care nurse is usually responsible for inducing the hypothermic state and monitoring the patient during this therapy, she must be aware of the physiological manifestations of the various phases of body cooling.

Phases of Hypothermia

I. COOLING PHASE

For the conscious patient, lowering body temperature is at best a most unpleasant experience. It goes without saying that adequate explanation and support for the patient and his family is an integral part of his nursing care.

Although the method of inducing hypothermia will depend upon the situation and the equipment available, there are essentially two ways to proceed — surface cooling or the more direct method of bloodstream cooling. The latter is the method employed during open-heart surgical procedures when the blood passes through the cooling coils in the cardiopulmonary bypass machine. Surface cooling with the use of blankets circulating a refrigerant is the method usually employed in critical care units. The cooling blanket may be placed directly against the patient, or more esthetically a sheet can cover the blanket and be tucked under the mattress to hold the blanket in place. (This should not negate turning the blanket with the patient to maintain skin contact with the cooling device.) The important point here is to avoid placing any degree of thickness between the patient and the blanket, as this will serve as an insulator and impede the cooling process.

When cooling is initiated, one blanket may be placed under the patient and another placed on top to hasten the cooling process. If a top blanket is used, care must be exercised in observing the patient's respiratory status, as the weight of the cooling blanket may limit chest excursion. Keeping the blanket in contact with areas of superficial blood flow such as the axilla and groin will also expedite cooling. In the event that a cooling device is not available, ice bags can be used to initiate the cooling process, utilizing these same principles.

The body's initial reaction to exposure to cold is an attempt to conserve body heat and to increase heat production. Skin pallor that occurs is due to a vasoconstrictor response which limits superficial blood flow and thus loss of body heat. Intense activity in the form of shivering occurs to maintain body heat. The effects of these compensatory responses will be reflected in the vital signs, and it is important that the nurse understand these transient variations and consider them in evaluating the patient.

During the first 15–20 minutes of hypothermia induction all vital signs increase. Pulse and blood pressure rise in response to the increased venous return produced by vasoconstriction. Respiratory rate increases to meet the added oxygen requirements of increased metabolic activity produced by shivering and to eliminate the additional carbon dioxide produced. If the patient hyperventilates with shivering, respiratory alkalosis can develop. The initial rise in temperature is a reflection of this increased cellular activity.

Since the patient requiring hypothermia usually has an existing cellular oxygenation problem, the increased oxygen consumption induced by shivering is undesirable. For this reason, chlorpromazine (Thorazine) may be given at the beginning of induction to reduce hypothalmic response. Hypoglycemia is a potential occurrence during vigorous shivering, as increased glucose is required for the increased metabolic activity.

After approximately 15 minutes the vasoconstrictor effect is broken by means of a negative feedback loop, and warm blood flow is reestablished to the body surface. This accounts for the reddened skin color following initial skin pallor. This same phenomenon can be demonstrated by holding an ice cube in the hand for a short period of time.

As superficial warm blood flow is reestablished, body heat is lost and body temperature begins to drop. The temperature is best monitored by a rectal probe taped in place which allows for frequent or continuous readings. Fecal material should be removed before inserting the probe. Because blood cooled at the body surface continues to circulate through the body core, "downward drift" of the temperature usually continues for approximately one degree after the cooling blanket is turned off. In the obese patient, a greater degree of drift may be experienced. For this reason, the cooling device should be turned off before the desired hypothermic level is actually attained. Close temperature monitoring will be necessary to determine if the trend remains downward or whether an increase in temperature will be noted requiring use of the blanket again.

Skin care becomes particularly crucial due to the presence of cold and its circulatory effects. Position can be changed to eliminate pressure points, taking care to move the blanket with the patient so that body contact is maintained with the cooling device. Experience has indicated that the skin can be protected by applying a thin coating of lotion followed by talcum powder which does not appear to impede the cooling process. The application can be repeated in accordance with the skin care program, but the skin should be gently washed at least every eight hours to remove the accumulated coating.

II. HYPOTHERMIA

When the desired level of hypothermia is achieved, usually around 32°C (89.6°F), a number of other physiological changes become apparent. The vital signs at this stage are all diminished. The development of respiratory acidosis is a real possibility, since at deeper levels of hypothermia ventilation falls off more rapidly than does reduced carbon dioxide production. Also, with increasing hypothermia the oxygen dissociation curve shifts to the left, and at lower tensions oxygen is not readily released by hemoglobin to the tissues. Because of the developing circulatory insufficiency and increased metabolic activity due to shivering, metabolic acidosis is also a possibility. Secretion of antidiuretic hormone is inhibited and an increase in urine output may be noted with a drop in the specific gravity. During hypothermia, water shifts from the intravascular spaces to the interstitial and intracellular spaces. This results from sodium moving into the cell in exchange for potassium and taking water with it. This fluid shift produces hemoconcentration, and nursing measures must be taken to prevent embolization. Such measures would include passive range of motion exercises and frequent change of position.

In hypothermic states, for every degree of temperature below normothermic levels, cerebral metabolism is decreased 6.7 percent. At 25°C (77°F) the brain volume is reduced 4.1 percent and extracellular space increases about 31.5 percent. The sensorium fades at 34 to 33°C (93–91.4°F). This becomes increasingly significant for the nurse working with the neurological patient who already has a depressed sensorium. She must then rely on other measures to evaluate changes in the patient's level of response. This may be accomplished by evaluating purposeful or nonpurposeful movements in response to painful stimuli and the degree of painful stimuli necessary to elicit a response.

As all cellular activity diminishes with hypothermia, cerebral activity decreases and hearing fades at approximately 34–33°C (93–91.4°F) due to reduced cochlear response. At 18–30°C (82.4–86°F) there is no corneal or gag reflex, and pulse irregularities may be noted due to myocardial irritability, which probably occurs as a result of potassium moving into the cell. Ventricular fibrillation is a common occurrence at this level, and consequently the patient is usually maintained at a hypothermic level around 32°C (89.6°F) to avoid cardiac problems.

Drugs tend to have a cumulative affect in the hypothermic patient. Decreased perfusion at the injection site and decreased enzyme activity result in slower chemical reactions. Therefore the intravenous route is preferred, and intramuscular or subcutaneous injections should be avoided. If a drug must be given hypodermically, it should be given deeply I.M. and vigilance maintained during the rewarming phase for accumulative effects.

Another potential occurrence in hypothermia is that of fat necrosis. This results from prolonged exposure to cold and decreased circulation which allows crystals to form in the fluid elements of the cells, leading to necrosis and cellular death. Nursing measures which can minimize this occurrence are turning the patient frequently, massaging the skin to increase circulation, and avoiding prolonged application of cold to any one area.

When the patient has reached the desired hypothermic level, vital signs will also level out at reduced values. Changes in vital signs must therefore be evaluated in light of the patient's hypothermic state. For example, if you are caring for a neurosurgical patient cooled to 32°C (89.6°F) and if his vital signs have decreased as you would normally expect, an increase in pulse, respirations, blood pressure to "normal levels" must be interpreted in view of the hypothermic state. For example: Is an infectious process present? Are changes occurring in the patient's neurological status? Is intracranial pressure increasing?

If the patient is to be maintained at the hypothermic level for a prolonged period of time, this can be accomplished in a number of ways. The patient (after his temperature has risen several degrees) may need to periodically be placed on the cooling blanket and returned to the desired level. Nursing measures should be carried out gently, with a minimal degree of activity to the patient to prevent an increase in body heat, such as providing passive range of motion exercises. Bathing of the patient should be done with tepid or cool water to avoid increasing temperature in this manner. It cannot be overemphasized that prevention of pulmonary problems in the hypothermic patient is almost entirely dependent upon nursing care. Change of position allowing for postural drainage, measures to promote adequate ventilation and suctioning to remove accumulated secretions are all extremely important in this patient.

III. REWARMING

Once it is determined that the patient no longer requires the hypothermic state, rewarming can be accomplished by a number of methods. These methods include surface rewarming, bloodstream rewarming, or rewarming naturally. Allowing the patient to rewarm naturally is the preferred method. The cooling device is removed. Blankets may be used to cover the patient but no artificial heat is used and the patient is allowed to warm at his own rate. As the patient approaches normothermic levels, it is to be anticipated that vital signs will return to precooling levels due to reversal of the physiological events. One of the hazards of artificially inducing rewarming is that of warming the skin and muscles before the heart. The heart remains in a cooled state and is unable to pump sufficient blood to meet the oxygen demands of the superficial areas. Further warming increases the dilatation of peripheral vessels and blood pools, resulting in decreased circulating volume, decreased venous return, and therefore decreased cardiac output. This sequence of events can be avoided if the heart is warmed first, as in the bloodstream method or by allowing the body to rewarm naturally. Other complications which may occur during the rewarming process are hyperpyrexia, shock (for reasons just cited), and acidosis. The acidosis occurs as a result of the increase in metabolic activity in those areas already warmed and an insufficient circulation to meet the metabolic requirements of this increased activity. Oliguria may also result, probably due to antidiuretic hormone secretion. During this rewarming phase the patient must be monitored closely for indications necessitating recooling. Using the patient's normothermic status as a baseline, these indications would include a fading sensorium, greater increase in pulse and respirations than would normally be expected with the warming process, and a drop in the blood pressure. Another important facet to be monitored is the cumulative effect of drugs given previously.

The necessity for interpreting clinical changes in the patient on the basis of the physiological changes brought about through cooling and then rewarming cannot be overemphasized. The nurse must anticipate changes and findings based on the patient's pathology and other variables present which would alter those findings. When those findings that she is anticipating do not occur, and when there is a deviation from the anticipated, the critical care nurse must be prepared to ask the question *Why?* and go about systematically determining why the anticipated change is not present. Only when she is able to do this, can she render optimum nursing care.

15

Assessment Skills for the Nurse

M. LYNN McCRACKEN, R.N., M.S.

NEUROLOGICAL NURSING ASSESSMENT OF HEAD-INJURED AND STROKE PATIENTS

Nursing care of the neurological patient must be approached with the attitude that the patient can resume a useful life and be an asset to society. To do this, nursing assessment must be done completely and systematically to establish a baseline of function and to identify when change has occurred. Understanding the physiology involved in change allows for proper nursing judgments on the appropriate intervention. Certainly a proportion of head-injured and stroke patients die or function at less than their potential, not from their pathophysiology, but from nurse-allowed or nurse-induced complications. Nurses must become accountable for nurse-induced disability. To this end, assessment will be discussed so that disability is abolished so far as possible and not induced (or allowed to occur). The objectives for neurological crisis care are (1) to maintain and support life, (2) to prevent complications and further neurological deficit, and (3) to help the patient to accept and adjust to his limitations.

Thrombus, Embolus, Hypotension, Spasm

The thrombus-caused CVA usually occurs while the patient is quiet, activity-wise. Atherosclerosis is frequently the cause and the patient fits into the atherosclerotic risk profile. This patient often has had transient ischemic attacks (small strokes). Some of these premonitory symptoms consist of falls or dropping attacks for no reason, blurring of vision or transient monocular blindness, transient paresthesia, ataxia, dysphasia, nerve palsies, disorientation, vertigo or lightheadedness, or behavior change noted by family and friends. (Incidentally, if the nurse or the layman had been sensitive to these

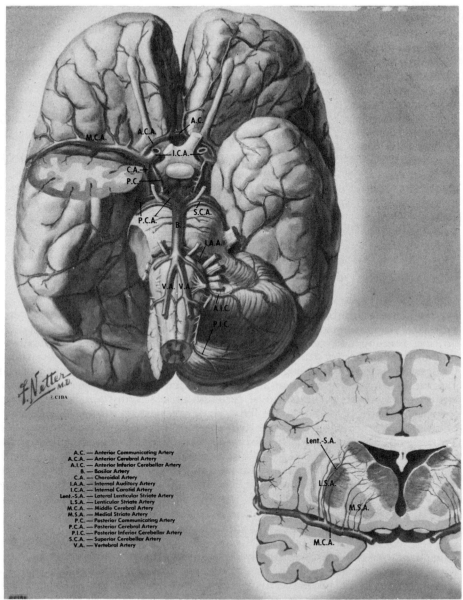

Fig. 15-1. Blood supply of the brain. [© Copyright 1953, 1972 CIBA Pharmaceutical Company, Division of CIBA-GEIGY Corporation. Reproduced, with permission, from THE CIBA COLLECTION OF MEDICAL ILLUSTRATIONS by Frank H. Netter, M.D. All rights reserved.]

warning signs and directed the patient to appropriate medical care, this CVA might have been prevented.) The embolus-caused CVA is usually related to primary heart disease, (chronic atrial fibrillation, rheumatic valve disease, or the mural thrombus of a myocardial infarction). Hypotension from acute blood loss, myocardial infarction, hypotensive drugs, or cardiac arrhythmias are other causes of CVA's. The thrombus, embolus, or hypotensive-caused CVA will cause similar symptoms as will those related to arterial spasm. Symptoms vary depending on the site of interference with the blood supply to the brain. (See Fig. 15-1.)

TABLE 15-1
SYMPTOMS OCCURRING DURING
TRANSIENT ISCHEMIC ATTACKS (TIA'S)

CAROTID OCCLUSION	VERTEBRAL-BASILAR OCCLUSION
1. Aphasia	1. Vertigo or dizziness
2. General or focal seizure	2. Hearing loss or tinnitus
3. Contralateral weakness or numbness	3. Visual graying or loss
4. Ipsilateral migraine-type headache	4. Diplopia
5. Transient blurring of vision or blindness in ipsilateral eye	5. Dysarthria
6. Homonymous visual field loss	6. Dysphagia
	7. Hemiparesis
	8. Occipital headache
	9. Homonymous visual field loss

Hemorrhage

Hemorrhage, while probably less frequent, is more likely to occur on exertion. Hypertension and atherosclerosis are often involved. The patient may have severe headache, nausea and vomiting, more severe motor deficit, and frequently may be comatose. If there is blood in his spinal fluid, he will have signs of meningeal irritation (nuchal rigidity, positive Kernig's sign, photophobia—see last page of this section).

Recognition of the above patterns will assist the nurse in collecting data for the physician who will make the diagnosis. The point is not for the nurse to make the diagnosis, but in planning appropriate nursing care, the nurse needs adequate data. The patient with intracranial hemorrhage will be treated so as to avoid any re-bleeding. The Valsalva maneuver is avoided as is anything that might elevate the blood pressure. CVA's due to other causes will be treated initially with more aggressive patient activity toward rehabilitation.

The hemiplegia of the stroke patient is the result of an upper motor neuron lesion. It follows the general rule that upper motor neuron lesions yield spastic paralysis, while lower motor neuron lesions yield flaccid paralysis (Fig. 15-2).

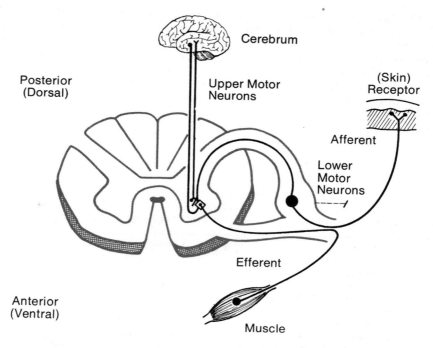

Fig. 15-2. Upper motor neurons vs. lower motor neurons (spinal reflex arc). (Courtesy of Sylvia Meeks.)

The spinal reflex arc (lower motor neurons) when interrupted yields a flaccid paralysis. When the efferent nerve in the arc is interrupted, this also prevents stimulation or inhibition from the upper motor neuron (arising in the intracranial central nervous system) for voluntary motor function. When the upper motor neuron is interrupted (as in stroke or traumatic brain damage) the spinal reflex arc remains intact. Thus whenever the afferent nerve is stimulated in the arc, the corresponding efferent function occurs.

Accordingly, stroke patients develop spasticity because of the interruption of the upper motor neuron influence. The pyramidal and extrapyramidal systems are also both involved in the control of resultant tonus.

The nurse must recognize that while occasional upper motor neuron lesions may yield a permanent flaccid paralysis, this is relatively rare. The initial flaccid paralysis is caused by a state of "shock" or depressed reflex function that occurs with sudden nerve damage. Soon spasticity will appear. Exercise will maintain joint range of motion as well as "fatigue out" some muscle spasms. It must be brought to the patient's attention that exercises will maintain muscle tone and joint function and reduce disability, should significant function return. The nurse must also teach the patient that frozen, flexed joints, particularly in the upper extremity, (1) are painful, (2) reduce social acceptance when one is unable to wash the axilla, (3) inhibit one's dressing with a shirt or slip, (4) do not allow for the assistive functions that even a paralyzed limb has to offer, such as stabilizing objects while the other hand works on them. Exercise in controlling spasticity is very important to the patient's maximum rehabilitation.

A stroke patient's motor deficit (hemiplegia or hemiparesis) is on the

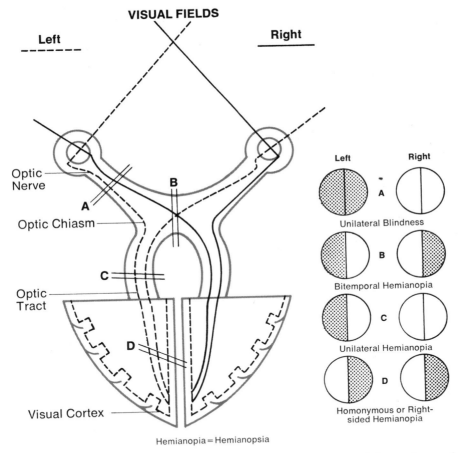

Fig. 15-3. Neural pathways for vision. One can see that some of the pathways for vision cross. By creating a lesion in the occipital area (visual cortex) as in a CVA, one creates a half-blind state in both eyes on the opposite side as the brain damage. This is called *homonymous hemianopsia* (or hemianopia) (Lesion D). Note that the visual field defect is on the same side as a stroke patient's motor deficit. [Adapted from W. B. Youman, *Fundamentals of Human Physiology,* 2nd ed. (Chicago: Year Book Medical Publishers, Inc., 1962) p. 198.]

opposite side to the brain damage when the middle cerebral artery is affected because the pyramidal tracts (the voluntary motor nerves) cross at the level of the medulla (Fig. 15-3).

What should the nurse observe for and expect to find with a right hemiplegia versus a left hemiplegia?

You will recall that the areas of the cortex controlling the sensory and motor aspects of speech are found in the frontal, temporal, and parietal lobes of the dominant cerebral hemisphere. The majority of the population (90 percent) are right-handed with the dominant hemisphere on the left.[1] One can generalize that right hemiplegics are more likely to have expressive and/or receptive aphasia (lack of ability to communicate). Left hemiplegics, on the other hand, tend to have a form of agnosia (lack of ability to interpret sensory stimuli or to integrate them with past experience). Pigott and Brickett[2] describe this phenomenon as visual-spatial neglect. The nondominant parietal lobe serves the visual-spatial functions of orientation of self in space as well as psychologic awareness of oneself as a spatial entity. This loss, which is often combined with homonymous hemianopsia on the paralyzed side, leads to complete denial of that side of the body. For instance the patient might dress only his nonaffected side. Trying to teach a patient to care for his paralyzed side of the body is extremely difficult when he denies that it exists.

It is helpful in assessment to know, either from the patient or his family, his dominant hemisphere as determined by his right- or left-handedness.

To evaluate visual field defects, try letting the patient read something of adequate size (the larger print of a newspaper). It is wise first to ascertain that he is literate, had no preexisting visual problems, and is not obviously asphasic. You could also observe what part of his meal tray he utilizes.

Appropriate placement of objects and teaching the patient to rotate his head and scan horizontally with his eyes are methods of intervention for the hemianopsic patient.

The remainder of neurological crisis assessment for the stroke or head injured patient is as follows:

1. Airway with adequate oxygenation must be the first consideration immediately and long-term. An unconscious patient should never be unattended in the supine position without a cuffed tube in his trachea. In addition, both immediately and continuously any hypoventilation resulting from accumulated secretions or related to respiratory difficulties due to brain damage may produce hypoxia, hypercarbia, and acidosis with resultant cerebral edema and secondary brain damage. These patients need excellent basic respiratory care measures. Hypoxia causes altered permeability of cell membranes, promoting exudation of fluid into the tissues. Hypercarbia ($\uparrow$ pCO_2 = respiratory acidosis) causes dilation of cerebral blood vessels, increased blood flow, and consequently contributes to cerebral edema. Respiratory acidosis also is accompanied by decreased blood pO_2 and consequently only a small amount of extra oxygen is available to be released at the tissue level. On the other hand, if hyperventilation caused by brain damage goes unchecked, respiratory alkalosis decreases the blood pCO_2, causing con-

striction of the cerebral blood vessels, decreasing available oxygen, and also increasing cerebral edema.[3]

2. Assessment of neurological status (sensorial status, vital sign and motor function) is mandatory as a baseline from which to detect change. Observations must be purposeful and systematically thorough or the nurse will be uncertain when change develops. Subjective involvement can easily sway judgment when observations have been hastily and carelessly made.

(a) *Level of Consciousness*

Is behavior appropriate? Is the patient oriented to time, place, and person? Explain to patients why you are doing this. It is particularly frustrating for the patient who can hear your request but is unable to respond. Remember that with each request to which the patient is unable to comply you are reinforcing the reality of their disability. Some patients may become so angry that they elect to "turn off" and stop trying. Repeated explanation and reassurance will help as will varying methods of gathering the same data.

(b) *Vital Signs*

Graphing of vital signs is a part of the observations relative to assessment for increased intracranial pressure. Changes in the level of arousal are often the first signs of increased intracranial pressure and should not be missed because one is looking for the classic vital sign changes. Written and verbal communication describing the patient's level of arousal should be done on a stimulus/response basis. One should describe the stimulus exactly (moderate pressure at the base of the fingernail) and the response specifically (forearm and arm were withdrawn). Use of broad terms such as *stuporous, semicomatose,* and *comatose* should be used only when they are clearly defined in writing and universally accepted and utilized by all the physicians and nurses involved. Because this is a difficult consensus to reach, the use of stimulus/response charting is easier.

Note in Figure 15-4 that the changes to be noted in evaluating BP are an elevation of systolic pressure with a decreased diastolic pressure yielding a widened pulse pressure. Note also the corresponding drop in the pulse rate. These are the classic Cushing's reflexes. One may also see marked instability of the vital signs as the initial crisis.

When systolic BP is elevated, the vagus nerve is reflexly stimulated, slowing the pulse rate and allowing more time for cardiac ventricular filling and stretching of cardiac fibers, in turn yielding increased strength of cardiac contraction in an attempt to get more oxygenated blood to the brain, which is becoming hypoxic.

Relative to the patient's vital-sign status will be observations for cardiac arrhythmias. Pressure on the brain stem as well as the accompanying blood gas changes which may occur with brain injury, may precipitate arrhythmias. Cheyne-Stoke's or Biot's[4] breathing are equally significant danger signals (respirations that come in couples,

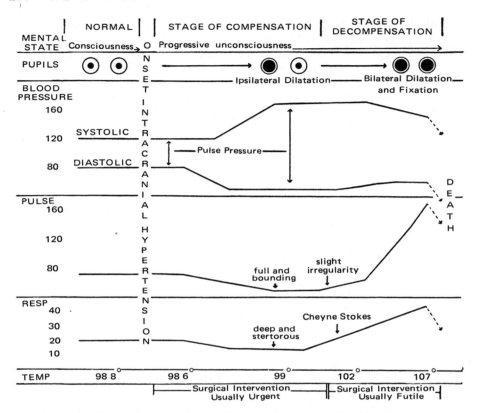

Fig. 15-4. Chart showing changes in mental state, pupils, blood pressure, pulse rate, respiratory rate, and temperature before and after the onset of fatal increase of intracranial pressure.

triples, and quadruples without varying in depth and rate and with apnea between) (see Fig. 15-5). Pupillary changes will be discussed under cranial nerves.

(c) *Voluntary and Involuntary Motor Function in All Four Extremities*
The upper extremities can be assessed by requesting the patient to grasp firmly. (The nurse should use only nonringed fingers to avoid being hurt.) When weakness is suspected, but may be subtle, ask the patient to extend his arms in front of him with his eyes closed. If weakness is present, one arm will drop or drift before the other.

The Babinski sign is present if dorsiflexion of the toes is elicited in an individual approximately 2 years or older when stroking the lateral part of the foot and moving across the base of the toes with a closed safety pin or retractable pen. Any withdrawal attempt of the lower extremity may make the test invalid, but otherwise the test indicates damage to the pyramidal (voluntary motor) tract.

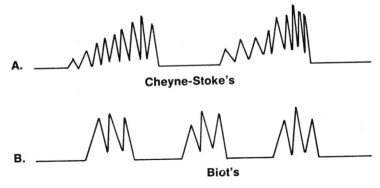

Fig. 15-5. Types of periodic breathing.

Lower extremity motor function is assessed by requesting the patient to plantar flex against the nurse's hand. Note that one must be observant for any twitching or rhythmical motor abnormality that may be indicative of seizure activity.

(d) *Sensory Loss*

Sensory loss should be assessed without scratching or bruising patients. Pressure at the base of the fingernail in the half-moon portion, and pinching the trapezius muscle or the Achilles tendon will demonstrate sensation if motor function is present. One should attempt to maintain consistency of stimulation when assessing sensory loss. For communication purposes utilizing the stimulus/response method, one should attempt to describe levels of stimulus required so that a trend of increase or decrease in response can be noted. One cannot be exact, but perhaps words such as *minimal, moderate,* and *severe* in describing stimulus would promote better communications.

(e) *Cranial Nerve Assessment*

Another method of making further systematic observations is to consider the function of the twelve cranial nerves and the implied nursing care when dysfunction is noted.

    I. *Olfactory*—smell is usually not tested in the critical care unit. However, deficits in this function should be recognized so the patient may be taught about his loss of defensive mechanism. (Have you noticed with upper respiratory infections how difficult it is to tell if food is spoiled?)

    II. *Optic*—observation for visual field defects has been discussed.

    III. *Oculomotor*—the most important functional abnormality of the oculomotor nerve for which to observe is dilatation of one or both pupils. The third cranial nerve carries the parasympathetic innervation to the iris which results in constriction of the pupil. Increasing intracranial pressure compresses the third nerve, leaving the sympathetic innervation dilating the pupil and decreasing its reaction to light until it may become fixed. Dilatation of the pupil usually occurs on the same side as the brain damage. With severe pressure, both pupils dilate and become fixed. Pupillary changes indicate impending herniation of the uncus into the tentorial ring, which in turn compresses the medulla into the foramen magnum compromising all the maintenance functions of the medulla. Damage to a portion of the brain stem (pons and midbrain) can paralyze the sympathetic fibers and cause bilaterally constricted pupils.

III.
IV. *Oculomotor, trochlear, and abducens* — these three control the motion of the eye via their appropriate extraoccular muscles.

V. *Trigeminal* — The sensory portion controls sensations of the face and cornea while the motor portion controls the muscles of mastication.

VI. The doll's-eye phenomenon, which is movement of the eyes conjugately (together) to the opposite side of the turned head, remains intact unless damage is present in the frontal or brain stem eye fields. If these three nerves are functioning properly, the eye on an unconscious patient should move in the opposite direction from the way the head is moved, just as doll's eyes do. When the eye does not move to the opposite side, there is nerve dysfunction.[5] If you wish to separate out which nerve is involved, consult an anatomy and physiology text.

VII. *Facial* — controls the muscles of facial expression. Loss of the corneal reflex (V) or blinking ability (partially controlled by VII) requires means to prevent drying and ulceration of the cornea. If closure of the eyelid is used, assure that there are no inverted eyelashes. Sterile normal saline drops can be used until an order for artificial tears (methyl cellulose or mineral oil base) can be obtained. Scotch tape or any of the non-allergic tapes can be used to close the eye. An eye patch can be made out of exposed X-ray film and taped tightly, but without pressure on the eye, so that normal condensation will keep the cornea moist. Any other type of eye patch should be applied without pressure and with the eye taped closed before applying the patch so that corneal abrasion is avoided. The eye should not be "fiery red" before the nurse takes action. Remember that the pupil of the closed eye should still be checked for function and symmetry.

VIII. *Acoustic and vestibular* — hearing and equilibrium are functions of this nerve. Loss of hearing should not be confused with receptive aphasia or auditory agnosia. Problems with equilibrium will be most troublesome with ambulation of the patient.

IX. *Glossopharyngeal, vagus*—these two nerves are considered to-
X. gether because of their close anatomic relationship and function, which relates to the gag reflex and phonation. Prevention of aspiration and maintenance of airway are obvious problems when dysfunction exists.
XI. *Spinal accessory*—control of the trapezius and sternocleidomastoid muscles results in ability to shrug the shoulders, which is most important to the use of assistive devices by quadriplegics.
XII. *Hypoglossal*—controls the motor function of the tongue which is important to patients who have lost function of the muscles of mastication. It is efficacious to teach them to use their tongue to clean out the "weak" side of their mouth after eating.

(f) *Meningeal Irritation*

The nurse should also observe for signs of meningeal irritation provided there is no suspected cervical injury. Nuchal rigidity is a most prominent symptom. A positive Kernig's sign is elicited when pain occurs in the neck and back upon extension of the lower leg while the thigh is flexed on the abdomen. Meningeal irritation, due to the presence of blood in the spinal fluid, usually also causes fever, headache, photophobia, and nausea.

Spinal cord injuries or dysfunction would be assessed with all of the same considerations which have been discussed. Sensory loss becomes especially important in these patients. The nurse should realize that because the pathways carrying pain and temperature sensation cross in the spinal cord, it is possible to lose pain and temperature on one side and motor function on the opposite side (Brown-Sequard's syndrome).

Adequate assessment of the neurological patient cannot only prevent unnecessary complications and disability, but is the first ingredient for optimum rehabilitation. It can be a most rewarding "game" to play.

REFERENCES

1. New Jersey Regional Medical Program, East Orange, N.J., *A Manual on Stroke*, Monograph No. 2 (July 1970), p. 24.
2. Richard Pigott and Florence Brickett, "Visual Neglect," *American Journal of Nursing*, January, 1966, p. 102.
3. L. Claire Paisons, "Respiratory Changes in Head Injury," *American Journal of Nursing*, November 1971, pp. 2187–2190.
4. Arthur C. Guyton, *Textbook of Medical Physiology*, 3rd ed. (Philadelphia: W. B. Saunders Company, 1966), p. 602.
5. Jeanne Holman Quesenbury and Pamela Lembright, "Observations and Care for Patients with Head Injuries," *Nursing Clinics of North America*, Vol. 4, No. 2 (June 1969), pp. 237–247.

A Specific Crisis Situation

16

Disseminated Intravascular Coagulation Syndrome

JOHN H. ALTSHULER, M.D.

INTRODUCTION

Disseminated intravascular coagulation syndrome has the singular distinction of being the oldest universally accepted hypercoagulable clinical state known. The many faces of this syndrome have led to synonyms so that it is known as consumption coagulopathy, diffuse intravascular clotting, and the defibrination syndrome. In most "clotting circles" however, the syndrome has become honorably dubbed "DIC" and will be referred to by this nickname throughout this chapter.

Unfortunately, DIC cannot be understood without a working knowledge of the clotting mechanism both *in vitro* and *in vivo* (as they differ). Lest the reader be discouraged by the thought of this task, let me assure him that the mystery of clotting will be sequentially and simply outlined for you in the pages that follow.

THE BLOOD COAGULATION MECHANISM

A. In Vitro Mechanism

If blood removed from a patient could remain unaltered in a syringe, it would not clot. However, upon exposure of blood to any surface outside of a blood vessel lining, (i.e., a syringe) changes in clotting factors start immediately. These changes are irreversible and cannot be stopped without the addition of inhibitory chemicals to blood. The changes that occur bear the relationship of enzyme (organic catalyst) to substrate (specific substance upon which an enzyme acts). The initiation of change referred to above is as yet unknown, although evidence suggests that exposure of blood to a foreign surface causes molecular alteration in one clotting factor. The unaltered clotting factor, known as a proenzyme, is thus converted to an altered state—an active enzyme (Fig. 16-1). One molecule of enzyme acts upon specific substrate which is also a proenzyme clotting factor. The single active enzyme molecule is capable of converting not one but perhaps thousands of specific substrate molecules into other active enzymes. This is but a single event in what is to become an entire series of enzyme-substrate reactions. Hence a chain reaction is born whereby activation of a single proenzyme molecule may lead to activation of the entire clotting mechanism. The chain reaction involves at least nine well-defined clotting factors with 34 others reported as being involved in disputed points along the way. During the in vitro clotting process, at one place the reaction is known to be self-perpetuating so that a vicious cycle of clot activation ensues causing clot formation to accelerate rapidly. The cascade of events may be paralleled with a waterfall as represented in Fig 16-2.

Understanding the basic concepts of clotting far outweighs knowledge of technical factors involved. However, some of these factors must be known. The first factor to be activated in clotting is inactive XII. The active enzymatic form of XII is annotated XIIa. The enzyme XIIa acts upon the next clotting proenzyme factor—inactive factor XI—converting it to the active enzyme XIa, and so on. Diagrammatically the clotting sequence may be represented as in Fig. 16-3.

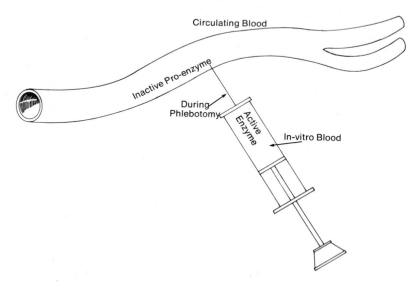

Fig. 16-1. *In vitro* clotting mechanism.

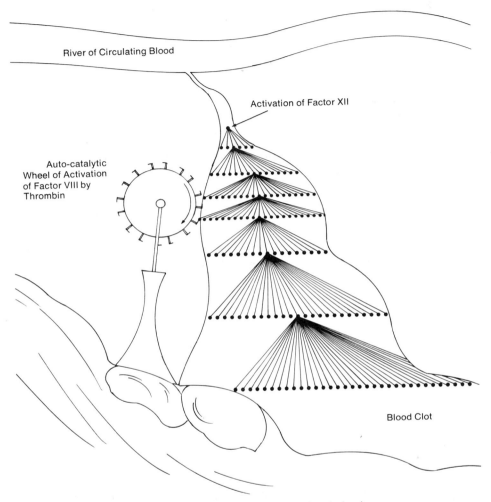

Fig. 16-2. Waterfall sequence of blood clotting.

Note that the activation of factor X requires factor VIII, and activation of factor prothrombin requires factor V. Furthermore, a fatty (lipid) substance derived from platelets (platelet cofactor −3) must be present at the site of activity of both factors VIII and V. The self-perpetuating effect in the mechanism takes place by creating the vicious cycle of activation of factor X through the effect of thrombin on factor VIII. Thrombin is a very potent enzyme converting fibrinogen to fibrin clot. The initial fibrin clot is further stabilized by yet another clotting factor (XIII).

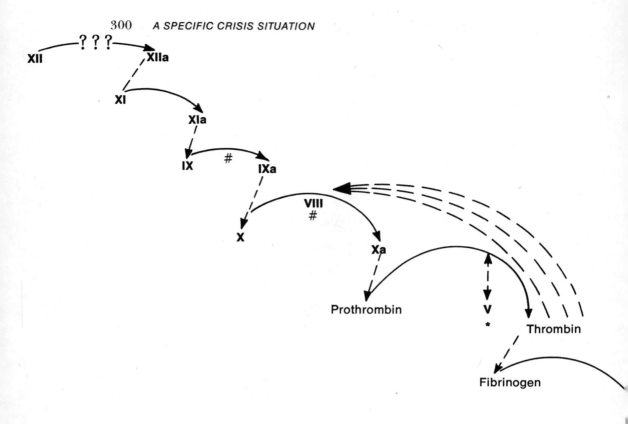

Fig 16-3. Clotting sequence. [#—calcium ion required; *—calcium ion and fat (lipid) substance derived from platelets—both required.]

As in most biologic orders, a system antagonistic to the clotting mechanism exists—the fibrinolytic system. Again, a series of proenzymes, when activated, are converted to enzymes which are capable of dissolving blood clots. The dissolving or lytic enzyme is called *plasmin* and is derived from the proenzyme *plasminogen* normally present in whole blood. Unlike the coagulation mechanism, the fibrinolytic system is not activated by withdrawal of blood from the body. Nonetheless the state of the fibrinolytic system may be determined *in vitro* by assaying plasmin levels.

B. In Vivo Mechanism

In the normal state, the coagulation mechanism is inactive. Due to normal wear and tear of blood vessel linings, holes occur through which blood leaks out. The hole, however, is promptly plugged by the adherence of platelets to the hole, thus preventing blood leakage outside of the vessel. The seepage of tissue juice into the rent in the vessel wall attracts platelets and causes the latter to adhere to the hole, effectively plugging up the leak. This phenomenon is further enhanced by the platelet's own ability to release a chemical (adenosine diphosphate — or ADP). Because platelet plugging may interfere with normal smooth flow (laminar flow) of blood through the vessel, eddy currents are set up which tend to activate the intrinsic clotting mechanism. Such activation would cause clots to form on top of the platelet plug, releasing thrombin in the process of clotting, further attracting platelets to the clot site, and causing additional clot to form at the local site of vessel leak. Total vessel occlusion by clot would occur if it were not for the fibrinolytic system which keeps a delicate balance between clot formation and clot lysis. (See Fig. 16-4.)

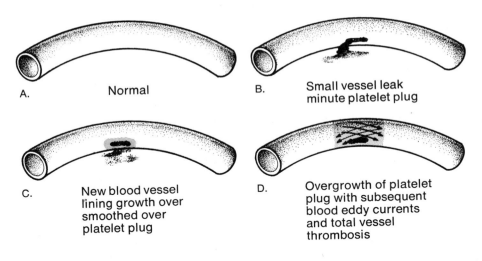

A.   Normal

B.   Small vessel leak minute platelet plug

C.   New blood vessel lining growth over smoothed over platelet plug

D.   Overgrowth of platelet plug with subsequent blood eddy currents and total vessel thrombosis

Fig. 16-4. Sequence of thrombus formation in blood vessels.

A well-controlled balance between clotting and lysis is established in man. Diagramatically, a seesaw plank depicts coagulation control (Fig. 16-5). On one side of the plank are the clotting factors (CF) and on the other side are the fibrinolytic factors (FF). Note that the plank may oscillate in a normal range. It is important to remember that the range of fluctuation may increase to a point where laboratory tests are abnormal but clinical evidence of pathologic bleeding or clotting is not seen. Obviously, when this warning fluctuation range is exceeded, the patient will demonstrate overt clinical evidence of thrombosis or hemorrhage.

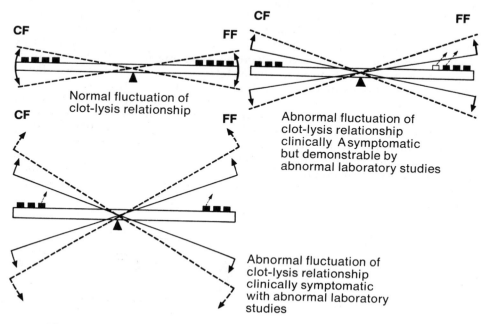

Fig. 16-5. Normal and abnormal fluctuations in clot-lysis relationships.

The balance may be upset by:
1. Decreasing clotting factors as in classic hemophilia where clotting factor VIII is low and the patient has a bleeding tendency.
2. Increasing fibrinolytic factors causing excessive bleeding.
3. Decreasing fibrinolytic factors causing pathologic thromboses.
4. Increasing clotting factors causing hypercoagulability (still debated).

DISSEMINATED INTRAVASCULAR COAGULATION SYNDROME (DIC)

DIC is a syndrome of transient coagulation causing transformation of fibrinogen to fibrin clot, often associated with acute hemorrhage. The syndrome is secondary to a whole host of diseases and diversity of etiologic factors. Paradoxically, DIC is a bleeding disorder resulting from an increased tendency to clot. Although the causes are varied, the syndrome itself has many common factors regardless of etiology. Almost uniformly, patients have arterial hypotension often associated with shock resulting in arterial vasoconstriction and capillary dilatation. Blood is then shunted to the venous side, bypassing dilated capillaries due to the opening of arteriovenous shunts. The dilated capillaries now contain stagnant blood which accumulates metabolic byproducts (pyruvic and lactic acid) rendering the blood acidotic. Further, the precipitating factors in DIC frequently cause release of procoagulant substances into the bloodstream (e.g., free hemoglobin, bacterial toxins, thrombosis-promoting placental tissue, amniotic fluid, cancer tissue fragments). We thus have three concomitant procoagulating effects in capillary blood: (1) acidosis—a potent coagulation activator, (2) blood stagnation, (3) presence of coagulation promoting substances in blood.

ARTERIOLE - CAPILLARY - VENULE RELATIONSHIP IN NORMAL AND DIC

NORMAL

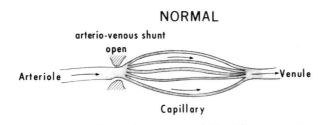

Capillary perfusion is normal, blood flow is rapid.

DIC

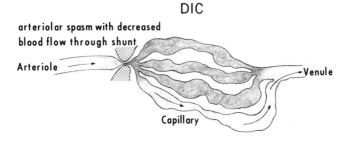

Capillary perfusion is impaired, blood flow is slow,
intracapillary thrombosis occurs with blood stagnation and acidosis.
Cells nourished by capillaries die of ischemia due to blood clotting.

Fig. 16-6. Effect of A-V shunting in DIC.

A special event in DIC may be the activation of clotting factors in cardiopulmonary bypass due to contact of blood with the extracorporeal apparatus. The result of DIC to this point is the accumulation of clot in the body's capillaries, the length of which exceeds 100,000 miles in the average adult.

Thus the amount of blood clot sequestration in capillaries in acute DIC is enormous. Because of the rapidity of the process, clotting factors are effectively used up in the capillary clotting process at a rate exceeding factor replenishment. Circulating blood hence becomes depleted of clotting factors. With such depletion, the patient can no longer maintain normal hemostasis, therefore bleeding follows. Hemorrhage starts from needle and incisional sites, respiratory, genitourinary and gastrointestinal tracts. Blood cells now become suspended in serum rather than plasma—serum being the liquid portion of blood minus the clotting factors used up in clotting. Not all clotting factors are used up in clotting, although the platelet blood cell is totally removed in clotting. Table 16-1 shows the difference between serum and plasma.

TABLE 16-1
DISTRIBUTION OF CLOTTING FACTORS
IN SERUM AND PLASMA

CLOTTING FACTORS	PLASMA	SERUM
XII	†	†
XI	†	†
IX	†	†
VIII	†	0
X	†	†
V	†	0
Prothrombin	†	0
Fibrinogen	†	0
XIII	†	†
(Platelets)	(†)	(0)

† present; 0 absent; ( ) cellular component of blood.

Stress has a significant role in DIC as the former activates the fibrinolytic system. As stress is a primary cause of increased fibrinolysis, the DIC patient bleeds not only as the result of consumption of clotting factors but to some degree because of increased fibrinolysis. This effect not only brings about lysis of clots already formed but also causes production of certain degraded products of fibrin which further add to the bleeding diathesis. As may be recalled from the previous discussion, the clotting process elaborates thrombin, the most potent of all coagulation enzymes. In DIC, abundant intravascular thrombin is produced, rapidly converting fibrinogen to fibrin clot. When in the course of DIC fibrinogen is entirely used up, circulating thrombin persists in the intravascular space, just waiting for its substrate fibrinogen to arrive, converting it to clot. This arrival occurs either by additional body production of fibrinogen or by transfusion of blood, plasma, or fibrinogen, all of which serve to perpetuate the syndrome and worsen clinical hemorrhage. Although the body has naturally occurring antithrombins which inhibit thrombin activity, in DIC antithrombins are practically absent. The most important, *antithrombin (III)*, is not even present.

A summary diagram of the vicious cycle of DIC is given in Fig. 16-7.

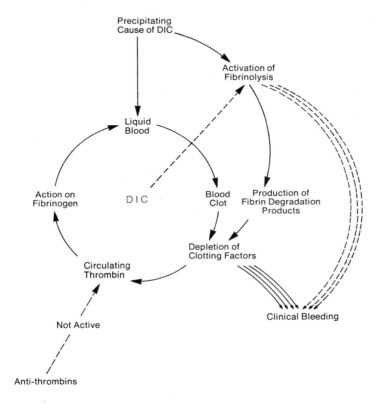

Fig. 16-7. Self-perpetuating cycle of clotting and hemorrhage in DIC.

Now that the pathogenesis of DIC is understood, let us discuss how the laboratory can aid clinicians in diagnosing DIC. Below is a list of the clotting factor and cell abnormalities found in DIC.

1. Clotting factor depleted plasma, hence the following clotting factors are reduced:
   (a) Fibrinogen
   (b) Factor VIII
   (c) Factor V
   (d) Prothrombin
2. Platelets markedly reduced (thrombocytopenia)

3. Absence of antithrombins
4. Abnormally high blood thrombin levels
5. Abnormally increased fibrinolytic activity
6. Abnormally increased fibrin degradation products

In classic DIC, the tests given in Table 16-2 are abnormal.

TABLE 16-2
LABORATORY FINDINGS IN CLASSIC DIC

TEST	DIRECTION OF ABNORMAL VALUES	RATIONALE
Prothrombin time	Prolonged	Factor V and prothrombin are measured.
Partial thromboplastin time (PTT)	Prolonged	Factors V and VIII are measured and to a lesser degree—fibrinogen.
Platelet count	Low	Thrombocytopenia present.
Fibrinogen level	Low	Patient with DIC has reduced fibrinogen.
Euglobulin lysis time (ELT)	Shortened	ELT measures fibrinolytic activity.
Antithrombin III level	Low	Antithrombin III is absent in patient with DIC.
Thrombin time	Prolonged	Fibrinogen is indirectly measured by thrombin time.
Fibrin degradation products	Elevated	These products are increased in DIC.

Recent investigation (unpublished data) suggests that clot tension strength is altered in DIC from a normal of 30 to 10–15 dyne/cm. These data are of prognostic importance because clot tension in patients recovering from DIC returns toward normal before conventional laboratory tests show normalization.

TREATMENT OF DIC

The backbone of therapy consists of removing the cause of DIC. If your kitchen is flooded by a broken pipe, adjacent flooding will not be averted by mopping alone. One must turn the water supply off to the broken pipe. If the cause of DIC cannot be removed (as in intravascular dissemination of cancer) therapy of the syndrome may control but not cure it.

Control of DIC is brought about by stopping the vicious cycle of thrombosis-hemorrhage as shown in Fig. 16-7. Heparin does this three ways. First, it is antithrombin in activity and will neutralize free circulating thrombin. Second, heparin prevents propagation of thrombi that have formed in capillaries—in which capacity, heparin is functioning as an anticoagulant. Third, heparin has an inhibitory effect on the activation of blood clotting *in vivo*, principally due to its effect on factor IX.

In DIC, heparin should be given only *intravenously* for four reasons:

1. Dosage regulation is far easier via I.V. rather than subcutaneous administration because the absorption rate from tissue is affected by amount given, depth of injection, temperature of the patient and his cardiovascular status.
2. Local hematoma formation when given subcutaneously may severely alter absorption of the drug.
3. The dose in severe, acute cases may be too large for proper blood levels to be obtained by any route except intravenously.
4. The time lag for therapeutic effect of subcutaneous heparin is too great compared to the immediate effect of the drug I.V.

The amount of heparin to be given for acute DIC is not established. Most adults are given between 10,000 and 20,000 units (100–200 mg.) every 2–4 hours. Ideally, the stat dose of heparin is 2–2.5 mg. per kilo body weight with follow-up doses which keep the circulating level between 0.5 and 1 mg. per kilo body weight. The dosage may be determined by calculating the disappearance rate of heparin in the patient and giving a calculated dose every 2 hours to maintain the patient in the therapeutic range. The dosage of heparin required to treat DIC must be tempered by the clinical status of the patient as heparin is eliminated from the body by renal excretion (in both an altered and unaltered state) and by heparinase activity in the liver. Patients with renal failure, inadequate liver perfusion or both will thus have an abnormally prolonged heparin half-life requiring far less heparin to control the DIC patient. The author has experienced such cases in which a heparin dose of 1 mg. (100 units) every two hours was sufficient to control acute DIC.

The author's experience suggests that continuous drip of heparin does not work well in keeping the patient properly heparinized. Of course, once the primary precipitating cause of DIC has been removed and clinical and laboratory evidence suggests that the patient is on the way to recovery, heparin should be discontinued. In early acute DIC, a single large dose of heparin will arrest the DIC process if the primary factors have been eliminated.

Recent unpublished observations suggest that low doses of heparin in the range of 5 to 10 mg. (500–1000 units) every 2 hours is enough to inhibit thrombin in the patient with active DIC. This inhibitory activity will break the cycle of clotting and hemorrhage.

The role of acidosis in this syndrome is sufficiently great to add another treatment goal in this disorder—the prevention of acidosis. Frequently patients in shock with DIC are acidotic, and correction of this acid-base imbalance should be part and parcel of the treatment of DIC bleeders.

Some authorities have recommended the use of epsilon amino caproic acid (eACA) (trade name, Amicar) in acute DIC. The rationale is to take advantage of the potent antifibrinolytic effect of eACA, hence reduce the fibrinolytic component of bleeding in acute DIC. Let us not forget that eACA is a double-edged sword. It not only inhibits pathologic but normal fibrinolysis as well, hence inhibiting a protective mechanism in the clot-lysis balance. Remember that DIC is after all a hypercoagulable state and eACA may render a patient even more hypercoagulable by destroying the lytic side of the balance. Certainly if one desires to control the pathologic element of fibrinolysis, eACA must not be given unless the patient is adequately heparinized, and then only with great caution.

Thus far we have discussed the acute bleeding episodes of DIC. However, this syndrome occurs both in a subacute and chronic phase. In the subacute stage bleeding may not be clinically obvious; however, at this stage the patient is in great danger of becoming an overt bleeder (acute DIC). Treatment of the subacute stage is important only to prevent the acute stage from occurring. The chronic form of DIC is usually unassociated with hemorrhage or abnormal clotting tests. The *only clue* may be a sudden *drop in hematocrit* in the absence of any demonstrable blood loss. It is assumed that hemoglobin is sequestered as clot in capillaries. Due to the slow replacement of red cell mass in circulating blood, the only manifestation of chronic DIC is a drop in circulating blood hemoglobin. Blood volume is kept normal with rapid plasma replacement. The typical chronic DIC patient is the one with a sudden episode of coronary shock with hemoglobin loss as a single occurrence.

"All that glitters is not gold." Likewise, all that bleeds is not DIC. All too often every bleeding crisis is diagnosed as DIC. There are numerous bleeding situations that mimic DIC and they should not be forgotten. To name a few—acute fibrinolytic activation, clotting factor depletion secondary to massive hemorrhage, and acquired clotting factor inhibitors. Unfortunately, routine laboratory data do not differentiate these syndromes with ease. Because treatment of the different bleeding disorders varies, correct diagnosis is essential if the act of living is to be prolonged. Incorrect diagnosis, hence improper treatment will hasten the act of dying.

Summary

1. DIC is secondary to primary disease or symptom-sign complex.
2. DIC is a serious bleeding disorder resulting from a hypercoagulable state.
3. Massive capillary thrombosis leads to platelet and clotting factor depletion and hence, hemorrhage.
4. Simultaneous events in DIC include
    (a) Arterial hypotension
    (b) Opening arteriovenous shunts
    (c) Capillary blood stagnation
    (d) Acidosis
    (e) Capillary thrombosis.
5. Stress associated with DIC increases fibrinolytic activity.
6. Treatment of DIC requires a twofold approach:
    (a) Remove etiologic factor(s) causing DIC
    (b) Heparin use as outlined above.

Professional Practice
in the Critical Care Unit

17

Planning for the Training and Development of the Critical Care Nursing Staff

NAOMI D. MEDEARIS, B.S., M.A., M.B.A.

A CASE IN POINT

As the charge nurse of the critical care unit replaced the telephone in its cradle, she silently prayed enough people would respond to the Cor Zero page. She had been having these feelings of panic more frequently of late. She could not accurately anticipate the number of people who would respond. Sometimes there would be too many, sometimes there would be too few.

Without hesitation she moved into action and began dealing with the crisis. Fortunately enough people began to appear. The right things began to happen. The patient began to move out of crisis. Things began to ease off a bit.

It was then that she really began to have the shakes. "What if enough people had not shown up? What if they had not accurately assessed the situation? What if people had hesitated to do the things that needed to be done?"

That night while nursing her exhaustion and recalling the events of the day, she thought of the crisis and the panic it caused. "Why," she said to herself, "should I push the panic button every time there is a crisis on the unit? Is such wear and tear on the nervous system implicit in the job? Isn't there something I can do to reduce the tension and anxiety? Maybe I should give it more leadership. Maybe I should do more staff training."

She began thinking back over the critical care course she attended some months ago. She recalled a training session focused on the teaching role of the nurse in the critical care unit. The instructor spoke of the growing trend to decentralize inservice training programs. She had said, "The rapid change

313

in medical and nursing knowledge and the new techniques and procedures which evolve from these changes have created the need to decentralize training and share on-the-job inservice responsibility with professional nurses working in clinical areas. Ask your inservice educator to assist you in developing this new facet of your role as a nurse. She can help you acquire the knowledge and skill you need for teaching and developing your staff."

What the instructor said didn't seem to fit at the time. The hospital had an inservice program which seemed to be getting the job done. When she went home she talked it over with the inservice education director and they had set up a course on critical care nursing for the entire hospital. They set up lectures by clinical specialists in nursing service, physicians, and school of nursing faculty; demonstrations of equipment by salesmen and distributors; practice sessions in reading monitor strips, and lots of reading materials.

Things went better after the training, too. Cor Zero situations were pretty well handled. The right number of people usually showed up and did their part with few questions and with little or no hesitation. She had been pleased with the results of the training and had felt that the problem was solved.

What had happened since then? Things were certainly different now. As the charge nurse reflected on her situation, she began to suspect that several things had happened: For one thing, the inservice training program had been a "one shot" event—there was no follow-up. For another, there had been a number of staff changes in the nine months since the event. She couldn't prove this was a factor since she had never known for sure who had taken the training. Still another thing that seemed to have happened was that she had too easily assumed that everyone who had attended the inservice training would magically appear when they heard Cor Zero. And obviously this was not the case.

Even though she had been charge nurse for almost three years now she had never taken time to give such matters much thought. Nursing administration obviously had assumed she had the qualities needed for the charge nurse job; she had accepted the promotion with the same assumption. Since they hadn't talked to her about her need for supervisory training, she hadn't given it much thought.

She began to feel angry about her dilemma and her feeling of incompetence to train and develop her staff. She asked, "How can I change this situation?"

Perhaps you empathize with the charge nurse described above. Everyone has been there at one time or another—either in reality or in his imagination.

AN OVERVIEW

Alvin Toffler in his book *Future Shock* described what happens to people when they are overwhelmed by change. The acceleration of change produces a fantastic stress on people. Handling such stress demands special coping mechanisms. The case in point symbolizes such a situation.

To cope with job stress, the charge nurse decided to use education as a strategy for managing change. This decision became significant for three reasons. First, it challenged inservice education and the way it was organized to serve nursing personnel. Second, it expanded the role of the charge nurse and the way she developed nursing resources. Third, it changed the dynamics of staff involvement by offering each staff member different ways to respond to learning needs related to his job.

For your guidance, the first part of this chapter describes the changing focus of inservice education and its decentralization; the second part outlines the process of training and developing staff. The approach to content is presented as a guide for charge nurses in critical care units.

In describing the implications that decentralization of inservice education has for clinical areas, certain assumptions have been made regarding the charge nurse. She is a person who is competent in her nursing knowledge and skills. She is comfortable supervising the work of other people. She is aware of the acceleration of change in her unit. She is curious about potential alternatives to cope with needed changes. And she is willing to explore the possibility of decentralized inservice education and experiment with the role of teacher-learner (or co-learner).

THE CHANGING FOCUS
OF INSERVICE EDUCATION

What needs to take place in the modern hospital organization to improve inservice education of personnel working in acute settings?

Some background data on the development of inservice education will clarify its current status and support the premise that inservice for the critical care units should be decentralized to clinical areas.

Current Administrative Structure of Inservice Education

In a few hospitals you will find that staff development departments are emerging which incorporate inservice functions. These departments have expanded services to facilitate the development of both the professional nursing staff and the paraprofessional staff. However, you will discover that the usual inservice department today is locked into a system which limits its effectiveness. Inservice education has struggled to establish a viable program within nursing service, and it has struggled against unbelievable odds. However, a new role for the inservice educator is gradually evolving.

Over the years, many of the time-consuming reports and surveys, disciplinary actions requiring counseling, have been assigned to the inservice director, along with functions that range from conducting fire drills and updating procedural manuals to presenting films, lectures and nurse aide training programs.

Another handicap has been the budget. As a rule, the budget has been limited to the salary of the inservice director, and perhaps a part-time clerical. Operating expenses for the inservice program were "taken out of" the nursing service budget.

Physical facilities were limited to office space and an occasional classroom. Frequently the cafeteria or administrative conference rooms were utilized for training sessions.

Another deterrent to effective inservice education was the fact that the inservice educator lacked not only a realistic job description and adequate support but also the relevant educational preparation.

As you can see, it has often been an impossible job. When you combine a potpourri-type job with minimum financial support, inadequate facilities, and an underprepared inservice director, the need to reorganize administration of inservice programming is evident.

Program Characteristics of Inservice Education

If you take a moment to review the characteristics of most inservice education programs, you will discover another reason why clinical inservice should be decentralized to the unit level.

Some of the unique characteristics of inservice programs have evolved from mass education and the medical education model.

From mass education, designed to meet the needs of "anybody and everybody," classic inservice has drawn its form and methodology. It has characteristically assumed that all participants have the same abilities and interests in the subject being offered. Posters, public-address announcements, and pressure on head nurses to "send any one who can be spared from the floor" provided criteria for selection of learners. The successful inservice program was measured by the number who attended. As in the typical academic classroom, the basic purpose of education was simply to transmit information and assume content was assimilated by the learner.

In following the medical model, inservice programming often got trapped into equating role status with credibility of information. Thus it often relied on lectures, slide presentations, papers, and the like, usually presented in the language of medicine. The programs were presented to an audience of nonmedical listeners, namely nurses and paraprofessional nursing personnel who were scheduled for inservice. The intent of such programming was to teach by presenting information in an authoritative manner by an authoritative status figure. And the expectation was that everyone who attended would learn.

When you look for coordinated inservice programming in most hospitals, the evidence is at best minimal. Some of the reasons for this lack include the absence of long-range, collaborative programming with staff and prospective participants; the lack of relating each inservice activity to specific learning objectives for the participants; and the sporadic attendance of personnel who seem powerless to alter their working schedule to attend a planned sequence of inservice programs. As a rule, only persons on the day shift attend. It is still a rare inservice program that is offered "live" to personnel on all three shifts. Such fragmented learning significantly weakens the chances of the learner to acquire either knowledge or skill.

Confronted with these realities, it is impossible for the inservice coordinator to follow up on inservice sessions to see whether or not the knowledge has been effectively utilized throughout nursing service. Therefore the relevance and applicability of clinical inservice offered on a mass scale to nursing personnel is at best fragmented, superficial, and transitory. Combine these facts with the explosion of new techniques, procedures, medications, equipment, and material in a multiplicity of clinical settings within the hospital and you find that the need to restructure inservice is inescapable.

Consequently, you, as a charge nurse in the critical care unit, may want to pursue the prospect of developing a training and staff development program of your own. Such a program would be tailored to meet the needs of *your* unit, *your* staff, and *your* patients. Hopefully, the description of decentralization of inservice to clinical areas will offer data upon which you can base a decision to undertake such a task.

A Look at Decentralized Inservice Education

ASSESSING FEASIBILITY OF DECENTRALIZATION

To answer the question of feasibility you will need to gather data upon which to base your decision to add inservice and staff development to your job responsibilities. You will need to assess your current functions. To accomplish this assessment, the following suggestions are offered:

1. List the responsibilities for which you hold yourself accountable. By writing out a detailed list of these functions you will develop a concrete picture of what you do.
2. Next, rank-order these functions according to your own priorities. Perhaps this will be difficult to do, for you can easily convince yourself that everything you do is equally important. However, by numbering 1, 2, etc., you lay the foundation for the next important step in your job assessment.
3. Critically evaluate each of these functions. Consider: "Should you delegate, discontinue, reschedule or reorganize the function—or should you retain the function as it is?" The outcome of this evaluation will provide data for reallocating your time and redesigning some of your job, so that you can assume the new training functions.
4. Now, going back to your priority listing of responsibilities, insert inservice and staff development functions in a realistic position. By doing this, you crystallize your intent to engage in creating new job functions and your willingness to allocate time and effort to do so.
5. Evaluate the personal resources you bring to this new function of train-

ing and development of your staff. Again, write down the teaching you are already doing. Find answers to questions like, what help do I give new employees and floats? How do I introduce new ideas, procedures, equipment, supplies? After attending a meeting, conference, or intensive course, how do I share the information? When a critical incident occurs, how do I deal with it? When I am working side by side with my staff in a crisis situation, what is my staff learning from me? When the census is low, how do I use the time? Do personnel on the other shifts understand and follow nursing care plans that I write? How is "report" given and received? What plans do I make prior to calling a staff meeting, and how does my staff respond? What do employees learn in the periodic performance appraisals?

Add questions to this list which occur to you and more completely analyze the teaching and learning that is going on in your unit at the present time. The process of disciplining yourself to write down what you do, will help you (1) determine the training currently done, (2) recognize and build on the teaching you are already doing, and (3) clarify those areas that you may want to change to maximize the learning potential.

The next data you will need to assemble come from other people whose functions relate to your own. These people include the Director of Nursing Service and the Director of Inservice Education. Following the pattern used in assessing your own resources, list the administrative resources available to you that will provide the needed support for launching your inservice program. Consider specifically the interest, style, and leadership, as well as the contribution the Director of Nursing Service could offer you in your undertaking. Your observations, based on such questions as these, will help you list available resources: What is the attitude of nursing service toward experimenting with new ideas, new functions, new programs? What position does nursing administration take when plans do not work out as predicted? What kind of financial support would administration give if either additional coverage, compensatory time, or overtime pay were indicated in my staff development plan? Would money be available for outside consultation should such consultation resources be needed? Would administration underwrite costs for continuing education (tuition, fees, travel, lodging, and the like) outside our hospital to prepare me and members of my staff to increase our clinical competence as such opportunities arise? What kind of space do we have to hold staff conferences and how available is this space to us?

Next, assess the resources that the inservice education department offers. What support will the Director of Inservice Education give a decentralized inservice program? What materials are available to me, such as film and tape catalogues, programmed instruction materials on clinical aspects of nursing related to my specialty service? What unique resources such as persons within the hospital, related health agencies and associations, colleges and universities, and health consumers, are available to me?

As a result of this assessment of resources available from nursing administration, the inservice education department, and your own personal resources, you will have a basis of deciding whether or not it is feasible to continue your exploration of decentralization. If it shows promise, you are ready to pursue the study of the characteristics of a decentralized inservice program that is tailored to meet the needs of the adult learners in your unit.

CHARACTERISTICS OF DECENTRALIZED CLINICAL INSERVICE EDUCATION

The most unique characteristics of a reality-based inservice program in a clinical unit are its flexibility, spontaneity, timing, relevance, its conscious exploitation of daily situations for learning, the active involvement of everyone present, and the supportive nonjudgmental climate. A brief descriptive statement of each of these characteristics may help you get a feeling for the dynamic nature of a small, interdependent staff, meaningfully involved in meeting their own learning goals and the general goals of their unit.

A flexible program implies that even though there are thoughtfully developed training plans to meet long-term goals within a predetermined time block, changes can be made in the light of unexpected developments which offer viable learning opportunities, but *now. Flexibility* is the freedom to change the master training plan, to improvise on ongoing training, or to alter priorities based on new data or needs. If the charge nurse and members of her staff develop an awareness of freedom to deviate from the training prescription in the light of pertinent facts, and then exercise this freedom, flexibility to move to meet the needs becomes evident. Appropriate action will then follow.

Spontaneity might be described as generating learning from daily on-the-spot incidents, or when the inspiration occurs. No plan exists. Out of a situation grows the opportunity to acquire insights, identify new knowledge, or recognize new skills. Sensitivity to the learning inherent in what is happening all the time can be developed in your staff. This quality spawns spontaneity and unexpected or surprise opportunities to learn. It makes learning fun!

A *sense of timing* is essential to planning inservice and designing individualized staff development. Respect for careful and thorough long-range programming is a vital part of sequencing learning activities. On the other hand, a quick, perceptive response to a current situation has a profound effect on timing. If you can develop a feeling for the pulse of what is happening in the unit and if you can feed in either programmed or spontaneous learning experiences, you utilize time effectively and your staff responds positively.

Every potential training event should be assessed very specifically to see how directly it relates to the patient, the staff, and the unit. To validate *relevance* of potential learning, identify such basic issues as (1) how this information will be used, (2) why it should be offered, (3) what changes it will require, (4) what changes will individuals need to make, and (5) what results are expected. Taking time to articulate these relationships of learning will pinpoint their relevance to patient service, to the situation, to staff capacity, and to the goals of the unit.

In looking at the *exploitation of the daily situation for learning purposes,* you select those situations that occur infrequently or offer unique content and experience. Another criterion for selecting a situation is the opportunity for everyone involved to see the same occurrence and share their different perceptions of it and how they experienced it. From this it is possible to create new procedures, anticipate similar problems, and check out the understanding of what might be expected the next time a comparable event occurs. It affords an opportunity to demonstrate role and task relationships. The art of managing time, staff, and the situation creates meaningful involvement and learning for each person present.

Active involvement of everyone present has been alluded to in the aforementioned characteristics. However, active involvement of the total person in the teaching-learning process deserves to be lifted out for special emphasis. Research on the learning process shows people remember

> 10% of what they read
> 20% of what they hear
> 30% of what they see
> 50% of what they see and hear
> 80% of what they say
> 90% of what they say as they do a thing*

A nonjudgmental *climate* supports a creative inservice program in the clinical unit. Such a climate allows moderate risk-taking on the part of staff who want to grow personally and professionally while working, and who want to accept responsibility for their experimentation and are willing to be held accountable for the results. This climate permits more self-direction, once the level of competency has been identified cooperatively by the worker and members of the staff and the charge nurse. It creates a support system of interdependence when each member clearly sees the situation, the role and level of competency of his co-workers, and understands and accepts his relationship, level of competency, and responsibility in the unit. A nonjudgmental attitude supports the staff as they learn to move toward higher levels of competency. The emphasis is not on what is right or wrong, but rather, what is the most effective way to accomplish the task. Perhaps this attitude is the most significant one to develop when undertaking a new training program which is based on involvement of the staff.

Even though these descriptions of characteristics have been given separately, they are in fact blended, balanced, and counterbalanced in a well-conceived inservice program. To the degree that you develop your skill in integrating these components in your inservice and staff development programming, you can measure the degree of artistry and effectiveness you have in handling this responsibility.

*Special survey/research project conducted by the Industrial Audiovisual Association.

Expanded Role = Charge Nurse in Critical Care Unit + Learning Specialist

Probably the most exciting part of your new role in assuming responsibility for training and developing your staff is the fact that there is little precedent for it. Part of the reason for this is the recent major shift in emphasis from "teaching" to "learning." Becoming a learning specialist in the critical care unit offers a unique opportunity to pioneer—develop the role as you live it.

In writing about this change in education the eminent psychologist Carl Rogers points out that as a teacher he discovered he couldn't teach anyone anything. He believes the student learns what *he* wants and needs to learn. This fact imposes a significant change in the role of the teacher. Rogers believes his role as teacher is to help the student learn. To provide the kind of help the student needs in order to learn, the teacher will need to assume the new role of co-learner. As a co-learner, the teacher is free to learn many things about the learner, from the learner, and with the learner.

In the process of learning these things, the teacher will assume her part of the responsibility in the teaching-learning process—that is, planning and organizing learning activities and materials which have as their goal the satisfaction of learner needs. The teacher's responsibilities center around having "the right resources and materials, at the right time and in the right place" so that the learner can learn when he is ready.

Transferring this concept to the teaching and learning activities in the critical care unit, your role as teacher does not carry full responsibility for training and developing your staff. In fact, you and members of your staff will enter into a co-learner relationship in the teaching-learning process. You will need to learn together. Their role as learner will change from passively listening to you, as teacher, to actively assuming responsibility for what they want and need to learn, and when they need to learn it.

Employees are more than workers, they are adults who want to learn. Powell and Aker point this out (bracketed material added):

> Adults do not need, nor do they wish, to be overly directed or controlled in their learning experiences. They are self-directed, autonomous human beings, and desire a strong sense of dignity and individual worth. Nothing will offend this sense of dignity more than to have an individual throw bits of information at them, like raw chunks of meat, and demand that they accept them.
>
> The adult is a learner; as such, the responsibility for learning should be placed upon him. He will choose, if allowed, what he learns and how he learns it, and will also decide the rate and speed at which he learns best. He will need helpful advice and suggestions, however, as to how he should best continue his self-directed learning ... and this is where the teacher [charge nurse] comes in, as a helpful aide who is prepared, not to answer the student's [employee's] every question, or to solve his problem, but to help him develop the skills to solve his own problems. *The teacher* [charge nurse] *should not attempt to play God.* Her adult students

> [employees] are as mature as she, and in certain ways probably more so. With a deep interest in the student [employee] the teacher [charge nurse] can help him find his own way, but find his own way he must.[1]

If you embrace this concept of the role of teacher, you will probably have to unlearn many of your preconceived ideas about how you train and develop your staff. If, however, you can engage in this newer concept of the teaching role, the excitement of sharing responsibility for learning activities with your staff will bring its own rewards.

Characteristics of effective learning specialists include the following: (1) they spend considerable time planning; (2) they individualize instruction and make it practical in terms of the interests, needs and wants of their employees; (3) they are highly flexible; and (4) they use a wide variety of methods and techniques.

Planning is needed in order to develop unit goals, staff goals and individual goals; planning is needed in order to determine which method or technique or material will facilitate the achievement of objectives, and planning helps develop criteria for evaluating progress and change. Much of the planning, however, can be shared with staff members, as can the instructional responsibilities. The good teacher carefully plans the learning experience on the one hand but is extremely flexible on the other — by being able to use various techniques and resources to achieve the overall objectives as opportunities arise. A sensitive teacher constantly adjusts and changes the plan for the learning experience as new opportunities for doing so are presented and as "feedback" is obtained from the staff.

Many techniques and methods are available to you. Your choice of technique will be governed by the learning need and the situation. A brief summary follows:

1. *Presentation techniques:* lecture, television, videotape, dialogue, interview, group interview, demonstration, slides, dramatization, recordings, exhibits, trips, and reading.
2. *Discussion techniques:* guided discussion, article or book-based discussion, problem-solving discussion, group-centered discussion.
3. *Simulation techniques:* role playing, critical-incident process, case method, games, participative cases.
4. T-Group (sensitivity training).
5. Nonverbal exercises.
6. Skill-practice exercises, drill, coaching.

The best way to develop a repertoire of techniques is to experiment and evaluate the effectiveness. Keep in mind the objective, and match the technique with it. Certain techniques are more effective in bringing about behavioral change than others. Another point to remember is the principle of participation. If you have a choice between techniques, choose the one that involves your staff in active participation.

To increase your knowledge and skill in the teaching-learning process and your knowledge of adults and how they learn, read the current professional journals. An increasing number of journals present innovative ideas and writers share their experiences in using action learning approaches.

Dynamics of Staff Involvement

As you become increasingly aware of the teaching-learning process as it applies to the responsibility you and the staff of your unit share, it becomes obvious that the staff will actively participate in the training and development enterprise. If you can release the need for achievement, reduce the fear of failure, enhance the curiosity drive, develop new interests and stimulate the desire for learning and self-fulfillment, you will have effectively performed your tasks and fulfilled your role as charge nurse-learning specialist. To accomplish these tasks, several principles may make your job easier. These principles, taken from Powell and Aker, support the concept of active participation and staff development programming. If you bear these principles in mind, they will provide a viable guideline for securing participation that is meaningful to staff and productive in good achievement.

PRINCIPLES OF ADULT LEARNING

1. *Adults learn better when they are actively involved in the learning process.* The more they participate through discussion groups and in other group techniques, the more responsibility they are given for what happens in a learning situation, the more effectively they will progress.
2. *Adults can learn materials which apply to their daily work more quickly than they can learn irrelevant materials.* Adults will be receptive to new information only if they are sure it is useful to them immediately.
3. *Adults will accept new ideas more quickly if these ideas support previous beliefs.* Adults come to learning situations with a well-fixed set of values and beliefs, regardless of whether or not they verbalize them. They tend to reject information which attacks or destroys their beliefs.
4. *An adult's needs and background must be understood and integrated into his learning experiences as much as possible. Out of feelings of inadequacy, many adults believe they cannot learn.* This belief will be evident in their attitude toward learning situations and toward themselves. Before they are placed in a learning situation, adults should first feel encouraged enough to attempt to learn; otherwise they are likely to fail before they begin.
5. *To the extent possible, adults should be allowed to pursue their own areas of interest at their own rate, and to find answers to questions on their own.* Regardless of how they may react to an authoritarian learning atmosphere, adults are not likely to grasp knowledge that is forced upon them. A teacher should act as a resource person, available to guide or discuss a problem with the learner. The teacher should *not* have all the answers, or even pretend to have them.

6. *Adults, because of possible unhappy past experiences, should be prepared for learning so it will be a pleasant, rather than an unpleasant experience.* Drill and repetition of material will not help them to learn. It will only make them dislike the learning experience even more than they did before.
7. *Adult learners should be rewarded immediately for success, and should never feel as if they are being punished for making a mistake.* When rewarded, they will want to continue the experience. If punished, they are apt to reject the entire situation either by leaving it physically or by refusing to become involved.
8. *Adults learn in a series of "plateaus";* that is, they do well for a while, then level off in performance, but they will move on again if they have not become discouraged. This is a natural process, and adults should understand that it is, so that they will not give up.
9. *An adult should always know why he is learning and toward what goal he is aiming.* He should understand what steps are necessary to reach a particular learning goal, and in what order they should come. If he becomes confused about where he is going, or why he is going there, he will lose interest in going any place.[2]

In summary, the decentralization of inservice education and staff development to the critical care unit offers the charge nurse an opportunity to experiment with innovative ways of meeting the learning needs of her staff and achieve a higher level of nursing service for her patients. The characteristics of a decentralized training program, built on sound adult education principles and supported concretely by nursing administration, provide a framework upon which the charge nurse can begin to create a new role for herself—co-learner and learning specialist. The risks in undertaking this task should be moderate and the rewards should be great . . . for staff and charge nurse alike.

Moving on to the second part of this chapter, the process of training and staff development is outlined for the purpose of providing a practical and systematic approach which may prove useful to the charge nurse in a critical care unit.

THE PROCESS OF TRAINING
AND STAFF DEVELOPMENT

Training has as its primary purpose the discovery, development, and change of employee behavior and attitudes in such a way that job performance will be improved. Staff development includes this purpose of training as a component, but adds another vital purpose—staff development is predicated on meeting some of the employee's need for self-worth, growth and development, and satisfaction through his work.

If you, as charge nurse, undertake the responsibility for training and developing members of your staff in the critical care unit, you will need to give careful thought to these two components of staff development and their implications for your leadership style. It will mean integrating the needs and goals of the critical care unit with the personal growth needs and goals of members of your staff. For only by blending and balancing these diverse needs can you hope to achieve the ultimate goals of delivering appropriate and effective care to each patient and his family, as well as growth opportunities for you and your staff.

To provide some background for your orientation, consider the contribution of progressive industrial management.

For the past two decades many industries have experimented extensively with ways of dealing with both organizationl needs and objectives, and employee needs and objectives. Researchers have attempted to discover and develop the key to releasing motivational energy of employees toward achievement of company objectives. As a result of the research findings, the concentrated effort on the part of management and the willingness to participate on the part of employees resulted in participative and collaborative planning in job and staff development. Over a period of time the results of these cooperative efforts in job and staff development have been measured in cold cash — lower operating costs, lower turnover, creative product development, new marketing techniques, new management techniques, and increased profits.

Shifting from industry to health care systems, and to hospitals in particular, the problem of tapping the full potential of the people-resources is of genuine concern. With the increased pressure to deliver more effective health care to the community, control costs to patients, and to more fully utilize the unique capabilities of employees, hospitals must look for alternatives to the narrowly conceived assembly-line way of delivering health service to patients.

There was a tendency (and still is in some cases) for hospital administration and nursing service to buy into the assembly-line, minute-division-of-labor approach to organizing work which stems from Henry Ford's mass production concept, and was almost written in stone by Frederick W. Taylor in his scientific management theory.*

With the number of professional specialties and skilled technicians in the health sciences multiplying like rabbits, the challenge to integrate into the health care system persons who come with special educational preparation and rich and varied work experiences is somewhat overwhelming. To this complex situation add the fact that each one of these people comes initially with a desire to make maximum use of his special expertise and the need to keep growing in his job life as well as his personal life. It appears that the

---

*Taylor assumed that the majority of employees were undereducated and unskilled. Therefore a system which divided the task into routinized fragments which relatively unskilled workers could perform adequately under close supervision would maximize production. This theory also assumed a high need for control and centralized decision making. This theory may be useful in some industrial processes, but is not useful in the delivery of health care. In fact, it seriously inhibits and curtails the service to patients as well as stunts the growth and development of the professionals and paraprofessionals involved.

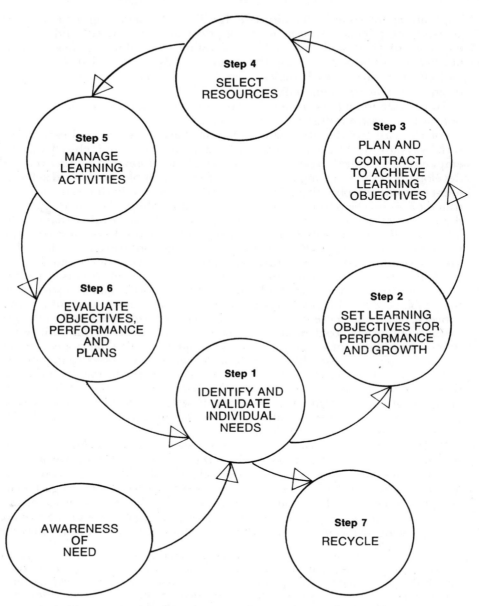

Fig. 17-1. Process model for training and staff development.

key to genuine motivation rests within the employee and is released when his need to keep growing on the job is met. How to release this energy in the interests of providing effective health care to patients is the focus of practical and realistic training and staff development.

The need to respond to a different concept of management confronts not only hospital administrators but also directors of nursing administration, and specifically supervisors of direct patient care.

Experience in training and developing a small group of people into an organization acknowledges the reality of interdependence, the need for mutual work goals, and an awareness of the process needed to achieve both organization and individual goals. It utilizes the participative decision-making process in those areas of work that directly involve the resources of the employee.

The process model for training and staff development is offered as a means of facilitating the planning of specific, realistic, and needed training which can be made manageable and measurable (Fig. 17-1). By familiarizing yourself with the process model, you can begin to develop an overall program for your unit. In addition, you will find it equally applicable in designing your own personal and professional developmental plan, and it will serve you well as a guide for working and planning with each member of your staff. Moreover, it will provide a continuing framework for training and developing staff through its recycling design. The process model uses seven steps:

Step 1. Identify and validate individual needs.
Step 2. Set individual learning objectives for performance and growth.
Step 3. Plan and contract to achieve learning objectives.
Step 4. Select resources.
Step 5. Manage learning activities.
Step 6. Evaluate performance and learning plan.
Step 7. Recycle.

Perhaps right now, as a result of the assessment you made of your personal resources, you are very much aware of how good you feel about the training you are already doing in your unit; however, you are also becoming increasingly aware of the value of involving your staff more actively in planning training which will meet some of their own needs. From this new awareness, a healthy dissatisfaction with the present way you are functioning as a teacher may trigger your taking time to validate the need to change the way you handle training in terms of staff involvement. This initial awareness is shown in the model (Fig. 17-1) in a kind of free form. It represents the consciousness of a need, but this need lacks validation which is necessary to determine whether or not it is a viable learning need.

Step 1—Identify and Validate Individual Needs

How do you determine what the needs are?
How do you check them out to make sure they are real?

Are they educational needs that can be met through training or staff development?

In reply to the question, "How do you determine what the training needs are?" your best source of information on needs will be the people with whom you work in delivering care to patients in the critical care unit. Different needs will come from each shift and from persons who "float" or "relieve" on the days the regular staff is off.

You can obtain data on needs in many ways; however, here are three with which you are familiar: interviewing, observation, periodic performance evaluations.

INTERVIEWING

If the individuals in the critical care unit are interviewed either formally or informally, on a one-to-one basis, or as a group, data based on "conscious needs" will be collected. Preparation on your part prior to interviewing will facilitate gathering specific data and guide the discussion; however, the use of some open-ended questions will permit some free-flowing input from employees and provide data that otherwise you would miss.

OBSERVATION

Gather data based on guided observations of the job performance of each member of the staff, on their interactions with patients and with each other. Observe staff contacts with persons who provide direct services to patients in the critical care unit, but who are not a part of the critical care staff. As a professional nurse in charge of nursing care delivered in the critical care unit, your observations are those of the expert. Your perceptions provide the criteria for determining the required level of competence for effective performance. Therefore, base your observations on a set of criteria which you prepare prior to making your observations.Your observations will reveal the "unconscious needs"—those needs that were not revealed in the interviews, but are evident from the point of view of an expert.

PERIODIC PERFORMANCE EVALUATIONS

Data on these reports provide an indication of the needs and resources both you and the employee are aware of and have dealt with in some way. In some cases, reports may cover several years and reflect changes in the performance level of an employee. In studying these data, consider the abilities and skills each employee demonstrates, as well as his attitude toward himself and his job.

Now, to refine the needs which the data produced, a suggestion from Malcolm Knowles will help pinpoint how the educational need is defined.

He states that need is defined as the gap between present level of competency and a higher level required for effective performance as defined by the individual, the organization or society. His concept is illustrated in Fig. 17-2.

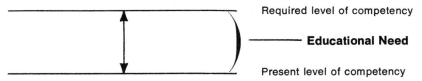

Fig. 17-2. Definition of an educational need.

In reply to the question, "How do you check it out to make sure it is real?" the issue becomes one of validating the need. Validation requires that you seek out sources of data that verify the reality and the extent of the need — it supports the fact that the gap, or educational need, exists and justifies further consideration. The best source for validation and the one most frequently overlooked is the person for whom the training is being planned — the learner himself. Sources such as the supervisors, administration, research studies, speakers, and consultants usually provide verification. In some instances their input is essential; however, the learner must not only be aware of the need to increase his competence, he must want to do it — for his own reasons. Therefore the learner provides one of the soundest answers to the question, "How do you check out the need to make sure it is real?"

Knowles phrases it like this:

> The more concretely an individual can identify his aspirations and assess his present level of competencies in relation to them — the more exactly he can define his educational needs — the more intensely will he be motivated to learn. And the more congruent the needs of the individual are with the aspirations of the organization . . . [and vice versa] the more likely will effective learning take place.[3]

Now for the last question: "Is it an educational need that can be met through training or development?"

Assuming that the need identified and validated is an educational need, the capabilities of the critical care unit and its staff must form the first criteria to determine whether or not the need can be met. The probability that training needs can be best met in the unit is a basic assumption. To increase the effective level of competency on the job, the reality situation offered by the unit provides the best learning laboratory. If the need is more long-range in nature, staff development may be the logical approach to meet the need. This may involve assistance outside the critical care unit.

One of the final considerations you will want to deal with is determining the priority of needs that result from your assessment. You would be wise to involve the staff in helping to establish priorities. This practice will begin to create the expectation that they share responsibility in the training and development program. Another thought to bear in mind in setting priorities is the desirability of a successful first experience. If the first need is "bite size" and chances of meeting it are very good, you probably have a winning combination to move to the next step in the process.

Step 2—Set Individual Learning Objectives
for Performance and Growth

The second step in the process model is concerned with setting goals and objectives so that the training efforts will have direction. For purposes of this model, goals will be identified as long-term and broad in scope. For instance, a goal for a training and staff development program might be stated:

> To involve each staff member in planning and implementing an inservice program for the critical care unit.

Another might be

> To provide more effective nursing care to patients in the critical care unit by helping to increase the level of competency of each person who gives direct patient care.

Although these goals are rather explicitly stated, and in fact provide guidelines upon which to structure a training program, more specific objectives are needed to insure achievement of the goals.

These more specific learning objectives are usually stated in behavioral terms which describe outcomes or results.*

For example, these short-term objectives usually include these characteristics: they represent behaviors that are observable by others; they are specific, limited in scope, and include certain conditions, such as time and method, and they are measurable.

As an example, an objective for a learning experience designed for a new associate degree nursing graduate who has been employed as a staff nurse in a coronary care unit might be stated:

> Given basic instruction on the use of monitoring equipment by the head nurse, within five days be able to prepare a patient and properly attach equipment.

As an approach to involving your staff in setting their own objectives, such questions as these may stimulate their active involvement: What would I be doing differently if I were accomplishing my goal? How might someone else know that I have changed? When will I be doing it? Where would I be doing it? What will I need to know and do to actually reach my goal? What can I do for myself? What help will I need from others? Who, specifically?

After each employee has identified his goal or goals, co-workers can review their goals with each other. With the help of feedback, each employee can clarify his goal, making it more specific, more realistic, and more observable.

In one training situation the author suggested that each participant do a little dreaming about what they would want as a goal if they could utterly divorce themselves from reality. Each participant was encouraged to go off to himself, away from the distractions and work on it. Most of the participants were able to do the assignment and found it a rather useful means of getting a goal initiated. The next step suggested was that of refinement of the goal.

---

*For a programmed instruction book on writing learning objectives, see Robert F. Mager, *Preparing Instructional Objectives* (Palo Alto, Calif.: Fearon Publishers, 1963).

Participants were encouraged to get together in pairs and share their goals with each other. In the process of sharing they could sharpen each other's goals by asking each other questions about them, and by trying to determine what kind of goal it was. Was it a "must" goal? Was it a "want" goal? Was it attainable? Was it an ideal goal that could never be attained, but one that set a direction for the maker? Was it a maintenance goal which merely keeps the performance on an even keel? Or was it a growth goal which partakes of the ideal and at the same time is close enough to reality to be attainable?

To get the goals broken down into workable units, or objectives, each participant was given the assignment of assembling the blocks that stood in the way of the attainment of the goal. He was also encouraged to assemble all of the assets he had going for him.

After having listed all the "blocks" and the "assets" to deal with these blocks, each participant was asked to state an objective, or outcome, to deal with each block he had identified. He was asked to state the objective as simply as possible, and in terms that could be measured when the time came to evaluate the outcomes.

While the learning experience proved to be a lot of hard work, each participant found it a useful discipline. Some considered it very difficult to develop a goal that could be broken down into objectives. But when it was finally possible to get the goals broken down into objectives, the participants could see the practicality of the process. They could understand how functional objectives can be in generating action that is aimed directly at the target of the problem addressed.

The step of goal-and-objective formation is probably the most difficult of the steps, but is essential and should never be overlooked. As your staff becomes more comfortable working together in planning the initial steps which need to be taken to lay the groundwork for Step 3, goals and objectives may change. It should be remembered that this element of change is implicit when you work with the concept of process.

Step 3—Plan and Contract to Achieve Learning Objectives

ACTION PLAN

In order to reach objectives, you will need to develop a strategy that will zero in on the restraining forces which slow down learning. There is a natural resistance to change, and the removal of this resistance is essential if the desired learning is to take place. Honestly acknowledging the existence of resistance to learning and accepting it as a normal phenomenon will remove some of the resistance. This strategy helps the learner identify the reasons he is resisting, and this awareness makes it easier to move him toward building on his assets, abilities, and strengths that will support his learning. Encourage him to specifically identify the resources he can use or request that will help him overcome the blocks to learning, and free his energy to accomplish his own goal. Help him identify the driving forces—those things that tend to propel him into action, and move him toward his learning goal. These forces provide the motivation. When he capitalizes on these and applies his personal resources to offset the resistance to learn, he is ready to develop a plan for determining responsibilities others share with him in supporting his goal achievement. Work with him in assigning specific responsibilities to you, and other resources he anticipates calling upon. Help him clarify his self-assignment of responsibilities. In each instance, encourage him to identify the specific contribution each person is expected to make in his learning plan.

CONTRACT

One of the most helpful elements of collaborative plans for achieving learning goals is the concept of a contract or working agreement among those involved. The contract is not of a formal nature. It evolves as you, your staff, and individuals openly discuss expectations of each other in terms of what needs to be done to achieve learning. For instance, in discussing the assignment of responsibilities, the dialogue clarifies what is needed and why a particular resource seems most relevant. At this point, agreement to accept the responsibility is sought from the resource person. As a part of clarifying the assignment, the persons involved need to discuss reasonable checkpoints and set deadlines. This practice provides specific data for mutually shared expectations. As you can see, the agreement takes on the overtones of a contract to which you, the staff, and individuals are committed. This agreement provides the mechanism that anyone who is involved in the work of achieving learning can use to check the progress that is being made, the status of assignments, problems encountered, renegotiate the agreement, and deal with other matters that center around the achievement of learning objectives.

If you keep in mind that the development of a strategy to help adult learners understand and accept the tension between their desire to grow and their desire to remain the same, you will help them move through the process of unlearning, learning, and relearning.

Adults resist unlearning things which have worked for them in the past, or seemed to be adequate in most situations. In the process of really giving up familiar ways of responding to situations, the adult accepts the necessity of learning new ways that increase his competence. However, learning is not enough; the adult needs to internalize the learning—make it a regular part of his behavior. Thus he needs the opportunity and time to relearn or "refreeze" the new learning so that it becomes his typical response to a situation.

RISKS AND PAYOFFS

One of the basic factors in the learning process is the power and influence of risks a learner takes and the payoffs he receives. Since learning imposes change, you will want to make sure that the risk the learner takes is a moderate one. Moderate risks result in a fair degree of safety and a good chance for success. Knowing the degree of risk he is taking enables the adult learner to accept responsibility for learning. Equally important to the adult learner are the payoffs in store for him. Frequently these payoffs are taken for granted, but you will want to plan very carefully for genuine payoffs for the learner. An open discussion of "both sides of the coin" of the learning experience—the risks and the payoffs—will make it much easier for the learner to buy into a learning experience and for you and his co-workers to support him during the learning process. He will have a gauge by which he can anticipate the results of his changed behavior as he strives for increased competency or self-fulfillment.

One further point: adults want immediate payoffs in return for learning. They want to be able to use the learning *now,* not at some future time. Being able to use the learning effectively and feeling competent in using it is probably the most valued payoff. Coupling this with your recognition of effective performance doubles the payoff.

Step 4—Select Resources

After the action plan has been developed, and even as it is taking shape, the identification of appropriate learning resources follows. You will want to look for situations, people, and materials that will enhance learning opportunities.

Situations offer unique resources. For example:

1. *Participative learning as a resource.* Unstructured learning groups provide rich resource material for learning about "people things." Task groups are useful for integrating theory inputs into operational objectives.

2. *The learner as a resource for planning and implementing programs.* The creative and practical forces generated by employees who accept the role of learner, release resources that can only be obtained from such involvement.

3. *Daily living experiences as a resource for learning.* When employees accept role playing and role training as a way of improving their competency, daily happenings in the unit provide the content for the learning situations. These offer a rare potential for reality-checking attitudes, values, habitual responses to situations and afford the opportunity to try on different behaviors. This enables employees to expand their behavioral repertoire of meeting common experiences. As a resource, it is one of the most stimulating and exciting.

4. *Spontaneity as a resource in learning.* When spontaneity is present, learning is precious, stimulating, and fun. The problem becomes one of how to develop spontaneity, how to make room for it, and how to capitalize on it. Spontaneity develops in a supportive, nonevaluative climate. The norms which govern behavior in the critical care unit hold the potential of inhibiting the development of spontaneity.

5. *Conflict as a resource for learning.* From genuine differences in values, expectations, techniques, roles, priorities, comes the grist for conflict.

Working through these differences to resolve the conflict provides another viable resource for learning. Here again the issue is how to develop a climate in which people can learn from conflict; to create a norm where conflict is legitimatized or sanctioned; to set ground rules so that the conflict can be resolved. Probably one of the most effective resources for learning is found in the differentness that can be openly dealt with.

6. *Failure as a resource for learning.* If the staff within the unit can lower the sensitivity, or help desensitize, so that the person who believes he has failed can learn from the experience, failure can become a motivational force to learn new ways of handling situations or performing certain procedures. Role training is helpful in assisting the learner to find new ways of approaching the problem. Using an approach of "how would you do it differently," may help the learner develop spontaneous responses which he can capitalize on later.

RESOURCE PEOPLE

Selecting competent resource people requires careful planning. Criteria for this selection is threefold: (1) Consider the resource person's ability to adapt his professional knowledge and expertise to "layman-type listeners." This ability is essential if the resource person is to be understood and his expertise utilized. (2) Consider his ability to adapt his "expertise" to your objectives. Unless the resource person has been given a well-developed set of objectives for his appearance, he will need to fall back on his own experience and perception of what your staff needs to know. This may subvert the achieving of your learning objectives. (3) Consider his ability to listen to and respect the knowledge and experience your staff members bring to the session. The assessment of this quality places a special responsibility on you. If the resource person believes in the competence and effectiveness of your unit and communicates his respect for you and your staff, and builds on this, he will be an acceptable resource.

Organizing the inservice program will mean carefully preparing resource people and employees to work together in the learning activities. Resource people will need well-prepared answers to questions like these: Why me? How do I fit in with your overall inservice training? What do you want from me? What are the people like that you want me to work with? What will they want to know? What do you expect to happen when it's over?

These, or similar questions, need to be answered for staff members involved in the inservice and staff development program. They, too, provide a reservoir of resources that needs to be tapped. To tap such resources, however, your people will need to know honestly what is in it for them. In other words, what's the payoff? If they can see a payoff, they will be motivated to learn and to become involved and to accept the change that learning creates and demands.

MATERIALS

With the help of your inservice educator and learning laboratories in schools of nursing which may be in your vicinity, you can locate excellent materials to use in group sessions for your staff; materials for individuals to work through on their own, such as programmed instruction units; reading materials for personal reading or group discussions.

In summary of resources, select the resource for achieving specific learning objectives, and keep in mind the work situation, the timing, and the learner. Accommodating all of these elements becomes an art, so allow yourself time to develop this particular ability.

Step 5—Manage Learning Activities

Once the potential resources have been selected, the next step in the process model is managing the learning activities in such a way that learning objectives and unit objectives are achieved. To gear learning to the work cycle in a practical and realistic manner demands sheer artistry in juggling the components that shape a satisfactory learning experience. These components include time, place, material, equipment, situations, and human resources. You may have to settle for something less than the ideal educational setting and schedule learning in conjunction with work in progress. As these functions become more complementary, you will use less time and energy in their integration.

READINESS OF THE LEARNER

To manage opportunities for individual learning, you will need to be thoroughly familiar with the level of performance of each member of your staff. In addition, you will need to be aware of the explicit learning objectives which will lead to his increased competency on the job. His readiness to learn is important. Recognizing this, you will need to schedule training for a specific time, or rely on the possibility that training can be done in the process of the day's activities on an unscheduled basis. Here again you can manage through specific teaching assignments, and the use of a variety of techniques, if you choose. Your responsibility is really to see that training happens when the learner is prepared and ready to learn, and that appropriate techniques have been used.

You will need to provide periods of time for learning which are long enough to capitalize on the learning potential of the employee. Consider the fact that each time the learner experiences a new behavior he is in effect relearning it in each new situation. Becoming aware of this fact will help you taper off any coaching or special attention when it becomes evident that the new behavior has been well integrated into his performance.

SITUATION

When you tune in to the daily experiences within the critical care unit which offer content for learning, your readiness and spontaneity facilitate learning. Getting people together and orienting them to the situation and content to be presented require presence of mind and quick action. At first this practice will be awkward, but as your staff becomes comfortable with it, such cooperative effort can be directed or suggested by any person. Being sensitive to feedback (which comes in the employee's verbal and nonverbal response to the learning situation) allows you to adjust your teaching as the activity progresses. This flexibility in your style of managing the situation and yourself will increase the potential for learning.

CONTENT

Handling content can pose problems for the instructor. Several cautions in managing content may save time and effort. So often the tendency is to tell the learners what you want them to know and rarely to take time to find out what they already know—or even need to know. The usual response of the learner in this situation is mixed; he feels put down by the instructor, or is bored and tunes out the instructor. The possibility of his missing important information is real. A guideline might be to take time to find out "who knows what" and build from there.

When you need to provide a considerable amount of information or content, organize it into a sequence of segments that can be grasped by the learner. An overload of information with little or no breathing space between inputs discourages the adult learner. When extensive content in a particular sequence is indicated, look at the potential resources within your staff. If sharing responsibilities for training is expected on the part of the employees, they can prepare specific content in collaboration with you. In this way you can decrease your responsibility and increase the versatility of your unit's resources. This approach to managing content will give you more time to manage the overall critical care unit and direct the resources toward both unit goals and growth goals of individuals.

HUMAN RESOURCES

This subject is covered rather extensively in Step 4. However, a point that bears repeating is this: Take time to carefully prepare your resources—outside resources, hospital resources, staff resources, as well as yourself. Check out the guidelines suggested in Step 4.

A great deal of the success and effectiveness of the resource person depends on how you have managed the scheduling, the goals for the event, the information announcing the session, the rationale for the content and method of presentation, the plan to involve the learners, the preparation of the learners, and the setting in which the session is to be held.

Attention to these details creates a climate which supports the teaching-learning activities and those actively involved in them.

PLACE, MATERIAL, AND EQUIPMENT

One asset not to be overlooked is the dual function of the critical care unit. It serves as a treatment area and as a learning area. This fact simplifies your management problem of providing an educational facility. The standard equipment and materials used in the unit serve the needs of both patient and employee-learner. As you begin to blend the service of nursing care to patients with on-the-spot teaching, you will develop a keen appreciation of the versatility, efficiency and capacity of the critical care unit.

Step 6—Evaluate Performance and Learning Plan

The next step is to evaluate the learning which in effect means measuring the degree of change in the performance of persons who have been involved in the training activities; it also means measuring the degree to which the learner's own objectives have been achieved. These changes may be observed in terms of overt behavior. Your guided observation over a period of time will result in the evaluation of the employee's ability to integrate the new learning into the performance of his job.

Another form of evaluating learning is open staff meetings. This allows the staff to give feedback on the significance of the learning opportunity and how they have been able to utilize what they learned. In this process, evaluation of the effectiveness of how the staff functions can be made. Successes, failures, conflicts, creative solutions—all these data are part of the evaluation process and contribute information essential to developing objectives for the next sequence of training activities.

Another facet of evaluation is determining the adequacy of the objectives. After evaluating the degree to which they were achieved, some objectives may need to be modified, others have to be phased out because they have been met, and new ones have to be developed. Still others must be discontinued because they were unrealistic or the situation had changed.

The action plan will need to be evaluated. How effectively the learning forces were identified and handled will be the focus of this evaluation. The resources used by the learner will be evaluated in terms of how effectively they overcame the blocks to learning. The working agreement and deadlines will be reviewed in terms of how they contributed to the accomplishment of the learning objectives.

How well were the learning activities organized in terms of the working situation, the readiness of the learner, the preparation of the resource people or materials, and the timing, will be grist for the evaluation mill.

Perhaps the most difficult one to measure will be the results. If you can gather data that will support such long-term results as lower turnover, effective patient care on a cost basis, a high level of staff competence based on specific learning activities, you will be a winner. To facilitate the gathering of these data, use resources such as the hospital's personnel director, inservice educator, and cost accountant. There may also be a researcher on the hospital staff that could help you design such an evaluation tool. Local colleges and universities will have resource people who could help design such an evaluation.

Use feedback from everyone involved in the learning activities. Data from these sources of information will provide viable information to use in moving into the recycling process, which is Step 7.

Step 7—Recycle

This last step requires us to start all over again. Based on the validation of new needs or unmet needs which emerge from the evaluation process, and from changes which have evolved during the intervening time, recycling inservice in the critical care unit begins.

All of these steps in the process model involve other people. In the final analysis, the process model is also a participative model as you have discovered by now.

CONCLUSION

After reading this chapter, and reflecting on how adults learn to cope with significant changes in their professional and personal lives,
    GO!
        GROW!
            LIVE TO LEARN!
                LEARN TO LIVE!
                    COLLECT THE PAYOFFS FOR LEARNING!

REFERENCES

1. Toni Powell and George F. Aker, "Teaching and Learning in Adult Basic Education," unpublished paper, Department of Adult Education, Florida State University, Tallahassee, Florida, 1971.
2. *Ibid.*
3. Malcolm Knowles, *The Modern Practice of Adult Education* (New York: Association Press, 1970).

BIBLIOGRAPHY

Argyris, Chris, *Integrating the Individual and the Organization.* New York: John Wiley and Sons, Inc., 1964.
———, *Interpersonal Competence and Organizational Effectiveness.* Homewood, Ill.: Dorsey Press, 1962.
Blansfield, Michael G., and Rachel Ayers, *The Professional Nurse Looks at Appraisal of Personnel.* Washington, D.C.: Leadership Resources, Inc., 1966.
Herzberg, Frederick, "One More Time: How Do You Motivate Employees?" *Harvard Business Review,* January–February, 1968.
Kindall, Alvin F., and James Gatza, "Positive Performance Evaluation," *Harvard Business Review,* November–December 1963.

Knowles, Malcolm, *The Modern Practice of Adult Education.* New York: Association Press, 1970.

———, and Rachel Ayers, *The Professional Nurse Looks at the Learning Climate.* Washington, D.C.: Leadership Resources, Inc., 1966.

Levinson, Henry, "Management By Whose Objectives?" *Harvard Business Review,* July–August 1970.

Likert, Rensis, *New Patterns of Management.* New York: McGraw-Hill Book Company, 1961.

Mager, Robert, *Preparing Instruction Objectives.* Palo Alto, Calif.: Fearon Publishers, 1963.

McGregor, Douglas, *The Human Side of Enterprise.* New York: McGraw-Hill Book Company, 1960.

Medearis, Naomi D., "Creativity or Conformity in Performance Appraisals," *Journal for Operating Room Nurses,* September 1971.

———, and Elda S. Popiel, "Guidelines for Organizing Inservice Education," *Journal of Nursing Administration,* July–August 1971.

Miles, Matthew B., *Learning to Work in Groups.* New York: Teachers College Press, 1959.

Morton, Robert B., "Straight from the Shoulder—Leveling with Others on the Job," *Personnel Magazine,* November–December 1966.

Powell, Toni, and George F. Aker, "Teaching and Learning in Adult Basic Education," unpublished paper, Department of Adult Education, Florida State University, Tallahassee, Florida, 1971.

Rogers, Carl R., "Personal Thoughts on Teaching and Learning," *Improving College and University Teaching, National Journal,* Graduate School of Oregon State University, Eugene, Ore., 1958.

18

Legal Responsibilities of the Nurse in a Critical Care Unit

VIRGINIA S. WARD
EXECUTIVE DIRECTOR OF
COLORADO NURSES' ASSOCIATION

The legal responsibility of the registered nurse in the critical care unit does not differ from the legal responsibility of the registered nurse in any work setting. Five principles to which the registered nurse adheres for the protection of both patient and practitioner are:

1. A registered nurse performs only those functions for which she has been prepared by education and experience.
2. A registered nurse performs these functions competently.
3. A registered nurse delegates responsibility only to personnel whose competence has been evaluated and found acceptable.
4. A registered nurse takes appropriate measures as indicated by her observation of the patient.
5. A registered nurse is familiar with policies of the employing agency governing nursing functions, and practices within these policies.

Nurses need particularly to be reminded that they can be as liable when they fail to take necessary action as when they act in a negligent manner. There have been numerous cases in which a nurse has been held liable for inaction. This is especially true when a nurse fails to act appropriately based on her observation of the patient. A typical situation might involve a patient with recognizable signs of acute cardiac embarrassment for whom the nurse fails to call for the immediate attention of a physician.

Nurses can be found liable of *misfeasance*, *malfeasance*, and *nonfeasance*. These terms will be considered in relation to the administration of medications so that they may be more understandable.

Misfeasance is an act which is lawful in itself, but in so doing results in injury to the patient. Thus a nurse may be legally administering sulfisoxazole under the written orders of a licensed physician, but may fail to recognize signs of toxic reaction. If she continues to give the drug until the patient sustains kidney damage, this would constitute misfeasance.

Malfeasance is the doing of an act which should not be done. For example, if a patient's chart indicates that this patient is allergic to penicillin, and a physican is informed over the telephone that the patient has symptoms of a postoperative infection, the physician may order a medication containing penicillin. If the nurse proceeds to give the medication despite further warning from the patient about his allergy to penicillin, this action on the part of the nurse would constitute malfeasance.

Nonfeasance is the omission of doing something which ought to be done. Thus if a medication vital to the patient's survival is not administered by the nurse, the nurse is liable for nonfeasance.

There are five ways in which functions once the exclusive prerogative of the medical profession become an accepted part of nursing practice. Frequently, procedures are absorbed by nursing when the physician finds them repetitive and time-consuming. When this occurs simultaneously throughout the community, it has become "standard practice in the community." Opinions of the state board of nursing or state board of medical examiners stating that there is no violation of either practice act, can expand nursing responsibilities. A legal opinion of the attorney general on a specific practice can determine the legality of the act; and statements of the professional nursing association will resolve whether or not specific practices fall within the purview of nursing practice. Of the four ways mentioned thus far, all are subject to reversal in a court of law. The fifth method would be legislative action amending the medical practice act to permit other categories of practitioners to perform functions which only physicians are entitled by law to perform.

The law covering extreme emergencies is broad in its protection of the nurse when there is no physician present to make judgmental decisions. If the nurse believes the situation critical enough to call for immediate action on her part, she should take the following steps: (1) evaluate the relative hazards of action and inaction, and (2) determine whether there is a reasonable chance of success.

If the hazard of inaction is greater than that of action, and if there appears to be a reasonable chance of success, the nurse should not hesitate to act for fear of possible legal implications.

All nurses should carry malpractice insurance. There seems to be a common misunderstanding that the employer, rather than the nurse, would be liable. It is true that a joint suit might be filed naming both the employer and the nurse as defendants, however, the fact remains that the nurse as a professional practitioner is responsible, at all times, for her acts in relation to other people. However, nursing malpractice insurance does not cover the nurse if she is performing functions which only a physician is licensed to perform.

The pitfall the nurse must assiduously avoid is to be pressured into performing functions for which she feels herself unqualified. The nurse must have the courage and integrity not to permit herself to be stampeded into unwise acts as a matter of expediency. The nurse's primary concern must always be the life of the patient.

Index

Page numbers in *italics* indicate illustrations.